BF 199 B67

Brown, Judson Seise   ior

The motivation of behavior

1548

The Motivation of Behavior

McGRAW-HILL SERIES IN PSYCHOLOGY

HARRY F. HARLOW, *Consulting Editor*

John F. Dashiell was Consulting Editor of this series from its inception in 1931 until January 1, 1950. Clifford T. Morgan was Consulting Editor of this series from January 1, 1950 until January 1, 1959.

THE MOTIVATION
OF BEHAVIOR

JUDSON SEISE BROWN

Graduate Research Professor
University of Florida

McGRAW-HILL BOOK COMPANY

New York   Toronto   London   1961

THE MOTIVATION OF BEHAVIOR

Two major aims have served as guideposts throughout the writing of this book. The more important of these has been to develop a tightly reasoned, systematic analysis of the concept of motivation, with special emphasis upon its relative utility as an explanatory component of general behavior theory. The lesser goal has been to formulate the analysis in such a manner as to make it intelligible to the advanced undergraduate or beginning graduate student in psychology.

In principle, if all behavior is motivated, any book about motivation should encompass all of psychology, at the very least. Since such inclusiveness is patently impossible, an author is forced, in reducing his task to manageable proportions, to neglect certain topics of special interest to particular readers. He must be selective, therefore, and in the absence of widely accepted criteria for evaluating the importance of each and every area, the process of selection must be governed primarily by idiosyncratic factors. In the succeeding pages, for example, almost no consideration is given to the topic of sexual behavior. This omission should not be construed, however, as reflecting the belief that there are no significant motivational aspects to sexual behavior. Rather it is a consequence of the conviction that while much is known of the effects of hereditary and environmental variables upon sexual behavior, especially in lower mammals, the *concept* of sexual motivation has thus far played only the vaguest of roles in behavior theory generally. This point is underscored by the observation that the terms *drive* and *motivation* are almost never used in published works on reproductive activities, even when such works have been written by psychologists. To be sure, students of reproductive activities are concerned with motivated behavior, but they have shown little interest in the construct of sexual motivation. Similarly detailed justifications to support my neglect of other topics, such as hoarding behavior, taste preferences, and the vast Freudian literature on unconscious motivation, would lengthen this preface unduly. It need only be said, therefore, that in some instances I was unable clearly to discern the motivational implications of the research, in certain cases my fund of knowledge was inadequate, and in others the existing literature seemed both adequate and extensive.

Some readers may feel that I have paid undue attention to Hull's multiplicative-drive theory of motivation. Here I must plead guilty to the belief that this conception, augmented by other theorists' emendations, is the most explicitly structured of existing views, and, at present, probably the most useful theory of motivation we possess. So far as I am aware, no other conception of the motivational process has generated so much experimental work or led to such varied theoretical inquiry. Nevertheless, on a number of occasions I have suggested, and sometimes defended, the possibility that Hull's conception is either inadequate or noneconomical. Rather generally throughout the book, and particularly in Chapter 4, serious and sympathetic attention is given to alternative, nonmotivational interpretations of the effects of so-called motivational variables upon behavior.

Grateful and enthusiastic acknowledgment is made to the many individuals who, as the result of their careful and intelligent reading of early versions of the manuscript, did much to improve its clarity and precision. In this respect, I. E. Farber's penetrating and constructive review of the entire manuscript was of inestimable value. The unusually discerning and appropriate criticisms of Bettina Bass, Richard deCharms, Kenneth P. Goodrich, Leonard E. Ross, Charles C. Spiker, and Allan M. Wagner evoke not only my warmest thanks but also, frankly, my envy. Robert S. Witte, who used a preliminary draft of the manuscript in his motivation classes at Cornell College, Mount Vernon, Iowa, relieved some of my qualms concerning the suitability of the material for undergraduates, and in addition made numerous positive suggestions for the improvement of the manuscript. Kenneth W. Spence repeatedly guided me to important references and concepts, and our informal discussions have been of great value in helping me toward clearer conceptions of difficult problems.

I am especially grateful to my wife, Julia S. Brown, for her cheerful and painstaking assistance in the preparation of the final manuscript and for her scholarly criticisms both of my phraseology and of certain of my arguments. The high-level secretarial assistance provided at various times by Betty Jean Stoner, Jean Hansen, and Sandra Wood is a pleasure to acknowledge, as is the bibliographic work of Marigold Belloni.

Some of that priceless commodity, time to think and to write, was provided by the Graduate College of the State University of Iowa in the form of a Graduate Research Professorship during the period from September 1956 to January 1957. Much of the theoretical development and some of the unpublished experiments cited in Chapter 8 were supported by a small grant (M-1789) from the National Institutes of Health.

Permission to reproduce figures and to make quotations were granted by individual authors and their work is credited in each instance as a citation to the list of references. Permission to quote and reproduce figures was also granted by the University of Nebraska Press, Yale University Press, the New York Academy of Sciences, the Journal Press, the *American Journal of Psychology*, the *Journal of Personality*, and the American Psychological Association. The cooperation of all of these authors and organizations is gratefully acknowledged.

Judson S. Brown

CONTENTS

CHAPTER 1

The Psychologist's Task and the Problem of Motivation

MOST PRESENT-DAY PSYCHOLOGISTS would probably agree that their principal task is to study and to strive to understand the behavior of living organisms, both human and subhuman. To accomplish this aim, the psychologist, if he wishes to proceed in a scientific manner, must begin by making dispassionate, careful, and repeated observations of the activities of organisms in a wide variety of circumstances. He must observe the movements they make, the sounds they utter, the objects they manipulate, and their interactions with other organisms. Moreover, these observations must be recorded in a relatively permanent manner so that they can be evaluated and analyzed long after the behavior has ceased and the process of observing has been terminated. Initially, therefore, the psychologist's task is to observe the actions of organisms and to record what he has seen in as precise and accurate a manner as possible. These recorded bits of information constitute the basic data with which he begins his work.

The psychologist concentrates his attention primarily upon the *behavior* of living organisms, not upon their physiological func-

tions, their anatomical structure, or their physical-chemical com-
position. Psychological data are thus derived from one class of
events and the data of other sciences from different classes.
Because of this one may maintain, with some justification, that the subject matter of psychology is unique in comparison
with the subject matter of other disciplines.

But we must also remember that there is almost nothing unique
or characteristically "psychological" about the *methods* by which
the psychologist collects his raw data. His observational techniques
are, in essence, the same as those of the zoologist, the physiologist,
and the physicist. Sometimes the only equipment he uses is a
pencil and paper. He notes whether a rat turns right or left in a
maze; he counts the motorists who do or do not stop for a red
traffic light; he tabulates the swallows a baby makes while drinking a bottle of milk; he records the number of mistakes made by
a student on an intelligence test. On other occasions, however,
the psychologist's observations cannot be made without the help
of much more elaborate equipment. He may use a stop watch to
measure the time taken by a student in completing a questionnaire; he may employ an electronic instrument to detect and record
changes in the resistance of the skin due to loud sounds or painful
stimuli; he may use the physicist's gauges to measure the force
of a manual movement. But whether the equipment is simple
or complex, in all of these instances the psychologist is using the
well-known, well-standardized methods of the natural sciences.
He measures the vigor of a movement and expresses its force in
physical units such as grams or pounds; he times the duration
of a movement in seconds or minutes; he counts the frequencies
of events of many kinds and records the results in standard numerical notations. His raw data, therefore, when tabulated and recorded
are simply the frequencies with which certain events occur, their
magnitudes, their rates, or their durations. Considered in this
restricted sense, as frequency counts, quantities that change with
time, amplitude measurements, and the like, the basic data of
psychology are identical with the basic data of all other sciences.
Psychological data could not be obtained, of course, save for the
existence of living organisms, but the fundamental observations
are made by methods common to all sciences and are couched in

the language of the natural scientist, not in any special-purpose psychological jargon.

Defining the Responses of Organisms. Since we have maintained that the student of behavior begins by observing the actions or responses of organisms, we must next consider the problem of how to specify or define a response. While difficulties may arise at the conceptual level, in actual practice few problems accompany the delineation of events that will be called responses. Responses are whatever movements or classes of movements or actions we decide to record or measure. A response is a member of a class or set of objectively recordable events attributable to whatever organism we are observing. But if different observers are to agree that a response has occurred (and such agreement is a necessary condition for scientific analysis), they must all be governed by rules of observation that specify precisely what activities are to be included in a response class. For example, two observers will usually agree that a rat has turned to the right at a designated point in a maze if it turns sharply through an angle of 90°. But what if the animal veers only 20° to the right of its original line of movement? Is this a right-turning reaction? It is or is not a "right turn" depending upon what limits have been placed upon the class of movements to be designated right turns. The selection of particular limits is a matter of choice at the outset, being governed by hunches or prior knowledge. It is only when our response-defining criteria have been shown to be unworkable or useless that they must be revised. Thus one may decide to call a movement to the right a right turn if it describes an angle of at least 80 but not more than 100°. Once such class boundaries have been specified, any competent observer can decide whether a given turning movement does or does not fall within the prescribed limits. If it does, he makes a tally mark on his record sheet and the response is said to have occurred.

From time to time various writers (Bakan, 1953; Nissen, 1954; Hall and Lindzey, 1957) have suggested that information about eliciting stimuli is essential to an adequate definition or description of any response. This appears to be true only when the phrase "adequate definition or description" is treated as though it were synonymous with "adequate scientific explanation." Few will deny that every observable action of an organism is antedated by complex chains of related events, some of which would unquestionably qualify as "stimuli." Quite obviously, therefore, any complete scientific *explanation* of a response would necessarily contain some reference to correlated or eliciting stimuli.

But a scientific explanation of a response is one thing, and its definition or description, for purposes of scientific observation, is something else. The activities of organisms are physical events occurring in the physical world, and agreement among competent observers as to the occurrence or nonoccurrence of these actions can be achieved through precisely formulated observational rules. A response is adequately defined when the criteria for its observation have been specified in detail. For this purpose information about the nature or presence of eliciting stimuli is completely irrelevant. In making his raw tally marks, an investigator need have no knowledge of the stimulus events that are correlated with the behavior; it is required only that he know the rules of observation and how to operate his measuring or recording equipment. In fact, the behavior scientist can spend his entire life investigating behavior and determining whether it is lawfully related to other data without ever getting involved in the question of whether he is indeed studying instances of what others might call responses. Incidentally, the assertion that an action, a response, or a reaction can be defined, specified, or described independently of correlated stimuli does not imply that the behavior has no stimulus correlates. It means simply that the behavior can be identified and recorded even though its eliciting stimuli may never be discovered.

Alternative Definitions of Response Classes. As we have seen, the task of defining a response is not especially difficult provided observational criteria can be specified with sufficient precision. No two responses are ever exactly alike, however, and hence our criteria of observation must encompass a class or group of responses. This necessity raises the further question of exactly where the boundaries of the response class should be fixed. Prior to extensive study we have no way of knowing whether the response domain should be broad or narrow. Important laws might be obtained with one criterion of class membership but not with another. In the absence of information provided by experience, the boundaries of response classes are determined by the best available guesses as to which settings will prove most fruitful in the long run. Psychologists' guesses in these matters have differed widely, however, and considerable controversy has been the result. Because of this difference of opinion it is necessary to examine the problem in greater detail. This can best be done, perhaps, by considering several of the alternative response-class definitions that have been advocated by various investigators. Somewhat similar discussions of response classes will be found elsewhere (e.g., Davis, 1953; Logan, Olmsted, Rosner, Schwartz, and Stevens, 1955).

In the first place, some students of behavior are quite satisfied to work with a very limited class of reactions such as those provided by a *single muscle group or gland*. Pavlov (1927), in his extensive studies of salivary conditioning in dogs, used a response-classification scheme of this kind. A dog was said to have "behaved" or "responded" whenever a drop of saliva was seen to fall from a tube attached to an externalized opening of its salivary gland. Hilden (1937), in studying conditioned finger withdrawal in human subjects, recorded electrical potentials originating in the muscles controlling the finger. A "response" in this instance was defined as an action-potential burst of a given magnitude. Because of the method employed, a subject was said to be reacting even when no overt movement of his finger could be detected. If definite rules were prescribed for reading the graphic records of electrical muscle activity, different observers would have little difficulty in reaching an agreement as to whether a response had or had not occurred. The psychologist who restricts the class of recordable reactions to the activity of a single muscle group or gland has adopted about as simple a classification scheme as he can use and still maintain that he is studying "behavior." To move farther back into the mechanisms underlying behavior, by investigating, say, the neural events preceding the contraction of a muscle, would take one into the traditional field of physiology.

A second, broader way of categorizing behavior would be to limit one's observations to *the overt movements of a single limb*. Thus one might tally the occurrence of a response, in an avoidance-conditioning situation, if a dog were to lift its leg at least ¼ inch from the floor during a certain interval following the presentation of the conditioned stimulus. This way of categorizing behavior differs from the first in that different muscle groups might be involved on each occasion when the leg is lifted. But by following the specified rules one can make repeated observations of the "same" behavior, where "sameness" is defined as any upward movement of the foot of at least ¼ inch. Such repeated observations are, of course, essential in any scientific investigation. The isolated occurrence of a single muscle twitch or a single movement or a single act of aggression is of little value to the student of behavior. Whether the criterion of movement is set at ¼ inch, 1 inch, or any other value is entirely up to the psychologist who conducts the experiment.

A third way of classifying responses is to *combine all activities that have the same end effect upon the environment, regardless of which specific limbs or muscles are involved.* Thus, in studying the behavior of children or adults, any action resulting in injury to another person, regardless of how the injury was produced, might be classified as an *aggressive* act. Or, in studying the behavior of rats in a Skinner box, any depression of the bar might be treated as a *bar-pressing response* irrespective of whether the bar is pressed by the rat's foot, tail, head, or body. Different effectors and different kinds of neural integrations would be involved in each case, but the reactions could all be treated as identical for the purpose of counting responses. In every instance of this kind the experimenter must specify the criteria to be met by the reaction if it is to qualify as a recordable member of the response group under study. If aggression is defined in terms of injury to others, then the child who throws an object at his toy box, but misses and hurts a second child, is exhibiting aggression. A bar-pressing response of less than some predetermined amount may or may not be included as a member of the class of bar-pressing acts. It would not be included if it does not activate the food magazine or the automatic electric counter that tallies the actions. Skinner (1938) carries this procedure to its logical extreme. His experimental situations are often structured so that it is impossible, even should one so desire, to observe how the rat actually does press the lever or to see whether partial responses are being made. Skinner is satisfied to determine whether a response, defined and identified in quite an arbitrary manner, varies lawfully with changes in laboratory operations. If the response does not manifest lawful variation, which might be the case if the force required to depress the bar were markedly increased, then the response class must be redefined and a new set of data collected.

Psychologists who observe in detail what an animal or child does in a lever-pressing or problem-box situation may be impressed by either the uniformity of behavior or by its variability. Guthrie and Horton (1946), for example, in studying the behavior of cats in a puzzle box, found their subjects' reactions to be highly stereotyped. If the cat got out of the box by hitting the release pole with its tail on one trial, it was likely to perform substantially the same set of movements on the next trial. Others, such as Tolman (1932), have been struck by the fact that, with regard to the muscle groups involved, behavior is highly variable from trial to trial. It is asserted, as a consequence, that the animal is not learning to make responses mediated by activity of the same efferent channels and the same muscular or glandular effectors. Each of these points of view is, in essence, a statement of faith as to how behavior should be classified if one is to attain to the highest level of understanding, lawfulness, and predictive efficiency. As will be noted shortly, those for whom the variability of the underlying mechanisms looms large are impressed by the constancy of the end result. Such writers often favor the view that the behavior is "purposive." For them the animal seems to know that regardless of which foot is used to press the lever the food will be forthcoming.

A fourth way of classifying responses is to combine *all actions leading to the satisfaction of the same psychological or biological need.* Suppose, for example, that we have developed a method for making reliable determinations of an individual's "need to be aggressive." Conceivably, this need could be satisfied by physical assault upon other persons or upon inanimate objects, by verbal insults, by self-inflicted injury, and by a wide variety of other actions, including imagined attacks upon others. If each of these quite different types of behavior leads to the satisfaction of the same need, they might all be included in a single response class. Similarly, an animal could satisfy its need for water by lapping up any of several different kinds of fluid mixtures containing water, by eating wet food, or by licking water from its paws. Behavior of this sort is even more variable than that included under our third method of classification, since it involves variations in both effectors and goal objects. Because of this it is even more likely to be called "purposive" by those who favor the use of such a term.

As a fifth way of grouping actions into classes for purposes of study, one might treat as class members *all reactions involving the same determinants or causes, regardless of the specific needs satisfied, the environmental objects affected, or the limbs or muscle groups involved.* For instance, if one could decide unambiguously that certain actions are controlled by the "will," and if other observers could concur in these decisions, it might be useful to allocate the responses to a "voluntary" category. Or if one could ascertain which actions are governed by the organism's intentions, these could be brought together into a class of purposive actions. One might also be able to decide that certain activities are determined by personality traits such as anxiety, rigidity, or honesty and thus be able to achieve useful groupings.

In concluding this discussion of criteria for classifying responses, it should be noted that as we progress from the first through the fifth method, it becomes increasingly difficult to get different observers to agree that a given action has been correctly classified. Actions can be defined independently of any potential or actual stimulating conditions, simply by setting up criteria for counting or measuring. But the criteria must be such that other impartial observers can obtain similar results by applying the criteria under essentially comparable conditions. Such application is not especially difficult with the first three methods, but it becomes a relatively serious problem with the last two.

Incidentally, there is no reason why a single observer could not apply more than one of these methods of response classification to a single set of behavioral data. In making his observations, if an experimenter has included a wide variety of actions and stimulating conditions and if these have been carefully recorded, he can, on later occasions, select several subsets of actions in accordance with specific but different criteria. He is then free to utilize whichever subset proves most useful or interesting.

Once criteria have been chosen for use in recording the occurrence of responses, the psychologist's next step is to search for what may be loosely described as the "causes" of behavior. In attempting to understand behavior it is not enough to record behavior and nothing else. One could note, in the most minute detail, the thousands of responses made by an organism throughout its life and yet have little or no understanding of why the behavior occurred. To understand behavior one must look for *environmental or organic conditions, for other responses of the organism, or for any other events that can be related in some meaningful way to the observed behavior.* One must record events or quantities other than the behavior under study: quantities such as temperature, humidity, degree of illumination, sounds, physiological states of the organism, number and kinds of previous experiences, and, on many occasions, other reactions of the same or different organisms. Because the task of defining and specifying these additional events leads to some controversy among psychologists, we digress briefly to consider the problems involved in defining the stimulus.

On the Definition of Stimuli. Some authors have maintained that the stimuli for behavior can be defined only in terms of the reactions they evoke. Because of this limitation they have argued further that meaningful relations cannot be formulated between responses and stimuli since the two variables of an empirical law must be independent. From one point of view these are correct assertions, but they must be carefully interpreted and extensively qualified.

In the first place, by using the methods of the physical sciences, we can specify or describe a multitude of physical phenomena in an entirely objective manner. Moreover, this can be done quite adequately *without referring to the behavior of the particular organisms we are investigating.* We can measure the temperature of the air that surrounds our subjects, the brightness of lights to which they are told to respond, the intensity of sound produced by a thunderclap, the number of grains of ragweed pollen per cubic foot of air, the amplitude of radio waves, and so on. These environmental events and many more are external to, and independent of, the presence or behavior of the subjects of our psychological experiments. For the moment let us describe these phenomena by the term *physical incidents*.

We can also include in this category additional incidents attributable to organisms other than our subjects. The patterns of light and shadow provided by the movements of another organism, the assorted sequences of sounds it produces, or its physical movements, are phenomena that can be recorded and measured by the same methods one uses for other physical incidents. These incidents do originate in the behavior of an organism, but they can be observed and measured independently of the particular organisms that serve as our subjects. For some purposes it may be desirable to distinguish this second group of incidents from the first, but both kinds of physical occurrences can be measured and defined by the methods of the natural scientist. Assertions about the presence of any one of these incidents, about its duration in time, or about its intensity or extensity, depend solely upon objective physical measurements; such assertions are not contingent upon the presence of the organisms whose behavior is under study, though they do depend upon the presence of the observing and recording scientist.

In order to simplify this discussion we have ignored the possibility that certain responses may have physical consequences that can be correlated with subsequent responses. These response-generated physical events can, in principle, be measured in the same ways that we measure events external to our subjects, but practical techniques for doing so remain to be perfected.

A strong case can be made for the view, therefore, that the raw data with which the psychologist works consist, *in part*, of (1) a set of quantities obtained from physical measurements of the actions of his subjects, and (2) a set of independent quantities obtained by measuring or counting physical incidents originating outside of his reacting subjects. The psychologist's goal is to understand the first set of quantities, and to date the most fruitful procedure has been to search for relations between elements of the second set (the environment) and elements of the first (behavior). At a low level of complexity, the ability to state lawful relations between the elements of these two sets of quantities constitutes scientific explanation in psychology.

As the process of formulating and discovering dependable relations between these two sets of quantities progresses, the psychologist finds that some physical incidents are correlated with actions of the observed organisms and some are not. For example, he may note that a subject exhibits a vigorous startle reaction whenever a loud, sharp sound is presented. On the other hand, a relationship may never be found between intensity of cosmic radiation reaching earth from outer space and any recordable bit of behavior. Both the loud sound and the cosmic rays are physical incidents, but, so far as we now know, only the sound is closely and consistently related to behavior.

As a consequence of numerous observations, the psychologist can point to a great many physical incidents that are related, though in varying degrees, to behavior. Moreover, he frequently knows how long the physical incidents must endure, how intense and how close they must be to the organism, and what other characteristics they must possess if they are to correlate with a subject's behavior. On the basis of his investigations, therefore, the psychologist can define a new subclass of physical incidents which, though they differ radically from one another, have as a common characteristic a known relatedness to actions. *It is to this subclass of physical incidents that the name stimuli is often given.* Thus, to describe a physical incident as a *stimulus* is simply to assert that it is, as a consequence of empirical findings, known to be related, or to have been related, to the behavior of some organism in some way. The assertion that a stimulus must be defined in terms of a response stems from the fact that responses are involved in the process of attaching the name stimulus to a given physical incident. But *the inherent physical properties of such a physical incident are not defined by appeal to responses, but by reference to physical measurements.* Whether a physical event is to be called a stimulus thus depends on its being related to responses; but *what it is as a physical event* does not. The term stimulus is simply a convenient shorthand expression for the fact of relatedness. It is a renaming that does little, in and of itself, to advance our understanding of basic relations.

In connection with the general problem of deciding which physical incidents might be chosen for inclusion in the special class, stimuli, the following may be said: The responses used in empirical demonstrations of relationships to physical incidents may be of several different types. One may select any of the response classes discussed above or may penetrate more deeply into the physiological reactions of the organism. For example, one may wish to assert that a response has been elicited by a physical incident, which can then be called a stimulus if any afferent activity whatever was noted when the incident occurred. If a faint light leads to electrical activity in a subject's optic nerve, even though no overt muscular movements occur, one may say the light was a stimulus. Alternatively, one may choose to call the light a stimulus only if its presentation results in the subject's saying "I see something." In either event, reclassifying the light as a stimulus is a consequence of observed concomitant action exhibited by the subject. At present, there are apparently no clear-cut reasons for choosing one kind of action over another.

Before turning to a further discussion of the task of the psychologist, we should note that irrespective of which kind of activity or response is used as the criterion for relabeling certain physical incidents as stimuli, the relatedness itself is dependent upon a great many variables whose presence must be considered. Thus a light may qualify as a stimulus if it is brighter than a certain minimal value, if it is within a certain distance of the subject, if it is located at a certain angle, if the subject is not too fatigued or too bored, if response A is used rather than B, and so on. If one or more of these conditions is not fulfilled, the light may not evoke a measurable reaction, and if it does not, then at that moment it does not meet the conditions for membership in the class, stimuli. A thorough understanding of behavior requires that we know precisely when and under what conditions a given physical incident is indeed related to action. The task of discovering the nature of these relations and the conditions under which they occur, constitutes an extensive and important part of the psychologist's field of endeavor.

Types of Functional Relations Studied by the Psychologist

As soon as the psychologist begins to observe both behavior and the environmental circumstances within which it occurs, he becomes involved in determining the empirical laws that hold between and within the two sets of quantities. In the following subsections we shall describe several kinds of these empirical laws.

Stimulus-Response Relations. Perhaps the simplest kinds of empirical laws with which the psychologist is primarily concerned are those in which the reactions of a subject (or subjects) to systematically varied stimulus conditions are recorded. As an illustration, suppose one were to measure the mean reaction time of a group of subjects to each of several different intensities of a visual signal provided by a light. If some regular change in reaction time (R) were found to accompany the variations in light intensity (S), a functional connection of the sort commonly called an S-R law would have been obtained. *Thus an S-R law is an empirical relation between measured changes in some aspect of the physical environment and measured variations in some property or characteristic of responses,* other factors being held constant.

An actual S-R relation obtained in a study by Hovland and Riesen (1940) is shown in Fig. 1:1. As can be seen from this figure, these investigators found that mean response amplitude increased as the intensity of the tone was heightened. The response was a decrease in skin resistance, and the stimulus was a 1,000-cycle tone whose intensity above the subjects' thresholds was expressed in decibels.

In actual practice a function of this kind could be obtained either from repeated tests of the same subjects, using the five different stimulus values, or from tests of a different group of subjects with each value. In either case the resulting S-R function constitutes a summary of the results of all the tests. The S-R laws obtained from individual subjects would probably differ considerably from an averaged function like that of Fig. 1:1.

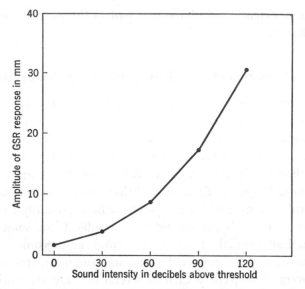

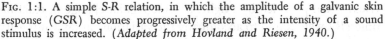

FIG. 1:1. A simple S-R relation, in which the amplitude of a galvanic skin response (GSR) becomes progressively greater as the intensity of a sound stimulus is increased. (*Adapted from Hovland and Riesen, 1940.*)

R-R Relations. A second kind of empirical law frequently obtained by psychologists may be described, following Spence (1944), as an *R-R* relation. Such a law is obtained by plotting one set of response measures against another. Suppose we administer an arithmetic aptitude test to three college students, who are required to solve as many addition problems as possible in five minutes. Suppose further that student *A* solves 20 problems, student *B* solves 15, and student *C* solves 10. These scores constitute one measure of the responses of each student to the stimuli provided by the test situation. Now imagine that the same test is given to the same three students a day later, and the scores of 23, 18, and 13 are obtained by *A, B,* and *C,* respectively. The results of these two administrations of the same test, if plotted graphically, would look like Fig. 1:2. This constitutes an *R-R* law of an extremely simple and elementary sort.

Nevertheless, this law contains the essential ingredients for making predictions of a relatively primitive variety. From a knowledge of how a student performs on the first day's test we can predict, with a certain margin of error, how well he will do on

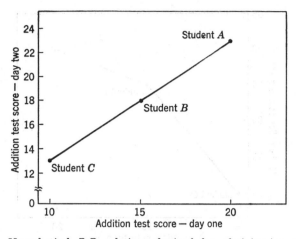

Fig. 1:2. Hypothetical R-R relation obtained by administering the same addition test to the same subjects on each of two successive days.

the second day. This assumes, of course, that the relationship between the performances on days one and two is essentially stable. To the student acquainted with elementary test-construction methods it will be apparent that this simple R-R law is identical in form to the relation obtained when one determines the test-retest reliability of a test. If an individual gets approximately the same absolute or relative score upon repeated administrations of the same test, or comparable forms thereof, the test is said to be *reliable*. It measures the same capacities or abilities each time it is administered.

Different R-R laws will of course be obtained if the two responses are measured under different environmental conditions and by different tests. To illustrate, the three students of the preceding example might all have taken the same elementary mathematics course, and student A might have received a grade of 90, student B a grade of 85, and C a grade of 70. When these course grades are plotted against the first day's addition-test scores for the same students, the resulting R-R law might be of the form shown in Fig. 1:3.

An R-R law such as this, assuming again that it proves to be stable, has considerable utility. From a knowledge of a student's score on the addition test one can predict his course grade, and

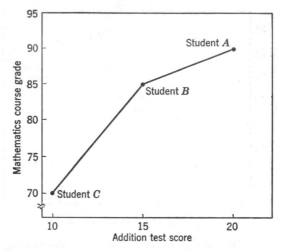

Fig. 1:3. Hypothetical R-R relation between the scores obtained by three students on a simple addition test and the grades they received in an elementary mathematics course.

vice versa. Readers familiar with elementary statistics will immediately recognize this relation as a very simple scattergram like those used in connection with the computation of coefficients of correlation. R-R relationships like this are extensively employed by psychologists who work in the areas of vocational guidance, personnel selection, and industrial psychology. If one can successfully predict, from the results of a short, written test, how well an employee will do in a certain job or how well a student will perform in college, substantial savings in time and money can be effected.

These two examples of R-R laws may be thought of as lying at the extremes of a continuum. At one end the same test items are presented on two separate occasions in the same environment, and nearly identical responses are recorded. At the other extreme neither the responses being recorded nor the two test situations are markedly similar. By making the test conditions and/or the responses the same or different we can achieve a wide variety of R-R laws that may be placed at appropriate positions on this continuum. The same kinds of responses might be recorded on the two occasions, but the testing situations might be quite different. Or the situations might be identical, but different reactions might be recorded. When both the reactions and the testing situations differ, as in our second example, the resultant R-R function is like those obtained in the process of *validating* a test.

O-R Relationships. A third type of function that psychologists seek to establish may be described as an O-R law (Spence, 1944). This designation refers to a relation in which *the independent variable is some measurable organic characteristic, property, or state of an organism (or of different groups of organisms), and the dependent variable is some reaction or response.* An O-R law differs from an S-R law in that the independent variable in the S-R relationship is usually a physical event in the external environment, whereas in the O-R law it is some bodily state of an organism. An example of an O-R law is given in Fig. 1:4 where the R variable is the number of times female rats crossed an electrified grid to reach a male and the O variable is the stage of the estral cycle as defined by histological examinations of the vaginal mucosa. In this experiment (Warner, 1927) all of the subjects were first tested in the obstruction box and were then classified into separate groups according to the results of the histological tests. In a sense,

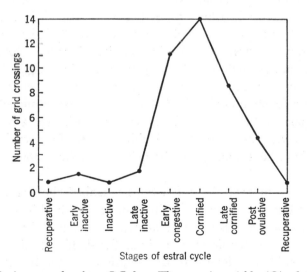

Fig. 1:4. An example of an O-R law. The organic variable (O) plotted on the base line is the stage of the female estral cycle, and the response variable (R) on the ordinate is the number of times the female rats crossed an electrified grid to reach a male. (*Adapted from Warner, 1927.*)

estrous level was thus varied by choosing subgroups of subjects who fell at each stage.

Specific values of an O variable are usually determined by means of standardized physical methods of measurement. For instance, the basic method used to compute percentage of alcohol in the blood of automobile drivers charged with intoxication probably involves chemical analyses of blood samples. Under certain conditions, however, comparable results could be obtained from behavioral data. Thus if a reliable functional connection (empirical law) has been established between alcohol percentage and scores on a line-walking test, then O values can be estimated from scores on the behavioral test.

Other Varieties of Functional Relations. The S-R, R-R, and O-R relations discussed above are among the most common empirical functions obtained by the research psychologist. There are several others, however, which, because of the ways we have chosen to apply our labels, do not qualify precisely as S-R, R-R, or O-R functions. For instance, the familiar learning curve relating some measure of performance to number of trials has not been cited here as an example of an S-R law, though it is often so regarded, since the physically defined properties of the stimuli in the learning situation are not systematically varied over trials but are held as constant as possible. Likewise, relations in which behavioral changes are plotted against the passage of time, e.g., speed of movement as a function of chronological age and sensitivity to light as a function of time in darkness, cannot be subsumed easily under any of the types of laws already considered. One could readily invent new alphabetical abbreviations for laws such as these, but the advantages to be gained therefrom appear to be slight.

Although in each of the functions described above a response measure was plotted on the ordinate of the graph, this is not true of all psychological laws. For example, the psychologist might be interested in determining the visual thresholds of his subjects under conditions where *both* the duration and the brightness of a test light are systematically varied. The empirical function resulting from such an experiment might look like the graph in Fig. 1:5. Here the intensity of the test light is plotted along

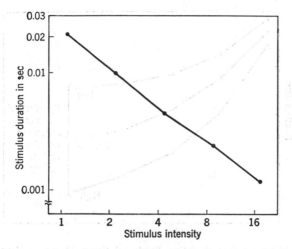

FIG. 1.5. An empirical relation in which physically measured values of the stimulus are plotted on both dimensions. Each point on the curve represents a visual stimulus whose duration and intensity are such that it is seen just 50 per cent of the time. (*Adapted from Braunstein, 1923.*)

the abscissa and its duration on the ordinate. The empirical points tell us which combinations of duration and intensity result in the subject's seeing the test light 50 per cent of the times on which it is presented. Thus the light will be seen for half the time if it is brief and bright, or for half the time, even when it is dim, if it is presented for a longer time. This type of relation differs from the S-R variety in that physically measured quantities occupy both the ordinate and the abscissa. Moreover, the plotted points do not represent different magnitudes or frequencies of a response. Because of these differences, this particular sort of function might best be described as a modified S-R relation.

Finally, it should be noted that functions more complicated than either the simple S-R or O-R laws can be obtained by simultaneously varying both the condition of the organism and some characteristic of the stimulus situation. Relations obtained under such conditions might be termed SO-R laws, since the dependent variable (the response) is a joint function of both an organic variable and an environmental one. A hypothetical example of this kind of relation is presented in Fig. 1:6. In preparing this graph it has been assumed that reaction time decreases as a

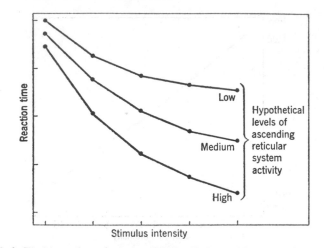

FIG. 1:6. Fictitious data depicting *SO-R* relations. The dependent variable (reaction time) is shown as varying both with stimulus intensity and amount of general neural activity in the ascending reticular activating system.

function of increasing stimulus intensity but that the function relating the two variables takes a different form depending upon the average level of activity of the brain-stem reticular formation. In this case stimulus intensity is the principal independent variable, and reticular-system activity, though also classifiable as an independent variable, would usually be described as a *parameter*. This combination-type law exemplifies a phenomenon which statisticians describe as an *interaction*. By this they mean that the effect of stimulus intensity upon reaction time depends upon the particular level of the third factor, reticular-system discharges. Although the curves of Fig. 1:6 have been called an *SO-R* relation, three simple and distinct laws are actually plotted on one graph. Each law, considered alone, is an *S-R* law specific to the magnitude of neural excitation present at the time of its determination. Level of reticular outflow could, with equal justification, have been plotted on the base line as the major independent variable, with different values of stimulus intensity constituting the parameter. To maintain a consistent terminology, compound laws of this latter type should probably be termed *OS-R* relations.

The reader should note that if the three values plotted vertically at any point on the abscissa of Fig. 1:6 were to be replotted as a separate graph, the result would be an O-R law relating reaction time to three values of the independent O variable (reticular activity), with stimulus intensity held constant. Similarly, a re-plotting of the values at any abscissa point on an OS-R relationship would yield an S-R law, the value of O being held constant. The complexity of any of these relationships could be increased by introducing other factors as additional parameters. The two-dimensional curves of Fig. 1:6 could be expanded into three-dimensional surfaces by simultaneously varying some other factor in addition to stimulus intensity and reticular outflow. The number of variables that might be included is limited only by the experimenter's ability to control and measure them and to analyze and comprehend the results.

General Approaches to the Study of Behavior

As noted in our introductory paragraphs, the psychologist's fundamental task is to study and to attempt to understand the behavior of organisms. Although some progress toward this goal might be attained by a careful study of historical and literary writings, most students of behavior believe that primary reliance should be placed upon objective observations of the activities of organisms and of environmental or other factors that are correlated with such actions. When the data obtained from such observations are collated and organized, the results are empirical relations of the several varieties we have just described.

But no matter how many functional relations are established by the psychologist, he is seldom satisfied to cease his inquiries at that point. He may be pleased to learn that reaction time decreases as a function of increasing stimulus intensity, but he is even more pleased if he can gain additional insights into the factors that determine this function. Hence he strives to learn precisely *why* reaction time declines as stimulus intensity increases. In his efforts to understand behavior, therefore, he often finds it rewarding to go beyond his initial empirical data, to speculate about relations not yet discovered, and to search for new facts and new contingencies.

Given a well-established empirical law, the psychologist may follow two principal paths toward the enrichment of his understanding of the law. One of these, which involves detailed analyses and descriptions of the bodily mechanisms of behaving organisms, is usually described as the "physiological approach." The second, often characterized as the "behavioral approach," leads to further study of the range of conditions under which the law holds and to the search for "explanatory" laws in which only behavioral and experimental variables are contained. These two approaches are not mutually exclusive, and many investigators follow both, but they are sufficiently different to warrant separate discussion.

The Physiological Approach. The student of behavior who adopts this general plan of action tries, where possible, to interpret his empirical laws by appealing to known facts concerning an organism's physical structure and its functions. He endeavors to explain his findings in terms of knowledge and concepts derived from the work of the physiologist, the physiological psychologist, the anatomist, the biochemist, and the biophysicist. Given an empirical relation between a response measure and a stimulus variable, he may inquire into the details of the receptor mechanisms by which the organism senses the stimulus, or he may try to trace the neural connections intervening between the receptor and the final response. This approach is primarily favored by those who concentrate on the study of the sensory processes of vision, audition, olfaction, and gustation. Its value is indicated by the tremendous strides toward the understanding of such processes that have been made during the past few decades. And the desirability of continued work along these lines is strongly supported by the widespread conviction among behavior scientists that living organisms, though descriptively unique and astonishingly complex, are nevertheless physical systems or assemblies of such systems. There are many reasons for believing, therefore, that in the future our explanations of complex human and animal behavior will be considerably broadened by the identification of the neurophysiological and physicochemical systems whose functions make that behavior possible.

The Behavioral Approach. Investigators whose activities exemplify the behavioral approach typically do not concern themselves with the question of why an empirical law is what it is in the light of the structural characteristics of the behaving organism. They do not, as a rule, apply the terms or concepts of the physiologist or anatomist to the explication of empirical relations between behavior and other variables and seldom refer to such specific bodily entities as muscles, tendons, glands, and nerve fibers. Instead, their attention is concentrated upon what they may describe as *molar* behavior, meaning relatively gross movements or goal-oriented actions of the entire organism. For the psychologist who favors this approach reasonably satisfactory explanations of behavior can be wrung from a knowledge of the wide assortment of experimental variables that affect behavioral laws, from information as to the kinds and magnitudes of these effects, and from supraordinate laws that tie simpler laws together in a meaningful fashion. Gaps in this network of explanatory laws are filled, in part, by "guessed-at laws" (Spence, 1948) and by the introduction of "explanatory" concepts such as intelligence, personality traits, ego-involvement, associative connections, inherited reactive tendencies, unconscious desires, cognitions, motives, and drives. These terms refer, though often in a relatively vague fashion, to properties, states, predispositions, or characteristics of organisms that function as determinants of behavior. Their basic meanings, for purposes of communication within the context of the scientific vocabulary, can be given by explicit definitions, but failure to provide such definitions is commonplace. The broader meanings of these terms, in their roles as integrative or explanatory elements of interpretive networks or theories, derive from the varieties and kinds of empirical and conceptual relations into which they enter as constituents. In following the behavioral approach, therefore, one deals primarily with molar rather than molecular behavior; one investigates the ways in which an assortment of variables affects behavior and modifies the laws relating it to other variables; and in attempting to explain behavior, one tends to appeal to postulated processes or intervening variables whose principal function is that of summarization and integration. The concepts of drive and motivation, to which we now turn, are often encountered in the writings of those who subscribe to the behavioral approach, and generally speaking, occupy a position of considerable importance therein

The Problem of Motivation

There is no question but that the idea of motivation or some similar notion appears in almost every systematic account of behavior. Contemporary psychological theorists as well as their more philosophically oriented predecessors have frequently relied upon some kind of moving, pushing, driving, or energizing force or agency. The ubiquity of the concept of motivation, in one guise or another, is nevertheless surprising when we consider that its meaning is often scandalously vague. It is not our intention to tabulate all of the many motivationlike terms that have been used or to summarize the history and development of the concept. Such summaries may be found in the writings of Troland (1928), Young (1936), Gardiner, Metcalf, and Beebe-Center (1937), Lindzey (1959), and Madsen (1959), as well as in widely scattered briefer discussions. It will be sufficient to note that, depending upon the particular writer consulted, motivation can be conscious or unconscious; it can be the same as, or different from, drive; it may or may not guide behavior; and all motives can be either learned or instinctive. Moreover, arguments can be found to support the view that motivation is both crucial to behavior and a useless concept, that it is simply the energy that moves the body, or that it is identical with the neural discharges of specific central nervous-system structures. We thus find ourselves in the position of trying to deal with an allegedly vital factor in the face of violent disagreements as to its origins, its essential nature, and its particular roles as a behavior determinant. The evaluation and reconciliation, where possible, of these divergent opinions and contradictory views is of central concern to the student of motivation and is a significant facet of the problem of motivation.

Within the field of psychology, broadly defined, factors or variables known to affect behavior in one way or another are grouped into a number of loosely defined classes, to each of which, by more or less common agreement, a distinguishing name is assigned. These names frequently coincide with the traditional chapter headings of our elementary texts. For instance, when behavior is found to vary with changes in sensory stimulation, the psychologist says he is concerned with the problems of *sensation* or *perception*.

If frequency and diversity of previous experiences prove to be important variables, the area of study may be labeled *learning* or *fatigue* or *adaptation*, depending on other information. If verbally administered instructions influence behavior, the research is concerned with *set* or *expectancy*. In like manner, other areas of investigation are given names such as conflict, emotion, transfer of training, remembering, and of course, motivation or drive.

Although significant and relevant variables have been successfully isolated and identified in some of these areas, this is less true for motivation than one might wish. Many of the fundamental problems in this field arise when serious inquiries are launched into the nature of motivational variables. To bring order into our thinking we need criteria for deciding that a given variable is indeed affecting behavior "motivationally"; we need to know whether motivational variables can be identified in terms of intrinsic properties as well as by means of their effects on behavior; and we need to identify variables that may function both motivationally and nonmotivationally. The task of obtaining such knowledge is clearly relevant to the general motivational problem, and much of the remainder of this book is concerned with this matter.

It is also necessary to note that in recent years more and more investigators have raised the serious question of whether a concept of motivation is really required by a comprehensive theory of behavior. The student of motivation must also devote a portion of his time, therefore, to the analysis and evaluation of arguments and evidence bearing on this issue. This means that he must concern himself not only with the problem of motivation but also with more generally comprehensive behavior theories. The construction and evaluation of theories in which motivation plays an important role is as much a part of the general problem of motivation as the gathering of empirical data and the identification of significant variables.

Summary

In this chapter we have tried to set the stage for our subsequent discussions of motivation by describing in general terms some of the activities, procedures, and goals of the student of behavior.

The attainment of satisfactory explanations of behavior is described as the psychologist's principal aim and the observing and recording of the activities of organisms as his initial task. The raw data with which he works consist of tabulations of the frequency of occurrence of certain actions, their magnitude, their rate, or their duration. These data are unique in that they are contingent upon the presence of living organisms, but the methods used in collecting them are essentially identical with those of the natural sciences.

Since no two responses are ever exactly alike, the investigator, in gathering his basic data, must deal with classes or groups of responses. The boundaries of the class may be quite restricted, as in the case where the activity of only a single muscle group or gland is recorded, or wide enough to encompass complex purposive and goal-directed acts. The setting of class limits is dictated solely by individual preference and by the scientific and/or practical utility of the research findings. Irrespective of where the boundaries are set, however, lawful regularities in behavior cannot be expected unless the conditions of observation have been specified precisely in advance.

Collections of raw facts, valuable as they are, do not contain all of the ingredients required for adequate scientific explanations. Unelaborated descriptions of a subject's behavior must be supplemented by accounts of environmental events, by records of previous experiences and reactions, by observations of the behavior of other organisms, and by measurements of physiologically defined states or characteristics of the subject. The discovery of dependable empirical laws relating behavior to other variables such as these is a necessary step toward explanation and understanding. Identifying abbreviations such as S-R, R-R, and O-R are often applied to special groups of these laws.

Because the component variables of any empirical relation must be independent of one another, it is sometimes held that one cannot legitimately speak of stimulus-response laws, since it is also alleged that responses and stimuli can be defined only in terms of one another. An analysis of this matter leads to the conclusion that, given precise criteria of observation, responses can be identified and recorded reliably even when observers know nothing of the stimuli that elicit the responses. Similarly, the conclusion is reached that environmental events such as lights, sounds, and odors can be identified and measured by physical procedures, irrespective of whether these events are correlated with responses. To apply the term stimuli to events having known response contingencies is simply to reassert the facts of dependency.

The discovery of empirical relations represents an important step toward scientific explanation, but the questions of why a given law holds or why it takes a particular form also demand answers. In seeking solutions some investigators find it profitable to study the physiological and neurological bases of behavior and may be said to follow the physiological approach. Others, in adopting a behavioral approach, confine their search for answers to data at the behavioral level of description. Their techniques involve the discovery and evaluation of further related laws, the manipulation of additional variables to determine the range of factors crucial to the stability of laws, and the introduction of summarizing or explanatory concepts such as habit strength, personality traits, intelligence, inhibition, and motivation. The meanings of these terms are given both by explicit definitions within the scientific language and by the variety of useful relations into which they enter as constituents.

Finally, although a concept of motivation or some similar notion is to be found in nearly every theoretical account of behavior, an amazing divergence of opinion exists as to the nature and function of motivation. A significant portion of the general problem of motivation arises, therefore, from the need to clarify, evaluate, and, wherever possible, to reconcile these disparate conceptions. Other critical aspects of the problem are the identification, selection, and manipulation of motivational variables, the critical appraisal of the utility of the concept, and the formulation of adequate theories.

‖‖

CHAPTER 2

Intervening Variables and the Definition and Measurement of Drive

As WE HAVE SEEN in the previous chapter, investigators who attempt to formulate systematic accounts of behavior often appeal to intermediary explanatory factors such as intelligence, personality, field forces, associative strength, libido, instinct, frustration, and drive. Various general names have been suggested for these intermediaries, e.g., symbolic constructs, explanatory concepts, and hypothetical constructs, but the term *intervening variables* (Tolman, 1932) is perhaps the most common. The qualifying adjective "intervening" is used to convey the notion that the postulated states, conditions, or processes intervene between behavior and its observable correlates or antecedents. Since these variables cannot be observed directly, their meanings are provided by explicit definitions and by their functional relations within the context of general theories of behavior. Inasmuch as the introduction of such conceptions is widespread, and since motivation is a prominent example, it is desirable at this point to consider the question of why students of behavior have felt impelled to make venturesome and sometimes unbridled speculations about such unseen entities.

One rather obvious reason for the use of intervening variables, even when ill defined and loosely connected to a theory, is that the users regard them as having real value as summarizing or interpretive concepts. The psychologist feels that he has explained behavior in a way that would otherwise have been impossible. Alternatively, some explanatory concepts (and certainly motivation is one of these) are elements of the nonscientific language of the layman and may have been passed uncritically from one generation of psychologists to another without regard for their scientific worth. One cannot, unfortunately, ask the psychologists of the last fifty years why they have felt the need to incorporate intervening variables into their theories. We can, however, examine the kinds of data with which they have worked to determine whether those data or their interrelations have special characteristics requiring the postulation of intermediary concepts. It is difficult to believe that the universality of such notions as associative strength, drive, and the like, can be due merely to chance, and it is possible, therefore, that intervening variables have, in a sense, been thrust upon psychologists by the nature of the empirical facts with which they have dealt.

Empirical Relations Tending to Evoke Motivational or Other Intermediary Concepts

The Evocation of Vigorous Responses by Weak Stimuli. Concepts such as drive, set, or expectancy are especially likely to appeal to psychologists when subjects exhibit violent reactions to weak stimuli. The creaking of a wind-blown shutter may evoke intense reactions of fear or escape from the timid explorer of an abandoned house; the faint nighttime stirrings of a sick child may galvanize its mother into action; and the smell of a female dog in heat may rouse the male to excited and extensive exploratory action.

Disproportionalities of this sort are common among S-R laws, and though they may assume a variety of forms, a single example will suffice. In this instance, the relation is such that increases in the intensity of the stimulus produce no response whatever until

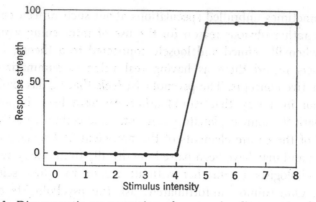

Fig. 2:1. Diagrammatic representation of a stepwise disproportion between the intensity of a stimulus and the strength of the response it evokes. The units on both axes are fictitious.

a certain level is reached, whereupon the reaction appears with maximum strength. Further increases in the strength of the stimulus have no effect upon the response. A *stepwise* function of this type is shown in Fig. 2:1, where the intensity of the stimulus has been plotted on the horizontal axis (abscissa) and the vigor of reaction on the vertical axis (ordinate). The units of both scales are fictitious. A function of this type might be obtained in the case of verbally presented instructions or commands. If the instructions are too faint to be heard, the receiving organism does nothing; but when they become loud enough to be clearly understood, the hearer reacts appropriately. Beyond the point of intelligibility, further increases in the intensity of the commands may have little or no effect on the behavior they elicit.

In dealing with a relation of this sort, the psychologist may entertain the view that the stimulus controls a separate source of energy which is released in the response, and hence may find it desirable to introduce a motivationlike concept. It must be emphasized, however, that disproportionality, as such, can also be explained, perhaps more adequately, by nonmotivational concepts such as set, expectancy, or associative strength. Motivation may be suggested by data such as these, but it is not required.

Variability of Response in the Presence of Constant Stimulating Conditions. The observation that an individual's behavior varies from time to time in an environment whose physical characteristics have not apparently changed is commonplace and provides strong inducement for the use of one or another intervening concept. Suppose, for example, that the running speed of a rat is measured in the same straight runway on three different occasions and that at each successive trial his speed increases. The elements of this situation are represented in Fig. 2:2, with the large S at the left of the diagram denoting the constant environment provided by the alley and the three Rs at the right, with their respective subscripts, indicating the running speeds as measured on the three trials.

Presented with data of this kind, the investigator may wonder why the rat did not run at exactly the same speed on the three occasions. Since the physical properties of the runway were identical throughout the experiment and the rat was presumably handled in the same way on each occasion, performance inequalities cannot be explained by appealing to variations in the stimulus situation. At this point the psychologist might assume that the rat differed from trial to trial with respect to some unknown state or characteristic, and that this characteristic was responsible for the recorded changes in running speed. As a first step toward accounting for his observations, therefore, he might postulate the existence of a behavior-determining factor which he simply calls factor X. This leads him to modify the relations in Fig. 2:2 to include three values of X. This alteration is shown in Fig. 2:3, where the greatest amount or degree of X, i.e., X_{high}, is associated with the highest speed (R_{fast}), the intermediate level of X with $R_{moderate}$, and low X with R_{slow}. From this, the scientist may wish to assert that speed of running depends upon level or amount of factor X.

Not much has been accomplished, of course, if the interpretive process stops at this point. A conception as bare as this must be strengthened and enriched

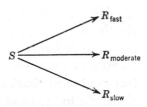

FIG. 2:2. Schematic illustration of intraindividual variation in response despite a carefully maintained constancy of the external environment (S). The subscripts to the three capital Rs indicate the running speeds of a single rat when tested on three occasions in the same straight-alley maze.

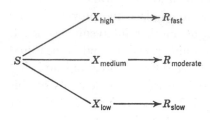

Fig. 2:3. Schematic diagram show-ing the postulated introduction of three levels of a hypothetical be-havior determinant (X) designed to "explain" differences in the re-sponses of a single organism that has been tested under identical stimulating conditions (S) on three occasions.

by additional assumptions as to the properties of factor X, the pre-cise ways in which it functions to determine speed of running, and its relations to experimental variables and other intervening con-cepts. These are matters of substantial importance to the behavior scientist, but their consideration must be postponed for the pres-ent.

Enlarging upon this example of response variation in the pres-ence of constant stimulus conditions, we note that the relation, in its basic form, applies to differences between the performances of different individuals as well as to intraindividual variability. Thus if one rat runs faster than a second, and the second faster than a third, when all are tested in the same situation, an inter-vening, performance-determining variable can perhaps be profitably invoked.

An instance of what seems to qualify as a special case of response variability in the presence of constant stimulation is found in the observation that, when food is presented to an animal, it some-times eats and sometimes does not; or, of two supposedly identical animals, one may eat and the other not. Skinner (1938), in his treatment of motivation, states that this is the basic phenomenon giving rise to the concept of drive. This particular behavior could be represented by separate diagrams like those of Figs. 2:2 and 2:3, but this is not necessary. Suppose, for example, that the rat whose performance is shown in Fig. 2:2 instead of running slowly, simply does not run at all. His failure to run might then be attributed to a complete lack of, or negligible strength of, factor X. If the behavior is exhibited, X is postulated to be present; if no behavior occurs, X is assumed to be effectively absent.

Equality or Constancy of Behavior in the Presence of Normally Effective Changes in the External Stimulus Situation. Under some

FIG. 2:4. Three different stimulus situations, i.e., the brightnesses of an alley on three different occasions, are represented at the left by the three Ss. It has been assumed that these unequal brightnesses all lead to equal (and moderate) rates of running in three individual rats, even though rats usually run faster (also assumed) under bright than under dim illumination.

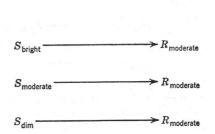

conditions subjects may behave alike even though they are expected to react quite differently, and an individual, in situations that typically lead to quite different responses, may show behavioral constancy. As in our preceding examples, empirical data of this sort tend to lead to the introduction of intervening variables. To give a specific illustration, imagine that, normally, the more brightly an alley maze is lighted the faster a rat will run. Suppose further that an available alley can be illuminated with three degrees of brightness and that three rats from the same litter are tested therein, one under each level of illumination. If all three animals run at the same speed, we would have an instance of *response equality in the presence of normally effective changes in the external situation.* This is represented schematically in Fig. 2:4.

Were such results obtained, the psychologist might be tempted to explain them by assuming that the three rats differed with respect to a factor X. He might postulate that the rat tested under bright illumination ran more slowly than animals typically do because its level of X was low. Similarly, the rat tested under dim illumination might have run faster than expected because of an excessive amount of X. By assuming that differences in X have counteracted the effects of illumination in this way one might explain the failure to obtain the expected differences in response. The elements of this interpretation are represented diagrammatically in Fig. 2:5.

In concluding this section, we must note that many additional examples might be cited of representative empirical relations that seem to call for the introduction of intermediary constructs. For example, as Skinner (1938), Hull (1943), and Miller (1959), among others, have observed, when several different experimental

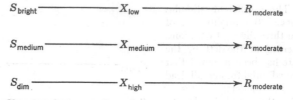

Fɪɢ. 2:5. Showing how equality of response in spite of normally effective variations in the brightness of a stimulus might be explained by postulating differing levels of an intervening variable, factor X. Variations in brightness and variations in factor X are inversely related when evaluated with respect to their effects on speed of running.

variables are found to affect behavior in the same way, the postulation of an intervening process common to all of them may prove desirable. Furthermore, intervening constructs should not be regarded as unique to S-R relations. Equally imperative reasons for the use of such concepts may arise from the study of O-R, R-R, and other relations.

Circular Reasoning in the Use of Intermediary Concepts

When properly introduced into a psychological theory, intervening variables often serve a useful function as conceptual devices. When carelessly defined and irresponsibly used, however, they not only contribute nothing to our understanding but may even be gravely misleading. In the preceding section, several examples were given of the kinds of empirical relations that seem to give rise to intermediary concepts, and it was observed that in attempting to explain such relations one might begin by attributing the behavior to variations in an unidentified factor X. One must go well beyond this point, however, to achieve satisfactory explanations. It is especially unfruitful to introduce different degrees of factor X on the ground that different responses are observed, and then to turn about and appeal to the inferred values of X to "explain" the variations in behavior. One may assume that some animals run faster than others *because* they have more of factor X, but this is trivially circular if the only basis one has for asserting they have more X is the fact that they run more rapidly. From this it becomes clear that the introduction of factor X in the manner diagramed in Figs. 2:3 and 2:5 has in only the most superficial sense explained the observed behavior.

There are many instances within psychology of circular reasoning in the use of intermediary constructs. For instance, one frequently encounters the statement that individuals behave in different ways in the same environment *because* their perceptions are not the same. This reasoning is typically circular since the perceptions are defined by the same behavior that is allegedly determined by the perceptions. Other terms such as ability, constitutional differences, personality traits, and motivation are likewise often introduced and used in this uncritical way. Psychology is not alone, however, in its occasional use of circular arguments. Social scientists, for example, have tried to explain the gregarious behavior of sheep by postulating an instinct to be gregarious (the herding instinct), but the existence of the instinct has usually been based entirely upon the observed gregarious behavior.

Defining Intervening Variables so as to Avoid Circular Explanations

As we have seen, the introduction of intermediary concepts into one's theory must be done in such a fashion as to avoid circular interpretations. This can be accomplished, in principle, by making certain that one's definition of an intervening variable is completely independent of the specific responses that are assumed to be determined by that variable. This requirement can be met by basing the definition upon (1) the subject's previous experiences, (2) the responses he makes in other test situations, (3) one or another of his organic states, or (4) the stimuli impinging upon him. Each of these ways of achieving independence in definition is examined in more detail in the paragraphs that follow, and in every case the intervening variable is simply called factor X. The problem of whether factor X should be described as drive, habit strength, cognition, set, or whatever, will be discussed at a later point in this chapter.

1. *An Intervening Variable May Be Defined in Terms of Differences in Experience Prior to the Test Situation.* In essence, this method of defining an intervening concept requires that we have

some knowledge concerning an organism's life history. For instance, if subjects who respond differently when tested in the same environmental situation can be shown to have had different experiences or treatments prior to the test, then those experiences can be used to define a factor X.

To illustrate, suppose we have carried out an experiment like that depicted in Fig. 2:2, using three rats rather than one, and have found that they all run at different speeds in the straight runway. Let us suppose also that our subjects are known to differ with respect to the amount of time that has elapsed since they were last fed. Perhaps the fast rat has not eaten for 48 hours, the moderate-speed rat for 24 hours, and the slow rat for 4 hours. This type of information satisfies our need for independent data upon which to base the definition of factor X. The deprivation histories of the animals in this case are correlated with, but *measured independently of*, running speed. Different degrees of factor X can be inferred from, or defined by, measured differences in time of deprivation, and differences in running speed can be "explained" by appealing to differences in factor X as thus defined. Figure 2:6 illustrates schematically the way in which several values of factor X would be inferred from the different deprivation histories of the three animals.

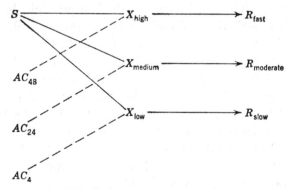

FIG. 2:6. A diagrammatic representation of the manner in which three different antecedent conditions, AC_{48}, AC_{24}, and AC_4, which designate 48, 24, and 4 hours of food deprivation, respectively, may serve as the basis for defining high, medium, and low levels of factor X, in turn. Differences in factor X defined in this way are assumed to be responsible for the fact that an identical stimulus situation (S) elicits fast, moderate, and slow rates of running from three otherwise comparable animals.

In this figure, which is simply a modification of Fig. 2:3, AC_{48} denotes the antecedent condition of being without food for 48 hours at the time of the running-speed test, and AC_{24} and AC_4 refer, respectively, to the conditions of being without food for 24 and for 4 hours.

2. *An Intervening Variable May Be Defined in Terms of Differences in Performance on Some Task Other than That Used in the Test Situation.* Consider again the laboratory situation in which the responses of different subjects are found to vary though the testing conditions are held constant, but suppose that we now have no way of determining the past history of our subjects. Under such circumstances it would be impossible to base our inferences about factor X upon differences in the antecedent conditions to which the organisms had been exposed. Such a situation is not so likely to occur, of course, in a laboratory where the animals are under constant supervision, but it often occurs with human subjects. In most cases we simply do not know what the distinctive antecedent events have been.

Whenever we are unable to control a subject's previous history or to get an accurate estimate of it, we can still achieve an independent definition of an intervening variable by *measuring the subject's responses in a second test situation.* For instance, we might take three rats and place them in separate activity cages and record the amount of activity they exhibit during a standard test period. Differences in amount of activity could then be used to define levels of factor X, and these, in turn, might be invoked to explain differences in running speed in the straight alley. This method of obtaining an independent definition involves the formulation of an R-R relationship, and is represented schematically in Fig. 2:7.

In this diagram S_2 represents the activity-cage situation, and S_1 represents the alley maze. R^1, R^2, and R^3 indicate high, moderate, and low levels of activity, respectively. The dashed lines from R^1, R^2, and R^3 to the three factor-X levels indicate the process of defining inequalities of this factor in terms of the responses exhibited in the activity cages.

3. *An Intervening Variable May Be Defined in Terms of Differences in an Organic Variable.* This way of attaining independ-

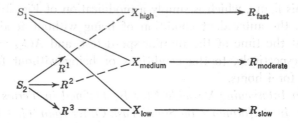

Fig. 2:7. A paradigm to represent the method whereby differences in intensity or vigor of response (R^1, R^2, R^3) in one testing situation (S_2) can yield independent definitions of the levels of an intervening variable. The defined levels of factor X then serve to "explain" variations in response to a different situation (S_1).

ent definitions involves the measurement of some physiological condition of the organism (O variable), such as per cent normal body weight, blood-sugar level, stage of estral cycle, total neural activity in the brain at some point, or skin resistance. Once such measurements have been obtained, they can be examined to determine whether they are stable indexes of inter- or intraindividual differences. If the three rats of our previous example were found to differ reliably with respect to blood-sugar level, such physiologically measured values could be used as the basis for an independent definition of factor X.

Although an O variable has been described as an organic state or characteristic of an organism, numerous instances of such states are difficult to distinguish from responses. To take a single example, a subject's heart rate might remain relatively constant over a period of inactivity and hence might be termed an O variable. But the individual contractions of the heart are clearly consequences of, or responses to, antecedent neural impulses. Similarly, *changes* in mean heart rate might appropriately be catalogued as responses. Were these responses used to define drive differences, the procedure would become an instance of the second method we have just considered. In cases like this the distinction between the second and third methods tends to disappear. Fortunately, this does nothing to destroy the independence of either method.

4. *An Intervening Variable May Be Defined by Referring to Differences in Stimulus Conditions.* When the characteristics of the test situation are not the same from subject to subject, or

from time to time for the same subject, these differences can be employed to obtain independent definitions of intervening variables. As an illustration, consider an experiment in which the eyeblink response is being conditioned to a faint light (CS) by paired presentations of the light and a puff of air (UCS) directed at the cornea. If a strong puff is used for one group of subjects and a weak puff for another, one can assert that the level of factor X is a function of strength of puff, the strong-puff group being defined as having a higher level of factor X than the weak-puff group. Thus the definition of factor X is independent of the resulting behavior, i.e., the frequency of conditioned eyelid responses exhibited by the two groups.

The important elements involved in this defining procedure are summarized in Fig. 2:8. Here the upper line denotes the conditions for the strong-puff group and the lower line those for the weak-puff group.

Thus far in this chapter we have discussed some of the reasons why behavior theorists tend to introduce intermediary constructs into their theories, the dangers of circular interpretations resulting from inappropriate definitions of intermediary constructs, and ways of structuring definitions so as to avoid such circularity. In the

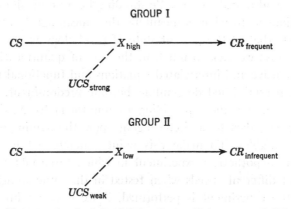

FIG. 2:8. Elements involved in defining factor X in terms of differences in the intensity of the unconditioned stimulus in an eyelid-conditioning experiment. The greater frequency of conditioned responses ($CR_{frequent}$) exhibited by Group I is attributed to the higher level of factor X resulting from the use of a more intense unconditioned stimulus (UCS_{strong}).

specific examples given, we have purposely refrained from substituting a specific label such as motivation for the colorless symbol, factor X. Our next task, therefore, is to consider the problem of how one decides whether, and under what conditions, particular names, such as habit strength, expectancy, drive, or motivation, might be substituted for factor X.

Naming Intervening Variables

Although meaningful names, instead of abstract symbols, are typically applied to intervening variables in theories of behavior, the use of such names is not necessary, and may sometimes be dangerous. The meaning of a factor X is given by explicit definition within the scientific vocabulary and by the nature and variety of laws of which it is a part. Moreover, the scientific meaning of any other term that might be substituted for factor X is given in precisely the same ways. Thus to say that factor X is "really" *drive* adds nothing to our understanding unless drive has already been more specifically defined or has acquired more significant secondary meanings within the broader context of behavior theory. It is possible, of course, that the use of a meaningful term in place of a symbol may facilitate communication among investigators, but it may also lead to misunderstanding because of different preconceptions as to what is meant by the "meaningful" term. It is also likely that in the present state of psychology words must be used because we lack so much in the way of quantification. Not until extensive and interrelated equations and functional relations have been established do symbols become predominant.

If one does set about providing a name for factor X, the name must be secondary to, and contingent upon, the naming of experimental variables. To make this point concrete, let us consider again the hypothetical experiment in which three rats are found to run at different speeds when tested in the same straight alley. When the experiment is performed, if we have no information about our subjects save that provided by the animals' behavior, we can neither define factor X appropriately nor rename it. But should we discover that the three subjects have been given different amounts of practice in running through the alley, then practice becomes a manipulated variable capable of providing an independent definition of factor X. And since practice, by convention, is said to affect learning, factor X might then be called a *learning* or *habit* factor. In like manner, if we were to discover that our subjects differ with respect to hours of food deprivation, factor X might be defined in terms of this variable, as in our first example of independent definitions, and might be renamed *drive*. Generally speaking, therefore, *the particular name one applies to any factor X stems from the variables used in its definition and from our customary ways of naming the effects of those variables on performance.* To describe factor X as a *motivational* factor implies that it has been defined in terms of certain variables, which, by common agreement, are said to have motivational effects. But agreements are not as common as one might wish, and we must turn, therefore, to the task of specifying possible criteria for the identification of motivational variables.

Criteria for the Identification of Motivational Variables

At the end of Chapter 1 it was observed that the numerous variables or conditions affecting behavior are customarily classified into several broad groups. In elementary textbooks, chapters on sensation and perception treat, in the main, of the effects on behavior of stimulus variables; chapters on instincts and development tend to stress genetic variables; and chapters on learning, transfer of training, and memory elevate the variables of practice and experience to a place of primary importance. Questions often arise as to whether certain variables belong in one or another of these groups, but apparently fewer differences of opinion exist as to the limits of group membership than as to the limits of the class of motivational variables. Attempts to identify motivational variables lead to considerable controversy, and widely accepted criteria for making decisions in case of doubt are nonexistent. The specific criteria listed below cannot, therefore, be regarded as either definitive or exhaustive, or as representative of all possible views.

1. *A Variable Is Often Said to Be Motivational if It Facilitates or Energizes a Wide Variety of Responses.* This criterion, which is probably more widely accepted than any other, stresses the fact

that the presence of certain variables may alter the frequency, latency, or vigor of a number of responses. For example, a moderate degree of muscular tension, produced by squeezing a hand dynamometer, is considered motivational because it facilitates verbal learning, mental arithmetic, the knee jerk, and a variety of other responses (Courts, 1942). Similarly, food deprivation appears to be motivating, especially in animals, since it often intensifies reactions of running, sniffing, exploring, clawing, biting, whimpering, and even drinking. Thus it is the nonspecific, broadly generalized effects of certain variables that seem to mark them off as motivational rather than something else.

2. *A Variable Is Commonly Said to Be Motivating if the Learning of New Responses Seems to Depend upon Appropriate Manipulations of That Variable.* This criterion involves the assumption that a reduction in the drive state associated with the variable is rewarding and that responses followed by such a reduction will tend to be learned. If a period of stimulation by an intense light is terminated as soon as an albino rat presses a lever, the probability of his making the same response on a future occasion may be increased. The variable of intense light is then a motivator because its offset brings about or is correlated with the acquisition of a new response.

3. *A Variable Is Sometimes Regarded as Motivational if Changes in That Variable Lead to the Weakening of Certain Responses.* Strong stimuli tending to elicit aversive or avoidant behavior are clear examples of variables that meet this criterion. A child may have a strong tendency to reach out to touch a brightly burning match, but the reaching response is likely to be abandoned if it is followed by a painful burn. This, of course, is the phenomenon typically subsumed under the heading of punishment, and the hot flame is treated as a motivational variable because of its efficacy in leading to the weakening of the reaching reaction.

4. *A Variable Is Occasionally Labeled Motivational Simply Because No Other Designation Seems Suitable.* If the results of certain experimental treatments cannot be explained by appealing to principles of learning, perception, genetics, or whatever, one may be tempted to assert that the treatments have led to changes

in level of drive. For instance, altering a variable such as deprivation time may result in relatively immediate and precipitous
changes in performance. If these changes are more abrupt than
we might predict from the suppositions that learning or inhibitory
processes are involved, we may wish to assume that the variable
is functioning motivationally. This criterion is perhaps the least
satisfactory of all, however, since the variable is named by exclusion. By this standard a variable is motivational if it is *not* affecting behavior as we would expect it to be affected by other
variables for which we already have meaningful names. For this
criterion to be of real utility, we would have to have much clearer
notions than we now have of what each of the many nonmotivational variables is and of how it functions as a determinant of
behavior.

It has been asserted in the previous section that, generally speaking, variables are regarded as motivational if they affect behavior
in ways that are commonly said to be motivational. The four
criteria listed above may be regarded as a tentative summary of
some of the "motivational ways" in which behavior may be altered by variables. At the present stage of our knowledge, of
course, it would be foolhardy to maintain that all students of behavior would approve of this list or that any one of its loosely structured criteria is entirely adequate.

Before leaving this topic we should note that certain criteria for
the identification of motivational variables are clearly not satisfactory. For example, an increase in the probability or vigor of a
single reaction following the manipulation of a variable is not
suitable since the same behavioral effect might be ascribed, perhaps with equal reason, to learning, expectancy, perception, or
whatever. Improvement in performance, as such, does not point
unerringly to motivation as the only responsible variable. It is also
clear that the intrinsic properties of a variable do not suffice to
distinguish it as motivational. An allegedly motivating electric
shock may be identical in its physical properties to a shock used
in studying tactual sensitivity. In like manner, one cannot rely
upon the descriptive properties of behavior alone for clear guidance
as to what is motivational. The appearance of an emotional tantrum in a frustrating situation may mean either heightened motiva-

tion or simply the transfer to that situation of a previously well-learned mode of adjustment to frustration.

One is under no obligation, of course, in doing research, to specify whether a variable is or is not motivational. One can, for instance, study the effect of failure instructions upon the performance of human subjects even when one is uncertain as to how the variable should be classified. Such instructions could operate as stimuli to elicit habits or sets; they could change the subjects' attitudes; or they could alter motivation. The theoretical implications of the research would perhaps be enriched if one could decide among these alternatives, but the empirical results would be valuable even if a decision were never made.

Operational and Significant Definitions of Drive

Operational Definitions. In an earlier section of this chapter, mention was made of several techniques for introducing constructs such as drive into one's theory without having to refer, in the definition itself, to the behavior to be explained by the construct. In exemplifying these methods the definitions were never formally presented, but each could have been stated in such a way as to qualify as an operational definition. The need for operational definitions of concepts and terms has been heavily emphasized in recent years by psychologists seeking a maximum degree of precision and rigor. While the phrase *operational definition* may sound formidable, it is essentially nothing more than a *clear* definition. It is a definition in which the conditions under which the concept is to be used have been clearly and unambiguously stated in terms of operations or activities of observing and recording that can be made by any competent observer. Thus the statement, "Degree of drive in the rat is defined in terms of the time during which the rat has been without food," is a good (operational) definition. It states precisely what operations, i.e., measuring and recording the time during which a rat does not eat, must be carried out to satisfy the definition. Presumably, all observers who have stop watches or other time-measuring devices can agree as to how much time has elapsed since the rat has been fed. From the definition, therefore, they can agree that rat X has a higher drive than rat Y if rat X has been without food for a longer time than rat Y. When a concept is defined operationally, therefore, it is defined *in terms of communicable, repeatable manipulations and observations that can be performed by any reasonably competent observer*. It is a definition whose meaning within the scientific vocabulary is clear because the meanings of its constituent words and symbols can be given in terms of observable properties of physical objects and the relations among them. Many of the definitions of drive that have been seriously proposed in the past fail to meet the test of operational precision, but allusions to them still appear frequently in psychological literature. Taken seriously and uncritically, nonoperational definitions lead to little but confusing and interminable arguments.

Although an operational definition of drive in terms of hours of food deprivation may seem sensible on intuitive grounds, many other possible definitions, though less obviously reasonable, are equally acceptable as to their operational bases. For example, there is no a priori reason why the strength of a man's drive cannot be defined in terms of the length of his nose as measured under certain carefully prescribed conditions. To assert that men with long noses have a strong drive and those with short noses a weak drive is a perfectly clear operational definition. It is operationally adequate because it specifies the conditions under which the terms *strong drive* and *weak drive* are to be used. Any person with a suitable ruler and a little patience can presumably measure the noses of a number of individuals, and the data he obtains will correlate positively with those obtained by other nose measurers. If the measurement conditions of the definition are carefully met, all members of a subject population can, with a high degree of agreement among observers, be separated into relatively long- and short-nosed groups. And the observers can then agree that, by definition, one group of subjects has a strong drive and the other a weak drive. In a similar manner, one could formulate operationally precise definitions of drive in terms of the color of a rat's fur, in terms of the ratio of its weight to the amount of curvature of its nose, in terms of the length of steps it takes while running, or, in fact, in terms of any conceivable quantities one could measure. As long as the measurements, discriminations, or other activities that must be performed by an observer are specified precisely by the definition, and those activities can indeed be executed in the same way and with the same outcome by independent competent observers, the definition satisfies the requirement that it be operational.

Significant Definitions. The mere fact that a definition is indeed operational does not guarantee that the construct thus defined will be generally useful or theoretically significant. Drive *can* be operationally defined in terms of the length of a man's nose, and nose length can be measured with reasonable precision. But it would be foolish to use such a definition for very long if one could not show that nose length meets one or more of the criteria of motivational variables or is meaningfully related to other variables. Thus, nose length provides a useless definition of drive unless it can be shown that long-nosed subjects behave as though they were more highly motivated than short-nosed subjects. Irrespective of the elegance of our operational definitions, they are of little value until the defined concepts have been shown to have sensible, clarifying relations to other concepts and to other facts. A definition is useful or significant when the laws of which the defined concept is a component fit meaningfully into a broader theoretical structure and serve to illuminate a variety of lower-order laws or functions. Nonoperationally defined constructs can probably never be scientifically significant; but a construct can be immaculately operational without being helpful in any way.

A distinction is thus drawn between (1) the basic scientific-vocabulary meaning of a concept, as the result of its having been defined in specific operational terms, and (2) the additional, more significant meanings it may acquire if it proves to be useful or helpful. A clear understanding of these two kinds of meanings (Bergmann, 1944; Spence, 1948) helps to eliminate confusion in dealing with psychological problems, and we shall have occasions throughout the remainder of this text to refer to them again.

Since drive or any other construct can be defined operationally in many different ways, decisions as to which definition will be used must rest upon the utility of the concept. Of several operational definitions, the one that is most useful or significant is clearly to be preferred. And whenever utility can be enhanced by altering a definition, then such remedial measures are clearly in-dicated. Unfortunately, we cannot state in precise language what is meant by maximum utility or significance, and hence cannot point to any single definition of drive as the one that is most use-ful. The process of evaluating significance and of refining defini-tions is an ever-continuing one, and widely satisfying answers can probably not be expected for many years. It is even possible that no definition of drive will ever turn out to be useful and that the concept will disappear entirely from our scientific vocabulary.

The Problem of Drive Quantification

General Considerations. The problems involved in attempting to quantify or to measure the strength of a drive or motive are extremely complex, and any comprehensive discussion of them would take us far beyond the intended scope of this book. But the "measurement issue" is repeatedly raised in discussions of motivation, and since it is closely allied to the definitional matters we have just considered, it seems desirable to examine it briefly at this point.

The bases of our concern with measurement, both in the affairs of our daily lives and in our scientific pursuits, have been discussed quite frequently and need only to be touched upon here. We are constantly making judgments about the properties or qualities of objects and situations, and our behavior is often guided by the outcome of these judgments. A room may be judged to be "too warm," so we remove our jackets; an automobile is seen to be approaching the intersection "too rapidly," so we step back until it has passed; our friends may be judged to be "too angry" at the moment, so we may defer a request for a favor. In many instances, judgments of this kind, in which we simply affirm or deny the presence of qualitative characteristics, provide adequate support for the normal activities of living. In other circumstances, however, and especially in the pursuit of scientific knowledge, we find it necessary to ascertain, if possible, the precise degree of the prop-erty or characteristic about which judgments are made. Thus we may need to know, not just that a rat has become heavier when fed certain foods, but whether it has gained 10 grams or 50 grams;

we may need to know whether a subject's skin resistance has changed by 100 or 1,000 ohms; whether one subject is more highly motivated than another, and if so, by how much.

In the case of motivation or drive, as in many other instances, answers to such questions as "how much," or "how intense," are fundamental to an increase in the accuracy of our judgments about motivation and to the discovery of comprehensive explanatory principles. Not until these answers can be given shall we be in a position to formulate principles or theories capable of being *unambiguously* confirmed or refuted (Cohen and Nagel, 1934). When we can say that an individual has a certain amount or strength of drive we have substituted *quantitative* distinctions for *qualitative* ones and have made an important first step toward the measurement of the attribute or property of drive.

Acknowledged authorities on the topic of measurement, though they differ with respect to a number of issues, hold comparable views as to what constitutes the essence of measurement. Broadly conceived, *measurement is the process of assigning numerals to events, objects, or the properties of objects, in accordance with clearly specified rules and procedures.* It is a process through which experimentally demonstrable properties or relations of objects or systems are juxtaposed against a numerical system having corresponding properties and/or relationships. As Stevens (1951) has so aptly phrased it, when we measure ". . . we deputize the numerals to serve as representatives for a state of affairs in nature . . ." (p. 23).

From these general statements about measurement, it follows, for example, that the heights of a number of discernibly different individuals have been measured when we have applied yardsticks or other length-measuring devices to these individuals in certain agreed-upon ways, and when, as a consequence of these experimental operations, we have allocated one numeral to each individual. By the same token, it would be permissible to say that we have measured the strength of a drive or motive when, by following certain operational procedures or rules, we have been able to assign numerals to different organisms that are presumed to possess different degrees of drive.

In actual practice, however, any of several different rules and procedures might be followed in attempting to assign numerals to objects or individuals possessing a certain property. As a consequence, one cannot speak simply of just one kind or variety of measurement. Typically, at least two, and sometimes four, types of measurement are described, depending on the kinds of operations that can be performed with the property being measured, on the existence of related numerical laws, and on the types of mathematical transformations that can be applied to the measured data.

Let us now consider several of these kinds of measurement as they might relate to the problem of quantifying drive or motivation.

Counting. Perhaps the simplest example of what some writers describe as a crude sort of "measurement" is that in which instances of the phenomenon under study are *counted* or *enumerated*. By the use of a standard set of ordered symbols, such as the series of numerals 1, 2, 3, etc., we can, by pairing off one instance of the phenomenon against each numeral, determine whether there are more instances of the event in one situation or under one set of conditions than in another. Thus we determine whether there are more students in classroom A than in classroom B by the simple expedient of counting the students in each room. Counting satisfies the broad criteria of measurement because it involves assigning the numeral 1 to a particular student, the numeral 2 to another, and so on, until all of the students have been given a number. If the last numeral assigned to classroom A stands higher in the series of numerals than the one last assigned to classroom B, we can conclude that A contains more students than B. This procedure will not be successful, of course, unless we have some means of unequivocally identifying the individual students so that no two students will be assigned the same numeral and no student fails to get a numeral.

This elementary method of measurement might be applied to the quantification of drive in the following manner. Since counting cannot be successful unless we can recognize the things or properties to be counted, our initial step must be to set up definite criteria for determining whether an individual is motivated. For this purpose we might choose a simple operational definition such as "an animal is motivated (has some degree of drive) if it is awake and walking about, but not if it is asleep." Since we can readily observe whether an animal is active and awake or asleep, we can apply the definition to each and every animal in a group. Thus we can recognize the presence or absence of the phenomenon we wish to measure and can go on to count the number of animals in the group that are, by the terms of the definition, possessed of drive. Should we be interested, we could then note whether colony A contains more motivated animals than colony B, whether the count of motivated animals is higher under one diet than another, and the like. Moreover, if it seemed expedient to do so, we could alter our initial operational definition of drive or choose a completely different one. By means of new counts we could then determine whether the use of the alternate definition yields more significant or more meaningful relations than did the original one.

The application of operational definitions and counting procedures in this suggested manner does not, of course, provide us with information as to the *relative* drive strengths of different animals or of different colonies. But the fact that we have been able to divide our animals into "driven" and "nondriven" groups and to enumerate the constituents of each group does mean that we have achieved one kind of drive quantification.

Ranking. The operational definition employed in the previous section, that an animal is motivated if it is awake and moving about, is an all-or-none type of definition. By applying it we can decide whether any one individual is motivated or not. But the definition does not provide us with a method for determining which of two motivated individuals is the more highly motivated. Assertions about the relative drive strengths of different individuals imply a different sort of measurement than that achieved by counting and involve different kinds of definitions and procedures. The outcome of such procedures is an *ordinal* or *rank-order* scale by means of which numerals may be assigned to individuals having varying degrees of the property or dimension of drive.

The first requirement to be met in constructing an ordinal drive scale is to develop standardized laboratory operations for arranging individuals in order with respect to strength of drive. We must, that is, find empirical methods to support decisions such as "A has more drive than B," "B has less drive than C," and so forth. But since drive is an intermediary construct, it again becomes necessary at this point to introduce an operational definition. Perhaps we might choose a definition such as the following: if two food-deprived rats are permitted simultaneously to run down adjacent straight alleys for food, then the rat that first reaches its goal has the higher drive. In principle, at least, the procedures specified in this definition can be carried out in the laboratory, and from the outcome it can be asserted that, with respect to any two rats, the drive of one is either greater than, less than, or equal to that of the other, by definition. The definition states that the rats are to be run simultaneously, and it is implied that the observer simply judges which rat is the "winner." However, the rats could be run individually, provided their comparative running speeds are evaluated through the use of stop watches or other timing devices. The two methods would yield identical estimates of relative running proficiency, and hence of relative drive strength, unless social or other factors were differentially involved in the two situations. Incidentally, other operational definitions than the above (e.g., definitions involving differences in antecedent conditions, organic states, or stimulus conditions) could be used with equal justification as the basis for the rank ordering of subjects according to drive level.

The logical requirements for quantifying any physical property or quality have been clearly stated by such writers as Campbell (1921), Cohen and Nagel (1934), and Reese (1943). Cohen and Nagel have listed the minimum requirements to be met in constructing an ordinal scale. In the following paragraphs each of these requirements is examined in relation to the problem of developing an ordinal scale of drive.

Given a group of individuals, A, B, C, etc., we must be able to arrange them serially with respect to the property (drive) so that between any two individuals, A and B, one and only one of the following relations holds: (a) A has more drive than B; (b) A has less drive than B; (c) A's drive equals B's. It must also be possible to show by physical operations that the relationship "greater than" and its converse "less than" (symbolized by > and <) are *asymmetrical* and *transitive*. The requirement for asymmetry is satisfied by demonstrating that if $A > B$, then $B \not> A$ (where $\not>$ means "not greater than"). Transitivity can be demonstrated by showing that if $A > B$, and $B > C$, then $A > C$. Satisfying these requirements at the empirical laboratory level, by comparing running times, for example, comprises the first steps toward constructing an ordinal scale of drive.

The actual task of scale construction is a relatively simple matter once we have found satisfactory physical operations for establishing the fundamental relationships listed above. To do so we must assign numerals to the individuals of the group in accordance with certain rules. If we have determined, by laboratory tests, that individual A has more drive than B, we must assign to A a numeral standing higher in the series of numerals than the numeral assigned to B. Conversely, if B has less drive than A, the numeral assigned to B must be less (lower in the series) than the numeral assigned to A. If A and B are equal with respect to drive, as experimentally determined, then the numeral assigned to one must be the same as the numeral assigned to the other. The numeral series is, by convention, an ordered series that exhibits transitive and asymmetrical relations. But until we have shown *empirically* that the relations among individuals with different drive strengths are also transitive and asymmetrical we cannot profitably use the numeral series to represent the rank orders of the individuals' drives.

Incidentally, although our operations may tell us that A has more drive than B there is nothing in these operations to indicate what specific numerals should be assigned to A and B. The rule merely states that the numeral assigned to A must be greater than that assigned to B. Any two numerals will do: 1 and 2, 10 and 20, or 37 and 99, so long as the second is the larger of the two. As Reese (1943) has pointed out, at this stage *we have no operations for determining how much more drive A has than B*, and hence the numerals we assign cannot mirror a relation that has not been determined. The ordinal scale we would obtain from assigning numerals in compliance with these rules would tell us nothing about the size of the interval separating any two individuals on the scale, nor would it yield any information as to the absolute amount of drive at any point. We can assign the numerals 2 and 1 to A

and B, respectively, if we wish, but we cannot maintain that A has twice as much drive as B, since the relation "twice as much as" has not been empirically demonstrated.

Once a rank-order (ordinal) scale of drive has been established, we can use it in a number of different ways even though no meaning can be attached to the statement that the drive of one individual is twice (or n times) the drive of another. For instance, any new individual can be assigned a position on the scale with respect to the original group used in constructing the scale. We can also use the scale to study the effects of any new variables upon relative scale position. Or we can relate position on the scale to level of performance on some new and different task. Thus, we can, from the scale, select groups of organisms with different drive levels and subject them to a learning task to discover whether their speed-of-learning scores stand in the same rank order as do their drive levels. A great many of the "qualities" of individuals that are "measured" by the psychologist, such as intelligence, honesty, and aptitude, etc., are measured only in the limited sense that different degrees of the quality can be arrayed in serial order. But it is also true that certain properties of purely physical systems, such as density and hardness, are also restricted to measurement of this kind. All of these qualities are commonly described as *intensive*, and when, for a given quality, physical operations have been worked out which satisfy the criteria listed above, one speaks of an *intensive dimension*.

In concluding this discussion, we must note that the major problem in constructing an ordinal scale of drive is to find satisfactory empirical methods upon which to base the assertion that individual A has more drive than individual B, or that individual A has more drive at one time than at another. The method used in our illustration, of defining drive operationally in terms of relative running speeds, would probably not be entirely satisfactory to most investigators. In principle, one *can* construct an ordinal scale of drive, but it will be of limited interest until a genuinely significant definition of drive can be formulated as the basis for the empirical process of rank-ordering subjects with respect to drive.

Extensive Properties and Fundamental Measurement. The ordinal type of measurement as applied to the problem of drive quantification can never tell us *how much more* drive one subject has than another. To obtain this information it would be necessary to demonstrate that drive intensity is an *extensive dimension* and susceptible, therefore, to what the physicist calls *fundamental measurement*. According to Campbell (1921), an extensive dimension is like an intensive one in that the characteristics of asymmetry and transitivity can be shown to hold among events having the extensive property. The two differ, however, in that a quality that is extensive possesses also the attribute of *additivity*. The property of objects which we call their length is extensive because experimental operations have been found by which one length can be added to another to produce more of the same property of length. It is because length is additive, primarily, that it is said to be extensive and to permit fundamental measurement.

At present there seems to be little reason for supposing that a property such as drive can ever be measured in this fundamental sense, since experimental operations for demonstrating additivity may never be found. It is conceivable, however, that satisfactory quantitative estimates of drive can eventually be obtained by what is termed *derived measurement*. We cannot pause to describe this method in detail here but it is applied by the physicist to dimensions such as *density* that do not exhibit the property of additivity.

Summary

The discussions in Chapter 2 have dealt with the general questions of why intervening variables such as drive are used in behavior theories, how such impalpable entities can be defined by reference to observable variables, how one might decide that a given intermediary variable is motivational rather than something else, and how such variables might, in principle, be measured.

In the first part of the chapter it was noted that intermediary variables or constructs are usually proposed in the hope that they will add to our understanding of obscure relations between behavior and other variables both inside and outside of the organism. Typical relations of this kind were cited with special emphasis being placed upon disproportions between the vigor of a response and the intensity of a stimulus, upon behavioral variability in the presence of constant environmental conditions, and on invariant behavior in the face of normally effective changes in the environment.

Intervening variables are sometimes defined in terms of the particular responses that are supposed to be explained by such variables. This practice leads to circular explanatory reasoning of an undesirable kind, as when a herding instinct, defined in terms of gregarious behavior, is alleged to be the cause of such behavior. To avoid such circularity an intervening variable can be defined in terms of variations in the organism's life history, in terms of other responses recorded in different testing situations, or in terms of organic variables and contemporary environmental conditions.

The scientific meanings of an intervening variable are provided by explicit definitions as to how the term shall be used in the scientific vocabulary and by the diversity and kinds of laws into which the variable enters. It is not necessary, therefore, that the constructed variable be given a name that is also meaningful to laymen. Usually, in such an attempt, the choice of a particular name seems to depend primarily upon the independent variables used in defining the construct and upon traditional ways of naming the effects of such variables upon performance.

Although opinions differ as to the nature of motivational variables, several criteria for their identification are suggested in this chapter. Thus a specific variable tends to be regarded as motivational (1) if it tends to facilitate or energize several different responses, (2) if its termination or removal following a new response leads to the learning of that response, (3) if sudden increases in the strength of the variable lead to the abandonment of responses, and (4) if its effects on behavior cannot be attributed to other processes such as learning, sensation, innate capacities, and sets.

In later sections of the chapter we have pointed out that intermediary constructs, including drive or motivation, must be defined with sufficient clarity so that investigators with comparable training can understand what the terms mean. This goal can be attained if construct-names are defined either in terms of directly observable things, or in terms of words that have been so defined. Definitions of this kind are said to be operational, and the scientific-vocabulary meaning of the construct is thus given by the operations or manipulations used in its definition. A construct may be clearly defined, however, and yet have no value as an element of a theory of behavior. The student of motivation, therefore, must face the problem of how to formulate a conception of motivation that is both operationally immaculate and generally useful. When functioning as an integral component of a behavior theory, a construct acquires, from its interrelations with different constructs and laws, other meanings than those provided by its operational definition. A construct can have operationally clear meanings without these secondary meanings, but not the reverse, save perhaps in highly developed physical theories.

Some elements of the problem of drive measurement are reviewed in the final section. There it is observed that measurement, in essence, is the assignment of numbers to objects and events in accordance with certain rules and conventions. Counting is one way of assigning numbers, and if operations for detecting the presence of drive can be devised, then the frequency with which "driven" subjects appear in a given population can be determined. At a more advanced level, an ordinal scale of drive can be devised, provided one can find physical operations for arranging individuals in rank order with respect to drive strength. No procedures have yet been devised by means of which drive may be measured in the *fundamental* sense that length and weight are measured, but the quantification of drive by what is termed *derived* measurement may eventually prove to be feasible.

CHAPTER 3

Primary Sources of Drive

IN THIS CHAPTER we shall deal primarily with experimental studies of the effects of certain alleged motivational variables upon the performance of animals in a variety of situations. The variables to be considered are those that are commonly said to be responsible for the arousal of the "primary drives." For reasons presented below, however, we have chosen to depart somewhat from conventional terminology and to speak, not of "drives," but of "primary sources of drive." Since these and other terms to be used hereafter require clarification, we begin with a brief terminological discussion.

Some Terminological Distinctions

Motivating and Steering Variables. With few exceptions, contemporary theorists make a distinction between independent variables that seem to have motivational effects upon behavior and those that direct or guide behavior (e.g., Tolman, 1932; Lewin, 1938; Hull, 1943; Spence, 1956). Moreover, two kinds of intermediary constructs are introduced that correspond with these two groups of variables. Thus, drives, motivations, conations, emotions, and libidos function as the activating agents; while cognitive maps, associative tendencies, and habit strengths serve, in conjunction with external and internal stimuli, to determine the direction behavior will take.

In some instances, however, difficulties arise in attempting to maintain these distinctions. Specifically, there are certain manipulatable variables that appear to exert both a motivating and a guiding influence upon behavior and hence cannot be put into a single classification. Peripheral shock is a good example, since it has sensory consequences in addition to its presumed drive-arousing effects.

Two solutions to this difficulty merit consideration. First, one might assume that a variable such as electric shock affects only drive, but that drive can function as both an activator and a director. This conceptual arrangement is represented in the upper half of Fig. 3:1. Unfortunately this solution seems unsatisfactory, since the directive function it ascribes to drive is precisely the same function traditionally reserved for cognitions or associative tendencies (lower half of Fig. 3:1). If both drive and habit are to be

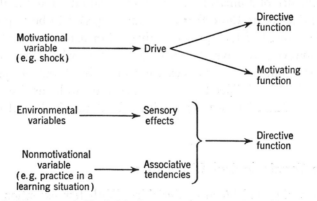

Fig. 3:1. The upper half of this figure represents one hypothesis as to how a motivational variable such as electric shock might have both directive and motivating effects upon behavior. For purposes of comparison, the directive effects of environmental variables and of practice in a learning situation, as mediated by associative tendencies, are included in the bottom half of the figure.

included in our theories, then the two should affect behavior in different ways; otherwise only one construct seems to be required. In the scheme of Fig. 3:1, habits (associative tendencies) operate as behavior directors but not as activators, whereas drive exhibits both properties. This interpretation thus seems to add little to the clarity of our understanding, but several theorists (McClelland, 1951; Young, 1955; Seward, 1956; Marx, 1956) use the term *motive* in essentially the way that drive has been used here.

A second solution that promises to be more useful is represented in Fig. 3:2. Here the dual-purpose variable (shock) is assumed to have two distinguishable consequents rather than one. It provides sensory stimuli which, in conjunction with associative predispositions, can impart direction to behavior, and in addition it affects drive, to which only the single function of motivation is assigned. This answer has the advantage of preserving unique functions for drive as well as for habit strength. On this view, which is tentatively adopted throughout the remainder of this book, the construct denoted by the words drive or motivation—these terms are used as synonyms here and elsewhere—is assumed to have no function as a behavior guide or director. Certain *variables* may thus be seen to have dual consequences, but *drive* is assumed to have only motivational effects and *habit strength* only directive functions.

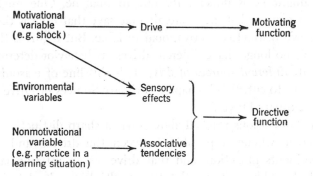

FIG. 3:2. Components of a second interpretation of the dual behavioral effects of a motivational variable. Here electric shock is assumed to affect drive, which serves as the sole motivating agent, and also to lead to sensory effects. These effects are essentially identical with those arising from other aspects of the physical environment and are presumed to function in conjunction with associative predispositions to direct behavior.

It should be clearly understood, however, that an adequate theory of directed behavior may not require both an activating and a steering agency. As we shall see in the next chapter, some theorists feel that a construct having an activating function can be dispensed with entirely, the assorted effects of the so-called motivational variables being explained by appeal simply to changes in stimuli and in associative strengths.

Drives or Drive? In current discussions of motivation it is commonplace to encounter the word "drives." For certain writers, this term apparently conveys the idea of multiple directedness. The hunger drive is said to be directed or to direct behavior toward food, the thirst drive toward water, and so on. But this terminology is confusing if, as we have argued, it is desirable to limit the function of a drive to that of an activator or motivator. If this latter position is adopted, drive can never be directed toward any specific goal, nor can it selectively activate one type of associative tendency to the exclusion of others, since this would indirectly involve a directive function. To speak of "drives" implies that the constructs so designated are alike, yet different. If they are exactly alike *when functioning as motivators*, then identical processes must be involved in all cases, and all drives, as activators, become one. If they are not alike as motivators, then each must be motivating but in a unique way. Just what these different yet comparable ways might be is difficult for one to imagine. One might suppose, of course, that drives are all alike save that each is the result of its own distinctive motivational variable. But if this is the case, then we no longer have different drives, as behavior determinants, but only *different sources of drive*. It is this line of reasoning that has led us to entitle this chapter "Primary Sources of Drive" rather than "Primary Drives."

The conclusions reached above, that a sharp distinction should be drawn, whenever possible, between the driving and steering determinants of action, and that drive, as an intermediary construct, should be unitary rather than multiple are clearly coordinate with a theory proposed by Hull (1943) in his *Principles of Behavior*. According to Hull, behavior is determined, in large measure, by two intermediaries, *drive* (D) and *habit strength* (H). Drive, for him, is a broadly acting, nondirective factor that functions exclusively to facilitate associative tendencies whether learned or unlearned. Drive results from the manipulation of certain variables, such as strong stimuli and the withholding of food or water. Furthermore, its capacity to facilitate all behavior is assumed to be independent of the particular antecedent condition of which it may, at the moment, be a function. For example, drive due to intense stimulation is indistinguishable, as an energizer, from drive due to food deprivation. At the theoretical level, drive is simply a numerical quantity multiplying associative quantities (habit strengths) to yield a further quantity, excitatory potential (E). This latter quantity, further altered by other factors, is in turn related by one or another postulated mathematical law to overt behavior.

The behavior-directing function is performed within Hull's system by the hypothetical associative tendencies, whether learned or instinctive, functioning in combination with both internal and external stimuli. An animal in a discrimination situation is steered or directed toward one stimulus object and away from another by its learned associative predispositions. But drive, being nondirective, is presumed to facilitate both movements of approach to the positive cue and movements away from the negative cue. Whichever reactive tendency is dominant at the moment is catalyzed into overt action by drive.

Primary and Secondary Sources of Drive. Although mention has been made of primary sources of drive, we have neither explained the meaning of the adjective "primary" nor contrasted such sources with those that are called "secondary." Broadly speaking, primary motivational variables are those that produce their effects through the action of inherited bodily mechanisms. When environmental conditions are altered in any of a variety of ways, the physiological mechanisms of an organism, even in the absence of opportunities to learn, tend to react in a corrective manner. At such times the organism is likely to behave as though motivated. The environmental changes or variables leading to these effects are called primary because they appear early in the developmental and phylogenetic sequences, not because they are necessarily more important than those labeled secondary. Such terms as homeostatic drives, biogenic drives, and physiogenic drives have been used as synonyms for what we are calling primary sources of drive. These terms serve further to emphasize the regulatory mechanisms involved and their relations to the genetic constitution of the organism. Examples of variables typically described as having primary motivational effects are the withholding of such commodities as food, water, or air for breathing. The removal of a mother's offspring—in some species only—is also described as a primary variable, as are deviations from optimal levels of environmental temperature and humidity, and pressures produced by the accumulation of bodily wastes. Any stimulus to which the organism is receptive may have motivational effects if it is intense enough. Electric shocks, bright lights, loud noises, pin pricks, and the like, are common instances. In the opinion of some authors, the withholding of opportunities to play, to be active, or to explore, also qualify as primary motivational variables.

The secondary drives, or, as we shall describe them, the *secondary sources of drive*, differ from their primary counterparts in that their efficacy as motivators rests largely upon learning. Specifically, if an individual has acquired a tendency to make a certain response to a particular environmental situation, the elicitation of that response may have motivational consequences; consequences, that is, resembling those stemming from primary sources of drive and consistent with one or more motivational criteria. Because human behavior is often said to be largely motivated by secondary or acquired sources of drive, these have come to occupy the attention of psychologists to an increasing degree. All of Chapter 5 is devoted to their analysis.

The remainder of the present chapter is concerned with a discussion of certain primary sources of drive and their effects upon behavior. Since hunger and thirst are the most frequently studied sources and since their strength is often believed to be reflected rather directly in the amount of consummatory behavior, we begin with the question of how such behavior is regulated.

The Regulation of Consummatory Behavior

Students concerned with the ways in which biological needs may serve as primary sources of drive have dealt extensively with the effects of such needs on performance in problem solving, discrimination, and conditioning tasks. In addition, considerable effort has been devoted to the study of the physiological mechanisms controlling consummatory behavior. Most of the relevant research in this latter area lies more properly within the field of physiology rather than in that of psychology; hence we shall consider it only briefly and in broad outline. For more detailed information the reader may wish to consult such sources as Morgan and Stellar (1950), Stellar (1954), Miner (1955), and Morgan (1957).

The Local Theory of Hunger and Thirst. When psychologists and physiologists first became concerned with the nature of hunger and thirst, they tended in large part to approach the problems from the basic position of the introspectionists. Looked at in this way, hunger and thirst were *sensations* experienced by the self-observing scientist, and the proper way to study them was to seek for meaningful relations between these sensations and other conditions such as time since eating or drinking and organic activities. Such an approach to the study of these needs is well illustrated by the work of the physiologist Cannon (1929). Over a period of many years, Cannon's research was directed toward discovering the physiological correlates of these sensations and toward elaborating and justifying his "local theory" of their origin. The essence of this theory was that thirst, or at least the sensation of thirst, was a consequence of a dryness of the mouth and throat caused by the body's need for water. Similarly, hunger was identified with sensory impulses arising from vigorous contractions of the empty stomach. The label "local theory" has been applied to this view because of its emphasis upon the peripheral, localized origins of the hunger and thirst sensations.

The evidence presented by Cannon and others to support his views was extensive and persuasive. If dryness of the buccal cavity is alleviated by rinsing the mouth with water, the sensation of thirst is also reduced, at least temporarily, even though no water passes into the body. And any one of a wide variety of events, such as tightening one's belt, smoking, or becoming frightened, may temporarily reduce or eliminate hunger contractions and thereby also alleviate the subjective pangs of intense hunger. Moreover, objective records of gastric contractions obtained from subjects who swallowed special recording devices (Cannon, 1929) were found to coincide with subjective reports of hunger pangs. Hunger also appeared to be related to level of overt activity, since the movements of sleeping subjects occurred at about the time of vigorous stomach activity.

The local theory of hunger and thirst thus seemed adequate to explain the origins of the sensations consequent to food and water deprivation. But with the growth of interest in the broader consequences of deprivation, especially in animals, it soon became clear that the local theory could not encompass all of the important motivational phenomena of hunger and thirst. Its inadequacy was due, in part, to the fact that introspective methods could not be used with animals, but more importantly to the finding that laws obtained when hunger and thirst were defined as sensations were different from, and apparently not as useful as, those obtained when hunger and thirst were defined in terms of consummatory behavior. For example, thirsty subjects do not cease drinking immediately after the first mouthful, even though only a small quantity of water is needed to moisten the mucous membranes of the mouth and throat and thus eliminate the sensations of thirst. Nor do subjects stop eating after their first few bites, in spite of the fact that their hunger contractions have doubtless ceased and their hunger sensations have been allayed. Hunger and thirst as sensations thus turned out to be different from hunger and thirst as regulators or motivators of eating and drinking.

Physiological Mechanisms Governing Consummatory Behavior. Amount or rate of consummatory activity has been used as the principal basis for estimating biological needs in a great many physiologically oriented investigations of basic mechanisms. A detailed review of factors responsible for the control of consummatory activity would take us far beyond the intended scope of this book (see, for example, Miner, 1955) but a brief summary of some of the major trends appears justified.

Concerning the factors that function to produce *cessation* of eating, Grossman (1955) has concluded that they may be divided, for purposes of analysis, into four components: (1) oropharyngeal factors, (2) gastrointestinal factors, (3) circulating nutrients in the blood, and (4) stored nutrients in the tissues.

The oropharyngeal component refers to the stimulation of sensory receptors in the mouth and pharynx produced by food in the mouth and by the subsequent movements of chewing and swallowing. Available evidence points to the conclusion that stimulation of these head receptors tends to produce cessation of eating, apparently through the mediating action of the medial portion of the hypothalamus. The neural impulses function, it would seem, as a kind of signal that, in cooperation with many other kinds of signals, tells the brain to shut off the mechanisms that initiate and maintain consummatory activity. The oropharyngeal control function, Grossman points out, is most effective when supplemented by the entry of food into the stomach. His studies indicate that neither factor operating alone will produce satiety. For example, if a portion of a dog's daily ration is placed directly into its stomach through a fistula, just before food is given ad libitum, voluntary intake is reduced, but the dog will still eat. This it would not do, clearly, if stomach distention provided sufficient inhibitory stimulation. However, the quantity of food ingested during the subsequent ad-lib feeding period is greater than if the pre-ad-lib portion is eaten in the normal manner. Thus the suppression of oral intake is greater when the head receptors are stimulated during the normal processes of eating and, in addition, the stomach is distended. Experimental studies by Berkun, Kessen, and Miller (1952) and by Miller, Sampliner, and Woodrow (1957) have also shown that consummatory behavior is reduced more when a given amount of food or water is ingested orally than when it is slowly injected directly into the stomach. When milk is very rapidly injected, however, the opposite effect is obtained (Smith, Pool, and Weinberg, 1959), suggesting that rate of injection may be a significant variable.

In some studies, involving the use of esophageal fistulas, food consumed orally is not permitted to reach the stomach. Animals that are given sham feeding in this manner generally eat more than their normal daily rations before stopping. This increase in intake, when the oropharyngeal cues are functioning in isolation, points to the need for supplementary control by gastrointestinal factors; but the fact that eating ceases even temporarily when stomach distention does not occur suggests that hunger drive, re-

garded as a determinant of eating, has suffered abatement. Grossman summarizes the situation as follows: "From these observations, we may hypothesize that stimulation of head receptors by
smelling, tasting, chewing, and swallowing, during eating, plays
an important role in bringing about satiety and suppression of
further eating, but that this factor is relatively ineffective when
it is not associated with entry of food into the stomach" (1955, p.
86.). On the basis of these and other studies it appears probable
that hunger, defined in terms of eating behavior, *can be controlled
by appropriate stimulation and its resulting neural activity.*

Apparently, knowledge as to the precise neural mechanisms
through which stimulation of the head receptors can reduce the
tendency to eat is not yet available. Experimental evidence (Anand
and Brobeck, 1951) is at hand, however, to support the view
that stimulation of the hypothalamus may lead either to hy-
perphagia (overeating) or to aphagia (undereating). Brobeck
(1955), in reviewing the evidence for neural regulation of hunger
and appetite, has hypothesized that the lateral hypothalamus may
be the facilitative and the medial hypothalamus the inhibitory
mechanism. On this view, when food is eaten, certain changes
occur within the body which either directly or indirectly affect the
hypothalamus. "These changes serve as signals to the brain, tending to suppress the activity of the lateral hypothalamus and thus
to decrease appetite, while they stimulate the medial or inhibitory
portion of the mechanism and thus promote satiety" (Brobeck,
1955, p. 48). As the food becomes absorbed into the body, the
situation tends to reverse; the lateral hypothalamus becomes more
active and the medial portion more inhibited. Under these conditions the animal's locomotor activity increases, and eventually
eating begins again if food is available.

Concerning the role played by nutrients in the blood and in
the tissues in regulating consummatory activity, we need only
note that physiologists have not yet agreed on the extent to which
either of these factors governs consummatory activity. Moreover,
the mechanisms of the alleged effects remain obscure (cf. Grossman, 1955).

Needs and Drive Distinguished

An interesting problem, arising in part out of these studies of the regulation of consummatory behavior, is that of the relation of physiological needs to drive. The term *need*, as it is usually used, refers to a bodily imbalance or departure from normality produced by any one of a variety of conditions. If food is withheld for a sufficient period of time, the chemical structure of the body is altered, and a need for food is said to exist because the ingestion of food is the necessary condition for the restoration of the original state. Other variables such as water deprivation, hormonal imbalances, extreme temperatures, and even noxious stimuli can be thought of as generating needs for conditions conducive to the restoration of equilibrium. When variables such as these are manipulated, behavior is often affected in ways that are consistent with one or another motivational criterion, and it is common, therefore, to identify these needs with drive. Moreover, it is often implicitly assumed that drive fluctuates concomitantly with needs as the latter are modified by the manipulation of appropriate variables.

Over restricted ranges of variation and for a limited number of needs, the identification of need with drive can perhaps be defended. But as many bits of evidence show, the two concepts must be distinguished under certain conditions. Consider, for example, the case of the rat from which all food is withheld until death occurs. If this animal's need for food is defined by reference to loss of body weight, then its need increases progressively up to the moment of death. But if, as is sometimes done, drive is independently defined in terms of the number of times the animal crosses an electrified grid to reach food, drive increases at first and then decreases. Decreases in number of grid crossings with prolonged starvation are usually ascribed, of course, to muscular weakness attending inanition. Nevertheless, the two quantities, need and drive, when defined in these two different ways, are not covariant save perhaps for the first two or three days of the deprivation period.

It is also obvious that the body may, as a consequence of improper diet, develop a physiological need for a specific chemical substance such as a vitamin. But an organism with a deficiency of this sort may not exhibit increased activity or other behavioral characteristics typical of increased level of drive (behavioral definition). The body's need for the vitamin may increase as a function of time, but drive, as estimated from changes in overt behavior, remains constant.

Other evidence to support the assertion that need and drive are not always covariant and hence should be differentiated comes from a variety of observations. It is generally accepted, for example, that the need for sexual gratification depends primarily upon the presence of hormones in the blood (Morgan, 1957). The satisfactory completion of the sex act, however, does not produce a direct or immediate reduction in hormonal concentration. Nevertheless, strength of sex drive, conceived as a general motivating tendency, is clearly reduced by copulation.

Studies of sham drinking and of sham eating such as those of Adolph (1943) and Janowitz and Grossman (1949) also point to the noncorrespondence of need and drive. Here the important fact is that an esophageal animal will temporarily stop drinking or eating even though no water or food is permitted to enter its stomach. For a brief period following sham ingestion, the animal's thirst or hunger drive, defined in terms of its willingness to engage in the consummatory act, is nonexistent. Yet the body's need, as measured by loss of weight, tissue conditions, or hours of deprivation, does not decline, and may even increase. Apparently, *consummatory activity itself may be drive reducing even though need is not thereby altered.*

These examples should suffice to support our contention that a need, as estimated from one set of observations, may vary independently of drive, when the latter is defined by appeal to a different set of data. Similar lacks of covariation may be found, of course, between two definitions of a need or two definitions of a drive, whenever the members of the pair are defined by reference to conditions of observation that are quite different. Thus tissue-condition-defined need does not correspond perfectly to drinking-behavior-defined need; and deprivation-estimated drive may not covary with activity-wheel estimates of drive. This failure of different definitions to coincide is one of the persisting problems facing the student of motivation. Its solution, as we have already suggested in our chapter on the definition and measurement of drive, probably hinges upon the formulation of definitions that are useful and significant as well as operational.

We conclude this section with the observation that a tendency indiscriminately to identify need with drive is frequent among those who seek to disprove the hypothesis that drive reduction is a necessary condition for learning. Arguments against the drive-reduction concept are sometimes based on evidence of the following sort: Rats rewarded with a nonnutrient solution of saccharin and water will learn a simple instrumental response more readily than rats rewarded with plain water. Empirically, therefore, the sweet-tasting solution is more reinforcing than the plain water in spite of the fact that the former is no more effective in reducing the body's need for water and has no food value. From this it is reasoned, assuming that the water needs of both groups have been equally satisfied and that their drives have therefore been equally reduced, that drive reduction is unnecessary for the growth of learned associations.

The suggestion that needs and drive should be differentiated provides one plausible answer to this type of argument. Thus saccharin-rewarded rats and water-rewarded rats might differ with respect to drive reduction, even though their need reduction was the same. The sweet-tasting saccharin solution would be expected to provide a greater amount or intensity of oropharyngeal stimulation than would plain water. And this, in terms of the neural inhibitory mechanisms described by Brobeck, could readily be followed by decreased appetite and increased satiety. Whether this is *the* drive-reduction mechanism of reinforcement we cannot say. But this analysis suggests that at least one kind of drive-reduction mechanism could be excited by saccharin even though need for water is not differentially affected. A recent observation by Smith and Capretta (1956), though nonsystematic, supports this interpretation. According to these authors, after rats have been injected with sufficient insulin to produce insulin shock, they are less likely to manifest severe shock symptoms if they are allowed to consume saccharin. Apparently the neural consequences of the sweet-tasting substance set into motion the same kind of compensatory machinery normally excited only by the ingestion of sugar.

Along this same line of thought, the mere sight or smell of food (stimuli usually described as secondary reinforcers) may be effective as rewards for new learning simply because they do lead to a reduction in drive. Because of the individual's repeated opportunities to see and smell food just prior to its ingestion, associations could be formed having the capacity to produce a temporary and partial decline of drive. Perhaps the cues provided by food come to evoke a competing reaction that interferes with events in the hypothalamus normally responsible for hunger-drive behavior. Direct experimental evidence to support this notion is lacking, but several writers (Mowrer, 1951; Osgood, 1953; Farber, 1954a; Brown, 1955) have hypothesized that such a relationship might exist. Even Tolman (1949), who seldom advocated the drive-reduction view under any conditions, maintained that subgoals antedating the final goal might, to a degree, be drive reducing. Moreover, Morgan (1957), who for reasons similar to those given above also maintains that drive and need should be distinguished, contends that a strong argument can be presented for the view that sensory stimulation can reduce drive. Neurophysiological evidence to support this position is also available and is discussed briefly in Chapter 9.

Performance as a Function of Variations in Primary Sources of Drive

Some students of behavior, as we noted earlier, are not vitally interested in the details of the physiological processes resulting from manipulations of primary sources of drive. Instead they are concerned with the observable effects of such manipulations on the behavior of their subjects in a variety of situations. Such research workers seek to determine the empirical laws relating the dependent behavior variables to independent motivational variables. Although few of these laws are as firmly established as might be desired, a considerable number of experiments have been directed toward their clarification and understanding. It is to the presentation and discussion of selected examples of these types of experiments that the remainder of this chapter is devoted.

The Effect of Deprivation Time on Consummatory Behavior. One of the basic research problems in the field of motivation is that of determining the relation between time of deprivation and consummatory behavior. For example, if an animal is deprived of food for varying periods of time before being allowed to eat ad libitum, what is the function relating duration of deprivation to rate of eating or some other index of voracity? Though such a problem is obvious and is perhaps logically an antecedent to other problems, few experiments have been directed toward its solution, and the precise nature of the laws for different species, different kinds of deprivation, and the like, remain to be determined in future experiments.

From available experiments, two may be cited as illustrations. The first, by Siegel (1947), seems to be among the earliest systematic studies of water consumption as a function of hours of privation. In his experiment, 60 male albino rats were used as subjects. They were housed in a thermostatically regulated environment marked by small temperature and humidity changes. On the first evening all animals were weighed and their intake of water was measured over a five-minute period. Since they had been maintained on an ad-lib drinking and eating regimen since weaning, the values obtained from these first measurements provided estimates of water ingestion following zero hours of water deprivation. The body-weight data were then used as the basis for dividing the animals into four groups of approximately equal weight. On the second and third days the animals were given an additional test to see how much water they would drink in five minutes. At the time of these tests, the four groups had been deprived of water for different lengths of time. These times were 6, 12, 24, and 48 hours. The results of these tests are summarized in Fig. 3:3, where mean water intake in milliliters (cubic centimeters) has been plotted against hours of deprivation.

It is clear from this figure that rate of drinking is for the most part an increasing, negatively accelerated function of time of privation for periods up to 48 hours. The initial portion of the curve exhibits a slight positive acceleration, but, as Siegel observes, this may well be due to chance. The fact that rate of drinking is

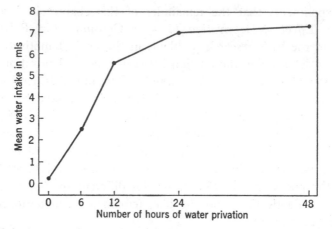

Fig. 3:3. Amount of water (in milliliters) drunk during 5 minutes by rats as a function of the number of hours since drinking was last permitted. (*From Siegel, 1947.*)

higher at the 48-hour than at the 24-hour point is of interest because earlier studies by Warden (1931), using the Columbia obstruction box, had implied that thirst decreased after 24 hours. There are various plausible reasons for the poorer performance of Warner's 48-hour animals, such as inanition or increased sensitivity to electric shock. Nevertheless, the fact remains that we have here another instance of noncorrespondence between two measures or definitions of drive.

A subsidiary finding of Siegel's also deserves mention. Just before testing his animals on the second and third days, he weighed them carefully to find out how much weight the groups had lost during their respective deprivation periods. From these data and from measures of drinking he was able to plot per cent of body weight drunk in five minutes against percentage of body-weight loss. This is shown in Fig. 3:4. In its general form this curve resembles one previously reported by Adolph (1941) relating sham drinking to body-weight deficit in dogs. It provides further confirmation of the observation that animals tend to adjust their intake of water to match the body's need for fluid. And incidentally the curve provides an excellent example of what was described in Chapter 1 as an O-R law, since body-weight loss reflects an organic state (O) and drinking is clearly a response (R).

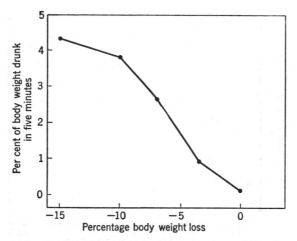

F_{IG}. 3:4. A functional relation between an organic variable (loss in body weight) and a response variable (amount of water ingested). (*From Siegel, 1947.*)

Our second experiment illustrating the effects of privation on consummatory behavior is one by Horenstein (1951). In her study, the subjects were 10 female rats that had been used in a previous investigation of the relation of drive to response latency. At the outset, the 23.5-hour feeding rhythm on which they had previously been maintained was reestablished. Then the animals were satiated on wet mash and returned to their home cages for the duration of the deprivation interval. At the end of that interval, the subjects were weighed, permitted to eat freely of mash for 20 minutes, and were finally weighed again. The quantity of food consumed was computed from the difference between these initial and final weights. The deprivation intervals were: 0, 0.5, 1, 2, 6, 12, and 23.5 hours. All of the animals were tested under each of the various deprivation conditions in a random order to balance out the influence of systematic factors such as learning, aging, etc. The results of these manipulations are summarized in Fig. 3:5.

As the curve of Fig. 3:5 clearly shows, mean food intake during the 20-minute test period was an increasing monotonic function of hours of deprivation. In contrast to Siegel's water-drinking data, the food ingestion curve of Horenstein's exhibits a rapid initial rise from zero to two hours of deprivation. This effect is apparently

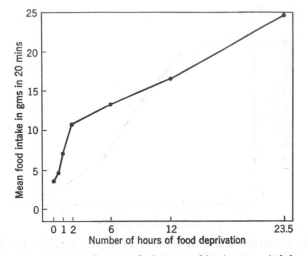

Fɪɢ. 3:5. Amount of food ingested during a 20-minute period by rats deprived of food for varying lengths of time. (*From Horenstein, 1951.*)

not specific to consummatory behavior since Horenstein obtained a similar result in her studies of the effects of deprivation time upon latency and resistance to extinction of a simple instrumental response. Moreover, the phenomenon had previously been reported by Koch and Daniel (1945) and by Saltzman and Koch (1948). Several possible reasons for this sharp increase in response strength during the first two hours are discussed by Horenstein, among them being cyclic factors and digestive mechanisms of the rat.

Concerning these consummatory-response studies of Siegel and Horenstein, two explanatory comments are indicated. First, no vigorous instrumental responses such as crossing a charged grid or pushing a bar, over and beyond those necessary for eating and drinking, were required of the animals. Since the performance of such nonconsummatory responses involves additional energy output, estimates of hunger or thirst requiring their performance might yield spuriously low values, especially at longer deprivation times, when the animal may be somewhat debilitated. Moreover, in Horenstein's experiment, the animals were allowed to eat wet mash instead of hard pellets, a substitution which would minimize the effort involved even in eating. Consequently the animals' performance level was probably not appreciably reduced by inanition,

The second comment on these studies has to do with their potential utility as estimates of drive (D) in Hull's sense of the term. If drive, as Hull assumed, serves to energize into overt action all reactive tendencies, whether learned or unlearned, then eating and drinking curves reflect the strength of D in a relatively direct manner, provided that the strengths of the *habits* to eat and drink are equal at the different deprivation intervals. Stimulus similarity is one of the variables believed to determine habit strength, but in order to explain how this variable might have affected Horenstein's results, we must digress briefly to discuss deprivation-induced stimuli.

Within Hull's system, deprivation, like electric shock (cf. Fig. 3:2), is assumed to generate not only D, the nondirective catalyst, but also, in most cases, distinctive internal stimuli. These stimuli are consequences, for example, of stomach contractions attending hunger and of dryness of the throat during thirst. These internal events have sensory components and, unlike D, *can* have a directive influence on behavior since associative connections can be formed between them and overt (as well as implicit) reactions. Hull used the term *drive stimuli* for these internal cues and symbolized them by the notation S_D. This designation is somewhat misleading, however, since the internal stimuli neither originate in nor bear any direct relation to drive (D) as such. It would be more appropriate, though less succinct, to call them *motivation-variable stimuli* $(S_{MV}s)$, since they, like drive, result from manipulations of so-called motivating variables.

Now in Horenstein's experiment, though not in Siegel's, the animals had been maintained for a good many days on a fixed dietary regimen, being fed every 23.5 hours. Because of this regularity, as Horenstein suggests, the tendency to eat may have become more strongly associated with internal stimuli characteristic of a 23.5-hour deprivation period than with cues arising from shorter privation times. Thus the fact that Horenstein's curve was highest at the 23.5-hour point and lower at increasingly shorter deprivation intervals might be due, in part, to differences in associative strengths. This would follow if as the privation periods became shorter and shorter, the internal cues became increasingly different from those of the 23.5-hour training interval, and if, with increasing disparity, there was a decrease in the associative tendency to eat. This sort of nonmotivational interpretation of data deserves serious consideration, and in the next chapter we shall discuss the matter at greater length. The important conclusion to be reached here, however, is that *changes in performance following the manipulation of a motivational variable cannot be ascribed solely to changes in drive unless there is reason to believe that associative strengths have remained constant.* In this respect Siegel's results come closer to providing a "pure" estimate of drive, since his animals were not habituated to an externally imposed drinking schedule prior to the experiment, and the drinking responses, therefore, could hardly have become associated with only one specific value of thirst-stimulus intensity. The ad-lib drinking schedule under which Siegel's rats were reared might have led, however, to the growth of associations between drinking responses and various low-intensity thirst stimuli. The presence of such tendencies would tend to encourage drinking at short-term privation test periods relative to long-term periods.

Estimates of drive strength based upon consummatory behavior may also be affected by the number of previous experiences the organism has had with deprivation and with the removal of deficits by eating or drinking. As Ghent (1957) has clearly shown, when rats are permitted to eat or drink after their first deprivation experiences, they do not immediately go to a familiar food dish or to a familiar water spout. But with repeated privations, eating and drinking latencies decrease markedly, and time spent in consuming food and water increases. Corroborative evidence to support this view that prior experience with deprivation affects consummatory responses has been reported by Young (1949), Baker (1955), and Lawrence and Mason (1955).

Instrumental Behavior as a Function of Deprivation. The two experiments we have just examined were chosen to illustrate the effects of deprivation upon behavior which, though probably learned in part, appears quite early in the organism's life and under conditions seldom controlled by the experimenter. In this section we shall review experiments in which the indicant reactions are instrumental to the obtaining of food or water and have been learned under the supervision of the experimenter. Thus we shall be dealing with the effects of motivational variables upon such responses as running, swimming, and lever pressing, which must be performed by the subject to obtain a reward. As in the preceding section, we shall make no attempt to review existing studies *in toto*, but will concentrate on a few of the more recent and more adequately controlled experiments.

One problem of central importance in this area is that of the *effects of different levels of a motivational variable upon the rate of acquisition of an instrumental response and upon terminal levels of proficiency.* In principle, the experimental design required for this problem is extremely simple: different groups of subjects are taught the to-be-learned reaction under different levels of the motivational variable, and their performance during acquisition is observed and recorded. Unfortunately, our psychological literature contains few studies of this simple, straightforward type.

An experiment by Fredenburg (1956), designed in essentially this way, yields evidence as to the effects of different deprivation levels upon the performance of a simple instrumental response. In her study two groups of rats were trained to run down a 4-foot alley for food. One group received this training after 3 hours of food deprivation, the other after 22 hours of deprivation. Two additional groups, also under 3- and 22-hour deprivation conditions, respectively, were trained in an 11-foot alley. Four trials per day were given to each rat for a period of 12 days. By means of photoelectric devices it was possible to measure both starting and running time on every trial. Starting time was defined as the interval between the opening of the starting-box door and the instant the rat had moved a distance of 1 foot out into the alley. Running time was the time taken to traverse the second, foot-long segment of the alley.

Acquisition curves for the two groups trained in the 4-foot alley are reproduced in Figs. 3:6 and 3:7. These speed curves were obtained from the starting and running times by converting each individual subject's time scores into reciprocals (by dividing each score into 1) and then averaging these reciprocals. As the curves in these figures show, the performance of the 22-hour deprivation group was superior to that of the 3-hour group in both starting and running speed. Comparable results favoring a long- over a

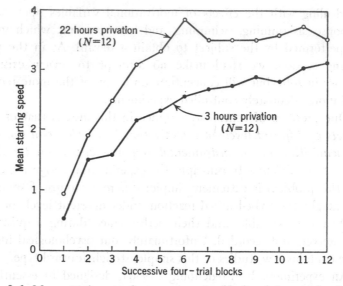

Fig. 3:6. Mean starting speeds over successive blocks of four trials of rats that had been deprived of food for 22 and for 3 hours. (*Adapted from Fredenburg, 1956.*)

short-deprivation group were also obtained in the case of additional animals that Fredenburg trained in the 11-foot alley.

The conclusion to which these data point is amply supported by other experimental evidence. For example, Loess (1952) found performance level during learning, as measured by speed of response, to be higher for a 22-hour group than for a 3-hour group. In his experiment the response was one of running from a starting compartment into a choice compartment to touch a small bar projecting from the back wall. Kimble (1951), Ramond (1954), Davenport (1956), and Bass (1958) have also shown that acquisition curves obtained after long deprivation intervals tend to reach higher final asymptotic levels than curves obtained following brief periods of deprivation. Moreover, performance of an instrumental running response is better under high than under low drive even when these conditions are induced in the same subjects on alternate days (Bass). We may take it as reasonably well established, therefore, that the heights of curves depicting the acquisition of a simple instrumental response vary directly with level of food deprivation over a limited range.

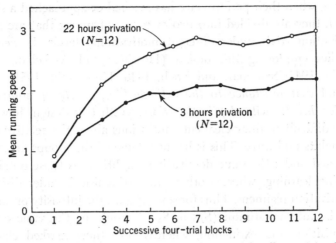

FIG. 3:7. Mean running speeds of rats in a short straight alley as joint functions of number of rewarded learning trials and of length of food deprivation. (*Adapted from Fredenburg, 1956.*)

In attempting to interpret the results of studies such as these one must proceed with caution. Performance may be better when a response is learned following long deprivation, but this may or may not mean that the manipulated variable (deprivation time) is functioning "motivationally." Actually, stronger associations or habits might be formed when an animal is hungry than when it is not, and if behavior is assumed to be a joint function of habits and drives, the observed disparities in performance might be due to habit-strength differences, not to drive differences. Alternatively, such results could be due to inequalities in both drives and habits or in drive level alone.

While few experimenters have studied the effects of a motivational variable upon the *acquisition* of instrumental responses, a great many studies have been performed in which such variables were manipulated during the extinction of a response. The problem under investigation in these experiments is that of *how different drive levels affect resistance to extinction resulting from non-reward.*

Experimental designs evolved to shed light on this problem have assumed a variety of forms. In a number of these, all subjects are given their initial training under the same motivational conditions,

Then, when their performance has reached or approached a stable level, they are divided into two or more subgroups that are given extinction trials under different motivational levels. In general, studies employing this design (Heathers and Arakelian, 1941; Perin, 1942; Saltzman and Koch, 1948; Horenstein, 1951) have found that *resistance to the extinguishing effects of nonreward varies directly with deprivation time.* With this design, however, it is difficult to draw clear-cut conclusions about the relative roles of habits and drive. This is because some of the groups are extinguished under the same deprivation conditions as those obtaining during learning, whereas others are extinguished under different deprivation regimens. Thus for some groups the intensity or quality of the internal stimuli (S_DS or $S_{MV}s$) would be the same during acquisition and extinction, whereas for others marked changes might be expected. Altering the nature of these internal cues would affect performance if the response under study had become associated with those cues. If all animals were trained under a high level of deprivation and separate subgroups were extinguished under that and lower levels, an observed decrease in resistance to extinction with declining motivation could be explained as an instance of weakened internal cues. Such an interpretation would qualify as associative rather than motivational.

The difficulties attending this design might be overcome by giving all subjects extensive preliminary training under all the levels of deprivation to be used during extinction. Provided that habit strength does not depend on drive, such diversified training should result in the instrumental response's becoming conditioned equally to the several intensities or kinds of internal deprivation-produced cues. Response strength manifested by subgroups extinguished at different privation levels would then not be distorted by uncontrolled variations in associative strength. To the best of our knowledge, no one has performed an experiment in precisely this way. The nearest approximation is a study by Cotton (1953). His subjects (rats) were first given preliminary training in a straight runway under a 22-hour deprivation schedule. This was followed by extensive training under deprivation times of 0, 6, 16, and 22 hours, administered in a random order within each four-day period. When running-speed asymptotes had been reached, further tests were carried out under the four different privation schedules. The measure of response strength was running speed on rewarded trials rather than resistance to extinction. When all test trials were counted, running time was found to decrease as a linear function of deprivation time. Quite a different function was obtained, however, when the trials on which animals made competing responses, such as stopping to sniff, were excluded. Under these conditions performance was but little affected by deprivation, a result that underscores the importance of the particular measure used in studies of this kind.

Some of the difficulties inherent in shifting from one motivational level during acquisition to another during extinction can also be overcome by the kind of design used by Yamaguchi (1951). He employed five different deprivation times (3, 12, 24, 48, and 72 hours), one group of animals being both trained and extinguished at each of these levels. Thus for each group, the motivation-variable-produced stimuli $(S_{MV}s)$ would be the same during both learning and extinction. The response was that of pressing a lever in a modified Skinner box, and the basic measure was the number of responses made during a series of extinction trials to a criterion of no responses in two minutes. As in previous studies, Yamaguchi found that the mean number of responses in extinction increased progressively as the period of privation was lengthened. He obtained means of 14.9, 15.8, 24.4, 32.2, and 40.0 responses for 3, 12, 24, 48, and 72 hours of hunger, respectively. Considerable confidence can probably be placed in the stability of these results, since the number of subjects in each of the five groups was quite large, ranging from 36 to 66. The possibility still remains, however, that associative strength depends, to a degree, upon level of motivation, and this would operate artificially to enhance the apparent energizing effects of extended deprivation times. Moreover, different results might have been obtained had the distribution of extinction trials been the same as that of the acquisition trials. In Yamaguchi's study extinction trials were massed, whereas the learning trials were given in a quasi-distributed manner: four trials per session, one session every five days.

As we have seen in our discussion of behavior strength as a function of time of deprivation, difficult problems arise in designing experiments on motivational variables, and since known investigations differ so widely with respect to subjects, responses, and procedures, no single function can be held to be uniquely representative of the relation between response strength and deprivation time. Nevertheless, three conclusions for which there is reasonable support may be tentatively stated. First, consummatory activities, as well as the speed and resistance to extinction of responses instrumental to consummation, tend to be enhanced by privation. The effect of any specific deprivation period is also a function, however, of such variables as the number of deprivation cycles preceding the test, the animal's body weight, and the relative familiarity of the testing environment. Second, curves depicting the course of acquisition of instrumental responses as a function of different deprivation levels tend to diverge during early learning trials and to maintain a constant separation with extended practice. Third, when performance is measured at its asymptote, behavior strength is found to rise rapidly after satiation (or shortly thereafter) up to privation times of about two hours and then to increase at a slower rate to periods of about 48 to 72 hours. With intervals longer than this, behavior strength declines, presumably as a consequence of inanition.

Instrumental Behavior and Level of Noxious Stimulation. While food and water deprivation are the most commonly manipulated motivational variables, our treatment of primary sources of drive would be incomplete without some mention of the ways in which intense stimuli may motivate instrumental responses.

In experimental work with animals, electric shock, because of the relative ease with which it can be applied and controlled, has been used more frequently than any other noxious stimulus. Experiments have also been reported, however, in which loud sounds, bright lights, intense olfactory and gustatory stimuli, and excessively hot or cold environments have been employed as motivators.

As the student of learning is well aware, noxious stimuli are used as unconditioned stimuli (UCSs) in studies of classical (Pavlovian) aversive conditioning with both human and animal subjects. Unfortunately, UCS intensity has seldom been systematically varied in animal experiments, and it is necessary, therefore, to rely upon instrumental conditioning studies for information as to the motivational consequences of this variable. In Chapter 7, the role of *UCS* intensity in classical aversive conditioning with human subjects will be discussed.

In research on noxious stimuli as motivators of instrumental actions, the situation is commonly arranged so that the subject, by performing either a previously established response or by learning a new one, can escape from or terminate the noxious stimulus. Proficiency in the performance of the designated response is then measured at different levels of the noxious stimulus. Experiments by Amsel (1950a) and by Campbell and Kraeling (1953) serve as examples of this general procedure.

In Amsel's study, two groups of hooded rats were given practice in escaping from a section of a straight alley with an electrified floor into a wooden-floored goal box. The two groups were satiated with food and water at the time of these trials and, save for the fact that one group was given weak shocks and the other strong, were treated identically. The performance of the two groups was evaluated by measuring the time they took to traverse the middle 4-foot section of the 60-inch alley. Figure 3:8 presents the median running times for the strong-shock and weak-shock groups as a function of 10 successive training trials administered during a single day.

From the data in Fig. 3:8 it appears that although the animals were not motivated by either hunger or thirst, the shock provided a strong drive to activate running, and its cessation following escape from the alley functioned as a reinforcing agent. Moreover, although both groups quickly acquired the new skill of running to escape shock, the strong-shock group maintained a consistently higher performance level (shorter running times) than did the weak-shock group. Amsel tried to prevent the rats from becoming negatively adapted to the shock by gradually increasing its strength, but the tendency for both curves to rise toward the end of a second day of training (not shown in Fig. 3:8) may indicate the occurrence of such adaptation.

The experiment of Campbell and Kraeling (1953) also shows that the performance of rats in an escape situation is facilitated by increasingly strong electric shock. Acquisition curves obtained from three groups of animals that were escaping from different

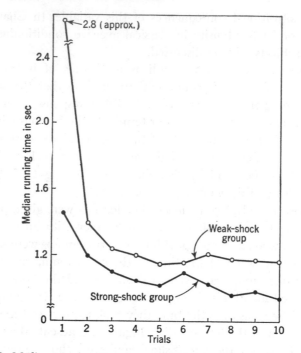

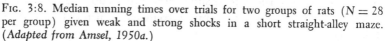

FIG. 3:8. Median running times over trials for two groups of rats ($N = 28$ per group) given weak and strong shocks in a short straight-alley maze. (*Adapted from Amsel, 1950a.*)

levels of shock into a neutral goal box are reproduced in Fig. 3:9.

As these data indicate, the strong shock provided a more powerful drive for running, even on early trials, than did the weaker shocks. In commenting on these and other groups run in their investigation, Campbell and Kraeling state that on the initial trials most of their subjects ran at a speed proportional to the intensity of the shock. Nevertheless, the performance level of the three groups differed but little by the time training was terminated. On the basis of statistical analyses of these data, Campbell and Kraeling concluded that rate of acquisition varied significantly with amount of shock reduction but that final running speed did not. They suggest that differences in response strength might have been observed if a different measure had been used. If all animals were running at or near their maximum speeds by the

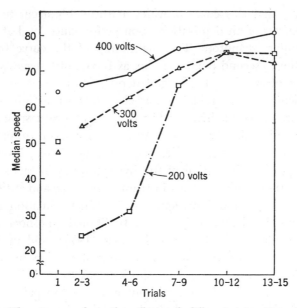

Fig. 3:9. These curves show the effects of different intensities of electric shock on the speeds with which rats run to escape shock. Speeds for trial 1 are plotted separately to indicate the effect of shock on running speed prior to the first successful escape experience. (*From Campbell and Kraeling, 1953.*)

end of practice, an artificial ceiling would be imposed on magnitude of response.

To the writer's knowledge, the only investigation in which a functional relation has been obtained between time of air deprivation and performance is one by Broadhurst (1957). Since there seems to be little question of the noxious nature of stimulation resulting from interference with breathing, studies of its motivational properties quite properly deserve mention at this point. The curve of Fig. 3:10 reproduced from Broadhurst's paper is, in large measure, self-explanatory. It shows that the speed with which rats swam under water through a short straight alley increased progressively as the period of air deprivation prior to their release was increased. Broadhurst used 20 rats in this portion of his experiment, all of them being tested at each of the several air-deprivation intervals. The subjects had had preliminary practice in underwater swimming before these tests, and it seems likely, therefore, that this curve provides a reasonably accurate picture of the effects of air deprivation upon performance level at or near the learning asymptote. The slight drop of the curve from the 20- to the 25-second point may be, as Broadhurst suggests, a consequence of anoxia at the longest deprivation interval.

Incidentally, a stimulus such as electric shock may function as a primary source of drive for the learning of new responses even when applied directly to the brain rather than to peripheral sensory surfaces. For example, in a study by Cohen, Brown, and Brown (1957) stimulation of the hypothalamus in cats served to motivate the learning of both instrumental escape and anticipatory (conditioned) avoidance responses. Central stimulation thus exhibits functional similarities to the traditional grid-shock UCS, a finding confirmed by Bower and Miller (1958), and by Roberts (1958), among others. The two methods of shock administration differ, however, in that central shock seems to lead directly to a motivating emotional state without arousing the pain that grid shock produces. Intracranial shock may thus be an instance of a motivational variable having minimal directive (stimulus) consequences and maximal motivating effects. This has important implications for the interpretation of experiments in which the onset

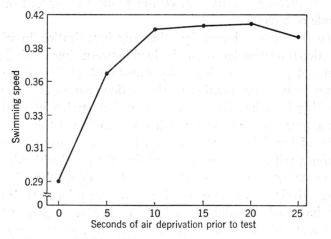

Fig. 3:10. The speed with which rats swim through an underwater maze as a function of the length of an immediately preceding period during which they have been deprived of air. The ordinal values are reciprocals of swimming times in seconds. (*Adapted from Broadhurst, 1957.*)

of central shock proves to be reinforcing rather than punishing, but we shall postpone our discussion of this topic until Chapter 9.

It seems justified, from these and other studies (e.g., Miller and Dollard, 1941; Kaplan, 1952; Ketchell, 1955; Spence, 1956), to conclude that under certain conditions intense stimuli can serve as a primary source of drive to motivate the performance of instrumental acts. Moreover, responses followed by the cessation of such stimuli tend to be learned, and the stronger the stimulus, within limits, the better the performance. Nevertheless, it is well to remember that the motivating and rewarding function of strong external stimuli is always complicated by their capacity to elicit specific responses. These reactions may be the correct ones in a given experimental situation, or they may be wrong and in competition with the correct ones, and their relative strengths may vary with stimulus intensity. As an example, if weak grid shock elicits responses of jumping and running in rats, oriented escape reactions will perhaps be readily learned. But with intense shock, crouching may become prepotent over running, and the process of learning to escape may be retarded even though level of motivation may be higher than before. Clearly, any conclusions as to the motivating function of strong stimuli should, in principle, include some reference to the associative (response-eliciting) properties of those stimuli.

Up to this point, our discussion of the effects of primary sources of drive has dealt only with relatively simple situations and simple responses. To round out the picture we turn now to the examination of a few selected investigations in which primary sources of drive have been varied in choice and discrimination situations.

Behavior in Spatial Choice Situations as a Function of Primary Motivational Variables. The simple T maze is one of the most frequently used experimental situations in which animals must learn to choose between two alternative goals or response sequences. Since the response to be learned is simply to turn toward and approach a goal on either the left or right, the T maze is sometimes described as a *two-choice spatial situation.* It is usually distinguished, therefore, from a *discrimination situation* in which the animal must approach a specific stimulus, such as a white card, regardless of its spatial position.

Choice of the correct side of the T maze may be induced in a number of ways. The animal may be rewarded on one side but not on the other; he may be given more frequent rewarded trials or larger rewards on one side; or he may be rewarded on one side and punished on the other. Sometimes animals are permitted to correct an error that has led to punishment or nonreward (correction method), and sometimes they are simply removed from the maze (noncorrection method). In all cases efficiency of performance is evaluated by counting the number of choices of the correct side during the course of learning, these data being supplemented occasionally by measurements of running speed in the stem or to the correct and incorrect sides.

Another practical device for studying the learning of choice reactions is the apparatus described by Logan (1952). The schematic drawing in Fig. 3:11 shows that the principal features of the apparatus are a starting box and a choice compartment. When the guillotine doors are opened, the rat must leave the starting box, enter the choice compartment, and touch one of the two small bars projecting out into the compartment from the back wall. When the correct bar is touched, a small pellet of food drops

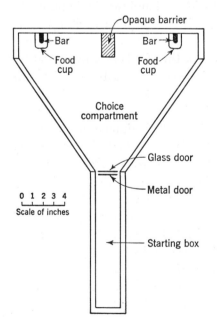

FIG. 3:11. Floor plan of apparatus used to investigate choice behavior in rats. At the experimenter's discretion, either or both sides of the choice compartment can be made distinctive by switching on lights above each of the bars. Response speed is obtained by measuring the time that elapses between the opening of the glass door and the moment at which the rat touches a bar. (*Adapted from Logan, 1952.*)

into the food cup below the bar and the bar is withdrawn from sight. As in the T maze, performance may be evaluated either from number of correct choices or from response speed. Speed is determined by measuring the time between the opening of the doors and the touching of the bar. While the T maze and the two-bar choice box differ in many respects, the same principles of learning and motivation may be applicable to both. Certainly the problem of immediate concern with both is whether proficiency in the execution of choice reactions is meaningfully and lawfully related to variations in the strengths of primary sources of drive.

Systematic experimental studies of choice behavior as a function of drive are relatively scarce, but the weight of evidence points to the conclusion that *selection of the correct side is unrelated to time of food deprivation.* This generalization seems to be restricted, however, to experiments in which the animals are not permitted to rectify their errors (noncorrection method) and in which they are forced to go to the incorrect (nonrewarding) side as often as they are permitted to go to the correct side.

The study we use to illustrate this conclusion is one whose different aspects have been reported by Teel and Webb (1951) and by Teel (1952). Four groups of albino rats, 21 per group, were trained in a single-unit T maze under food-deprivation periods of 1, 7, 15, and 22 hours, respectively. Of the four trials given each subject on each of 14 days, two were free-choice trials and two were forced. On free trials both choice-point doors were open, whereas on forced trials only one was open and access to only one arm of the T was permitted. This procedure was used to equate the number of reinforced and nonreinforced runs for all animals. The arbitrary criterion of learning was eight correct choices in succession.

Analyses of the data revealed that the mean number of trials required by the four groups to reach the criterion of learning did not decrease with increasing time of food deprivation. In fact, a small but consistent trend in the opposite direction was obtained. It was also found, as reported in the Teel and Webb paper, that when trials were administered under near-satiation conditions, level of performance was not significantly reduced. Again, this indicates that performance in a choice situation, as estimated by correct reactions, is unrelated to deprivation time. Data tending to corroborate those of Teel and Webb have been reported by Loess (1952), who used the two-bar choice box; by Champion (1954), who employed a *T* maze; and by Carlton (1955), who trained his subjects on an elevated Y-like maze.

These studies are consistent in finding choice proficiency to be unrelated to level of deprivation, but other experiments in which different procedures were followed have produced positive results. For example, Ramond (1954) found, with the two-bar choice box, that rats under 22 hours of food deprivation performed significantly better than others under 4 hours of deprivation. His subjects, however, were given twice as many reinforced trials to one bar as to the other, and his performance measure was the percentage of times the more frequently rewarded bar was chosen. Thus, frequencies of left- and right-bar choices were unequal, which was not the case in studies with negative findings.

Additional evidence for a positive relation between strength of motivation and behavior in simple and multiple choice situations may be found in the investigations of Siegel (1943), Tolman and Gleitman (1949), Miller (1948*b*), and Davenport (1956). In all of these studies, however, as in Ramond's, the procedures were such that the number of responses made to the correct and incorrect sides of the apparatus were either purposely made unequal or were permitted to become unequal during the course of learning. As Spence (1956) and Ramond (1954) have pointed out, one would not expect a variation in drive to affect choice behavior unless the training methods produce differences in the strengths of the habits corresponding to the two reactions. If the habits are kept equal by the use of forced trials, drive differences arising from changes in deprivation should not affect percentage choice. The explication of the details of this prediction is rather lengthy, and hence it will be postponed to the next chapter, where we shall be concerned more directly with such matters.

Behavior in Discrimination Situations as a Function of Primary Motivational Variables. As we have noted, it is customary to apply the term *discrimination learning* to situations in which an animal must acquire a specific response to an environmental cue having no fixed spatial location. For instance, in a black-white discrimination the positive stimulus is usually presented equally often in the right and left positions in the apparatus. Hence, success in the performance of the discrimination cannot be achieved unless tendencies to prefer one side or the other are overcome. It is in this principal respect that discrimination situations differ from the spatial-choice problems we have just examined.

It is somewhat regrettable, from the point of view of understanding phenomena in this area, that investigations of the role of motivation in discrimination learning are even less plentiful than those concerned with simple choice reactions. Perhaps the earliest relevant study is one by Yerkes and Dodson (1908), who examined the relation of shock intensity to performance on visual-discrimination problems of varying levels of difficulty. One of the principal findings of this investigation was that performance on easy discriminations tended to improve progressively with shock intensity. But on difficult problems performance was poorer with weak and with strong shocks than with shocks of intermediate strength. This latter finding led them to propose a general principle, since known as the Yerkes-Dodson law, to the effect that there is an optimal motivational level for learning, which tends to decrease as problem difficulty increases. Subsequently, Dodson (1917) performed a follow-up experiment, in which rats were taught a light-dark discrimination under several intensities of hunger. The results obtained were coordinate with those of the first study, since performance improved for values of food deprivation up to 41 hours but became worse when the period was extended to 48 hours. Shock was also used for some animals in the second study and was found to be most efficacious when neither too strong nor too weak.

More recent studies of the relation of hunger to performance in a discrimination situation are those by Dinsmoor (1952), by Eisman (1956), and by Eisman, Asimow, and Maltzman (1956). In Dinsmoor's investigation, rats were trained initially to press a bar while starved down to 85 per cent of their normal body weight. Then they were given further training in making the discriminatory response of pressing the bar in the presence of a light and not pressing it in the dark. Final tests were carried out with satiated animals and with animals maintained at 100, 95, 90, 85, 80, and 75 per cent of normal weight. The tests with percentage weights of 80 and 75 represent a greater food need than that in effect during original training, and the weights of 90, 95, and 100, as well as the satiated condition, constitute weaker need values. The results of the study are presented in Fig. 3:12. Of principal interest here is the finding that the *difference* between the number of responses to the positive stimulus (light) and negative stimulus (no light) increased as hunger was heightened above the level used in training. Thus an increase in hunger, even after fairly extensive training has been carried out, seems to lead to improved proficiency in responding *differentially* to the positive and negative cues. Dinsmoor's data also indicate that differences between responses to the two cues decrease as hunger is reduced, with the total number of responses declining also. Dinsmoor's animals were trained, as has been pointed out, at only a single level of deprivation, a procedure that may have permitted associative (habit) as well as motivational (drive) variables to affect his results. As we shall see in the next chapter, associative factors provide a reasonable basis for explaining the convergence of the curves as drive level is reduced but not their divergence as drive is increased. Dinsmoor's

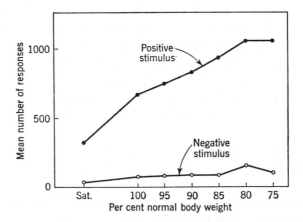

FIG. 3:12. Data obtained in a study of the effects of varying degrees of hunger on behavior in a discrimination situation. The ordinate shows the number of lever-pressing responses made to the positive stimulus (light) and negative stimulus (no light) during a 90-minute test period. The initial points of the curves were obtained following a period of continuous feeding (satiation). (*From Dinsmoor, 1952.*)

experiment, therefore, seems to support the earlier conclusion of Dodson that the performance of a (simple) discrimination task is facilitated increasingly by heightened hunger.

The remaining two experiments of Eisman, Asimow, and Maltzman and of Eisman provide further evidence for a positive relation between discrimination-task performance and level of motivation. In the first of these experiments, rats run in a black-white, Y-type discrimination apparatus under 46 hours of food deprivation made fewer errors and required fewer trials and reinforcements to reach a learning criterion than did rats trained under 22 hours or 4 hours of deprivation. The 4-hour and 22-hour groups did not, however, differ significantly with respect to any of the three measures. This rather unexpected finding was interpreted by supposing that the rat's stomach takes about four hours to empty following eating, and that after this further deprivation has no effect upon drive. On these assumptions, the drive levels of the 4- and 22-hour groups should have been identical.

But the fact that the 46-hour group was superior to both of the others could not be explained without additional assumptions. As a consequence, Eisman (1956) suggested that drive level also depends upon the general severity of the deprivation schedule under which the animal has been maintained. This variable which he termed "hours of deprivation during a unit of time" is believed to operate jointly with the more conventional factor of "time since eating." Thus one is led to the expectation that if two groups have been fed, say, 22 hours previously, but if one of them has been maintained on a 46-hour deprivation schedule, it will have a higher drive level than one maintained on a 22-hour schedule. Eisman's experiment, designed specifically to test this hypothesis, yielded clear confirmatory results. More directly related to the topic under discussion, however, was Eisman's finding that high-drive groups, defined by reference to the severity of the maintenance schedule, performed more efficiently on a black-white discrimination problem than did low-drive subjects.

It might seem justifiable, in the light of the evidence provided by these studies, to conclude that, in general, performance in the learning of a discrimination reaction improves as a function of heightened motivation. But exceptions to this conclusion are to be found in the performance of the 4- and 22-hour groups of the Eisman-Asimow-Maltzman study and in an unpublished study by Myers (1952). This latter investigator found no relationship between drive differences due to 4 and 21 hours of food deprivation and performance in a T-shaped brightness-discrimination apparatus. Meyer (1951) has likewise found that in experiments with monkeys rather large differences in time of deprivation do not affect performance in a discrimination-reversal situation. Until these negative findings have been satisfactorily accounted for, the wisest course of action is to withhold final judgment. Further studies of the relations of changes in primary sources of drive to discrimination learning and of the conditions determining specific outcomes are urgently needed.

Summary

The first sections of this chapter were concerned primarily with the elucidation of various terms frequently encountered in discussions of motivation. Initially it was observed that a distinction is commonly made by theorists between motivating or activating variables and variables that function to guide or direct behavior. The terms drive, conations, emotions, and motivation have been used in conjunction with members of the first class, and cognitions, associative bonds, and habit strengths with the second class. Certain variables, however, are difficult to classify because they appear to function both as directive cues that elicit specific responses and as relatively nonspecific motivators. To reduce confusion it was suggested that such variables be conceptualized as leading to two intermediary processes having the nonoverlapping functions of behavior direction and of motivation, respectively.

As a further step toward terminological clarity, it was proposed that the use of the plural word "drives" be dropped in favor of the singular form. This suggestion was supported primarily by the contention that the so-called drives can be differentiated with respect to their individual antecedent variables, but not in terms of their postulated effects upon behavior. The phrase "multiple sources of drive" is proposed in place of the word drives.

In accordance with current practice, a distinction was also made between sources of drive that achieve their motivating effects through the operation of inherited homeostatic mechanisms and those whose effects are largely contingent on prior learning. The former are here termed "primary sources of drive" and the latter "secondary sources of drive."

The variables of food and of water deprivation have been studied more extensively than any others by students of primary sources of drive. And since intakes of food and water have often been used as indexes of the resulting drive, the problem of how such intakes are regulated becomes of considerable significance. Contemporary thinking in this area places primary emphasis upon two factors: oropharyngeal stimulation produced by chewing and swallowing, and stomach distention. Each of these processes exercise some control over ingestion when operating separately, but neither is alone sufficient to account for all consummatory behavior. Thus stimulation of receptors in the mouth and throat serves as a signal tending to produce cessation of eating or drinking, but unless aided by additional signals from the stomach, the control of ingestion is incomplete. Circulating nutrients in the blood and stored nutrients in the tissues probably also play a role, but the specific mechanisms involved have not been clearly detailed.

In the context of our discussion of factors controlling ingestion, it was observed that a distinction can be profitably made between need and drive. This is because drive can apparently be reduced by variables that cannot possibly modify a physiological need and because a need arising from deprivation may continue to increase until death, whereas the resulting drive increases and decreases with time. It was also noted that the maintenance of this distinction may clarify the interpretation of experiments directed against the drive-reduction hypothesis of learning.

The major portion of the chapter dealt with studies of the effects of primary sources of drive upon consummatory behavior, upon instrumental responses, and upon performance in discrimination situations. Concerning the relation of deprivation to oral intake, available data indicate that consummatory activity increases as a monotonic function of hours of deprivation up to periods of the order of two or three days. Beyond these limits ingestive activity declines, presumably as a consequence of general bodily weakness. Estimates of drive strength based upon consummatory responses are complicated, however, by learned tendencies to eat or drink at certain times and by the kind of deprivation schedule in effect prior to the test.

Studies of the effects of deprivation upon responses instrumental to securing food or water support the conclusion that the speed of these responses and their resistance to extinction tend to be enhanced by privation. Learning curves for different privation levels tend to diverge at a relatively early stage of practice and to maintain a constant separation thereafter, asymptotic performance levels being directly related to deprivation duration from about 2 to perhaps 72 hours, but not beyond.

Noxious stimuli appear to provide a convenient primary source of drive, and performance under a variety of conditions, especially those in which escape responses are investigated, is directly related to stimulus intensity. The fact that exceptions are common, however, indicates that noxious stimuli may sometimes elicit competing responses and may thereby lead to performance decrements.

Experiments on the learning of spatial-choice reactions, as in T mazes, are relatively consistent in showing that performance is unrelated to privation when the associative strengths of the alternate response tendencies are deliberately held equal. When one response is more frequently reinforced, however, choice behavior becomes more proficient as motivation is increased. In visual-discrimination problems the effects of drive variations remain obscure, since high drive sometimes facilitates performance and sometimes does not.

Motivational and Associative Interpretations of "Motivated" Behavior

FROM TIME TO TIME in the preceding chapters we have noted that changes in behavior following the manipulation of motivational variables can sometimes be explained by other than motivational concepts. Moreover, we have stressed the view that any experiment purporting to demonstrate motivational effects is not convincing unless the influence of other factors has been eliminated or controlled. Altering a so-called motivational variable may indeed modify drive strength; but it may also lead to changes in the intensity and kinds of effective stimuli, in degree of learning, or in the physiological condition of the organism. Whenever variations in factors such as these provide acceptable explanations for the observed behavior the concept of drive may become expendable.

The question arises, therefore, whether a specific drive construct is needed at all by an adequate theory of behavior. Certainly, if drive adds nothing to the clarity of our explanations or to the breadth of our understanding, the principle of parsimony would argue for its complete elimination. This possibility is tempting to motivational theorists, and in recent years it has claimed their attention to an increasing degree. Our purpose in the present chapter is to evaluate the relative merits of the views that dispense with, and appeal to, a drivelike concept.

To facilitate the discussion we have chosen to describe the alternative views by the terms *motivational* and *associative*. A motivational theory is one containing, in a role of central importance, a unique construct to which a specific label, e.g., drive, may be attached. It is a theory in which the behavior-determining properties assigned to the drive construct are clearly different from those ascribed to cognitions, habits, excitatory tendencies, and other constructs. Hull's theory, which we have already considered briefly, is a good example of a motivational theory because it contains the construct D and because of the special properties assigned to D. However, a motivational theory, by our definition, is not one that appeals only to motivational mechanisms in attempting to explain behavior. Nor must it place primary emphasis upon such mechanisms to the exclusion of others. It is simply one that provides specific room for a motivating mechanism as well as for associative, excitatory, inhibitory, and other mechanisms.

By way of contrast, the type of theory we shall label *associative* contains no reference to concepts having such motivational-sounding names as drive, tension, or libidinal energy. An advocate of this type of theory would maintain that a separate drivelike intermediary is not needed, and that most, if not all, of the consequences of motivational variables can be explained by invoking altered associative connections and their complex interrelations. If this kind of view is to prove successful in interpreting the known facts of motivated behavior, while maintaining an adequate degree of internal consistency, it must not introduce additional constructs having drivelike titles. Moreover, the functional properties of the constructs in an associative theory must be different from those of the drive construct in a motivational theory. Renaming drive with a nondrivelike title will not suffice. Actually, highly detailed and specific versions of associative theories are just beginning to appear, but the basic position has gained increasing numbers of adherents in recent years, and it deserves, therefore, serious consideration.

Motivational Interpretations

Hull's Multiplicative-drive Theory. Probably the best known and most influential motivational theory is that of Hull (1943). As we have already seen in the previous chapter, Hull assumed that behavior is determined primarily by two major intermediary factors: the nonspecific drive state (D) and a variety of learned and unlearned reactive or associative tendencies. Unlearned reactive tendencies are denoted by the symbol $_sU_R$, and learned tendencies (habit strengths) by $_sH_R$, the S and R subscripts being used to indicate the functional association of stimuli and responses. We have chosen to apply the label "multiplicative-drive theory" to this conception because Hull assumed that drive combines multiplicatively with any reactive tendency to yield a response-determining resultant called *excitatory potential* $(_sE_R)$. Expressed in the form of a simple equation with the subscripts omitted, $E = D \times H$, where E stands for excitatory potential, D for drive, and H for learned associative tendencies. If the reactive tendency were unlearned, U would be substituted for H in the equation. Within the system, excitatory potential, modified by inhibitory and oscillatory processes, governs the speed with which a response will be made, its resistance to extinction, its amplitude, and so on.

This assumption that behavior is determined by the combined operation of drive and associative tendencies has several implications that should be made explicit. In the first place, since drive is conceived simply as a numerical multiplicative factor, it clearly cannot determine the direction behavior will take. Such direction-controlling functions reside in the reactive tendencies which may be loosely described as blueprints for action, or as the organism's "know how." Moreover, D as a nonspecific activator has only the one multiplicative function irrespective of the source from which it springs.

A second implication of the multiplicative hypothesis relates to the distinction commonly made by learning theorists between *learning* and *performance*, where learning denotes the unseen hypothetical changes produced by training and performance refers to overt behavior. This distinction has arisen from the observation that organisms sometimes do not perform well or perhaps do not perform at all even when there is no good reason to suppose that they have forgotten the skills requisite to a successful reaction. In Hull's system, learning is represented by habit strength, and performance is determined by excitatory potential. On the assumption that drive and learned reactive tendencies combine multiplicatively, it is possible for him to maintain that when either D or H has a value of zero, the product of the two is zero (i.e., $E = 0$) and no overt behavior should be exhibited. Thus an organism can "know" what to do (i.e., H can be greater than zero) yet never exhibit this "know how" in its performance if the value of D is zero. Such a conclusion could not be reached if D and H were assumed to combine by addition rather than by multiplication.

A further consequence of Hull's hypothesis is that one cannot, from the manifest characteristics of overt behavior alone, make accurate estimates of the relative contributions of the two intermediaries, D and H, unless a number of tests are given under a variety of conditions. Any particular response could be due to the presence of a strong drive combined with a weak reactive tendency or to a weak drive and a strong reactive tendency. When behavior does become manifest, both determinants are assumed to be present. But if no response is exhibited, one cannot decide, without additional information, whether a reactive tendency is present and drive is not, or the reverse. If a response suddenly fails to be exhibited where formerly it was commonplace, Hull's position would suggest that associative tendencies are present but not drive, since the former are assumed to be relatively permanent and not subject to abrupt fluctuations.

Practical Implications of the Multiplicative-drive Theory. From Hull's assumptions as to the manner in which a variety of different antecedent conditions (motivational variables) contribute to drive, and from his hypothesis of drive as a multiplier, a number of practical implications may be derived. In so far as these implications can be supported by research findings, the drive concept gains in acceptability.

For one thing, the theory implies that any motivational variable can, within unspecified limits, be substituted for another since the D provided by each is identical. Thus if a response has a high probability of being elicited by a stimulus when a subject is hungry, it should also be elicitable, though not necessarily at the same strength, when a subject is thirsty or in pain. In principle, the response could be either learned or unlearned, because both kinds of responses are affected by D in the same way. If positive results are obtained, the theory tends to be supported. But negative results, as we shall see at a later point in this chapter, may be inconclusive since the shift from one drive-producing antecedent condition to another may have modified the cues to which the response was attached.

A second implication of the theory is that variations in strength of drive produced by changing, say, time of food deprivation, should ordinarily alter the quantitative but not the qualitative features of a response. Increasing D should increase the speed, amplitude, frequency, and resistance to extinction of a response; but its specific direction should remain unaltered. Here again, either learned or unlearned behavior could be studied, but positive results would be expected only if the motivational variable does not lead to marked changes in stimuli (S_{MV}s) in addition to changes in D.

The drive theory also implies that a wide variety of responses should be enhanced by an increase in drive and weakened by a decrease in drive. This is an obvious expectation from the hypothesis that D multiplies all reactive tendencies. This prediction might be tested experimentally by determining which response is most likely to occur in each of a variety of different situations when the subject is operating under a given level of drive. An increase in drive produced by suitable manipulations of the antecedent conditions should ordinarily lead to the enhancement of all of these maximum-probability reactions. Conversely, all such reactions should be weakened when drive is lowered.

The Multiplicative-drive Theory Applied to Various Kinds of Behavioral Data. In order best to understand how the multiplicative theory functions in the interpretation of behavior, let us apply it to some experimental data of the kind described in the previous chapter. Later on we shall show, for purposes of comparison, how an associative theory containing no concept of D might account for the same results.

Consider first an experimental result such as that reported by Koch and Daniel (1945). These investigators trained rats to depress a bar to obtain food in a modified Skinner-box apparatus. At the time the response was acquired, the subjects were motivated by 22 hours of food deprivation, and upon the completion of training, the response was strongly established. After being thoroughly satiated with food, however, the rats would scarcely press the bar at all. The median number of responses elicited from the 32 subjects prior to a five-minute no-response interval was only one. From this result, Koch and Daniel concluded that the effective response strength under conditions of satiation was essentially zero.

Now according to Hull's theory, the strength of the reactive tendency (habit) to press the bar is not weakened by the operation of satiation. The animal has forgotten neither how to make the response nor where the food is located. Rather, the failure to act is a consequence of the marked decrease in D accompanying satiation. Suppose the associative tendency is given an arbitrary numerical value of 5, and the D resulting from 22 hours of deprivation a value of 10. Multiplying these two quantities together yields an excitatory tendency (E) with a value of 50. Since the animal *does* react under these conditions it must be presumed that E is above threshold. But if the drive is reduced through relatively complete satiation to a value of, say, 1 unit, the product of D and H is only 5, and the threshold may or may not be exceeded. If the threshold lies above 5, the animal will not respond at all. The less complete the process of satiation, the smaller the reduction in the value of D and the less the performance decrement. In this way, then, the multiplicative-drive theory attempts to account for the fact that an animal will display a previously learned response when it has been deprived of food, and not, or to a lesser degree, when satiated.

In addition to affecting D, the operation of satiation doubtless eliminates some of the internal stimuli (S_{MVS}) produced by food deprivation and may also introduce new cues arising from stomach distention. As we have already observed in our discussion of Horenstein's and Siegel's experiments (Chapter 3), these interoceptive cues may function importantly as determin-

ants of behavior under changing conditions of deprivation provided they have become associated with critical responses. A "pure"
motivational interpretation cannot appeal to such internal cues.
To do so would be to invoke a nonmotivational (associative)
explanatory mechanism. In the foregoing interpretation of the
Koch and Daniel results, no such associative mechanism was
found necessary.

As Koch and Daniel have pointed out, however, the almost
complete lack of responses by their animals is apparently inconsistent with Hull's assumption that other primary sources of drive,
e.g., sexual deprivation, also contribute to nonspecific D. Their
subjects had been deprived of all recent sexual experiences, yet
D, which should have resulted from this deprivation, seemingly
did not multiply the bar-pressing tendency when hunger was
eliminated by satiation. The theory asserts that D, considered
solely as a multiplier, is unrelated to the source from which it
springs. Consequently, a shift from one primary source of drive
to another should result in almost perfect response transfer, provided that the second primary variable contributes as much to D
as the first, and provided the change involves the introduction
of no competing tendencies. To explain instances in which a shift
from one deprivation condition to another results in little transfer,
other principles must be introduced. The animals of Koch and
Daniel were not, of course, shifted from one primary source of
drive to a second. Rather their D was reduced from a level produced by hunger plus sex (and other factors) to a level dependent
only upon sex and other factors. Studies of the effects of gonadectomy upon the activity level of rats (e.g., Richter, 1933) suggest that sex does make some contribution to general drive level.
It may be, therefore, that in the Koch and Daniel study the
motivating effects of sexual deprivation were overridden by competing tendencies to rest induced by the extreme degree of satiation.

The effects of changes in deprivation conditions upon the
behavior of animals in a spatial-choice situation constitute a second
typical observation to which the multiplicative-drive theory may
be applied. As was noted in Chapter 3, the experimental procedures used to study behavior in these situations may be such

that the number of responses to each of the alternatives is either equal or unequal. The multiplicative interpretation yields a different prediction for each of these situations, and it is instructive to consider them in turn.

Ramond's (1954) study with a two-bar choice box (see Chapter 3) provides us with an example in which twice as many reinforced trials were given to one bar as to the other, separate groups of animals being trained under 22 and 4 hours of food deprivation, respectively. If we assume, following Hull, that the strength of a habit depends upon the number of times the response has been reinforced, then the habits to approach and touch the two bars in this experiment should have been unequal, and since both habits are multiplied by the same value of D, the corresponding excitatory tendencies should also have been unequal. Therefore, the animal should choose the more frequently rewarded alternative, since the dominance of one mode of reacting over another is assumed to be determined by absolute differences in the strengths of the corresponding E values. Thus an observed dominance of one mode of action over another is attributed by this theory to *differences in habits or reactive tendencies.* Drive makes it possible for the "know how" to be exhibited in overt performance, but it does nothing to alter the ranks of two (or more) reactive tendencies. Drive has no inherent capacity to steer behavior into one channel rather than another.

To continue the analysis, let us consider the effect on performance in the two-choice lever box of *differences in D.* Here Hull's assumption of a multiplicative relation between drive and habit leads to conclusions quite in accord with Ramond's findings. That is, the *relative superiority of a stronger over a weaker excitatory potential increases as drive is strengthened, and is reduced as drive is weakened.* To see precisely how this works let us assign an arbitrary value of 10 to the habit tendency to press the left bar, and a value of 5 to the right-bar tendency that has been reinforced less often. If the drive due to 23 hours of deprivation is assumed to be 4 units, the resulting E values obtained by multiplying Hs of 10 and of 5 by 4 are 40 and 20, respectively. The absolute difference between these E values is 20, with the left-bar excitatory potential the stronger. But suppose that when the animal has been partially satiated the strength of D drops to 2 units. In this case, the absolute difference between the E values is decreased to 10, since the E value for the left bar drops to 20 and that for the right bar to 10. If the number of correct responses, i.e., depressions of the more frequently reinforced bar, is determined by the absolute difference between the two Es, performance should become poorer under the partial satiation conditions. Conversely, of course, performance should improve as strength of drive is increased. *Because changes in drive intensity may thus lead to either better or poorer performance, drive, in an indirect sense, does have an effect upon the direction behavior will take.* It exerts this effect, however, not by virtue of a steering function inherent in drive itself, but through its power to change the absolute difference between the strengths of competing excitatory potentials.

An experiment by Teel (1952), described in Chapter 3, illustrates the application of the multiplicative theory to behavior in a spatial choice situation (T maze) where practice in performing the two responses has been equated. In this study, it may be recalled, four groups of rats were trained under food deprivation times of 1, 7, 15, and 22 hours, respectively. Each rat was forced to run to one side as often as to the other to equate practice in running to the rewarding and nonrewarding sides. When performance was evaluated in terms of the number of trials required to reach a learning criterion of eight successive correct choices on the free trials, all four groups learned with equal facility.

This finding can be handled by the multiplicative theory, as Spence (1956) has shown, provided one makes the assumption that the forcing procedure which produced equal runs to the two sides of the maze resulted in equal habit strengths to approach the rewarding and nonrewarding arms. This assumption, it should be noted, is not one that Hull would have made, since he believed that habit strength is built up only on reinforced trials. Rather it is the kind of assumption made by those who hold that mere contiguity of stimulus and response is sufficient to produce learning (e.g., Guthrie, 1935). On the supposition that the habit strengths are equal, the multiplicative theory would predict no change in the relative frequency of correct and incorrect responses as a function of differences in D, since the two E values obtained by combining D with the two Hs would be identical regardless of strength of D. This was the result, as we have seen, of Teel's investigation. To explain the fact that animals do learn to perform correctly under these experimental conditions, resort must be made to other factors, e.g., anticipatory goal reactions, which are unequal for the two sides of the maze (cf. Spence, 1956).

An additional and quite important implication of the multiplicative theory is that *performance will be degraded by an increase in drive whenever the reactive tendencies corresponding to incorrect responses are stronger than those corresponding to correct reactions.* In Ramond's experiment, for instance, if the more frequently touched bar were actually the wrong one from the experimenter's point of view, intensification of D would lead to an increase in errors and hence to a decline in proficiency. Moreover, lowering D *should tend to make performance better*, a prediction that is apparently unique to the multiplicative-drive conception.

In this context it should be noted that the theory cannot, in its "pure" form, explain a drop in performance following a supposed increase in drive if there is reason to regard the correct habit as stronger than the wrong one. When such results are obtained, appeal is customarily made to the presence of competing tendencies, a solution that is essentially associative in nature. This is legitimate, of course, provided independent evidence can be presented to indicate that the motivational variable which led to an increase in D also led to an increase in the strengths of interfering habits or to an increase in the intensity of stimuli associated with such habits.

In summary, a motivational theory such as Hull's explains certain relatively simple behavioral phenomena by introducing an explicit construct of *drive* (D). This factor is assumed to combine in a multiplicative fashion with habitual or instinctive reactive tendencies (Hs or Us) to yield the excitatory potentials (Es) of which behavior is said to be a more or less direct function. When a specific overt reaction occurs as a consequence of an operation such as food deprivation and does not occur following satiation, the multiplicative theory holds that D has been raised by deprivation and the value of the corresponding E has been elevated above a threshold. Since D itself is not regarded as a director of behavior but only as a broadly acting energizing process, the occurrence of one response rather than another is explained as being due primarily to differences in the strengths of simultaneously present reactive tendencies. When two or more such tendencies are present, an improvement in performance following an increase in deprivation is accounted for by the assumption that, as D is increased, the absolute difference between the strengths of the stronger correct E and the weaker competing E is increased. But if the wrong habit is dominant prior to the increase in drive, then raising the level of D should lead to poorer performance. When the correct tendency is believed to be dominant initially, but increased D is followed by a decline in performance, it must be assumed that other, incorrect habits have displaced the correct ones at the top of the hierarchy of habits.

Other Motivational Theories

Hull's theory has served as the focal point for our discussion of motivational interpretations because it is perhaps more widely known than others and has been carried to a relatively high level of systematic refinement. Numerous other theories, however, might also qualify as motivational interpretations, and although we cannot take time to show how each might be applied to experimental data, a brief mention of several is appropriate at this point.

In its principal elements, Spence's (1948, 1956) theory parallels Hull's since the construct of drive (D) is retained along with the assumption that it multiplies associative tendencies. Spence holds that drive is a direct consequence of deprivation, but that variables such as unconditioned stimuli (for instance, air puffs in eyelid-conditioning experiments) and electric shocks affect drive *indirectly via the elicitation of an emotional response*. Since drive strength is taken as proportional to the vigor of this response, such descriptively different factors as individual differences in emotional reactivity to stress, the number of prior exposures to aversive stimuli, and stimulus intensity can all affect drive and hence performance (Spence, 1958).

Spence's interpretation also departs somewhat from Hull's in placing more emphasis upon a second motivational construct termed incentive motivation (K). As a behavior determinant, K is assumed to combine with D in an additive manner, and like D, therefore, it multiplies reactive tendencies. The variables determining K, however, are different from those upon which D depends. Specifically, K is a function of magnitude of reward, of the number of times the reward has been experienced, its palatability, the length of the chain of responses, and perhaps also of the time between the initiation of the response and the receipt of the incentive. As to its underlying mechanism, K is the consequent of the occurrence of a classically conditioned partial consummatory goal response (r_g). After an animal has been repeatedly fed in a given situation, it will tend to make anticipatory chewing and salivating responses prior to obtaining food. It is these responses $(r_g s)$ in anticipation of reward that provide the motivational increment described as K. Because these responses are largely learned, they qualify as secondary sources of drive and will be discussed in greater detail in Chapter 5.

Other writers who have followed Hull in their treatments of motivation (e.g., Brown, 1953a; Farber, 1954a; Taylor, 1956a; Amsel, 1958) are readily identified as motivational theorists, but it is more difficult to categorize those who fall outside the Hullian tradition. Within Tolman's (1932) early system, for example, *demands* (sometimes identified with purposes) tend to be equated to drives or motivations and to occupy the status of intervening variables. But demands, or at least drives, though they are initiated by physiological conditions, consist in part of a sign-gestalt readiness (a sort of perceptual-ideational process) which at other times is said by Tolman to be a constituent of *cognitions*. Thus Tolman is a motivational theorist in postulating intervening variables named *drives* or *demands*, but the behavior-determining properties of these variables are neither clearly specified nor carefully differentiated from those of cognitions. In certain of his latest formulations, Tolman (1951, 1952) seems to have moved even closer to a concept of a general, nondirective drive, since he introduces a *libido need* that has no specific goals of its own but is capable of controlling the energy that is available for the satisfaction of other specific needs.

Duffy (1934, 1951, 1957) has insisted for many years that a

clear distinction should be made between the factors that determine the *direction* behavior will take and those that govern its *intensity*. Her use of such terms as "arousal," "activation," and "energy mobilization," in reference to the dimension of behavior intensity is clearly congruent with a concept of a nonspecific motivating agency such as Hull's D. Moreover, she has also maintained that the concept of activation aids in erasing an unwarranted distinction between "drives" and "emotions," a view that can readily be related to theories of fear as a learned source of drive (Miller, 1951) and to the view that diverse environmental variables arouse drive through a mediating emotional response (Spence, 1958). Malmo (1957, 1958) has taken a position much like Duffy's, though he has tended, where she has not, to identify arousal level with specific physiological variables.

Among physiologically oriented psychologists, Morgan (1943, 1957) might be described as having espoused a motivational interpretation because of his concept of the *central motive state* (c.m.s.), which he defines as the neural integrative activity underlying motivated behavior. On the antecedent side, the c.m.s. is aroused by receptor-mediated stimuli and by chemical hormonal conditions. The latter are believed to affect the c.m.s. by direct stimulation of certain brain centers or in such indirect ways as by the excitation of internal receptors. Regarding its functional properties, the long-perseverating c.m.s. appears to serve in part as a nonspecific energizer, since it leads to general activity. It also is capable, however, of "emitting" particular responses even in the absence of specific stimuli, and can sensitize the organism to respond selectively to certain stimuli rather than to others. Morgan has listed four ways in which the c.m.s. might be reduced or negated: (1) by removal of the initiating humoral or stimulus events; (2) by the release of other "humoral messengers" having the capacity to reduce the c.m.s. directly; (3) by the excitation of sensory receptors; and (4) by the performance of certain acts generated by the c.m.s. As we have already noted in Chapter 3, Morgan is among those who hold that drive (c.m.s.?) may be controlled by sensory stimulation. Items (2) and (3) and perhaps (4) of the above list clearly reflect this view. Morgan has not, however, presented a formalized treatment of the c.m.s. or applied it to experiments in which motivational variables have been expressly manipulated.

Stellar (1954) has accepted Morgan's c.m.s. as the central nervous mechanism underlying drive and has suggested that it be assigned a definite physiological locus in the hypothalamus. In broad terms, motivated behavior thus becomes dependent upon the level of activity in "certain excitatory centers of the hypothalamus."

Lindsley (1951, 1957) and Hebb (1955), both of whom have been struck by the nonspecific activating effects of excitation in the ascending reticular system of the brain, might also be tentatively listed among the motivational theorists. Hebb, in particular, has identified the arousal function of the reticular formation with a general drive state and has urged that the energizing function be distinguished from the "S-R or cognitive functions that are energized." Neither of these writers, however, has presented us with a formal system in which the precise role of the arousal mechanism has been delineated. A brief resumé of physiological findings bearing on the concept of a nonspecific drive, as cited by these and other writers, will be found below in Chapter 9.

Finally it should be noted that concepts such as Freud's (1905) *libido*, McDougall's (1917) *instincts*, and Woodworth's (1918) *drive* suggest that these authors might be classified as early advocates of motivational interpretations. By certain standards, of course, these formulations may seem relatively unsystematic but clear anticipations of many of our present-day views can be discovered therein.

Associative Interpretations of the Role of Motivational Variables

Although motivational theories clearly have merit, there are other reasonable interpretations of the same phenomena which, because they make no reference to a construct such as D, may be described as nonmotivational or, more specifically, as *associative*. The ideas basic to any associative view are well known to students of motivation, and suggestive allusions to them may be found in various sources. Fundamentally, an associative view would hold that the manipulation of a motivational variable leads to *changes in the stimulus conditions effective at the time performance is measured*. The altered stimuli, in turn, would affect behavior through *changes in the number, relative strengths, or kinds of associations between those stimuli and overt reactions*. To the author's knowledge, however, the specific steps involved in the development and application of associative interpretations have rarely been presented previously. The following discussion represents the writer's preliminary attempt to formulate and evaluate several versions of an associative theory.

An examination of existing hypotheses as to factors responsible for variations in associative strengths suggests that three relatively distinct versions of an associative theory might be developed. The basis of the first is that motivational variables alter behavior because they lead to the *addition or removal of critical stimulus elements* and hence to the modification of *existing* habit strengths. In the second, motivational variables are assumed to operate by changing the *quality or intensity of critical stimuli*. This, in turn, produces variations in associative strengths in accordance with the specific hypothesis of habit-strength generalization. In the third version, central prominence is given to the likelihood that *new* habits, capable of either facilitating or interfering with the old are brought into effective action by the manipulation of motivational variables.

Attributing the Effects of Motivational Variables to the Addition or Subtraction of Critical Stimulus Elements. To illustrate this first form of an associative interpretation, let us refer again to the Koch and Daniel (1945) experiment wherein animals were trained to press a bar under long-term deprivation and were then tested in the same situation under short-term deprivation (satiation). In this case, the empirical phenomenon to be explained is the decrement in performance produced by satiation.

According to the view under consideration, the original training may be thought of as producing associations between the bar-pressing responses and a constellation of both internal and external stimuli. This assumption is represented in the upper part of Fig. 4:1, where stimuli S_1, S_2, S_3, and S_4 represent internal cues, S_E represents all the external cues of the testing situation, and H

indicates the associative connection of all cues to the bar-pressing response. When tests are conducted under conditions of complete or partial satiation, some, though probably not all, of the internal stimuli originally conditioned to the reaction would presumably be eliminated. This possibility is expressed in the lower half of Fig. 4:1, where only S_1 and S_2 of the original set are indicated as present. Now if we make the explicit assumption that the strength of an existing habit is directly related to the number of elements that are present from the originally conditioned stimulus aggregate, then the deletion of S_3 and S_4 should weaken the bar-pressing habit, and level of performance should decline. In effect then, this view holds that *behavior occurs when stimuli appropriate for its elicitation are present and does not occur when they are absent.* Thus, the facilitative effect of long-term deprivation as contrasted with the effect of satiation is explained without reference to the energizing or multiplying effects of a general D.

This version of an associative theory cannot, however, easily explain the facilitation of performance that might occur when training has been carried out under short-term deprivation and tests are then made under long-term deprivation. Loess (1952), for example, found that speed of response in a two-bar choice box increased when time of deprivation was shifted from a training

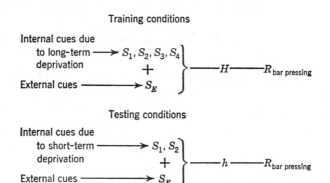

Fig. 4:1. Elements of an associative interpretation of a decline in performance following a shift from a long-term to a short-term deprivation schedule. The loss of stimuli S_3 and S_4 occasioned by the shift in schedule is assumed to weaken the original associative tendency. The stronger habit is indicated by H, the weaker by h.

value of 3 hours to a testing level of 32 hours. The hypothetical factors involved in this series of events are shown in Fig. 4:2. The upper portion of this figure represents the assumption that the response of approaching and touching a bar has become strongly attached (H) to the combination of S_1, S_2, and S_E. If at this point the deprivation period is lengthened, stimuli S_3 and S_4 should be added to the complex (lower part of Fig. 4:2). But if these new cues have never been previously associated with the response of approaching and touching the bar, their addition to the stimulus complex cannot explain the observed improvement in performance. In fact, as deprivation increases, the internal stimulus complex should become progressively more unlike that present during original training; and if we accept current views as to the role of stimulus similarity in determining associative strength, we must conclude that the tendency to make the original reaction should become weaker, not stronger, as the difference between the original and subsequent stimulus complexes is increased. This possibility is indicated in the bottom portion of Fig. 4:2 by the lower-case h. It thus appears that, granting the above assumptions, we must conclude that this particular associative interpretation cannot

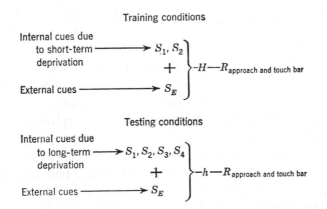

FIG. 4:2. The application of an associative hypothesis to behavior observed when original training is carried out under a short-term deprivation schedule and subsequent tests under long-term deprivation. From these assumptions alone it would be predicted that, as deprivation is enhanced, the addition of S_3 and S_4 to the stimulus complex would lead to a weakening of the association and hence to poorer rather than better performance.

readily deal with the case where original training has been administered under short-term deprivation and improved performance is then observed under long-term deprivation.

Special-purpose modifications of the theory might be introduced, of course, so as to make it work more convincingly. Thus, one might maintain that S_1 and S_2 become more intense with extended deprivation and are therefore more likely to exceed a threshold, or that S_3 and S_4 have the power, as the result of previous learning, to facilitate rather than interfere with the approaching response. Modifications such as these, however, raise additional problems, which when carefully analyzed may convert the theory into one or the other of the two forms to be described below.

Our first associative hypothesis can, however, deal adequately with decrements in performance attending a shift from one need condition to another. Here it would be presumed that a change from thirst to hunger, for example, results in the partial elimination of the thirst stimuli associated with the response during training. The fact that the response occurs at all under hunger would be explained on the grounds that some of the original internal (thirst) stimuli were still present at the time of the tests under hunger. The theory is also satisfactory as an interpretation of the effects of deprivation upon the acquisition of simple instrumental responses (cf. Fredenburg's data, Figs. 3:6 and 3:7). One would probably assume, in this case, that many more internal cues are present under 22 than under 4 hours of deprivation and that running can become more readily conditioned to a CS complex consisting of many elements than to one with few components. Thus performance differences would be explained in terms of differences in habit strengths.

In attempting to extend this type of associative theory to choice situations in which one or more associative tendencies are simultaneously present and in which the deprivation conditions are altered, reference would again be made to the addition or deletion of stimulus elements. If a rat has learned to turn right in a T maze when strong need-produced stimuli are present, its performance would be expected to suffer if the need were reduced through satiation. On the other hand, if the reaction has been conditioned to weak need stimuli, there is no clear-cut prediction from the theory that performance will improve when the need is increased. As in the case of the single reaction considered above, it is difficult to see how performance could be improved by suddenly adding irrelevant internal cues to the conditioned-stimulus aggregate.

Motivational-variable Effects Ascribed to Changes in the Strength of Habits in Accordance with the Principle of Stimulus Generalization. In order to explain this second type of associative interpretation, in which *changes* in motivational variables are assumed to affect the intensity or quality of stimuli rather than their mere numerosity, we must digress briefly to consider both the empirical phenomenon of *stimulus generalization* and the hypothesis of *generalized habit strength*.

The empirical phenomenon of stimulus generalization is nicely illustrated in an experiment by Grice and Saltz (1950). In this study rats were trained to traverse a short, straight black alley to obtain food from a small compartment in the center of a white disk located on the end wall of the alley. Seventy-five animals were trained to approach when the disk had an area of 79 square centimeters. Five subgroups of 15 animals each were then tested on disk sizes of 79, 63, 50, 32, and 20 square centimeters, respectively. These tests consisted of 25 opportunities to approach a disk, but no food was given on any trial. The strength of the approach tendency was measured by counting the number of times, during 25 trials, that an animal approached and touched the disk within 60 seconds. The results of these tests, reproduced in Fig. 4:3 (dashed-line curve), indicate that the animals approach disks that have never been used in training, but that as the size of the disk decreases, the tendency to approach becomes progressively weaker. The phrase *empirical stimulus generalization* denotes the fact that responses do occur to stimuli even in the absence of specific training with those stimuli. The phrase *gradient of generalization* refers to an observed decrease in response strength as the test stimulus differs progressively from the one used in training.

An additional 60 animals were trained by Grice and Saltz to approach and secure food from the stimulus with the smallest area (20 square centimeters). Four equal subgroups were then given extinction tests with disks having areas of 20, 32, 50, and 79

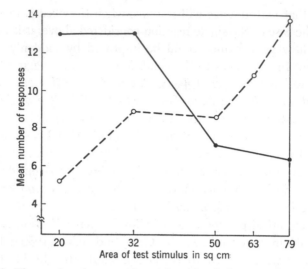

Fɪɢ. 4:3. The results of an experimental study of the generalization of instrumental responses to stimuli varying in the dimension of size. The dashed-line curve shows the number of extinction responses made by animals trained with the largest stimulus and tested on the others. The solid-line curve depicts the performance of rats that were trained on the 20-cm stimulus and tested on that and on larger ones. (*From Grice and Saltz, 1950.*)

square centimeters. Here also, stimuli never before associated with approaching elicited the response, and, in general, the more deviant the size of the test stimuli the less resistant the response to extinction. Data obtained from these animals are represented by the solid-line curve of Fig. 4:3.

This, then, is the empirical phenomenon of stimulus generalization: *after a response has become associated with one stimulus, it may be elicited, though often with a decrement, by other similar stimuli in the absence of specific training with those stimuli.*

In attempting to account for empirical data of this kind, Hull (1943) made the *assumption* that whenever a response is conditioned to a particular stimulus, associative strengths are automatically built up to (generalized to) other similar stimuli. Moreover, the greater the disparity between the conditioned and test stimuli the weaker the *generalized habit strength*. The specific details of his assumptions are shown in Fig. 4:4, where habit strength is indicated on the ordinate and a stimulus dimension on the abscissa. The conditioned stimulus (CS) is shown to have the greatest habit strength and the generalized stimuli (Ss with numerical subscripts) are shown to have progressively weaker habit loadings as their distance from CS increases in either direction along the base line. Hull assumed that the gradients of generalized *habit strength* will always have the general form shown in Fig. 4:4 irrespective of the particular stimulus dimension, provided the test stimuli have been located at subjectively equal distances along the abscissa. It is important to note that these curves do not represent experimental data but simply Hull's *hypothesis* as to the way in which the strength of an association changes with variations in the stimulus. It is an assumption advanced to explain the empirical phenomena of generalization. This assumption and the empirical phenomena must be kept separate in one's thinking if confusion is to be avoided.

Although the hypothetical curves of generalized habit strength differ considerably from the empirical curves obtained by Grice and Saltz, the latter do show a fairly regular decline as the distance between the conditioned and the test (generalized) stimuli is

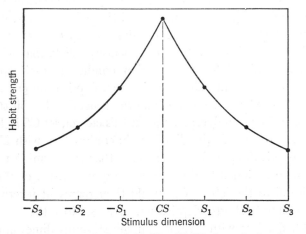

FIG. 4:4. A graphic portrayal of Hull's (1943) hypothesis of *generalized habit strength*. CS represents the stimulus to which a response has been conditioned, and the habit strength at that point is assumed to be maximal. The stimuli to the right and left of CS are assumed to be located at psychologically equal distances along the dimension, and the corresponding values of generalized habit strength are shown as decreasing with increased distance in both directions from CS.

increased. On Hull's hypothesis, the rats in the Grice-Saltz experiment approach white circles of sizes other than that used in training because habit strength generalizes to those other stimuli. The fact that the rats show less resistance to extinction as the test stimuli depart increasingly from the one used in training is attributed to the decline of habit strength with distance along the stimulus dimension.

Bearing in mind the empirical phenomenon of stimulus generalization and the hypothesis of generalized habit strength, we may now return to the associative interpretation to which we alluded at the beginning of this section.

For expository purposes we shall consider an experiment by Deese and Carpenter (1951) in which two groups of rats were given 24 training trials in running down a short straight alley for food. At the time of this training, one group had just been fed wet mash for 1 hour, whereas the other group had not eaten for 22 hours. At the end of this training period the drives of the two groups were reversed and 8 more trials were administered. Now according to the associative view we are considering, the early training should produce learned connections between the running response and a stimulus complex consisting of environmental cues plus the internal cues $(S_{MV}s)$. Turning first to the group trained under 22 hours of deprivation, the theory predicts that when the animals are shifted to near-satiation conditions their speed of running should decline, since the internal deprivation cues, if still present, should be much weaker and the generalized habit strength should therefore be reduced. To make this clearer, let CS in Fig. 4:4 represent the internal stimuli arising in conjunction with 22 hours of food deprivation, and let us assume that the running response has been conditioned to these cues along with those of the alley. The stimuli to the left of CS would then represent internal cues corresponding to shorter deprivation periods. Since the strength of the habit declines with distance on the stimulus dimension from CS, the strength of the tendency to run should also weaken as time since eating is reduced. The results of the Deese and Carpenter study are presented in Fig. 4:5, where it may be seen that the performance of the high-drive group (solid-line curve) did decline when deprivation was made less severe, though the drop is not extreme and performance becomes quite variable. This finding is thus consistent with the associative hypothesis under examination, but it also supports a drive theory such as Hull's.

An associative interpretation involving the assumption of generalized habit strength can thus explain a decrement in performance following a shift from long- to short-term deprivation. It is an explanation that stresses the role of stimulus variation in the determination of associative strength. In this instance, however, the stimulus is presumed to be internal rather than external, as in the Grice-Saltz experiment. Unlike the preceding associative interpretation, this one does not appeal to changes in the *number* of associated stimulus elements. Nor does it, like the multiplicative-drive theory, require the postulation of a general drive factor. In Chapter 3 an associative interpretation of precisely this kind was discussed as a possible alternative to the multiplicative theory in connection with Horenstein's experiment, though we did not, at that point, introduce the concept of stimulus generalization. By its very nature, incidentally, this associative view is applicable only to studies in which deprivation is shifted from one level to

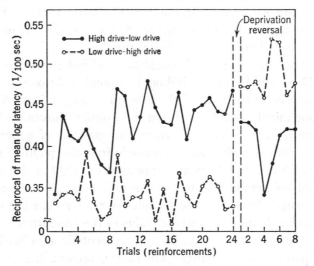

FIG. 4:5. Starting-speed scores for two groups of rats trained under long and short food-deprivation schedules, respectively, for 24 trials and then given 8 more trials with the deprivation durations reversed. (*Adapted from Deese and Carpenter, 1951.*)

another or to those in which one need is substituted for another.

From the relations depicted in Fig. 4:4, it may be seen that our second associative formulation, like the first, cannot easily explain the marked improvement in performance shown by the Deese and Carpenter animals that were trained initially under near-satiation conditions and were then shifted to the 22-hour deprivation regimen (dashed-line curve in Fig. 4:5). If CS in Fig. 4:4 now represents the internal cues characteristic of near-satiation at the time of initial training, stimuli to the right of CS would correspond to cues attending deprivation periods of greater and greater duration. As these stimuli become increasingly different from CS the corresponding habit strengths decline, and performance should become poorer. The unelaborated hypothesis of generalized habit strength, therefore, leads to the prediction that *performance will decline regardless of whether the deprivation period is increased or decreased from that used in original training*. Deese and Carpenter, however, found that performance improved immediately when deprivation duration was increased. Other experimenters have also observed that a sudden increase in deprivation leads to improved performance (e.g., Skinner, 1938; Loess, 1952; Hillman, Hunter, and Kimble, 1953; Davis, 1957; Barry, 1958; and Bass, 1958), though the magnitude of the effect varies with the response being measured and with situational variables.

The associative hypothesis could be modified to take account of the Deese and Carpenter findings by changing the basic assumptions concerning the form of the generalization gradients. Specifically, one might assume that when the stimulus dimension is one of intensity rather than of quality, the gradient of generalized habit strength actually rises progressively from the point of conditioning (CS in Fig. 4:4) to other points at the right of the dimension. But this would lead to the conclusion that the *generalized habit strength* for an intense stimulus is greater than the *conditioned habit strength* for a weaker value of the same stimulus even though the former has never been experimentally associated with the response. To the writer's knowledge, no one has seriously championed such an interpretation, but when test (generalized) stimuli are more intense than the conditioned stimulus, the *empirical* generalization gradients tend to be flatter than when the test stimuli are weaker than the conditioned stimulus (cf. Miller and Greene, 1954). A consistent associative theorist could not, of course, assume that strong stimuli have inherently more driving power than weak ones, since this would constitute a motivational rather than an associative conception.

Experiments in which an associative tendency is established under one motivational variable and performance is measured under another can also be interpreted in terms of habit-strength generalization. Here the underlying supposition is that the internal stimuli attending the substituted variable are similar to those present when the associative tendency was first established. Thus it might be supposed, with some reason, that hunger, thirst, and nausea all involve similar visceral stimuli. From the postulate of generalized habit strength the conclusion is reached that if a response has been learned when an animal is thirsty, the same response will be evoked, but with a decrement, when the animal is made either hungry or nauseated. Note once more that this associative explanation of the effects of interchanging motivational variables *does not rely upon the intensifying action of D but upon the concept of habit-strength variation as a function of degree of stimulus similarity.*

Among the relatively few studies involving an interchange of motivational variables, those by Miller (1948b) arc of special interest here because his interpretation of these phenomena is identical with the habit-strength generalization hypothesis.

In Miller's first experiment on this problem, rats were taught when thirsty to run down a narrow straight alley for water reward. They were then divided into two groups: one group was made hungry but was satiated with water; the other was satiated with both food and water. When these subjects were placed in the alley, the hungry but nonthirsty animals ran significantly faster and actually drank more water at the goal than did those that were neither hungry nor thirsty. Neither group, however, ran as fast or drank as much as they had when thirsty.

The fact that the running and drinking responses did transfer from a water-deprivation–food-satiation condition to a food-deprivation–water-satiation condition, though with some decrement, is explained by Miller in terms of generalization. The internal cues present during original learning are similar to, but not identical with, those present at the time of the tests for transfer. Transfer should occur, therefore, but to an incomplete degree. These same facts, of course, are perfectly consistent with the multiplicative-drive hypothesis, since habits acquired under thirst should also be evoked by the D due to hunger. As a matter of fact, Miller's finding that hunger seemed to facilitate even the consummatory response of drinking, which, on intuitive grounds, might be regarded as quite specific to thirst, fits the multiplicative theory very nicely. It is a finding clearly corroborative of the notion that D can catalyze any habit into action. Nevertheless, an associative interpretation, based on repeated preexperimental associations between hunger stimuli and drinking, would also be defensible.

In Miller's second study, hungry rats were trained on an elevated T maze to turn consistently to one side for food. After their learning had reached a high degree of proficiency they were thoroughly satiated on wet mash in an effort to eliminate hunger completely. They were then placed on the maze, where half of the animals in the original group were given a one-second electric shock and the others not. Since the shocked animals ran faster than the non-shocked ones and made significantly fewer errors on each of several successive runs, we may conclude with Miller that the shock served as an effective substitute for the absent hunger. Miller's associative view of this result is that the habit learned under hunger generalized to pain. The internal cues characteristic of these two states would seem to be so different, however, as to make a generalization interpretation difficult. To overcome this objection, Miller suggests that the generalization might be ". . . based indirectly on stimuli produced by similar states of muscular tension elicited by both drives, rather than upon common elements directly present in the drives themselves" (p. 165). That is, the animals made fewer errors when shocked because their vigorous running produced proprioceptive stimuli much like those present when they were hungry.

As a concomitant to the general problem we are considering, we should also note that the presence of a need state such as thirst can apparently increase the *resistance to extinction* of a response learned under hunger. Both Webb (1949) and Brandauer (1953) have shown that after hungry rats have been taught to perform a simple instrumental response for food they will continue to perform the response longer when they are thirsty and not hungry than when neither thirsty nor hungry. Moreover, the more severe the thirst, the greater the resistance to extinction. To explain these findings an associative theorist would probably assume that as thirst becomes more intense thirst stimuli become increasingly similar to hunger stimuli. This assumption is defensible if one considers only the dimension of stimulus intensity, but one might also insist that as thirst grows stronger its characteristic internal cues become qualitatively more distinctive and hence less similar to those of extreme hunger. Grice and Davis (1957), who were unable to confirm the findings of Webb and of Brandauer, have suggested that when such results are obtained they may be due to an increase in hunger induced by water deprivation.

Miller's theoretical treatment of the results of his T maze studies was restricted to the use of the stimulus-generalization hypothesis in explaining the degree to which one motivational variable could be substituted for another. The same principles, however, may be extended to the interpretation of behavior in complex choice situations following alterations in the strength of a single motivational variable. Without going into the matter at great length, let us see what might be predicted in the case in which a rat has learned to turn left in a T maze under a moderate period of deprivation and is then retested in the maze under either a long- or short-term deprivation schedule.

The basic assumptions regarding the habits acquired in the maze and the critical stimuli are shown in Fig. 4:6. If the left-turning reaction has been evoked more often than the right-turning one, the habit strength of the former (H) will be stronger than that of the latter (h). Both reactions, however, are conditioned to the same stimulus compound consisting of internal stimuli of moderate intensity (S_{IM}) plus stimuli at the choice point of the maze (S_{CP}).

Imagine now that at the completion of the initial training the deprivation period is lengthened (prior to a retest in the maze). This should result in an increase in the intensity of the internal stimuli. Conversely, if the deprivation period is shortened (partial

Fig. 4:6. Stimulus components and relative habit strengths presumed to be characteristic of a situation in which an animal has learned to turn left in a T maze for food under moderate deprivation conditions. S_{IM} = moderately intense internal stimuli; S_{CP} = stimuli at choice point of maze; H and h = strong and weak habits, respectively.

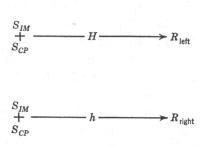

satiation), the internal cues should become weaker. Presumably these cues resemble one another in varying degrees, and they can be arranged, therefore, on a continuum from weak (S_{IW}) through medium (S_{IM}) to strong (S_{IS}). Such a continuum is represented graphically as the stimulus dimension in Fig. 4:7. According to Hull's postulates, the gradient of generalization for a strong habit would correspond approximately to the upper curve in the figure and the gradient for a weak habit to the lower curve. Since the moderately strong stimuli were present at the time of training, these cues would be more strongly associated with both left turning and right turning than would other intensities of internal stimuli. From the hypothetical relations of Fig. 4:7, it follows that the absolute strengths of both the right- and left-turning habits should decrease regardless of whether the deprivation period is increased (to produce S_{IS}), or decreased (to produce S_{IW}). Moreover, and this is the critical part of the analysis, a shift in the length of the deprivation period in either direction from its training value produces *a decrease in the absolute difference between the right and left habits.* In the figure it will be seen that the difference between H and h is larger than the difference between H' and h' or H'' and h''. If the proportion of correct turns (to the left) is determined by the absolute difference in the strengths of the two habits, it follows that *the efficiency of a rat's performance in the maze should decline as the intensities of the internal cues are shifted either up or down from an intermediate (training) point.* Although no one has apparently performed an experiment in exactly this way, Dinsmoor's (1952) study of discrimination learning (see Chapter 3) is most nearly relevant. He found, it may be remembered, that his animals did indeed perform more poorly as deprivation level—actually, he used per cent body-weight deficit, not hours of deprivation—was decreased from the value used during original discrimination training. This fits the generalized habit-strength view quite well, though it is also consistent with the multiplicative theory. But the performance of Dinsmoor's subjects *improved* when hunger was made more severe than at the time of initial training. This result does not follow from an unmodified generalization theory such as the one of Fig. 4:7, which predicts a decline in proficiency with lengthened deprivation. The multiplicative-drive hypothesis, however, does predict improvement. Apparently the generalized-habit view runs into the same difficulties in attempting to account for behavior in a situation involving two habits as it does in dealing with only one. Impairment in performance with reduced deprivation can easily be encompassed, but improvements in performance following increased deprivation cannot. The theory could doubtless be improved by

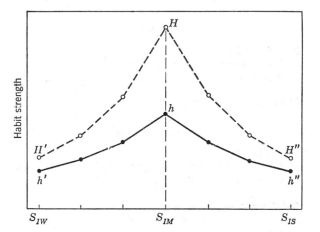

Fig. 4:7. Hypothetical generalization curves for a relatively strong habit (H) and a weaker competing one (h). Weak, moderate, and strong internal stimuli are plotted along the abscissa from left to right. It is assumed that both reactions have been conditioned to the moderately strong internal stimuli at the center of the dimension. With changes in the stimuli in either direction, the strength of each habit decreases as well as the absolute difference between them.

the introduction of special assumptions, but considerable additional data would be needed before a judgment could be reached as to its adequacy relative to a motivational theory.

Interpreting the Effects of Altered Motivational Variables in Terms of Competing or Facilitating Reactive Tendencies. The type of associative interpretation to be considered here rests on the assumption that the manipulation of a motivational variable produces behavioral changes through the evocation of habits that can either facilitate or compete with the habit under investigation. Fig. 4:8 indicates the stimulus elements, associative tendencies, and responses to which this type of theory might appeal in explaining performance decrements following a shift from long-term to short-term deprivation. It has been assumed that the response is one of learning to approach a goal for food under moderately strong hunger. The upper half of the figure shows that during original training the approaching response has become attached to a stimulus compound consisting of S_1, S_2, S_3, S_4, and S_E. When a shift is made to short-term-deprivation testing conditions, the important elements are as shown in the lower half of the figure.

Training conditions

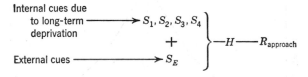

Testing conditions

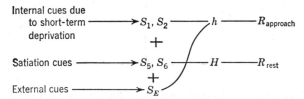

Fɪɢ. 4:8. Stimulus elements and associative tendencies assumed to characterize a situation wherein an approach response has been learned under long-term deprivation and tests are subsequently conducted under short-term deprivation. These are the components of an associative interpretation that relies upon competing habit strengths to explain the negative effects on performance of shifts to short-term deprivation.

For one thing, S_3 and S_4 are assumed to drop out under low motivation, which causes a weakening of the approaching habit (shown by the lower case h). So far, this is identical with the stimulus-deletion interpretation discussed in an earlier section of this chapter. The new feature of interest at this point is the addition of stimuli S_5 and S_6. These may be identified as the typical cues accompanying partial satiation, e.g., stimuli arising from a distended stomach. Now it might be assumed that as a consequence of past experience these cues have become associated with responses of resting, lying down, or being inactive. If such is the case, then *a decline in performance under the satiation regimen could be explained as a result of the introduction of the new tendencies to rest which compete with the tendency to approach*. Thus this interpretation relies on the assumption that overt performance will be weakened if tendencies to make incompatible reactions are simultaneously aroused.

The steps involved in applying this competitive-tendency view to the case where the deprivation term is changed from short to long are shown in Fig. 4:9. In the upper part of the figure, stimuli S_5 and S_6, with their already formed associated tendencies to rest

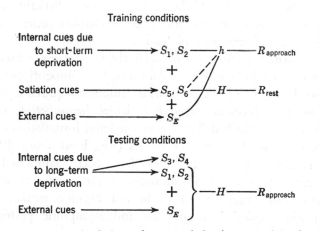

FIG. 4:9. Elements and relations of an associative interpretation of performance facilitation following a shift from short- to long-term deprivation. The presence of the tendency to rest during original learning is assumed to prevent the development of a strong approach habit. Under long-term deprivation, cues tending to elicit resting responses disappear and performance improves

are shown as present when the approaching response is being learned to the complete stimulus complex. If during the course of this learning the strength of the resting tendencies is never completely extinguished, the ultimate level of performance attainable under short-term deprivation would be reduced by an amount depending on the strength of the incompatible habits to rest. Thus the *net* associative tendency to approach is represented by a small *h*. Under long-term deprivation, stimuli S_5 and S_6 are eliminated, and the subtractive (interfering) effect of the competitive resting tendency (lower part of Fig. 4:9) disappears. As a consequence, performance might improve, provided the new stimuli S_3 and S_4 play an insignificant role, as they should since they have not previously been associated with approaching. In effect, then, performance facilitation may be explained by assuming that an increase in deprivation time functions to remove or eliminate reactive tendencies which have prevented performance from reaching its potential maximum. It is also possible, however, that if S_5 and S_6 acquired some habit strength to elicit approach behavior (dashed line in upper part of Fig. 4:9) during the original learning, their disappearance under long-term deprivation would tend to impair performance and perhaps to offset any gains due to the elimination of the resting responses. Strictly speaking, however, this is a stimulus-subtraction mechanism rather than one involving the interactions of habits.

Performance *decrements* following the substitution of one need for another could be readily explained by the competitive-tendency notion. In all such cases, *the only assumption required is that the new need produces new stimuli to which incompatible reaction tendencies are attached.* The competing-habit formulation can also be extended to the results of studies (e.g., Fredenburg, 1956) in which separate groups of subjects have been maintained under different deprivation levels throughout the course of learning. Perhaps interfering tendencies to rest become weaker as the deprivation period is lengthened and asymptotic performance level can therefore be elevated progressively.

When the competing-habit hypothesis is applied to behavior in situations such as the *T* maze, the interpretation might be structured somewhat as follows: If performance declines, following a shift from long- to short-term deprivation, it would be necessary to suppose that *competitive tendencies become stronger and interfere more with correct than with incorrect habits*. Conversely, if training is carried out under a short-term deprivation schedule, improvement following a lengthening of the deprivation period would be ascribed either to the elimination of competing habits or to the accrual of compatible ones.

As we have already noted, competing-habit interpretations of the effects of variations in deprivation conditions have not been formulated in detail. Clearly, the preceding suggestions toward such a theory are largely *ad hoc*, and much remains to be done in the way of refinement and extension. Especially needed are precise statements as to how associative tendencies compete with or augment one another, and useful ways of defining competing habits independently of the situations in which they are presumed to be degrading performance. Incidentally, it is conceivable that the most generally adequate associative theory would be one that incorporates all of the best assumptions of the three versions suggested here. Thus the notions of stimulus-element addition and subtraction, of stimulus generalization, and of competing tendencies might be combined into a single more potent theory of the effects on behavior of changes in motivational variables.

Advocates of Associative Interpretations

At the start of our discussion of the various forms that an associative interpretation might take it was noted that although no one writer has presented us with a full-blown theory of this sort, psychological literature contains numerous suggestions to the effect that the construct of drive may be superfluous. Postman (1953b), for instance, has clearly seen that since the manipulation of certain so-called motivational variables may affect drive stimuli as well as drive, it might be possible, and certainly more economical, to dispense with the concept of drive entirely and to base one's interpretations of motivated behavior solely upon changes in drive stimuli. Postman's (1953a) analysis of experiments on motivational selectivity in perception is consistent with this suggestion since, following the work of Solomon and Howes (1951), he has placed heavy emphasis upon the contribution to "motivated" perception of associative predispositions. It would be premature to attempt to identify Postman's views as characteristic of any of the three associative versions presented above, but he has appealed both to competing associative tendencies and to modified stimuli in his interpretations of the effects on perception of motivational variables.

Probably the most explicit associative theory of the effects of motivational variables is that of Estes (1958), who has extended his statistical theory of learning specifically to the problems of motivation. This development, which appeared after the preceding associative conceptions were written, and which can be presented only in broad perspective because of its specialized terminology, is essentially an extension and formalization of Guthrie's (1935) contiguity theory. According to this view, the probability that a response will occur depends upon the proportion of the stimulus elements in a situation that have been conditioned to the response. In the case of a variable such as food deprivation, the internal drive stimuli assume a role of relatively great importance. An increase in deprivation time has two principal consequences: (1) the probability of occurrence of a drive stimulus increases, and (2) the probability of occurrence of stimuli characteristic of satiation decreases. From these assumptions and from additional ones concerning the relative weights, as behavior determinants, of these cues, of conditioned cues, and of extraneous cues, Estes predicts the outcomes of several experiments in which deprivation has been manipulated. For example, the theory specifies that if training is carried out at a single level of deprivation, asymptotic performance will be higher the more severe the deprivation. It is also predicted that if a single group is trained at several deprivation levels, as in Cotton's (1953) experiment (see Chapter 3 above), asymptotic performance level should vary with deprivation if behavior on all trials is counted, but not if those trials on which competing responses occur are eliminated. The theory also predicts, as was true of the associative hypotheses we have just considered, that if training is carried out under a moderate level of deprivation, performance should become worse if deprivation is suddenly enhanced. This expectation follows from the assumption that an increase in deprivation will change the drive-stimulus complex by introducing new elements not previously associated with the response, and will thereby reduce the proportion of elements conditioned to the response. Since this effect is attributed to the tendency for the new elements to elicit interfering or competing responses, this aspect of the theory is comparable to the third associative interpretation presented above. But since the findings of such studies as those of Deese and Carpenter (1951), Loess (1952), and Hillman, Hunter, and Kimble (1953) contradict this theoretical expectation, the drive-stimulus conception may require modification. Bolles (1958) has also pointed out that the theory may encounter difficulty in explaining (1) the correlation of *vigor* of running with degree of deprivation when training has been administered at a single level of deprivation, and (2) the phenomena of incentive motivation. Nevertheless, Estes' formulation, which he has also applied to the problems of need combination and stimulus generalization, undoubtedly constitutes the most systematic attempt yet made to replace the concept of general drive with purely associative mechanisms.

Bindra (1959), expanding on Estes' (1950) original theory, has suggested that the interfering responses responsible for performance decrements following stimulus changes are actually "novelty reactions" and that the performance decrement, therefore, is due to, and directly dependent upon, the novelty of the test situation. Although Bindra does not relate this hypothesis specifically to the problem of motivational variables, it is apparent that it might be extended to the effects of changes of needs or to changes in deprivation severity. One wonders, however, whether it would be meaningful to suppose that a rat would ever find his own internal hunger or satiation stimuli to be novel even when they are considerably different from what they were at some previous time.

Other hints that motivational phenomena can perhaps be interpreted without reference to a drive construct may be found in the earlier writings of Hebb (1949), and in the theoretical interpretations of Child and Waterhouse (1953), Meyer (1953), McClelland, Atkinson, Clark, and Lowell (1953), Campbell and Kraeling (1954), Farber (1955), Davis (1957), Holder, Marx, Holder, and Collier (1957), and Meyer and Noble (1958).

Resumé of Evidence Bearing
on Motivational Interpretations

Although associative conceptualizations appear to possess the virtue of simplicity, it would be premature to conclude that the idea of a general energizing drive must, therefore, be rejected completely. One of the major reasons for retaining the hypothesis of a general drive is that certain variables such as strong stimulation and food or water deprivation have facilitative effects upon surprisingly diverse kinds of responses. Considering intense stimuli first, we find that electric shock or its aftereffects facilitates eating (Siegel and Brantley, 1951), drinking (Amsel and Maltzman, 1950), running speed and correct choices in a T maze after training under hunger (Miller, 1948b), wheel turning to an auditory signal (Nagaty, 1951), visual discrimination—when shock is administered intracerebrally—(Fuster, 1958), reaction time (Johanson, 1922), human eyelid conditioning (Spence, Farber, and Taylor, 1954), and of course, escape and avoidance behavior in many different situations. Moderate degrees of muscular tension also exhibit facilitative effects of considerable generality. Courts (1942), who has summarized these findings, states that all of the following have been shown to be augmented by tension: conditioned salivary responses in dogs, pursuit-rotor performance, the knee jerk, vibratory sensitivity, reaction time, mental arithmetic, tapping, startle responses, electric-shock thresholds, and ball throwing for accuracy. In the case of food deprivation, it is interesting to note that in addition to its familiar role as a facilitator of diverse instrumental acts and of general activity (Siegel and Steinberg, 1949; Hall and Hanford, 1954) it enhances reactions to intracranial electrical stimulation (Brady, Boren, Conrad, and Sidman, 1957), drinking (Miller, 1948b), escape from light (Bahrick, 1953), and the reinforcing effect of light onset (Davis, 1958). Moreover, as we have previously observed, loud noises, bright lights, and air deprivation also activate a variety of responses under particular conditions.

The important point in connection with all these observations is that each of the several motivational variables has the capacity to amplify activities whose manifest topographies and controlling stimulus complexes differ extensively. In some cases it may be reasonable to suppose that the internal (or other) cues produced by the variable have been associated with the reference response during previous periods of training. But it is difficult to imagine that this has occurred in every instance where facilitation has been observed. Wherever such associations cannot be invoked, a non-specific energizing drive becomes a reasonable alternative.

The fact that motivational variables sometimes cause decrements in performance must be noted, but it is not of crucial importance for either the motivational or the associative theories. Hull's multiplicative-drive theory interprets such findings by asserting that drive is indeed increased and that either (1) associative tendencies to make the wrong responses are initially dominant over the correct ones, or (2) that the motivational variable provides new stimuli to which overriding competitive responses are attached. The second of these is obviously the same conception upon which associative interpretations rely.

A second major line of evidence favoring a general-drive theory, as against a purely associative view, is provided by studies in which an increase in deprivation from that employed during training produces augmented performance. We have already reviewed these studies and have observed that none of the associative versions, unless modified by special *ad hoc* assumptions, can readily encompass this phenomenon. However, shifts from short to long deprivation sometimes lead to the decrements in performance predicted by associative theory (cf. Yamaguchi, 1952), and much additional research is needed to determine the direction and extent of the effects.

Other evidence consistent with the concept of general drive stems from studies in which the combination of two different motivational variables leads to better or more vigorous performance than does either alone. For instance, Amsel (1950a) reports that speed of running, as motivated by a conditioned pain-fear reaction, is enhanced when a primary need for food is added to the motivational complex. Similarly, Meryman (1952) has obtained clear evidence that unconditioned startle responses in rats are amplified more by a combination of hunger and conditioned fear than by either separately. Jerome, Moody, Connor, and Fernandez (1957) recorded the number of crossings made by rats from one side to another of a multiple-door shuttle box, and noted that the addition of hunger to an aversive light stimulus led to more crossings than did either hunger or light alone. Probability of error, however, proved to be unrelated to level of motivation. A satisfactory associative explanation of these findings might be developed, provided one could show that the motivation-variable stimuli had been previously associated either with the reference response or with responses capable of augmenting that response. But this may prove to be difficult, especially in the Meryman study, where one would have to suppose that the cues of hunger and fear had somehow become conditioned to vigorous startle responses during the normal cage life of laboratory rats.

Experiments in which two appetitive variables are combined have yielded conflicting results. Kendler (1945) found that the addition of moderate periods (up to 12 hours) of water deprivation to hunger led to an increase in the resistance to extinction of a food-reinforced bar-pressing response, but that a reverse effect was obtained when the period of water deprivation was increased to 22½ hours. Other studies, such as that of Verplanck and Hayes (1953), indicate that consummatory activities either of eating or drinking are reduced by the arousal of the opposite need; but Powloski (1953) reports that discrimination learning is as effective under both hunger and thirst as with either alone. In general, the findings of these and related investigations do not support Hull's view that two need states summate to yield a higher level of general drive. The discovery of interactive effects among needs, though not crucial to the concept of drive as a behavior determinant, suggests the need for changes in the functions that have been assumed to hold between drive and its deprivation antecedents.

It is also worth noting, as Spence (1956, 1958) has shown, that the specific hypothesis of a multiplicative relation between drive and habit strength has been supported in a variety of studies, specifically those in which performance curves obtained under different levels of deprivation or under different strengths of an unconditioned stimulus have been found to diverge as a function of training. Similar curves obtained under different incentive levels (i.e., magnitude of reward) also tend to diverge over training trials, and since incentive is assumed to determine a motivational factor, this too is consistent with the multiplicative interpretation.

In conclusion, it appears from the above summary of experimental evidence that many diverse findings are consistent with the concept of a nonspecific activating drive. Certain of these facts, however, can also be explained as instances of the operation of learned or unlearned associative predispositions. The principle of parsimony supports the wisdom of exploring fully the utility of associative interpretations, but until these theories have been more fully developed it seems wise to retain both an intermediary construct of general drive and associative mechanisms. In Chapter 9 additional evidence is presented from the field of physiological psychology that is consistent with the general-drive conception.

Summary

In this chapter we have analyzed two general approaches to the problem of how motivational variables function to modify behavior. One type of conception, termed a *motivational interpretation*, introduces, and places in a role of central importance, a unique motivational construct such as *drive*. In Hull's multiplicative-drive theory, which is used as the major example, drive is described as a nondirective factor that is aroused by a variety of antecedent conditions and becomes manifest in behavior through its capacity to multiply existing associative tendencies (habits). The multiplicative combination of drive with habits is assumed to yield a quantity termed *excitatory potential* which, though modified by other factors, is more or less directly reflected in behavior. Those who hold that intervening motivational constructs are useful also maintain that motivational variables have stimulus consequences in addition to their capacity to arouse drive and that responses of many kinds are, or can become, associated with these stimuli.

The principal implications of Hull's multiplicative theory are reviewed and are seen to be the following: First, the fact that behavior is exhibited when, for example, an animal is hungry but not when he is satiated is attributed to the multiplying effect of drive and the resulting elevation of the appropriate excitatory tendencies to a suprathreshold level. Likewise, correlations between the vigor of overt responses and time of deprivation are ascribed to level of drive, provided that habit strength is held constant. Second, if two or more reactive tendencies are present, the absolute difference between their respective excitatory potentials will increase as drive is strengthened and decrease as drive is diminished. This leads to the prediction that whenever the correct reactive tendency is stronger than any other, heightened drive will result in improved performance. But if an incorrect tendency is strongest, increased drive should lead to poorer performance. Conversely, reduced drive can lead either to poorer or to better performance depending upon which tendency is at the top of the response hierarchy. These predictions will not be fulfilled, however, if the motivational variable determining drive strength also serves as the source of stimuli to which competitive or facilitative responses have been associated. When the manipulation of a variable results in the introduction of salient cues, the hierarchical order of habit strengths can be radically altered, and predictions based upon the initial order must be modified appropriately. Third, if in spatial- or discrimination-choice situations the habits corresponding to the two responses are held equal, drive strength should be unrelated to choice of the correct alternative.

The second major type of conception considered in this chapter is one that rejects the need for constructs such as drive and appeals only to variations in associative strengths in accounting for the effects on behavior of changes in motivational variables. Because *associative theories* of this kind are just beginning to appear, it has been necessary to be somewhat speculative concerning the several forms that such theories may eventually assume. One possible version of an associative theory might stress the notion that performance is altered by a change in a motivational variable from that used during training because *some of the stimulus elements associated with the response have been eliminated and/or new elements have been added.* One might thus explain a decline in performance following a shift from hunger to near-satiation; but without additional assumptions, performance facilitation due to enhanced deprivation would be difficult to interpret.

A second variety of associative theory would emphasize the idea that changes in *motivational variables alter the intensity or quality of cues and that alterations in existing associative strengths would then occur in accordance with the principle of habit-strength generalization.* In effect, this principle is a guess as to how the level of a reactive tendency is altered as a function of specific modifications of the stimulus to which the response was originally conditioned. In the extension of this principle to motivational phenomena, emphasis is placed more upon the generalization of internal stimuli than upon changes in external cues. This associative model can encompass the effects of shifts from long to short deprivation, changes from one need state to another, and, with some additional assumptions, the transfer to a noxious stimulus of a response learned under an appetitive need. As was true of the first associative theory, however, the second encounters difficulties in attempting to interpret performance enhancement following changes from mild to severe deprivation.

A third associative interpretation might be developed which stresses the possibility that *new habits, either facilitative or competitive, are brought into effective action by manipulations of motivational variables.* On this hypothesis, the original habit is not changed to a major degree by the addition or subtraction of stimulus elements or by variations in the quality or intensity of the relevant stimulus complex. Instead, the motivational variable modifies the effective strength of the original associative tendency by evoking new habits and thus leads to different behavior. For this interpretation to become widely useful, specific principles of habit interaction would have to be developed and substantiated.

At the close of the chapter, evidence bearing on the concept of a nonspecific drive was reviewed, and the tentative conclusion was reached that although associative theories can successfully account for a number of motivational phenomena, the construct of drive is nevertheless supported by a wide variety of findings.

||||||||||||||||||||||||||||||||||||||||||||||||||||||||||||||||||||||||||||||||||||||||||||||||||||||||||||||||||||||||||||||||||||||||||||||||||||||||||||||||||||||

CHAPTER 5

Learned Responses as
Sources of Drive

As WE HAVE SEEN, particularly in Chapter 3, the various primary motivational variables may influence behavior in profound and widespread ways. In our society, however, with its high standard of living, the large majority of individuals are seldom racked by the pangs of severe hunger or by the tormenting sensations of intense thirst, and the experience of intense or prolonged pain is the exception rather than the rule. It is, in part, because of this melioration of man's condition that the tendency to regard biological needs and intense stimuli as the principal motivators of complex human behavior has waned in recent times. In its place the widespread conviction has arisen that the most significant source of motivation for human beings lies in the elaborate experiential structure produced by learning and acculturation. Human beings are said to be motivated to a significant degree by the so-called acquired drives for success, prestige, security, power, affection, money, property, and the like. As we shall indicate, it is questionable whether specific directed tendencies of this sort should be called "drives" at all, but it is clear that learning plays a major role in the activities described by these terms. The infant human organism certainly does not possess these tendencies, and it seems logical, therefore, to assume that they represent complex relationships among the diversified products of the learning process.

Before beginning our discussion of the acquired-drive problem, a word or two concerning terminology is in order. In earlier chapters it was pointed out that we are attempting to maintain a clear distinction between a nondirective, nonspecific motivating agency, e.g., Hull's D, on the one hand, and habits, with their corresponding responses, on the other. As a consequence of this attempt, we have avoided the use of the term "primary drives" and have spoken instead of "primary sources of drive." The primary motivating variables, it may be recalled, were assumed to affect behavior by contributing to drive, and/or by modifying the stimulus complex (S_{MV}) in certain ways.

This usage is continued in the present chapter and extended to the traditional problem of acquired drives. To do so, however, means that we shall seldom speak of acquired drives, in the plural. If the word "drive" is used to mean a nonspecific, nondirective, behavior-facilitating agency, then it is a construct to which unitary properties should be ascribed. Many variables may function motivationally, but since, in so doing, they are all affecting behavior in the same way, it is simpler to refer to them as "sources of drive," not as drives. This explains why the present chapter has been entitled "Learned Responses as Sources of Drive," rather than "Learnable Drives," or "Secondary Drives," or "Acquired Drives."

The Acquired-drive Problem

That both learning and motivation are significantly involved in secondary-drive phenomena is strongly implied by the words *acquired drive*. For many psychologists the outcome of learning is the acquisition of a response or a tendency to respond, and on this assumption what is acquired in the case of an acquired drive is a new or altered response. To have an acquired drive, therefore, an organism must have learned to respond, and when this response is evoked the organism's behavior must be affected motivationally.

Thus the so-called acquired drives may be described as *learned responses having many of the general properties of all responses, and, in addition, the capacity to affect other responses in the same ways in which they are affected by motivational variables.* Stated somewhat differently, the acquired-drive problem demands answers to the questions of how, and to what extent, the variables that govern the learning of one response function as though they were motivational variables when that response is interacting with other responses. Within the framework of a motivational theory such as Hull's, this idea is expressed by the assumption that some actions are capable of adding increments to drive and thereby of multiplying the habit strengths of other responses.

This conception of an acquired source of drive is represented in the upper part of Fig. 5:1, where the learned (motivating) response is shown as dependent upon learning variables and stimulus variables (at the left), and as leading to an increment in general drive (at the right). This drive increment, in turn, is assumed to multiply the habit strength of a reference or indicant response.

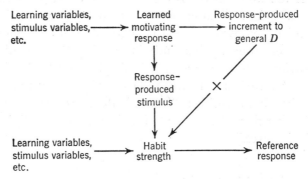

Fig. 5:1. Elements involved in two conceptualizations of an acquired source of drive. The three components at the top of the diagram indicate that the strength of a learned, motivating response depends primarily upon learning variables and stimulus variables and that this response may bring about an increment to general drive level. This drive increment may then affect a reference response by multiplying the habit strength of that reaction. However, the motivating response may also affect the reference response by providing stimuli capable of modifying the latter's habit strength. If reliance is placed upon the response-produced drive, the theory becomes *associative-motivational.* But, if the entire explanatory burden is placed upon the response-produced stimuli, the theory should perhaps be described as *associative-associative.*

Since both associative processes and the construct of general drive are involved in this interpretation, it may be appropriate to term it an *associative-motivational* conception.

Should one choose to omit drive entirely in dealing with the so-called acquired motivations, appeal could be made to the stimuli produced by the learned (motivating) response. These are shown in the center of Fig. 5:1 and are indicated as affecting the reference response by modifying its habit strength. Since the strength of the learned motivating response rests upon associative processes, and the mechanism of its influence upon the reference activity is also associative, this second conception might be termed *associative-associative*.

Thus for an associative-motivational theorist, learning variables have motivational-variable consequences by virtue of their effects upon the strength of a drive-producing response. But for the associative-associative advocate, learning and stimulus variables determine the original response and also mediate its effects, through response-produced stimuli, upon indicant reactions. In order to reduce our discussion to manageable proportions, we shall proceed throughout the remainder of this chapter on the assumption that an intermediary construct of drive is still desirable, thereby adopting the associative-motivational position as a working hypothesis. There are good reasons for believing, however, that the implications and ramifications of an associative-associative theory are worth extensive exploration. The development of such a theory would probably proceed along lines similar to those that characterize the associative theories described in Chapter 4.

In order to simplify our exposition, the above description of the associative-motivational view has been presented without mention of the general drive produced by variables other than the learned response. Within the theory, however, the strength of the motivating response and hence also the magnitude of the response-produced increment to D should depend upon other sources of drive. This raises the interesting possibility that the response-produced drive, when added to general D, can enhance the learned (motivating) response and hence itself. We shall make the simplifying assumption, however, that this does not occur, the response-produced drive being assigned the power to affect other reactions, but not itself. With respect to the latency of a motivating response, this assumption appears quite reasonable, since the time of onset of a given response can hardly be affected by a motivational increment that is contingent upon the appearance of that same response. It is by no means certain, however, that a motivating response, once it has become fully aroused, cannot enhance itself. An analogous self-augmenting process occurs in electronic circuits under conditions where "positive feedback" from output to input is possible, and the childhood temper tantrum may be a psychological instance of the phenomenon. Moreover, if we take the alleged motivating response of fear as an example, it would be premature to insist either that fear reduction cannot function to reinforce fear itself—perhaps this is why some fears are so remarkably persistent—or that the presumed increase in drive accompanying fear cannot act to inhibit fear. Miller (1951) has presented an illuminating discussion of certain aspects of these problems, but it is the writer's belief that our knowledge of such matters as the nature of reinforcement and the rise and fall of motivating responses with time is too meager to warrant further extensive speculation at present.

Although we have maintained that only learned responses or readinesses to respond qualify as secondary sources of motivational effects, this assumption is not as restrictive as one might imagine. It does not mean that attitudes, opinions, expectancies, perceptual readinesses, hopes, and the like, are necessarily eliminated from consideration as acquired motivators. But it does mean that the processes or events designated by these terms would have to be treated, within the theory, as responses or readinesses to respond. In many instances, this is not a difficult step. An attitude or an expectancy is not a directly observable entity. Therefore, useful inferences about expectancies or attitudes must rest ultimately upon the fact—if and when it is a fact—that indicant responses of such and such a kind have occurred in a specific environment. When subjected to critical analysis, therefore, attitudes, hopes, fears, opinions, and expectancies can probably all be reduced to learned reaction readinesses. And to the degree that these responses affect other behaviors as do motivational variables, they too would conform to our conception of acquired sources of drive.

The general way in which we have posed the acquired-drive problem may seem abstract and impalpable because reactive tendencies and even many responses cannot be observed in any simple and direct way. This need not be a matter for grave concern, however, since corresponding formulations of the problem can be couched in the purely descriptive language of the empirical psychologist or in the neurophysiological terms of the physiological psychologist. Thus, the empirically minded scientist may wish to deal only with directly observable relations between an organism's molar behavior and other variables in its training or environment. For such a psychologist the acquired-drive phenomenon would be typified by the observation that one response is affected in certain specifiable (motivational) ways by the kinds and amounts of practice, among other things, that an organism has had in making some other response. In the case of the physiologically inclined psychologist, the acquired-drive problem might be stated as a search for the neurological or other bodily mechanisms involved when one bit of behavior is affected in motivational ways by other, previously learned, reactions. The manner in which the acquired-drive problem is phrased will, of course, influence the kind of research one is led to do, but the basic relations and critical questions remain essentially unchanged throughout such transformations.

The foregoing analysis of the acquired-drive problem serves to set the stage for discussions to follow, but it also raises numerous questions for which satisfactory answers are not yet available. For example, one wonders whether motivating responses can be distinguished from other responses by a consideration of such manifest attributes as their latencies, durations, or anatomical bases. Or is the course of the acquisition and the extinction of a motivating response determined by the same variables (e.g., number of trials, degree of distribution of practice, percentage of reinforcement) that are now known to affect other reactions? Moreover, it would be important to know something of the nature of the neural and/ or chemical mechanisms by means of which motivating responses can influence other activities. And finally we shall eventually find it desirable to determine precisely which of the criteria for the identification of a motivational variable (cf. Chapter 2) have been met on any given occasion when an acquired drive is alleged to have been generated.

Conditioned Fear as a Source of Drive

Up to this point, our discussion of learned motivating reactions has, of necessity, been rather general. To make our analysis more specific we turn now to the consideration of one particular response that seems to be rather well established as a motivator for other responses. This is the response of conditioned fear, which, in its motivating role, has usually been described as "the acquired drive of fear or anxiety."

The general notion that a tendency to be fearful or anxious may have motivating effects upon other responses, though historically old, became significant for modern psychology through the writings of Cannon (1929) and Freud (1936). The translation of this general conception into the more specific language of the modern behavior scientist, however, was the work of Mowrer (1939). According to Mowrer, anxiety or fear is a learned emotional reaction to stimuli denoting the advent of a painful or noxious event. It is a reaction acquired in accordance with the associative laws of classical conditioning. Moreover, certain of its behavioral effects are comparable to the effects produced by such primary motivational variables as food deprivation and strong stimuli. Specifically, fear sometimes seems to function as a general energizer, and its reduction, following the elicitation of a new directed response, may serve to reinforce the learning of the new reaction. Since fear, described in this manner, is evidently learned, and since its effects upon other bits of behavior resemble the effects of motivational variables, it qualifies by our criteria as an acquired source of drive.

Procedures Used in Conditioning Fear Reactions. Although psychologists hold different views as to how fear is learned, all follow essentially the same procedures in attempting to produce conditioned fear in the laboratory. The training or conditioning trials always involve paired presentations of a neutral stimulus—the so-called conditioned stimulus (CS)—and a definitely painful or noxious stimulus. The painful stimulus fulfills the role of the familiar unconditioned stimulus (*UCS*). Quite frequently the *UCS* is an electric shock intense enough to produce overt signs of "emotional" excitement or disruption. In establishing conditioned fear reactions in rats, for example, a buzzer, light, or clicking sound may be used as the *CS*. It is presented for perhaps a second, though sometimes much longer, before the animal is given one or more short, strong shocks. Typically, the paired administration of the *CS* and *UCS* is said to result in the acquisition by the *CS* of a tendency to evoke an anticipatory emotional (fear) response that resembles, but need not be identical with, the pain-produced reactions to the *UCS*.

When the responses in a conditioning experiment can be directly observed and recorded, as in studies of eyeblinks or leg flexions, strength of conditioning is usually estimated in one of two ways. First, the *CS* may be presented alone, either following the completion of the conditioning trials, or at irregular intervals throughout the course of conditioning. A conditioned response is defined as the appearance on a *CS*-only test trial of a reaction of a certain (arbitrarily defined) magnitude and/or latency. Second, on any trial on which both the *CS* and the *UCS* are presented, a response having the defined characteristics may appear between the onsets of the *CS* and *UCS*, or after the onset of the *UCS*, but sooner than if it had been a response to the *UCS* itself. Such responses are tallied as conditioned responses.

These procedures are also occasionally used in studies of conditioned fear. For example, if the response being recorded is a change in heart rate or in skin resistance, the frequency or magnitude of these changes to the *CS* alone or to the *CS* in anticipation of the *UCS*, are commonly taken as indicating degree of conditioning. It is rather difficult, however, to measure the presumed autonomic components of fear in rats because of the animals' small size and because of their tendency to struggle violently against restraint. But since the laboratory rat is a convenient subject, investigators desiring to use rats have found it necessary to develop other techniques for estimating strength of conditioning in these subjects. Specifically, it has become common in recent years to *estimate the presence and strength of conditioned fear from observations of the manner in which some other reaction of known strength is modified by the presentation or by the termination of a CS that has been paired with a noxious UCS.* The response that serves as the indicator may or may not be one that a naïve observer would describe as "fearful." Reactions such as eating, drinking, bar pressing, urinating, defecating, jumping, turning a wheel, and crossing a hurdle have all been used as indicants of conditioned fear.

Studies of fear in which the more indirect methods are used may be divided into three broad groups according to the ways in which the CS is presented and the indicator response is affected. The experiments in one group, which are consistent with the concept of fear as an energizer, show that *the reference response, if elicited while the CS is on, tends to be enhanced or augmented.* Moreover, since degree of enhancement of the reference response, which is itself never conditioned to the CS, tends to increase with the number of CS-UCS pairings and to decrease during extinction trials, it is reasonable to suppose that the changes in the indicant reaction reflect strength of conditioning.

A second group of experiments consists of those in which, following fear-conditioning trials, *tests are made to determine whether the probability, speed, or amplitude of an indicant reaction increases over a series of trials on each of which an ongoing CS is terminated immediately after the response is evoked.* When learning of the reference response is demonstrated under these conditions, it is clear that the termination of the CS is reinforcing, and this event thus meets one of our suggested criteria for identifying motivational variables (cf. Chapter 2). And since the reinforcing power of CS-offset varies with the number of CS-UCS pairings, an associative variable, the conditions for an acquired source of drive have been met. Usually the further assumption is made that the CS arouses fear and that it is the reduction in fear due to the termination of the CS that functions as the reinforcing agent.

In a third group of investigations, it has been found that *the presentation of a CS that has been paired with a noxious UCS may inhibit or interfere with an ongoing overt response or response sequence.* By the proper choice of conditioning and testing methods it can be shown that the degree of interference suffered by the indicant response increases as a function of the number of CS-

UCS pairings, and that the reference reaction tends to regain its initial strength with repeated presentations of the CS alone as in the customary extinction procedure. If the reference response that is being weakened is followed by the onset of the CS, the conditions and the resulting effect meet one of the criteria for the identification of motivational variables. And since this effect also varies with associative variables governing acquisition and extinction, the picture is consistent with our general conception of an acquired source of drive. Where the time relations of response to stimulus onset differ from those mentioned here, however, the inhibitory effects can perhaps be attributed to response-produced stimuli and/or to CS-induced changes in the response hierarchy. We shall return to this problem at a later point in this chapter.

We turn now to an examination of some typical experimental studies from each of the three groups we have just described.

Studies of the Energizing Function of Fear. Although fear, at times, may serve as a debilitating deterrent to action, ample evidence from daily experience indicates that it often functions as a potent goad to action. The reader has but to recall the frequency with which frightened persons in stories, movies, and plays are depicted as capable of almost superhuman feats of climbing, leaping, and running, to realize that the notion of fear as an energizer is exceptionally widespread.

Within the body of scientific writing, this basic notion has been strongly supported by the physiologist Cannon (1929), whose studies of hunger and thirst we have already mentioned. According to Cannon, fear is an emergency reaction involving the mobilization of energy resources of the body and their effective utilization in expediting whatever responses are evoked by the situation at hand. This conception has been widely adopted during the past two decades, and it is only quite recently that the soundness of certain of its elements has been questioned. Incidentally, Cannon's views as to the dynamogenic properties of fear were not based upon evidence from studies of behavior at the molar level, but upon the biochemical and physiological consequences of fear.

Experimental studies by psychologists of the facilitating consequences of fear are of relatively recent vintage. Relevant data, though somewhat peripheral in origin, may be found in early studies of conflict and especially in supporting experiments on fear-motivated avoidance (cf. Bugelski and Miller, 1938; Brown, 1948). In these studies hungry rats were first trained to run down a short straight alley for food reward. They were then given electric shocks of various intensities at the goal and were subsequently tested without shock, when satiated, to determine how vigorously they would avoid the region where they had been shocked. The results indicated that the speed and vigor of the avoidance responses on test trials increased with strength of shock used during training. Since shock was omitted on test trials, it may be presumed that the avoidance was motivated by a learned tendency to be fearful, which should vary with intensity of shock and with other factors such as nearness to the point in the alley where the shocks had been administered.

A direct attempt to determine whether an alleged fear-arousing CS can intensify an overt skeletal response has been described by Brown, Kalish, and Farber (1951). From the assumption that fear as a learned source of drive should multiply existing reactive tendencies, and from clinical observations that anxious persons show exaggerated startle responses, these investigators reasoned that during the presentation of a CS that had been paired with shock, rats should exhibit intensified startle reactions to loud sounds. Accordingly, an experimental procedure was arranged with the aims of producing increasing fear during the course of fear-conditioning trials (i.e., CS-UCS pairings) and decreasing fear during extinction trials, and of providing an opportunity for fear to show spontaneous recovery during rest periods following extinction periods. Measurements were made at intervals throughout conditioning and extinction to determine whether the amplitude of the startle reaction varied concomitantly with the assumed variations in fear.

The apparatus used in this study was a *stabilimeter*, by means of which accurate graphic records of a rat's bodily jumps to a loud sound could be obtained. A drawing of this device is reproduced in Fig. 5:2. While confined in the rectangular box, the subjects could be presented with visual or auditory stimuli and mildly painful electric shocks. The fear-conditioning procedure involved seven paired presentations of a CS (consisting of a buzzer and a

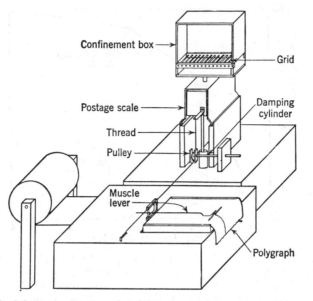

Fig. 5:2. Schematic drawing of stabilimeter used to measure the amplitude of rats' startle responses to loud sounds. (*Adapted from Brown, Kalish, and Farber, 1951.*)

light) and a UCS (electric shock) on each of four successive days. Three test trials were also given per day, interspersed among the seven fear-conditioning trials. On each test trial the CS was presented, but in place of shock a toy pistol was shot off to produce a loud, sharp sound. The sound of this pistol almost invariably elicited a definite startle response from the rats, even prior to training of any kind. No shocks were ever presented on test trials. The members of one group of experimental subjects were conditioned and tested in this manner. The members of a control group were tested in the same manner, but the temporal spacing of the CS and UCS during their training trials was designed to minimize or prevent the conditioning of fear to the CS.

The results obtained from tests interspersed among the conditioning trials are summarized in Fig. 5:3. The curves show how the animals of the two groups responded to the sound of the pistol shot on successive days. The plotted points are medians of 15 values, each of which is a mean of three responses. The values plotted at the zero point on the abscissa were derived from prelimi-

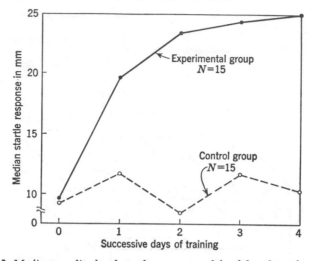

Fɪɢ. 5:3. Median amplitude of startle responses of fearful and nonfearful rats to a loud, sharp sound. The upper curve shows that experimental animals presumed to be fearful jumped more and more vigorously to the sound as the number of fear-conditioning trials increased. The responses of control (nonfearful) subjects, however, did not change progressively or significantly during the same period. (*From Brown, Kalish, and Farber, 1951.*)

nary measurements of startle-response amplitude on the day prior to the start of training. These data were used to equate the members of the two groups with respect to their inherent reactiveness to the sound of the pistol.

An examination of Fig. 5:3 shows that the magnitude of the startle responses evoked by the pistol shot in the presence of the CS increased progressively during the course of conditioning for the experimental animals but not for the controls.

The intervals between the CS and UCS and their orders of presentation were chosen, of course, so as to maximize conditioned fear in the experimental animals while minimizing it in the controls. It seems reasonable to conclude, therefore, that the CS elicited more fear in the experimentals than in the controls and that fear functioned as a drive to augment unlearned startle responses. Stated in other terms, this portion of the experiment provided evidence for an acquired source of drive, since an associative variable (number of conditioning trials) functioned as though it were a motivational variable in its effects upon a reference response which was itself not conditioned.

On three successive days following the period of fear conditioning, the animals of both groups were placed in the stabilimeter and were given 12 nonreinforced test trials. On each trial the CS was presented and the pistol was shot off, but the shock was omitted. Since these trials would qualify as fear-extinction trials, it was anticipated that fear would be weakened and startle-response amplitude would decline. The curves for day 1 in Fig. 5:4 confirm this expectation, since the startle responses of the experimental animals were relatively large at the beginning of the day, but diminished progressively with successive nonshock trials. By way of contrast, the control (nonfearful) rats started at a much lower level and showed a much smaller decline during the shot-only trials. As can be seen from the curves for day 2, the startle responses of the

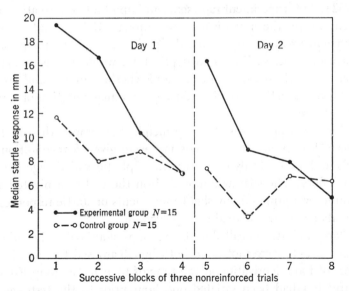

Fig. 5:4. These curves show the marked decline in startle-response amplitude exhibited by fearful (experimental) animals when a presumed fear-arousing CS is repeatedly presented without shock. The smaller decrease in response amplitude shown by the nonfearful control subjects appears to be the result of adaptation. The rise of the solid curve at the start of further extinction trials on day 2 may be due to the spontaneous recovery of fear in the interval between the two tests. (*From Brown, Kalish, and Farber, 1951.*)

experimental rats showed a spontaneous increase in strength following a day's rest. This phenomenon is clearly consistent with expectations from the laws of classical conditioning. If fear were undergoing extinction during the 12 nonshock trials of day 1, we should expect a period of rest to lead to some increase in its strength. And if fear serves as a source of drive to enhance startle reactions, a resurgence in the strength of the partially extinguished fear should be reflected by a rise in startle-response amplitude, as was indeed the case. Further support for the belief that fear is weakened by trials without shock is provided by the progressive fall of the solid curve during the nonreinforced trials of day 2. Additional test trials given on day 3 showed no further systematic effects, and they have been omitted from Fig. 5:4.

Another study supporting the view that conditioned fear may serve as a learned source of drive is that conducted by Meryman (1952). This experiment represents an important confirmation and extension of the investigation of Brown, Kalish, and Farber. Meryman was concerned with the problem of whether a primary source of drive, such as food deprivation, would intensify sound-induced startle responses in rats and whether hunger and conditioned fear together would produce greater augmentation of startle than either alone.

Meryman's apparatus was, in principle, the same as that used by Brown, Kalish, and Farber. His rats were given fear-conditioning trials and startle trials in a cylindrical, plastic-walled cage having a grid floor. The cage was mounted on the end of a pivoted aluminum lever arm and any slight movements or startle responses of the rats could be recorded on a polygraph.

Meryman's design called for four groups of animals. The animals in group F-46 were motivated both by CS-aroused fear and by 46 hours of food deprivation at the time of their tests; group F-1 was fearful but had been satiated one hour prior to the tests; group NF-46 was not fearful but hadn't eaten for 46 hours; and group NF-1 was not fearful and had been satiated one hour previously.

Following some initial adaptation trials to the sound of the pistol shot alone, all animals were given three trials at 20-minute intervals in the stabilimeter each day for ten days. On each of the first two trials the animals were individually placed in the cage and the

amplitudes of their startle responses to the sound of the toy pistol
were recorded. On the third trial of each day, the procedure of the
first two trials was repeated for the fearful groups (F-46 and F-1),
save that a brief electric shock was substituted for the sound of the
shot. This was calculated to produce an association between fear
and the tactual, visual, and olfactory cues provided by the stabilimeter cage. These environmental cues, rather than a buzzer or
light, served as the CS in this experiment. Thus the first two daily
trials provided measurements of startle responses as modified by
conditioned fear due to shocks received on the previous day or
days. The animals in the nonfearful groups (NF-46 and NF-1)
were also given two shot-only trials at the start of each day but
were not shocked when placed in the stabilimeter for their third
daily trial.

The results of Meryman's experiment are reproduced in Fig. 5:5.
The values plotted in this graph are means, based upon the two
daily startle responses to the shot for each of eight animals in each
group. Inspection of the curves reveals that on the first day, before any of the animals had had any shocks in the apparatus, all
four groups were about equal in their reactions to the shot. How-

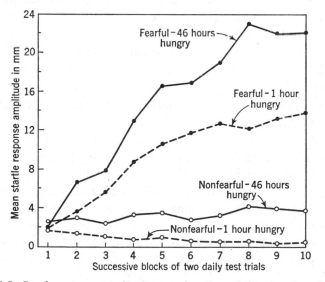

Fig. 5:5. Startle-response amplitude as a function of fear, no fear, intense
hunger, weak hunger, and their combinations. (From Meryman, 1952.)

ever, during the course of the ten days of training and testing, the responses of the two shocked groups (F-46 and F-1) exhibited a marked increase over their initial level. The responses of the fear-ful-nonhungry group (F-1) showed a considerable increase in am-plitude when compared with those of the nonfearful-nonhungry group (NF-1), and the fearful-hungry animals (F-46) exhibited an even more marked rise in their responses relative to the nonfearful-hungry (NF-46) rats. These results clearly support our conception of an acquired source of drive, since an associative variable (CS-UCS presentations) affected the startle response as if a motiva-tional variable had been introduced.

Two other findings by Meryman are of interest. First, the startle responses of the NF-46 group were significantly greater than those of the NF-1 group. This is important because it adds another re-sponse to the list of those that are facilitated by food deprivation, and because, to a degree, it allays the suspicion that startle, because of some unique relationship to fear, can be facilitated only by fear. Nevertheless, as the two middle curves show, fear, either be-cause it is strong or because it is innately associated with startle, is far more effective than intense hunger in enhancing startle. Sec-ond, a comparison of the upper three curves reveals that fear and hunger, when simultaneously present, are more potent than either one alone. Precisely what the mechanism is by which these two act in concert as facilitators is not clear. Conceivably, when hunger and fear are combined the result is simply an increase in level of general drive, multiplying the unlearned startle tendency. Or hunger might function somewhat less directly by augmenting fear and hence its capacity to affect startle.

In a subsequent study, Meryman (1953) has shown that the amplitude of the galvanic skin response (GSR) to a weak auditory click is enhanced by conditioned fear in human subjects. Fear was presumably established by pairing a brief auditory cue (a hiss-ing noise) with a mildly painful shock, an interval of 20 seconds separating the two stimuli. Because of this long interval, almost no conditioned GSRs were evoked by the CS even after a good many trials. But on the occasional test trials, when a click replaced the shock, the amplitude of the GSR to the test click showed a marked and significant increase throughout the course of conditioning. Since the click was never paired with shock, it cannot be argued that the click was itself becoming a conditioned stimulus for fear. Meryman concluded, therefore, that the noise had become a conditioned signal for fear, in spite of the long interval between noise and shock, and that fear intensified the unlearned tendency to respond to the weak click.

In addition to these experiments in which the dynamogenic effects of fear upon both startle and the GSR have been rather clearly demonstrated, there are several other studies that provide less direct support for the energizing conception of fear. Hunt and Otis (1953), for example, report that defecation in rats, during the presentation of a fear-arousing conditioned stimulus, increases progressively during conditioning and declines during extinction. They interpret this finding to mean that the CS acquired the power to "elicit" defecation as one component of the general emotional response. Alternatively, one might suppose that this is not an associative phenomenon but a consequence of the intensifying effect of fear-produced drive upon the defecation response when it is evoked in the emotional situation. This view is complicated, however, by the fact that another response, that of bar pressing, which was also elicited in the situation, tended to *decrease* as fear increased. Amsel (1950b) has also observed that during a period when rats are recovering from the emotional aftereffects of shock, defecation starts at a high level and declines, whereas drinking, which is initially inhibited, is gradually resumed. Thus fear can apparently facilitate one response and inhibit another at the same moment. Later on in this chapter we shall consider the implications of this seeming paradox.

Some investigators have applied the term *fear* to the general state of emotional excitement following the administration of electric shock, as well as to the conditioned emotionality aroused by a CS in anticipation of impending trauma. A distinction should probably be made, however, between these two presumed types of emotionality since their antecedent conditions, at least, are quite unlike. In particular, it is evident that postshock emotionality does not qualify as an *acquired* source of drive since a demonstration of its behavioral effects does not involve the manipulation of associative variables. Residual emotionality appears, however, to have drivelike energizing effects under certain conditions. Amsel and Maltzman (1950), for example, found that the consummatory response of drinking was enhanced following shock, provided the shocks were administered in a different situation from the one in which the rats were accustomed to drink. In a similarly designed study, Siegel and Brantley (1951) observed that if hungry rats were shocked in a separate place from where they were usually fed, eating was facilitated. In both of these studies, the conclusion was reached that postshock emotionality served as a source of general drive to intensify whatever reaction was dominant in the testing situation. Evidence contrary to this conclusion has been obtained, however, by Kabrick and Farber (1952), who report that postshock reaction times are lengthened in human subjects, and by Brown, Meryman, and Marzocco (1956), who find that amplitude of startle response in rats is diminished immediately after shock. These negative findings may be due to the elicitation by shock of competing responses, but further research is clearly needed to determine the range of conditions under which facilitation and/or interference can be obtained.

Studies of the Reinforcing Effect of Fear Reduction. All of the experiments in this group show that when a CS has been paired with a noxious UCS, terminating the CS after the evocation of a new response serves to reinforce the learning of that response. Since the capacity to function as a reinforcer is one of our suggested criteria for identifying motivational variables, and since this capacity varies in these studies with CS-UCS pairings (an associative variable) the operation of an acquired source of drive is strongly indicated.

The best-known experiment of this group (Miller, 1948a) has been quite influential in establishing the view that fear functions as a learned source of drive. The basic apparatus used by Miller was a rectangular box divided by a vertically sliding door into two separate compartments. One of these was painted white and had a grid floor, the other was black with a smooth floor. Twenty-five rats were given a series of preliminary training trials on which they were taught to escape electric shock in the white side by running through the open door into the black compartment. This training was also designed to produce a strong association between fear and the visual and tactual cues of the white box. During subsequent learning trials, the door was closed, but it would open automatically if a rat rotated a small wheel located directly above it. To determine whether reduction of the fear conditioned to the white box (CS) during the shock-escape trials would actually be reinforcing, Miller placed his rats in the white compartment without shock. Since the door was closed, they were faced with the task of learning to rotate the wheel in order to be released from the white box. The conditions were such that if an animal made the new wheel-turning response within 100 seconds, the door dropped, and the fear aroused by the white-box cues could be reduced by escaping into the black section. If the wheel-turning response was not made within this period, the animal was removed from the apparatus to await another trial.

The results obtained on the nonshock trials showed that if a rat succeeded in turning the wheel a number of times during the early part of the series, the new response was rapidly learned. According to Miller, escape from the fear-eliciting white-box cues served to reinforce wheel turning and to bring about a marked increase in the speed with which the act occurred. Actually 12 of the 25 rats did not turn the wheel often enough at first, and with repeated nonshock trials in the white side, their conditioned fear was extinguished before they could learn the new response. The 13 rats that did learn, however, also learned a second new response without any further shock trials. After wheel turning had been learned, the door was closed and the controlling circuits arranged so that a small metal rod had to be depressed to operate the door-release mechanism. During further trials with this arrangement, the rats gave up their earlier response of wheel turning, since it was no longer effective in leading to fear reduction, and acquired the response of depressing the bar. Shock was never administered on the learning trials, and Miller concluded, therefore, that fear was aroused by the white-box cues and that the elimination of those cues following escape into the black compartment led to a reduction of fear, which reinforced wheel turning and bar pressing.

Using Miller's study as their point of departure, Brown and Jacobs (1949) performed an experiment which provided further support for Miller's interpretation. From an analysis of Miller's

study, these experimenters reasoned that some other kind of reinforcement might have been operating in addition to, or instead of,
fear reduction. Specifically, during the initial training phase of
Miller's experiment, the animals had received a number of shock-
motivated trials in escaping from the white box to the black box.
Quite conceivably, therefore, during the subsequent learning trials
the animals may have been frustrated when prevented by the
closed door from further escape. If so, the anger or frustration
produced by interference with escape could have served as a drive,
and its reduction, following wheel turning and escape, could have
been reinforcing.

Following this line of thought, Brown and Jacobs designed their
study so that no escape responses were permitted or rewarded during the initial fear-conditioning trials. These trials were administered alternately in each section of a black-walled, two-compartment box. Each fear-conditioning trial consisted of the paired
presentation of a compound CS (interrupted tone plus blinking
light) and a pulsating electric shock (UCS). The animals could
not jump from one side of the box to the other on these trials, and
the durations of the CS and the UCS, as well as the interval between them, were completely independent of the animals' activities. In all, 22 trials of this kind were given, 10 on each of the
first two days, and 2 at the start of the third day. Half of the trials
were given in each side of the box so that fear, if it became conditioned to the cues provided by the apparatus, would be equal on
both sides.

Tests for the reinforcing effects of fear reduction were conducted
by putting the animals into one side of the box and turning on the
compound CS. At the same time, a guillotine door in the partition
separating the two compartments was lifted and the animals were
permitted to jump over a low hurdle into the opposite compartment. If they made this new response within 60 seconds, the door
was closed behind them and the CS was turned off. No shocks
were ever administered on these trials. It was anticipated that if
the CS aroused fear, its cessation following the hurdle-jumping response would be rewarding and the performance of that response
would improve. Animals not shocked during the initial trials
served as controls.

The time taken by an animal to jump over the hurdle after the door was opened provided the necessary performance data. Individual trial latencies were transformed into logarithms to normalize the distributions for statistical analyses, and the resulting means were plotted as in Fig. 5:6. In this figure the solid line shows that the hurdle-jumping latencies of the experimental (fearful) rats decreased progressively during the first 20 trials of hurdle jumping. The significant drop in these latencies suggests that the barrier-crossing responses of these rats were being reinforced by the cessation of the CS. The performance of the control-group animals contrasts sharply with that of the experimental rats. Whereas both groups crossed the hurdle with about the same latencies at first, the controls showed no tendency to improve their level of performance with additional trials. In fact, a statistical comparison of the first and last points of the dashed-line curve indicated that the performance of the control animals became significantly worse over the 40 trials. It was concluded from this study, therefore, that fear was developed in the experimental animals during the initial

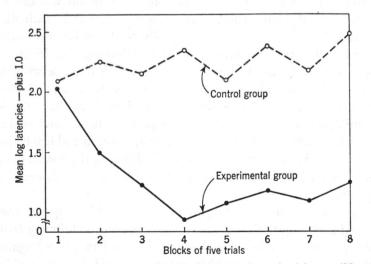

Fig. 5:6. Hurdle-jumping latencies for fearful and nonfearful rats $(N = 8$ per group) as a function of trials. The animals of the fearful (experimental) group show a marked decrease in latency (improvement in performance) during the first 20 trials, whereas the controls do not. The only reinforcement was that provided by the cessation of fear-arousing cues following the response. (*From Brown and Jacobs, 1949.*)

conditioning trials even though escape responses were neither permitted nor reinforced, and that the reduction of fear, following the cessation of the CS when the response occurred, functioned to strengthen the tendency to perform that response.

Kalish (1954), using procedures patterned after those of the Brown-Jacobs experiment, has carried out the most complete study of the effects on fear of varying numbers of acquisition and extinction trials. Previous experiments by Miller and Lawrence (1950) and by Gwinn (1951) had yielded somewhat obscure data concerning fear as a function of the number of shock-reinforced trials.

In his study Kalish used four principal groups of animals that were given 1, 3, 9, and 27 fear-acquisition trials, respectively, in a small, grid-floored, gray box. Each trial involved the presentation of a buzzer plus a blinking light (CS) for five seconds, with a one-second pulsating shock (UCS) being turned on during the last second of the CS. As in the Brown-Jacobs experiment, these acquisition trials were uncomplicated by the learning of escape or avoidance responses. Each of the four basic groups was divided into four subgroups. These were given 0, 3, 9, and 27 extinction trials (CS presented alone), respectively, following the initial conditioning trials. Immediately after extinction, the 16 groups were given a chance to learn a hurdle-jumping response with the CS-cessation providing the only reinforcement. Because of these procedures, the 16 groups should have differed, at the time the hurdle-jumping trials began, with respect to the amount of fear remaining after varying numbers of fear-acquisition and fear-extinction trials. Differences in proficiency in learning the hurdle-jumping response would be expected to reflect these differences in residual fear.

When the hurdle-jumping latencies for the 16 groups are combined according to the original number of fear-conditioning trials, irrespective of number of extinction trials, and are plotted against the trials, the four curves of Fig. 5:7 are obtained. Here we see that the group given the maximum number of fear-conditioning trials, i.e., 27, shows the greatest decrease in latency as a consequence of the reinforcement provided by the termination of the CS. As the number of conditioning trials decreases to 9, 3, and 1, the degree

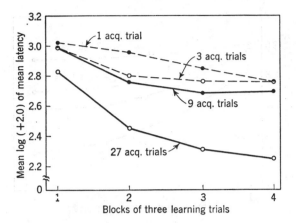

F<small>IG</small>. 5:7. Hurdle-jumping latencies on successive blocks of three trials during which the response was reinforced by the cessation of an alleged fear-arousing *CS*. Each curve was obtained by pooling the data from four subgroups of eight animals given differing numbers of extinction trials. (*From Kalish, 1954.*)

of learning in the hurdle-jumping tests declines, though some learning seems to have resulted from only a single fear-conditioning trial. Thus fear seems to be acquired very quickly, though its strength continues to rise with additional reinforcements up to at least 27 trials.

When the data from Kalish's experiment are regrouped to show the effects of variations in number of fear-extinction trials, the curves of Fig. 5:8 are obtained. Here again the findings accord well with expectation, since animals given no extinction trials learn most rapidly, and learning becomes progressively worse as the number of extinction trials is increased.

The procedures and findings of Kalish's study, it may be seen, are consistent with the concept of acquired sources of drive developed at the start of this chapter. Thus, number of acquisition trials and number of extinction trials, though clearly associative variables, affect the hurdle-jumping reference response, which was not elicited while these variables were being manipulated, much as we might expect it to be affected by a motivational variable.

Concerning data such as these, however, it must be remembered that although decreases in response latency provide evidence for the presence of fear, and differences among such decreases indi-

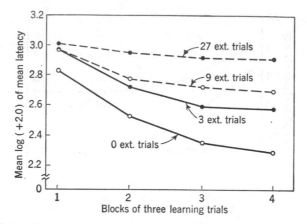

Fig. 5:8. Hurdle-jumping latencies for groups differing with respect to number of fear-extinction trials. The data from four subgroups of eight animals each, given different numbers of fear-acquisition trials, were combined to form each of these four curves. (*From Kalish, 1954.*)

cate differences in degree of fear, absolute reaction latencies do not reflect strength of fear in any direct manner. This is because the hurdle-jumping training is carried out in the absence of further shock trials. During such trials fear must be presumed to be undergoing extinction. Thus proficiency in the performance of the new response may be increasing, but this increase is occurring while the absolute strength of fear is doubtless declining.

The experiments described in this section on the reinforcing effects of fear reduction may be taken as representative of typical research in the area. Other studies by Miller and Lawrence (1950), Gwinn (1951), and Mowrer and Lamoreaux (1942) have also provided evidence that fear reduction is reinforcing.

Studies of the Inhibitory Effects of Fear. We have seen that if a reference response is elicited while a CS for fear is on, enhancement of the response may be observed. Under other conditions, however, especially when the CS is presented after a response (or response chain) has been initiated, activity may be inhibited rather than augmented. At first sight this negative effect seems to conflict with the notion of fear as a motivator. Nevertheless, it can be interpreted as an instance of an acquired source of drive, if one grants that the inhibition or abandonment of responses that are followed by the introduction of a motivational variable is a legitimate criterion (Chapter 2) for the identification of such variables. On this basis, evidence for an acquired source of drive would be provided by the observation that as the number of fear-conditioning trials (associative variable) increases, the likelihood that responses which are followed by the CS will be inhibited (motivational variable) should also increase.

One of the first experimental demonstrations of inhibiting effects of this kind has been reported by Estes and Skinner (1941). In their experiment rats were trained initially to press a bar to obtain a pellet of food. By presenting pellets at fixed intervals of time rather than after every response, the rats were taught to respond at a continuous rate. That is, they would depress the bar repeatedly even though only one pellet was given them every four minutes. Subsequently, fear reactions were conditioned (while the animals were pressing the bar) by turning on a tone (CS) for several minutes and giving the rats a strong shock at the time the tone was terminated. At first the rats continued to respond at their usual rate while the tone was sounding, but as the number of tone-shock trials increased, the onset of the tone produced a more immediate and more nearly complete cessation of bar pressing. Animals tested under low hunger drive did not exhibit this effect to as marked a degree as did others tested under a strong hunger drive. This latter finding is of special interest since it is consistent with the view that fear may be intensified by the presence of hunger. This possibility was suggested above in connection with Meryman's startle-response study.

The Estes-Skinner technique for investigating the behavioral consequences of fear has proved to be rather generally useful. Hunt and Brady (1951) and their associates, in particular, have employed the method repeatedly in their studies of the effects of electroconvulsive shock (ECS) upon fear. Though space does not permit a detailed review of their experiments here, these investigators have demonstrated rather clearly that the immediate aftereffects of ECS treatments are to abolish conditioned fear. Rats given ECS "therapy" are not deterred from repetitive bar pressing when a stimulus is presented that was formerly followed by strong shock.

Amsel (1950b) has shown that conditioned fear inhibits the consummatory response of drinking in thirsty rats, provided fear and the consummatory act have been associated with the same cues. In his experiment rats were given preliminary training in running from the larger of two similar white compartments into the smaller to drink from a calibrated water container. During this training, which was carried on for 24 days under a constant water-deprivation regimen, the amount of water consumed during a five-minute period on successive trials increased in a smooth, negatively accelerated manner until a stable level was reached. At this point the animals in one group were placed in the larger box and were given two shocks per day for four days. Control animals were also put into the larger section but were not shocked. Subsequently, when the animals of both groups were again permitted to run to water, those in the shocked group showed a sharp drop in water consumption. The water intake of the no-shock control group, however, did not change following the four-day no-drinking period. During additional no-shock test periods, the shocked animals exhibited a gradual increase in the amount of water drunk during the five-minute period. In interpreting his findings, Amsel assumed that fear was conditioned (in the experimental group) to the cues of the larger white box and generalized to the smaller white compartment. The decrease in water intake of these animals on the postshock trials was ascribed to the presence of "anxiety-motivated" competing responses. Thus fear did not facilitate drinking because its presence led to the appearance of new responses which interfered with drinking. One of these competing responses may have been emotional defecation, since, as we have previously noted, the frequency of defecation by the fearful animals was extremely high at the time when water consumption was low. Moreover, defecation decreased as fear was extinguished and water consumption rose.

This concludes our discussion of selected studies illustrating the inhibitory effects of fear upon other responses. Unfortunately, we are not yet in possession of a large body of experimental data in this area, and interpretations and generalizations must be cautiously proposed. We need, for example, more detailed information concerning the kinds of responses that are inhibited by fear, information as to the strengths of those responses relative to others, and information about the specific characteristics of those fear-conditioning situations that lead to maximum inhibition.

Fear as Both Inhibitor and Energizer. At the start of the preceding section it was noted that an apparent contradiction is implicit in the fact that fear sometimes functions as an energizer and sometimes as an inhibitor. However, it was asserted that within the framework of the present conception of acquired sources of drive these opposite effects are not paradoxical, since one of our criteria of a motivational variable is that its introduction following a response tends to lead to the abandonment or inhibition of that response. But this interpretation is applicable only when one can provide reasonable evidence that the inhibited response was indeed elicited *before* the onset of the fear-arousing CS. Unfortunately, this is usually not easy to do, especially in instrumental conditioning situations where the onset and/or termination of the CS may not be precisely controlled. The evaluation of this conception must be delayed, therefore, pending the accumulation of additional data.

An alternate hypothesis as to why fear has inhibitory properties can be developed along purely associative lines. Let us suppose, for example, that bar pressing is the reference response. If that response occurs consistently prior to fear conditioning, then the bar pressing habit must be stronger than other habits. Moreover, since bar pressing is not enhanced by the drive increment that might be produced by the first fear-conditioning trial, but is either slightly depressed or is unchanged, it must be further postulated that one trial is sufficient to shift some habit other than bar pressing into a position of dominance. Thus a tendency to freeze or to crouch or to move away from the region of the bar could have become slightly stronger than the tendency to press the bar. Whatever the nature of the newly dominant tendency, it must be regarded as one that can prevent or interfere with bar pressing. It could be either an innate or a learned response to fear-produced internal stimuli. As fear increases with training, the internal cues would be expected to increase in intensity, or more of them might rise above a threshold value, producing an increase in the superiority of the interfering tendency relative to the bar-pressing tendency.

Should one choose to do so, the construct of D could be added to this associative theory without changing its predictions. Both the new competing habit and the bar-pressing habit would be multiplied by the drive due to hunger and by the mounting fear-produced drive. Crouching or avoidance reactions and bar pressing should therefore both become stronger, but with the increase in drive and in the difference between the two habits, the strength of the interfering excitatory tendency would become progressively greater relative to the bar-pressing excitatory tendency. Consequently, *overt* bar pressing should decline, even though the absolute magnitude of its excitatory tendency was rising. As we have already seen, the multiplicative-drive assumption alone cannot explain declining performance under circumstances in which drive level is presumably increasing. One must further hypothesize that the variable leading to increased D also serves to bring a new, incompatible reactive tendency into a position of ascendance over the old. This is clearly an associative assumption, but its use permits one to retain the hypothesis of D as a multiplying agent even where an indicant reaction is becoming overtly weaker.

Variables Influencing the Strength of Fear. Some of the variables determining strength of fear have already been mentioned in our discussions of specific experimental studies of fear. There are numerous others, however, which, though they cannot be treated here in detail, are of sufficient importance to mention. For an excellent analysis of many of these the reader is referred to Miller's (1951) treatment of learnable drives and rewards.

The most general statement one can make concerning the strength of fear is that it is influenced by many of the same associative variables that determine the strength of other conditioned responses. For example, fear tends to become stronger as the intensity of the noxious UCS is increased (Miller and Lawrence, 1950). And if electric shock of near tetanizing intensity is used, with dogs at least, fear becomes so firmly ingrained that its extinction is accomplished only with great difficulty (Solomon, Kamin, and Wynne, 1953). Fear also tends to increase progressively as the number of paired presentations of the CS and UCS is increased (Brown, Kalish, and Farber, 1951; Kalish, 1954). Beyond a certain point, however, fear may decline with further conditioning trials. This possibility is suggested by Libby's (1951) finding that 80 fear-conditioning trials appeared to yield weaker fear than 40. Electric shocks of long duration may also produce stronger fear than short shocks, but the evidence is far from convincing (Mowrer and Solomon, 1954). Fear also is known to vary with the length of the interval between the CS and UCS (Libby, 1951; Murfin, 1954), and perhaps with degree of massing of fear-conditioning trials (Armus, 1954). Moreover, fear reactions may be more intense when an organism is hungry than when it is not (Estes and Skinner, 1941; Meryman, 1952).

Although existing studies of factors influencing strength of fear are illuminating, systematically gathered data in this area are still relatively meager. Much additional work certainly remains to be done before we can be reasonably certain as to what the optimum conditions are for the acquisition of fear. Investigations are rare, for example, of the generalization of fear or of the effects on fear of shock duration and changes in the characteristics of the CS. More data are also needed on fear as a function of the distribution of both acquisition and extinction trials.

Concerning the problem of the elimination or extinction of fear, it seems likely that any factor tending to increase strength of fear should also enhance its resistance to counteracting influences. As is well known, degree of resistance to extinction is often used as a measure of strength of fear and other responses. The procedures for the conditioning of fear are those of classical Pavlovian conditioning, and experimental extinction, therefore, is the basic method for eliminating fear. Thus, to weaken fear it is only necessary, in principle, to present the fear-arousing CS without the UCS. We have already seen from Kalish's study (1954) that fear declines progressively with the number of such nonreinforced presentations of the CS. Solomon and Wynne (1953) have suggested that fears often show remarkable resistance to extinction because the individual's avoidance responses remove him too quickly from the presence of the fear-arousing CS. Presumably, for extinction to be successful, fear must be more or less fully aroused by the CS and yet not be reinforced by the UCS. These authors have also hypothesized that traumatically strong shocks may produce conditioned fears that can never be completely eradicated by normal extinction procedures.

The process of fear extinction can be accelerated by massing extinction trials (Burros, 1949) or by permitting or persuading the subject to engage in appetitive activity while in the presence of the CS. This latter relationship has been demonstrated experimentally by Farber (1948). Those of his rats that ate in the fear-arousing environment lost their fears more quickly than animals that spent the same amount of time in the same environment but did not eat. In Jones's (1924) classic demonstration of this principle, a child's fear of a rabbit was overcome by first presenting the rabbit at a distance while the child was eating and by then bringing the animal closer and closer to the child on successive occasions.

Conditioned fear in rats can also be very nearly eliminated by the use of electroconvulsive shocks (Hunt and Brady, 1951), as we have already noted, and by the elicitation of audiogenic seizures (Brady, Stebbins, and Galambos, 1953). Moreover, alcohol, which is well known for its ability to reduce human fears and anxieties, tends also to reduce the fears of rats in laboratory conflict situations (Conger, 1951).

The problem of precisely which variables govern the learning of emotional reactions such as fear has engaged the attention of numerous theorists. For some, the learning of both emotional and nonemotional responses is governed by the same principles; others, however, hold that the known facts cannot be encompassed unless two or more different laws or principles are invoked. Marshalling and analyzing the evidence relative to this problem is a fairly lengthy matter, and we postpone it, therefore, to our final chapter which is devoted to theoretical issues of this sort.

Anxieties or Fears as Learned Sources of Drive in Human Behavior

Thus far our discussion of acquired-drive problems has been restricted, for the most part, to laboratory studies of, and theories derived from, conditioned fear responses in animals. We have followed this course because the most carefully controlled experiments have been done with animals, not because the study of their artificially induced fears is, in itself, to be regarded as of primary importance. The study of fear in animals is, of course, a perfectly legitimate area for scientists to explore. But most research workers wish to know whether functional relations obtained with one organism can be generalized to other organisms, including man. Actually, the process is a two-way one. We can learn important things about rats' fears from human beings, and vice versa. From everyday experiences with our fellow men and from laboratory studies, we often get hunches as to the ways in which certain variables affect behavior. But in testing out these hunches, we may find it desirable to use animals as subjects. This is often true when we desire to minimize the role of verbal mechanisms or when it is necessary to employ fear-arousing unconditioned stimuli of a traumatically intense nature. Studies such as those of Solomon, Kamin, and Wynne (1953) on traumatic-avoidance learning in dogs could never have been done with human subjects.

That human fears, anxieties, and feelings of insecurity have widespread effects upon behavior is almost universally acknowledged. In Freudian (1936) theory as in others, feelings of anxiety, guilt, and the like, play a major role in the interpretation of normal behavior. These feelings or reactions, moreover, are believed to constitute the cornerstones of the bizarre personality structures of the neurotic and the psychotic.

Human Fears as Learned Responses. Although tendencies to become anxious could conceivably be transmitted through genetic channels, human beings, by and large, must *learn* to be anxious. During a child's early years there are innumerable opportunities for it to acquire fears of certain stimulus objects in certain situations. We know little, unfortunately, about how these anxieties are learned, but it seems reasonable to believe that they are acquired in much the same ways as are conditioned fears in animals. For instance, the sight of a flaming match may serve as a CS, with the subsequently experienced burn providing the UCS. Since similar sets of events occur repeatedly, ample opportunities are provided for children to acquire fears of whatever objects society regards as dangerous. Indeed, in order to save children from injury, parents spend a great deal of time making certain that youngsters do become fearful at the sight of a hot radiator, an oncoming car, high places, deep ditches, electric outlets, and so on.

At first, when we try to inculcate these protective fears into our children, we cannot use language in any effective way. The words "hot," "hurt," "burn," and "ouch" mean nothing to the infant. During the early stages of training, therefore, most children must actually experience the trauma and pain provided by noxious stimuli. But with the passage of time the child experiences repeated pairings of warning words such as "hurt" with unpleasant or painful sensations. These warning words can thus come to arouse the child's anxiety or fear in the same way as do other stimuli such as the sight of the hot stove, the sharp razor blade, or the electric outlet. *The conditioning of fear to verbal cues of this variety is an extremely important step in providing the child with protective fears, since by this means the parent can arouse the child's anxiety in new situations to which the child has not been previously exposed.* The child may never have seen a soldering iron, but the parent can elicit fear and withdrawal simply by pointing to the iron and saying "hot" or "hurt." It would seem, therefore, that language serves, in this manner, the very useful adaptive function of eliciting fear and withdrawal in a large assortment of potentially dangerous situations. The widespread effects of this type of training are well illustrated by the behavior of a young child known to the writer who used the word "Ow!" as the name for flaming matches, cigarettes, bonfires, and stoves, long before she could give these objects their correct names. A child need not cut his fingers on a power-driven saw to acquire a fear and an avoidance of the whirling blade. But to do so without pain, he must learn to react with anxiety to certain verbal or gestural symbols, and these symbols must, in turn, be associated, sometimes repeatedly, with to-be-avoided objects or situations.

If we look at the technical details of this process, it becomes apparent that the initial step in associating fear with the warning words fits the pattern of classical conditioning precisely. But in new situations, where the child may not actually get hurt, the paradigm is different. The sight of the new object (CS) is not associated with pain but with the word "hurt," which, because it can arouse fear, now functions as a substitute UCS. By repeated pairings of the new CS with the fear-arousing word, the new CS also comes to evoke fear and/or withdrawal. This paradigm will be recognized as that of *higher-order conditioning,* a procedure described and successfully demonstrated by Pavlov (1927) and others. While the higher-order conditioning of salivary and skeletal responses in animals is rather difficult to establish and is somewhat unstable, it may be that the higher-order conditioning of fear can be more readily accomplished. Moreover, higher-order emotional conditioning of a strength and stability unattainable with animals can perhaps be produced in human subjects as a consequence of the operation of language.

Proceeding on the premise that human behavior is fraught with learned anxieties and fears, we must next consider whether, and to what degree, such anxieties can lie at the root of the so-called acquired drives for power, money, prestige, and the like.

Anxiety as an Element of the "Acquired Drive" for Money. Although the paradigm of classical conditioning seems to serve rather well for fear and anxiety, it cannot easily be applied to an analysis of the "drives for specific goal objects" that adult human beings are alleged to possess. Consider, for a moment, the so-called drive for money. If this is essentially a learned or conditioned response, we must first ask how it has become conditioned. But in seeking an answer we immediately run into difficulty, since we cannot specify any unconditioned stimulus capable of eliciting the money-seeking drive (or response) in the first place. If there is no stimulus that can elicit the response without training, how can we arrange for the response to become associated with a conditioned stimulus? Whatever the so-called acquired drive for money may be, it is not a simple, unitary response elicitable by a specific unconditioned stimulus and conditionable to other stimuli by the procedures of classical conditioning.

Part of the difficulty here arises from the use of the phrase "acquired drive for money." If, as we have suggested, it is desirable to use the word "drive" only when referring to a construct that is nondirective in its motivating effects upon behavior, then we cannot meaningfully speak of a drive *for* any specific goal, whether it be for money, prestige, power, or whatever. On this view, although both learned and unlearned responses may contribute to drive, one can have neither a learned nor an unlearned drive *for* anything. While working in factories, schools, stores, offices, and elsewhere, people do learn, of course, to perform a multitude of responses for which monetary rewards are provided. And in a certain sense money is the goal toward which these responses are directed. But unless our concept of drive is changed, the drive underlying those activities cannot itself be directed toward money; nor does it seem likely that those responses can serve as the source of drive to which reference is made in speaking of a "drive for money." In fact, it is precisely these day-to-day, work-situation activities that are themselves presumably motivated by the money-seeking drive, and we are forced to look elsewhere, therefore, for learned responses having the motivating properties we seek.

According to one interpretation (Brown, 1953*a*), anxiety might serve as a learned motivating agency for money-seeking responses if it is aroused by cues indicating the absence of money. On this view, *stimulus patterns such as those provided by an empty wallet or by an "overdrawn" notice from one's bank acquire, through learning, the capacity to elicit reactions of insecurity, uneasiness, or anxiety.* And because of the drive properties of such anxiety reactions, a wide assortment of specific stimulus-elicited responses can be affected as though some motivational variable had been manipulated. Moreover, a reduction in anxiety, should it occur following a particular response, would be expected to reinforce that response. At the heart of this interpretation, then, is the basic idea that an ". . . *important motivating component of many of the supposed acquired drives for specific goal objects is actually a learned tendency to be discontented or distressed or anxious in the absence of those goal objects*" (Brown, 1953*a*, p. 12).

If this analysis is to carry conviction, however, it is necessary to present the details of the process by which the reaction of anxiety becomes conditioned to stimuli signifying "no money" or "insufficient money." We need to know why we have learned to feel anxious, embarrassed, and uneasy if, for example, after ordering and eating a meal in a restaurant, we find that we have failed to bring sufficient money. By what process does anxiety become conditioned to the stimuli provided by the to-be-paid check in combination with the empty pocket?

Probably the most satisfactory answer to this question is that these anxieties are acquired through a process of higher-order conditioning, with verbal cues playing a major role, in essentially the same way that generalized fears of dangerous situations are learned. The initial stage in the process would consist of repeated childhood experiences in which pain has been associated with verbal or gestural cues of alarm or warning provided by adults. In their most general and common form, these are statements like "Look out, you'll get hurt," or "If you do that something bad will happen to you." Or the cues may be facial expressions of alarm, concern, and worry accompanying the verbal warnings. Following the paradigm of classical conditioning, these alarm-denoting cues might come to arouse the emotional reactions of dread, fear, or anxiety, even in the absence of actual pain.

The second stage of the process involves the further conditioning of anxiety to a wide variety of cues, all of which indicate a lack of money or its relative scarcity. Because of the nature of our society and the great significance of money for many of its members, ample opportunities exist therein for the occurrence of this secondary conditioning of anxiety. This could be accomplished in a number of ways. Consider the typical warnings given to children by parents. "If you get on a train and can't pay your fare, the conductor will throw you off," or, "If we run out of money before the end of the month, we may not have enough food to eat," or, "If you don't pay for your meal, the restaurant owner will make you wash all the dishes." Now in each of these statements, and in innumerable ones like them, an anxiety-arousing warning is paired with a statement about the lack of money. Through repeated pairings, by other children as well as by parents, of these two kinds of assertions, cues denoting a lack of money might come to arouse anxiety reactions. The cues become, in this way, the counterparts of the fear-eliciting CS used in animal experiments, and the anxieties they elicit may constitute an important motivational component underlying human money-seeking responses.

It is not necessary, according to this interpretation, to assume that one must have absolutely no money in order to experience anxiety. Being "broke" means different things to different in dividuals. The college professor may feel "broke" and anxious when his bank balance drops below, say, $25. But the multimillionaire, who owns numerous yachts, planes, estates, and cars, may suffer acute distress upon finding that he is "down to his last million." Just recently one of the richest men in the world was quoted as having said that ". . . after all, a million dollars isn't worth what it used to be."

One of the consequences of this view relates to the problem of the rewarding or reinforcing value of money. As we well know, sequences of action followed by monetary rewards tend to be learned by individuals in our society and tend to be abandoned if these rewards are withdrawn. One common interpretation of this phenomenon is based on the concept of *secondary reinforcement*, which was derived originally from Pavlov's work on higher-order conditioning. As usually stated, a stimulus object acquires secondary reinforcing properties when it has been closely and repeatedly associated with a primary rewarding event. Thus if a rat has been repeatedly fed in a white goal box, the box may act as a learned or secondary reward in other situations because of its association with the consummatory act of eating. Applied to money, the principle would be that money has become secondarily rewarding because it has been frequently exchanged for food, which in turn has led to a reduction of hunger. The behavior of chimpanzees in the well-known token-reward studies of Wolfe (1936) and of Cowles (1937) has commonly been explained as an instance of secondary reinforcement. These studies showed that initially neutral objects, such as poker chips, acquired a rewarding value for the chimpanzees if the chips could be exchanged by the animals for raisins or other preferred foods.

The foregoing interpretation of how anxiety may form the motivational substratum of money-seeking behavior leads to a different view of the process by which money acquires its rewarding value. If cues denoting the lack of money or its relative absence lead to anxiety, then the actual possession of money must lead to a diminution of anxiety. Moreover, if anxiety reduction functions to reinforce antedating responses, then some of the reinforcing value of money may be due to its anxiety-quelling properties. Thus *money may become a reinforcer, in part, because anxiety is aroused by stimulus events denoting a lack of money and because money in one's hand counteracts that anxiety.* Incidentally, this conception does not negate the value of the secondary-reinforcement theory. It serves, rather, as an additional explanatory mechanism, capable of operating jointly with secondary reinforcement.

Money, though of major significance, is by no means the only agent capable of eliminating the anxiety occasioned by cues denoting money's absence. Quite often people who are distressed by the knowledge that they are broke, or nearly so, escape from the disquieting cues by going to sleep, getting drunk, or going to the movies. Since these "escape" reactions are followed by anxiety reduction, they too tend to be reinforced, and as a result may become well established though unrealistic modes of reacting to a lack of money.

The essence of this interpretation has been summarized by Brown (1953a, p. 14) as follows: "In many instances, if not all, where adult human behavior has been strongly marked by money-seeking responses there appears to be little need for postulating the operation of a learned money-seeking drive. One does not learn to have a drive for money. Instead, one learns to become anxious in the presence of a variety of cues signifying the absence of money. The obtaining of money automatically terminates or drastically alters such cues, and in so doing, produces a decrease in anxiety. Money-seeking responses, or other reactions, appearing during the arousal of anxiety are strongly reinforced by the decline of anxiety attending the receipt of money."

As a final point we must emphasize that this conception is not restricted to the so-called acquired drive for money. Anxiety-arousing properties could certainly be acquired by stimuli denoting a lack of prestige or affection or power, and could thus provide a motivational mainspring for responses directed toward these goals as well. Moreover, this view of anxiety as a basic component of many of the so-called acquired drives is very similar to previously proposed conceptions. Tolman (1942), for example, has presented a somewhat similar explanation of the "drive of gregariousness." Thus he maintains that in gregarious species of animals, separation from the flock or herd results in an "internal sufferance" that is eliminated by rejoining the group. Clearly, this "internal sufferance" is functionally much the same as the anxiety we have been considering, and like anxiety can be aroused by cues indicating a special kind of deficit. A parallel line of reasoning has been followed by Dollard and Miller (1950) in their brief analysis of the anxieties experienced by a child when separated from its mother. Certain environmental cues, when not accompanied by the sights or sounds of the mother, are assumed to lead to the drive of fear, and the child's responses of seeking and approaching the mother are reinforced by the reduction in fear her presence provides.

Other Learned Responses as Sources of Drive

Anxiety doubtless constitutes a significant secondary motivating agency for human behavior, but there seems to be scant reason for regarding it as the only such learned motivator. Quite possibly other responses having motivational effects are learned by human beings, and some perhaps by animals. According to McClelland (1951), for example, human beings are driven as much by a "hope of success" as they are by anxiety or by a "fear of failure." Of the several attempts that have been made to develop theories of acquired motivators other than anxiety, three will be considered here. The first is the r_g–s_g "expectancy" mechanism of Hull and Spence; the second is the "affective-arousal model" proposed by McClelland, and the third is the writer's tentative hypothesis concerning the motivational role played by verbal self-instructions.

The r_g–s_g Mechanism as an Acquired Source of Drive. In some early theoretical articles, Hull (1931, 1937) made considerable interpretive use of what is described as the "expectancy" or r_g–s_g mechanism. According to Hull, when an organism is rewarded while making a consummatory goal reaction (R_G), such as eating, associations are formed by the process of classical conditioning between R_G and a variety of stimuli, both internal and external. Since some cues, e.g., those arising from the need for food (S_Ds), are present throughout all phases of the instrumental response sequence, there is a tendency for them to elicit R_G at every point in the sequence. But only certain portions or phases of the goal reaction of eating can be performed prior to the attainment of food. Responses such as seizing the food, biting it, chewing, and swallowing cannot move backward (appear at an earlier time) in the sequence since they lack, at those points, the necessary goal object (food) for their execution. Reactions such as sniffing, salivating, smacking the lips, and swallowing, however, can indeed be elicited before the goal is reached. Hull thought of responses like these as split-off portions of the goal reaction (R_G). He named them, therefore, *fractional anticipatory goal reactions* and denoted them by the symbol r_g. It should now be clear why the term *expectancy* is appropriate in connection with these responses. Observable responses of salivating, swallowing, and licking the chops, if exhibited by a pet dog, say, just before he is fed, constitute about as good an objective index of his "food expectancy" as can be found.

Now these fractional anticipatory goal reactions would be expected to give rise to characteristic internal stimuli, and Hull completed the picture by adding these stimuli (s_gs) to the r_gs. Thus the complete r_g–s_g mechanism was formed. In Hull's earliest use of this mechanism, the s_g portion played the principal role as a behavior determinant, serving both as a stimulus to which a variety of reactions could become conditioned and as a secondary reinforcer. On a number of occasions, however, Spence (1951a, 1956) has pointed out that *the fractional anticipatory goal response and its interoceptive and proprioceptive stimuli might operate motivationally as well as associatively.* Since the classically conditioned r_g is learned, it would qualify, by our criteria, as a secondary source of drive, provided it does indeed have the motivational effects suggested for it. In Spence's formulation, which we have outlined in Chapter 4, the strength of the r_g is dependent, in part, upon the magnitude of the food reward given an animal. And the intervening variable K, the *incentive-motivation factor*, is, in turn, a function of the strength of r_g. Within the system, K affects behavior in much the same way that D does. Thus the r_g–s_g mechanism and the related K factor are used to explain the fact that animals will run faster through a maze if they are expecting a large piece of food than if they are expecting a small piece. If they have been given large pieces of food, the r_g is stronger and, therefore, the habit of approaching the food is multiplied by a higher value of K.

As Spence has pointed out, a similar theory was proposed earlier by Crespi (1944), who, in interpreting his experiments on the effect of size of incentive, appealed to what he called an "emotional drive." In this so-called "eagerness" theory, variations in amount of reward were assumed to lead to differences in amount of anticipatory tension or excitement, and these excitement differences produced corresponding differences in motivation and hence in level of performance.

There are several avenues through which anticipatory goal responses and their interoceptive cues might exert their motivational effects. Within Hull's theory, for example, s_g could have a dynamogenic or energizing effect resembling that of intense external stimuli. The effect of stimulus intensity, per se, Hull called "stimulus dynamism." Or it may be, as Spence has suggested, that conflict would ensue when the tendency for r_g to occur at an early point in a response sequence is opposed by tendencies to make other responses. The excitement or tension produced by the conflict might have motivational consequences by adding an increment to the existing level of drive (D). This possibility is discussed in more detail in Chapter 6.

An interesting application and extension of the r_g–s_g concept appears in a study by Birch, Burnstein, and Clark (1958). During an initial 35-day training period, rats were allowed to eat dry food pellets from 5:30 to 7:30 P.M. each day. The purpose of this training was to develop an association between anticipatory eating responses $(r_g\text{s})$ and the internal cues characteristic of 22 hours of food deprivation $(S_D\text{s})$. On the assumption that the r_g habit strength generalized along the dimension of S_D intensity, one would expect that the $r_g\text{s}$ evoked by the combination of external cues and $S_D\text{s}$ would become progressively weaker with departures of deprivation time in either direction from the 22-hour training value. And on the further hypothesis that drive is monotonically related to the vigor and/or frequency of $r_g\text{s}$, drive should increase with deprivation up to the customary time of feeding and then decrease as deprivation is further extended. On this view, then, the strength of the rat's food expectation (r_g) is contingent upon how similar his interoceptive cues are to those that have usually been present at the time of eating, and his drive level is determined by the strength of his expectancy.

Data interpreted as supporting this conception were obtained from two behavioral measures. The first, which was the number of times the rats depressed the empty food trough during a 46-hour deprivation test period on the thirty-sixth and thirty-seventh days, showed that trough depressions, though relatively infrequent during the first 19 hours, increased rapidly during the period from 19 to 24 hours and then declined to zero at the 32-hour point, there being some suggestion of further increases in the period from 32 to 48 hours. This is consistent with the view that the expectancy-generated drive increased to a maximum at about the usual time for eating and then decreased with further deprivation. Unfortunately, the food troughs had been present in the cages throughout the 35-day training period, and hence tendencies to approach the troughs for food at deprivation times shorter than 22 hours may have become extinguished through nonreinforcement. Moreover, the rats' relatively weak tendency to depress the troughs at intervals longer than about 25 hours may have been due in part, as the authors note, to extinction's taking place during the middle periods of the 46-hour testing period.

The second behavioral measure, speed of running down a straight alley for food, showed that on the first trial speed tended to rise slightly, but not significantly, as deprivation time was increased from 15 to 37 hours. On subsequent trials, however, running speeds were markedly elevated for animals running under 22 and 25 hours of deprivation and depressed for those tested with 15 and 37 hours of deprivation. Birch et al. interpret these findings as supporting their hypotheses concerning the conditioning of r_g to S_D, and the contribution of r_g to D. However, all of their measures showed that performance under 25 hours of deprivation was superior to that at 22, despite the fact that the animals were never fed save at the 22-hour period. If generalization of r_g along the S_D dimension were the only factor involved, performance should have been worse at 25 than at 22 hours and there should have been no tendency for trough depressions to be greater at 46 than at 32 hours. Nevertheless, the experiment suggests that rhythmical feeding schedules may influence privation-motivated behavior, and that estimates of drive based solely upon time of deprivation may need to be modified when such schedules have been employed.

Before leaving this topic, we find it appropriate to note that Miller and Dollard's (1941) analysis of acquired drives also contains elements that are quite similar to those involved in the r_g–$s_g \rightarrow K$ mechanism. Thus they believe that any strong stimulus has drive value (cf. Hull's stimulus-dynamism concept) and that the *stimuli produced by learned responses constitute the basis for all acquired drives.* The learned responses of fear and anxiety are regarded as especially significant contributors to level of motivation (cf. Miller's experiment on fear in an earlier section of this chapter), but responses toward such "positive" goal objects as food, money, and sexual objects also provide drive-augmenting stimuli. The sight of food, for example, may elicit a learned appetitive response, and if the interoceptive stimulation attending that response is sufficiently intense it will serve as a drive to impel food-seeking (and other) responses. Moreover, all response-produced stimuli are said by Miller and Dollard to have cue value as well as drive-enhancing power. This aspect of their conception is identical with the notion that a variety of responses can be associatively connected to the s_g portion of the r_g–s_g mechanism.

The Affective-arousal Model. McClelland, Atkinson, Clark, and Lowell (1953), expanding upon some of McClelland's earlier work (1951), have made a serious attempt to solve some of the acquired-drive problems and have proposed what they call the *affective-arousal model* as a general theory of motivation. According to these writers, two affective states of the organism serve as important motivators. One of these is negative (fear or anxiety) and the other positive (anticipation of rewards, appetite). Since both of these motivating states are learned or conditioned reactions, they fit the authors' definition of a motive: "A motive is the redintegration by a cue of a change in an affective situation" (McClelland et al., 1953, p. 28). As shown in their example, if a buzzer is associated with the eating of a sweet substance such as sugar, the buzzer will eventually come to evoke (redintegrate) a state involving positive affective change. This positive affective condition is termed *appetite*. The corresponding negative affective state, *anxiety*, is conditioned in the same manner as is fear, according to our previous description. That is, a buzzer, if associated with shock, acquires the capacity to redintegrate a negative affective state that may have motivating effects on behavior. According to this theory, then, an individual learns to make anticipatory affective or emotional reactions to cues denoting the coming of both pleasant and painful events. And both the positive and negative affects are believed to have important motivating properties.

In their elaboration of this view, McClelland et al. maintain that *all motives* are learned. That is, unless the tendency to respond affectively in either a positive or negative manner is a learned one, it does not qualify as a motive. An unlearned primary affective state that provides the basis for affective conditioning is not in itself a motive, but the learned or redintegrated image thereof is a motive and is motivating. Following this line of reasoning, they arrive at the conclusion that a newborn rat, when it experiences a need for food (primary affect) for the first time, is not motivated, or at least its hunger *motive* does not develop until it has eaten food and the internal need-produced cues have come to function as conditioned stimuli to redintegrate an affective arousal like that experienced while eating. Unfortunately, McClelland and his collaborators do not tell us whether an unlearned *primary affect* has *motivating effects* even though it is not a *motive*. If it does, then their assertion that the hungry baby rat does not have a motive might be construed as having the same meaning as the statement (Brown, 1953a) that a newborn infant, though in need of food, cannot be said to have a drive *for* food. Apparently a motive, in McClelland's terms, is roughly equivalent to Hull's excitatory potential (E) in the sense that both conceptions are composites of associative (habit) factors and motivating (drive) factors. Just as Hull's E, which equals $H \times D$, would have a zero value if the habit strength (H) were zero, so too, McClelland's motive would be nonexistent until a habit had been formed, even though some primary affect (D?) were present. Identifying McClelland's motive with E makes it easier to understand why he insists that all motives *guide* behavior and are learned—this is the H part. It is uncertain, however, whether the *motivating effects* of McClelland's motives can be closely equated to D since no clear descriptions are provided of what a motive does in its role as a motivational determinant of behavior.

Comparing the affective-arousal model with some of the views already considered here is of some interest. As has been noted, the anxiety-conditioning paradigm of McClelland et al. is the same as that employed by Mowrer (1939), Miller and Dollard (1941), Brown and Jacobs (1949), and others, in their treatments of the acquired drive of fear. All of these latter writers, however, differ from McClelland in holding that both the learned fear and the original, unlearned pain-fear reaction have motivating power. Mc-Clelland's positive appetitive motive resembles in marked degree the Hull-Spence r_g–s_g mechanism. Both concepts involve learning, both are essentially expectancies of reward, and the conditions basic to their establishment are essentially identical. The concept of positive affective arousal also appears to be identical with Mowrer's (1950) emotion of "hope," which is said to be aroused by signs of forthcoming rewards and which, like fear, can energize response tendencies.

Verbal Stimuli as Acquired Sources of Drive. It is traditional to assert that human behavior differs from that of animals primarily because of man's capacity to use language. If so, then one is led to suspect that, in so far as human motivational systems are unique, language may be involved to a highly significant degree. Unfortunately, little research has been done on the relation of language to motivation and we have few theories as to how behavior may be affected by words. But since the ability to use words is clearly learned, it is interesting to consider the likelihood that certain words, probably by virtue of the learned responses they evoke, have motivating functions and that these responses, therefore, would qualify as acquired sources of drive.

To begin with, it is clear that some words when spoken by certain individuals can affect the behavior of others as though a motivational variable had been introduced. For example, verbal commands like "Hurry-up!" "Pay attention!" "Come on now!" and "Get ready!" when spoken by a parent to a child, tend to facilitate a variety of different acts such as eating, reading, dressing, walking, or doing the household chores. On some occasions these commands can be given in a relatively soft voice and still be effective. It seems unlikely, therefore, that the motivational effects of such stimuli can be due simply to their acoustic intensity, provided the commands are loud enough to be heard at all. Instead, it seems preferable to assume that *these verbal commands serve as conditioned stimuli to arouse learned responses that have motivating effects upon other responses.* Viewed in this way, words are analogous to fear-arousing CSs, and the learned reactions they elicit are functionally comparable to conditioned fear. Just what these reactions are is uncertain at present, but some promising candidates for the role will be considered shortly.

A distinctive characteristic of motivating words is that they do not, for the most part, provide cues capable of eliciting specific goal-directed acts. In a very real sense they have no definite content. When we tell a child to hurry we often need not specify the activities that must be performed more quickly. Such a goalless command, therefore, may function to speed up an assortment of very different actions. Whatever behavior is in progress, such as running, doing arithmetic problems, bathing, or working, will tend to be facilitated by the command "Hurry!" Because of their widespread power to energize almost any ongoing behavior, these motivating words bear a functional resemblance both to fear and to the so-called primary sources of drive.

Some verbal commands, of course, like "Drink your milk!" are quite specific and make direct reference to a definite concrete act. Such a command may speed up milk-drinking responses, but if this is its only effect it would scarcely qualify as a general motivator. Rather, we would tend to regard it as a specific stimulus to a specific learned response. It fits an associative interpretation better than a motivational one, though the intonation with which the command is given may have motivational effects. Perhaps, therefore, verbal commands serve as learned motivating agents only when they are essentially devoid of specific content.

Now if verbal commands like these, when provided by parents and other individuals, can exert widespread facilitative effects upon ongoing behavior, it appears reasonable to suppose that they would also be motivating when spoken by an individual to himself. For instance, if a person looks at his wrist watch, and sees that only a few minutes remain before he is supposed to meet a friend, he may tell himself to hurry. Presumably, these self-administered verbal commands, because of their similarity to commands from others, can impel the individual to walk more briskly, ride a bicycle faster, or drive his car at a higher speed. Those who engage in competitive activities doubtless often resort to self-exhortations like "I must do my best," "I must give it everything I've got," and "I can't quit now!" Because of the nonspecific nature of these instructions, it is possible, perhaps, for them to enhance whatever activity is being performed by the individual. And since all individuals of a given society tend to learn the same words, the same self-administered "pep talk" could facilitate the offensive and defensive play of a football hero, the pole vaulting of a track man, the cerebrations of a chess champion, or even the responses of an expert on a television quiz program. Moreover, the assumption that the commands can be self-administered means that motivation from this source can perhaps be aroused even in situations where the individual has had no previous specific learning experiences. Certainly people do instruct themselves in these ways in times of stress, and the tendency to do so is unquestionably learned. If such self-instructions can function as motivators, they may play a major role in human behavior as secondary sources of drive.

One of the interesting features of this proposal lies in its possible relations to the need-achievement motive studied by Murray (1938) and by McClelland, Atkinson, Clark, and Lowell (1953). According to the members of the latter group, individuals differ importantly in the degree to which they are concerned with personal success or are motivated to perform at a high level of proficiency in a variety of situations. They differ, that is, in the strength of their need-achievement motive. An individual is said to have *an achievement motive when either positive or negative affect results from his perception of his own performance relative to one or another standard of excellence.*

McClelland and his collaborators base their estimates of the strength of this motive upon subjects' imaginative responses to pictures like those of the Thematic Apperception Test. The subjects are told that the test is one of creative imagination and that their task is to write vivid and dramatic stories about each of the pictures. The stories are scored for degree of achievement motivation by noting whether affectively toned evaluative statements are made about the performances of individuals in the stories. McClelland has presented some evidence to suggest that high need-achievers are also those who habitually strive to succeed in various situations. If this is the case, then these should be the individuals who have best learned to make the kinds of responses that are consistent with their efforts to succeed. According to the view we are exploring, these motivating responses may be, in considerable measure, evoked by self-administered verbal commands.

Consider, for example, the student who tries to do well in every examination or classroom situation. Let us assume that whenever he finds himself being tested, the cues accompanying such situations elicit learned verbal responses such as, "I must try to do well, for if I fail, my family and my sweetheart will be deeply grieved." The phrase "I must try to do well," in this example is believed to function as a motivator in precisely the same way as do parental verbal commands like "Hurry!" or "Pay attention!" In short, *self-administered "try-hard" instructions such as these may constitute the basic "acquired drive" of the high need-achiever and may be used by him in a wide variety of circumstances.*

Our case for this interpretation would be strengthened if it could be demonstrated that high need-achievers are more likely than low need-achievers to provide themselves with instructions of this general sort, that all individuals are more likely to employ these self-instructions in times of stress than at other times, and that high need-achievers tend to use the "try-hard" instructions in a wide variety of different situations where efficient performance is expected of them.

Although self-administered commands have been assumed to operate motivationally because they evoke learned responses, we have not yet considered what these motivating responses might be like. One possibility is that *the commands or exhortations elicit an over-all increase in bodily tension.* As is well known from the experimental studies of Bills (1927) and Courts (1942), moderate degrees of muscular tension tend to facilitate not only performance in motor-skills tasks but even the learning of nonsense syllables. Thus the motivating effects of self-instructions to "try hard" or "to pay attention," might be ascribed to increases in general bodily tonus. Presumably, the steps in the learning process through which such increases in tension come to be associated with verbal commands could be outlined without great difficulty.

A second alternative is that *the "try-hard" types of self-instructions serve as conditioned stimuli for the arousal of motivating emotional states.* Suppose a student says to himself "I must study hard for this exam, because if I don't, I'll flunk out of school." Clearly, these self-instructions could evoke anxiety or fear of failure, which could have motivating effects of the kinds we have already considered. Or, if the verbal cues have become conditioned to fractional anticipatory goal reactions, these expectancies might provide the required motivational increments.

While the anticipation of an unpleasant event (anxiety) and the anticipation of a pleasant event (r_g or appetite) are thus seen, in addition to heightened tension, as possible sources of motivation when aroused by self-instructions, in any practical situation it may be difficult to tell whether one or all are functionally present. Probably all are frequently involved in complex situations with human beings. As McClelland and his collaborators have noted, the anticipation of a reward for good performance is often accompanied by the fear that failure will negate the reward, or even result in actual punishment.

Are Primary-need States Conditionable?

Occasionally people remark that they sometimes are not hungry until they find themselves in a familiar restaurant, whereupon they suddenly become hungry. Such casual descriptions cannot be taken too seriously, but they suggest the possibility that a stimulus might acquire the power to elicit hunger if it has been present on numerous occasions when an organism has been hungry. If hunger can thus be conditioned, and if it affects other responses in motivational ways, it obviously qualifies as a learned source of drive.

Although a number of early observations are consistent with this notion of the conditionability of hunger, none is entirely convincing. Skinner (1933), for example, believed that the phenomenon had been demonstrated in his studies of running-wheel

activity in the rat. He reports that rats, during their initial experiences on the wheel, when tested for six-hour periods would run
at a fairly constant rate for about the first three hours. But during
the last half of the period, their rates of running tended to decline.
If they were fed at the end of the six-hour running period for
several days, however, a "conditioned hunger cycle" was said to
have been developed, since the previously observed slowing down
now tended to disappear. Skinner reports that a number of rats
exhibited this effect, but the records of only a single animal are
presented, and apparently no suitable controls were run. The
phenomenon, therefore, though possibly genuine, need not be
interpreted as indicating that hunger has become conditioned to
cues accompanying the passage of time. Skinner's rats may simply
have been acquiring more skill in running, or cyclic feeding may
have led to the conditioning of motivating fractional anticipatory
responses which could counteract fatigue during the latter part of
the test period (cf. Birch et al., 1958).

A somewhat similar phenomenon, also suggestive of conditioned
hunger, has been reported by Slonaker (1912) and by Shirley
(1928) in their studies of spontaneous activity in the rat. According
to these investigators, when rats are fed at the same hour every
day, they develop a tendency to become increasingly active as
the feeding time approaches, and this activity rhythm can be
altered by changing the feeding schedule. Again, however, these
observations do not constitute acceptable proof of the presence
of conditioned hunger.

Perhaps the first experiment designed specifically to demonstrate
the conditionability of hunger was performed by Anderson (1941).
Since he believed that hunger could become associated with
external cues and aroused by them, he referred to conditioned
hunger as an "externalized drive." He used several groups of rats in
his studies, but only two groups are of special interest here. One of
these was given extensive training in running a multiple-unit maze
for food reward while hungry. A comparable group, that served
as a control, was given no maze training initially. Both groups were
then fed until satiated and were allowed to run through a second
maze but without food reward of any kind. The animals in the
pretrained group performed better in the second maze than did

the controls. From these results Anderson concluded that the second maze, because of its general similarity to the first, served as a stimulus to arouse a learned drive in the pretrained animals but not in the untrained controls.

Interpretations of the Anderson experiment are somewhat hazardous, since each group consisted of only five animals and no statistical evaluations of the differences were presented. Moreover, Siegel (1943), using a four-unit linear maze, could not confirm Anderson's results. Siegel's animals were given satiation trials interposed during the learning series, but neither time nor error scores on these trials exhibited the progressive decrement one would expect on the "externalized drive" hypothesis. As in the case of Skinner's experiment, however, Anderson's results may be genuine and yet due to factors other than conditioned hunger or externalized drive. For instance, the similarity of the two mazes could mediate the transfer of fractional anticipatory eating responses for the experimental animals, and these responses, rather than conditioned hunger, could provide the motivation for the second learning. Or the control animals, since they were not handled as frequently as were the experimental rats, might have run less well in the second maze because they were more emotional. It is also clear that the experimental animals, after having been repeatedly rewarded for running in the first maze, would have a stronger generalized tendency to run in the second maze, even though satiated. If so, they would tend to reach the goal box sooner than the controls, as indeed they did, and would thus be more immediately rewarded by the secondary reinforcing cues of the goal box or by being removed from the maze. And finally, the experimental animals, who had been on a deprivation schedule for many more days than the controls, might have had a greater bodily need for food. If so, the laboratory operation of inducing satiation in both groups might leave a greater residual hunger drive in the experimental rats than in the controls. Differences in residual hunger following apparent satiation—it is rather difficult, incidentally, to satiate rats completely—might account for the results if coupled with reinforcements provided by the goal-box cues or by removal from the maze.

Other attempts to demonstrate the conditionability of hunger have been reported by Myers and Miller (1954) and by Calvin, Bicknell, and Sperling (1953). In the Myers-Miller experiment, hungry rats were placed in the white side of the same box used in Miller's fear-conditioning experiments and were allowed to run into the black side for food when they touched the guillotine door. This preliminary training was designed to associate the cues of the white box with hunger. Three groups of rats were given 10, 30, and 70 food-rewarded trials of this kind. A fourth group of control animals received no comparable training. To test for the presence of an acquired hunger drive, the animals were placed, when thoroughly satiated, in the white box, and the operating mechanism was so arranged that if the rats pressed a small lever the door would open, and access to the black box would be permitted. Thus the problem was whether rats that had been quite hungry in the presence of certain stimuli (white-box cues) would, when satiated, learn to perform a new response, the only consequence of which was the opportunity to escape from those stimuli. If the white-box cues aroused a learned hunger reaction, escape from them should have resulted in a decline in hunger that might reinforce the learning of the new response. Since all four groups learned the new response about equally well, the results failed to indicate that the association of the white-box cues with hunger had led to the formation of a learned hunger drive. Through additional experimentation Myers and Miller were able to conclude that the learning was perhaps motivated by a tendency to explore unfamiliar places, but they rejected the notion that hunger, as such, was conditioned by their procedures.

There are a number of plausible explanations for these negative results. For one, hunger may be a slowly changing state and, therefore, unlike phasic responses, simply cannot be readily conditioned. For another, the animals in running from white to black were obviously exposed to both white and black cues when hungry, and hence the difference between the tendencies of the two sides to evoke hunger may have been extremely small. Or the process of satiating the animals, prior to testing, may be an operation that prevents conditioned hunger from occurring to any detectable degree. If one assumes, for instance, that conditioned hunger, if it exists, might be a response of the contractile portions of the stomach, it seems likely that complete satiation would so tightly fill the stomach as to inhibit any learned contractions.

In the experiment of Calvin, Bicknell, and Sperling, two groups of rats were given preliminary training in a very distinctive environment, consisting principally of a triangularly shaped box with black-and-white striped walls. The training consisted simply in placing the animals in the box without food for 30 minutes each day for 24 days. One group had been deprived of food for 22 hours at the time of these trials and the other had gone without food for only 1 hour. According to the authors, the tactual and visual cues of the box should have acquired more of a tendency to elicit conditioned hunger in the 22-hour group than in the 1-hour group. Tests for the presence of acquired hunger were conducted by noting the amount of food consumed by both groups when they were permitted to eat in the same box under an intermediate and identical level of food deprivation (approximately 12 hours). The four eating periods were 15 minutes long and were spaced over a two-day period at 12-hour intervals. Under these conditions, the formerly hungry group ate more in the triangular box than did the other group. Unfortunately, certain control groups necessary for an unambiguous conditioned-hunger interpretation were not included in the experiment. Because of this omission it is impossible to tell whether the 22-hour group's rate of eating was accelerated, as a consequence of its supposed acquired drive, or whether the 1-hour group's eating rate was depressed. Certainly, the possibility that the 1-hour animals had learned to lie down and sleep in the box, and that this response tended to interfere with eating, cannot be dismissed without further experimentation. It should also be noted that the major result of the experiment, however interpreted, was not confirmed by Siegel and MacDonnel (1954) in a careful repetition of the Calvin et al. investigation.

It would appear from this brief review of the principal literature in this area that only one conclusion is tenable at the present time: there is no convincing experimental evidence to support the contention that hunger, like fear, can, after training, be elicited as a learned response to a conditioned stimulus. Such evidence as does exist is either inherently inconclusive or can be interpreted with equal plausibility by other hypotheses than that of a learned hunger drive.

Summary

We have been concerned in this chapter with motivational systems that have traditionally been described by the terms "secondary drives" or "learned drives." These phenomena occupy a place of considerable importance in contemporary theories, there being many who hold that human behavior is governed more by these acquired drives than by biogenic needs. At the outset, however, it was suggested that the traditional terminology be discarded in favor of the phrase "learned sources of drive," since there appears to be little reason for supposing that the effects of motivation on behavior are multiple rather than unitary.

From a purely descriptive standpoint, a learned source of drive is defined by the observation that an associative variable affects responses other than the one being learned as though a motivational variable were present. Learned responses appear to have motivationlike effects upon other responses either because an increment is added to a nonspecific drive, or because distinctive cues are produced that alter habit strengths, or for both reasons. In any event, the major tasks facing the student of acquired sources of drive are those of discovering which kinds of learned responses function motivationally, of delineating the laws that govern the acquisition and extinction of these motivating responses, and of determining the breadth of influence of motivating responses and the mechanisms through which the effects are produced.

A major section of the chapter has been devoted to the analysis and discussion of studies purporting to show that conditioned fear or anxiety affects certain indicant responses as though it were a motivational variable. Three groups of investigations of this kind have been identified. Those in the first group show that if a reference response is evoked while a conditioned stimulus for fear is present, the reference activity tends to be enhanced or augmented. This is consistent with the activation criterion of motivation. Studies in a second group have repeatedly demonstrated that fear reduction, defined in terms of the cessation of a presumed fear-arousing CS, serves as a reinforcement for the learning of new reactions. The capacity to lead to new learning is also one of the commonly proposed criteria for the identification of motivational variables. A third group of experiments consists of those in which the evocation of conditioned fear results in the inhibition or abandonment of an indicant response. In so far as these studies involve the procedure of arousing fear after the elicitation of the indicant reaction, they, too, are consistent with general conceptions of what constitutes a motivational effect.

A summary of the variables of which fear seems to be a function indicates that these are, in many instances, associative variables of demonstrated significance for the conditioning of other responses. For example, number of conditioning trials, intensity of the UCS, number of extinction trials, and distribution of practice are all known to affect the strength of conditioned fear.

Although a large percentage of the experimental studies of fear have been carried out with animals, there are ample reasons for the belief that acquired anxieties also play a major role in the motivational structure of human subjects. The direct association of neutral and painful stimuli may account for certain human fears, but the acquisition of most of them seems to depend upon higher-order conditioning involving verbal cues in the roles of both conditioned and unconditioned stimuli.

The simple classical-conditioning paradigm, though moderately adequate for fear, cannot be applied directly to such so-called acquired drives as those for money, affection, power, and security. This is because one can neither identify the response that is supposed to have been learned in each case, nor specify an originally adequate unconditioned stimulus capable of eliciting the response at the outset. It seems likely, however, that anxiety plays an important role as the motivational basis for several of these alleged drives. In particular it is suggested that cues indicating a lack of affection, or of power, or of money, can acquire tendencies to elicit conditioned anxiety. Moreover, activities involved in seeking money, power, and so on, whenever they are successful, must inevitably counteract the anxiety-arousing cues occasioned by their absence, and hence will be reinforced by anxiety reduction.

The final sections of the chapter are devoted to the question of whether learned responses other than anxiety can be meaningfully said to have motivational effects upon reference activities. Three somewhat different answers to this question are considered. The first, a conception developed by Hull and Spence, assumes that consummatory goal responses become classically conditioned to cues present at the goal, and that fractional components of the total response complex can be elicited in advance of goal attainment. In addition to providing distinctive cues, these fractional anticipatory goal responses are assumed to add increments to the organism's total drive level and thereby to affect other reactions motivationally.

A second conception, McClelland's affective-arousal model, entails the fundamental assumption that all motives are learned and function both to guide and to motivate behavior. Motives are acquired as the result of the pairing of stimulus cues with changes in affect, the motive being a conditioned affectively toned expectation of the coming of either pleasant or unpleasant events.

The third conception of learned sources of drive, proposed by the writer, emphasizes the possibility that self-administered verbal commands might acquire, through a process of conditioning, the power to affect overt reactions motivationally. These verbal commands may produce their effects by leading to increased general muscular tonus, by evoking conditioned emotional responses, or by the production of stimuli to which facilitating responses have been attached.

In the final section of the chapter the question is raised whether a primary need such as hunger can become conditioned to a neutral stimulus and thereby come to qualify as a learned source of drive. Experimental attempts to demonstrate the phenomenon are reviewed and the conclusion reached that no convincing evidence for the conditionability of hunger has yet been presented.

CHAPTER 6

Motivational Consequences of Frustration and Conflict

IN RECENT YEARS motivational theorists have become increasingly concerned with the possibility that the thwarting of an ongoing response has behavioral consequences resembling those produced by the manipulation of motivational variables. The idea that response interference may be followed by emotional or motivational effects is not new, however, and references to the energizing and/or disorganizing effects of thwarting abound in literary and philosophical works. This same idea also appears in the writings of clinical psychologists and personality theorists, where it is common to encounter the statement that failure to achieve an expected goal may lead to an increase in emotional or other tension and that such tension may modify subsequent behavior. In psychoanalytic writings this general position is expressed in terms of the thwarting of libidinal energy and its redirection into new channels, culminating in the phenomena of conversion and sublimation.

We shall not attempt to trace in detail the history of the more technical formulations of this conception, but Lewin (1931) appears to have been among the first to present a relatively clear statement of the hypothesis. Thus, in his discussion of the consequences of conflict, he states that the opposed field forces in a conflict situation, especially when there is an outer barrier, lead to increases in total tension. Lewin did not refer specifically to the motivational properties of this heightened tension, but some such concept was probably intended, since augmented tension was said to produce restless behavior which, in conjunction with the directive characteristics (forces) of the specific situation, could lead to affective outbursts such as fits of anger.

Some years later, Miller and Stevenson (1936) advanced a similar hypothesis in an effort to explain some unexpected experimental findings. In their investigation, hungry rats were first trained to run down a short straight alley for food and were then given a number of nonreinforced (frustrating) trials. During these trials, it was observed that the animals exhibited an ". . . apparent energization of certain acts such as sniffing, tossing of the head, and cleaning of the whiskers. These acts frequently occurred in almost explosive manner—much more vigorously than during the first learning trials in the alley or than during the period in the cages immediately preceding the runs" (p. 227). In discussing these observations, Miller and Stevenson hypothesized that nonreward may have led to a conflict between the learned responses of eating and the responses elicited by the empty food dish. They assumed, moreover, that the conflict-produced, proprioceptive stimulation could have facilitated other actions much as hand tension was known to facilitate the knee jerk.

Subsequent to this proposal by Miller and Stevenson, somewhat similar hypotheses were advanced by a number of workers (e.g., French, 1944; Rohrer, 1949; Brown and Jacobs, 1949; Sheffield, 1950; Amsel, 1951; Brown and Farber, 1951; Spence, 1951b; Hull, 1952; Amsel and Roussel, 1952). The precise wording varies from writer to writer, but the essential similarity of the several views permits us to state the hypothesis in the following general form: *when stimuli normally capable of eliciting a response are present, but the response is prevented from running its usual course, behavior may be affected as though a motivational variable had been introduced.* Most versions of the concept (cf., e.g., Lawson and

Marx, 1958) include the specific assumption that frustration adds an increment to general drive, but as we shall indicate, the behavioral consequences of thwarting can often be attributed with equal justification to the operation of associative mechanisms.

Methods of Producing Thwarting

At first sight it might seem as though the simplest of procedures would suffice to bring about response interference and that its occurrence could be easily and unambiguously ascertained. Unfortunately, the process is not always so simple, and in any practical experiment, therefore, the frustrating procedures must be chosen and introduced with considerable care. Because of this necessity it is desirable at this point to consider some of the methods that have been used to prevent responses from running their usual courses. Throughout the remainder of the chapter the term *thwarting* will be used simply to mean response interference, while the term *frustration* will be retained to denote the state, condition, or response assumed to be produced by thwarting.

Physical Barriers as Frustrating Agents. One of the commonest ways of producing thwarting is by the use of physical restraint of one kind or another. With animals as subjects, these restraints may take the form of solid barriers in a maze path, restraining harnesses, delay chambers, treadmills, locked Skinner-box levers, and locked food-dish covers. Such restrictive devices may partially or completely prevent the subject's approach to a goal; they may be introduced at different points in the response sequence; and they may be interposed for varying lengths of time. If a response is to be thwarted and frustration is to result, blocking devices must be introduced into situations where cues normally capable of eliciting the to-be-blocked response are present. And from an ideal point of view the introduction of thwarting devices should result in the smallest possible change in the original stimulus complex. Thus, for example, it would be preferable to lock a formerly unlocked food-dish cover than to prevent the animal from having access to it by the interposition of an opaque door.

With the latter method many of the originally present cues are eliminated and new ones are introduced.

Thwarting Produced by the Removal of Maintaining Stimuli. A second frustration-inducing method involves the removal of some of the stimulus objects that normally function to support the response while leaving the remaining stimuli unaltered. For example, food may be removed from its usual position in the goal box of a maze or the lever may be withdrawn from the Skinner box. Under these conditions eating and bar pressing, respectively, are prevented from occurring, and thwarting should result since the residual cues still tend to elicit the response. This method may produce a more marked alteration of the stimulus complex than the first method, but in either instance the response is physically prevented from occurring. The two methods may be regarded as different, because they lead either to the blocking of different responses or to the blocking of the same response at different points. Thus if the cover of a food dish is locked, all of the responses of lifting the cover and of seizing, chewing, and swallowing the food are blocked. But if the cover is left unlatched and food is removed, only the responses of grasping and ingesting the food are thwarted.

Thwarting by the Elicitation of Incompatible Responses. A third way of preventing the appearance of a response is to introduce new stimuli known to be capable of eliciting reactions incompatible with the one to be thwarted. If an individual has been trained to lift his hand from a key when a red light comes on, the response may be inhibited if a green light, to which he has previously been told to press downward, is presented simultaneously with the red. These procedures define what is typically described as a conflict situation. It differs from the frustration situations we have just described in that the thwarted response is not inhibited or blocked by external restraints but by a competitive tendency to make an incompatible reaction. Conflict-induced thwarting of this kind could also be achieved by first associating a given response with one set of cues and then training the subject to perform an incompatible reaction to the same cues. Since this is what often happens in discrimination-learning situations, it serves to emphasize the view (Melton, 1941) that frustration is an almost inevitable accompaniment of all learning.

All of these response-interference methods may be used with either animal or human subjects. But because of the language facility of human subjects, additional techniques of thwarting may be employed with them that cannot be applied to animals. For example, an individual may be said to be thwarted if, after he has completed a task given him by the experimenter, he is told that his performance was very poor. In many such situations the subject's goal is to obtain the experimenter's approval. To withhold such approval or to tell the subject that he has performed poorly is to prevent him from reaching his goal. Verbal commands may also be used with human subjects (and after special training, with animals) to produce a cessation of ongoing behavior, to elicit conflicting response tendencies, and the like. Most such instances of response blocking correspond to what has just been described as the competing-response method, and hence no further discussion of them is necessary.

Criteria of Thwarting

The above methods for preventing the initiation, continuation, or completion of a response are commonly found in studies of frustration, but the use of one or more of them does not guarantee that the response has indeed been thwarted. Hence the conclusion that blocking has actually taken place usually rests, though often in an implicit manner, upon the satisfaction of one or more specific criteria of thwarting. The need for such criteria can be made clear by considering a specific example.

Suppose a dog is moving toward a bone on the other side of a room and that when we grasp him by the collar he stops. From such an observation we might conclude that his approach responses have been frustrated, but it is also possible that he was going to stop anyway at the instant we seized his collar. If the second alternative is true, then clearly the dog's approach behavior has not in fact been thwarted. It is improbable, of course, that the end of a response sequence and the thwarting operation will accidentally coincide in this manner on many occasions. But since the possibility does exist, it is desirable to have definite criteria for deciding whether a response has suffered interference.

Repetitive, Partial Responses as an Index of Thwarting. Perhaps the best basis for concluding that a response has been thwarted is the observation that the subject continues to make responses of the kind that were exhibited just prior to the introduction of the conditions designed to be thwarting. Thus if the dog in the preceding example lunges repeatedly against the restraint imposed on its collar, his behavior serves as an index of response interference. Although the lunges are truncated or fractional parts of the original approach behavior they provide support for the belief that if the restraint had not been imposed, the approach would have continued beyond the point of blocking.

Response Resumption as a Criterion of Thwarting. A second criterion of response interference involves the observation that the subject resumes his original behavior following the removal of the supposedly thwarting conditions. We might, for example, train a cat to approach a white square at the end of a short straight alley and then teach it, in a different situation, to avoid a black circle. If the black circle is now put into the straight alley beside the white square, the cat may not approach to the end as it did formerly. This change in behavior is suggestive of blocking due to a competing (avoidance) tendency. But we can be much more certain that the approach response was actually blocked by the competing response and was not momentarily weakened by other factors, if the approach behavior reappears upon removal of the black circle. Resumption of the original behavior thus seems to indicate blocking. But *a failure to resume the expected response cannot be interpreted to mean the absence of thwarting.* Interference might have occurred when the black circle was first introduced, but if the approach tendency were weak it might have been extinguished by even a relatively short exposure to the negative cue. In such a case approach would not reappear following the removal of the black circle.

Response Failure as a Sign of Thwarting. Still a third criterion is often used in practical experiments on frustration. Though less rigorous than the first two, it is easier to apply. Specifically, if a subject has always, or nearly always, exhibited a concrete bit of behavior in a given situation, and if we have observed this on a relatively large number of occasions, a sudden failure to perform in the expected manner suggests that thwarting may have occurred. The degree of confidence we may have in reaching this conclusion depends upon several factors. If we have observed the behavior on each of 100 different occasions prior to the critical frustration trial, we can be more confident that blocking has actually occurred than if we have seen the response on only five previous occasions. The higher the probability of response evocation, therefore, the stronger the conviction that response failure denotes thwarting. But it must be remembered that response failure, due to the removal of most or all of the original conditioned stimuli, is not a legitimate instance of thwarting. If the appropriate stimuli are eliminated, the tendency for the response to occur will be negligible, and by definition, neither thwarting nor frustration can be produced. Thus, for example, a hungry person who has been forbidden to eat should be far less frustrated in a bare room than in a food-filled restaurant. Presumably frustration will be maximal if a response is blocked in the presence of all the original stimuli with which it has been associated.

Associative Interpretations of Behavior in Frustrating Situations

Although motivational theorists favor the view that response interference leads to a state of frustration that functions, in turn, to increase level of drive, the behavioral consequences of thwarting can often be explained by associative rather than by motivational principles. The kinds of behavior requiring interpretation are usually said to include the following: trial-and-error reactions apparently directed toward the circumvention of obstacles, aggressive responses, escape or withdrawal responses, disorganized actions, anticipations of thwarting, and more vigorous or more persistent versions of the originally thwarted reactions. In broad outline, associative interpretations of these phenomena are identical with associative formulations of the kinds we have already evaluated in Chapter 4. Only a few comments are needed at this point, therefore, to clarify the application of associative theory to thwarting-induced behavior.

To reiterate, the conceptual core of any associative interpretation is the notion that behavioral changes are due to modified associative strengths resulting from changes in the stimulus situation. That such a conception can be applied to behavior in frustrating situations becomes clear when it is realized that response thwarting must inevitably alter external and/or internal stimuli to some degree. Existing cues to which the thwarted response is conditioned may be weakened or strengthened; new stimulus components may be introduced, bringing with them previously learned responses; and currently effective stimulus elements may be eliminated.

To take a specific example, consider Finch's (1942) observation that chimpanzees, who customarily obtain water from a spigot by depressing a plunger, tend to operate the plunger with augmented vigor when the water supply is turned off. As Brown and Farber (1951) have noted, several different versions of an associative theory can be applied to the interpretation of these observations. First, the chimpanzees may have learned from previous experiences with the same spigot or with similar ones that if water is not forthcoming after a gentle push, it will be produced by a strong push. On this view, vigorous responses are simply transferred from old to new situations because of the similarity of the stimuli in the two situations. Second, even when the external stimuli of the frustration situation appear to differ substantially from those which the subject has previously experienced, the transfer of learned responses to the frustrating situation could be mediated by internal cues characteristic of the state or condition of frustration. This mechanism may provide an explanation of the appearance of responses that seem to be maladaptive or inappropriate to the frustration-inducing situation. Moreover, internal cues uniquely characteristic of frustration could underlie one's ability to learn to differentiate between emotional states due to thwarting and other states such as fear or worry. Third, within the limitations of the frustration situation itself, behavior-modifying processes are at work, that may lead to the appearance of more vigorous movements. That is, the tendency to press the plunger gently may be the dominant reaction at first. But if water does not appear, the gentle reaction tends to become extinguished and may be replaced by responses having initially weaker associative strengths but greater inherent vigor.

Concerning other reactions to thwarting, such as trial-and-error behavior, and escape or withdrawal responses, there is little doubt but that many of these activities can also be explained without reference to special-purpose motivational conceptions. Generally speaking, these reactions fall within the province of the student of learning and have usually been interpreted in the light of the principles of transfer of training, reinforcement and extinction, stimulus generalization, and response competition or augmentation. Still other responses, however, are often described by such phrases as "persistent maladaptive reactions," "fixated responses," or by other terms carrying an "abnormal" flavor. Thus if the behavior is identical with, or resembles strongly, activities exhibited at an earlier stage of development or learning, it may be labeled "regressive." But even in these instances explanatory concepts other than those used by students of learning and problem solving may not be needed. Some apparent instances of regression, if not all, can be ascribed to the weakening effects of nonreinforcement upon initially dominant responses and to the subsequent appearance of weaker, previously learned, activities. Clearly, therefore, whenever an increase in drive appears to have been produced by blocking, serious attention should be given to the possibility that the observed behavioral changes are nothing more than instances of altered associative strengths. A paper by Holder, Marx, Holder, and Collier (1957) provides numerous additional examples of the application of associative principles to the interpretation of frustration behavior.

Motivational Theories of Frustration-situation Behavior

Purely associative conceptions may provide satisfactory accounts of many instances of frustration behavior, but the alternative view that thwarting leads to enhanced motivation as well as to altered habit strengths continues to be widely supported. It is appropriate, therefore, before discussing experiments purporting to have demonstrated the motivational effects of frustration, to review, for illustrative purposes, two rather representative motivational theories of frustration-situation behavior.

Brown and Farber's Formulation. The principal elements and relations comprising the Brown-Farber (1951) conception, which incorporates many of the basic assumptions of Hull's (1943) more general behavior theory, are summarized in the diagram of Fig. 6:1. Beginning with the intervening variables at the center of the diagram, we note that frustration (F), which is regarded as a hypothetical (defined) state or condition of an organism, is assumed to be produced when either an inhibitory tendency (I) or a competitive excitatory tendency (E_c) is aroused simultaneously with an ongoing excitatory tendency (E_o). Thus, on this view, either

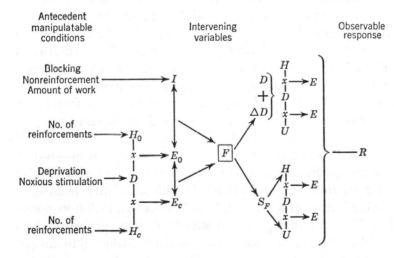

Fig. 6:1. This diagram summarizes the antecedent conditions and hypothetical variables of the frustration theory of Brown and Farber (1951). The state of frustration (F) is assumed to be produced by competition (indicated by double-headed arrows) between an ongoing excitatory tendency (E_o) and either an inhibitory tendency (I) or a competitive excitatory tendency (E_c). These interacting tendencies are shown to depend upon their respective habit strengths (H_o and H_c), drive (D), and upon the indicated antecedent conditions. The consequences of frustration are shown as either an increment in general drive (ΔD), or frustration-specific stimuli (S_F), or both. These factors are assumed to have, respectively, the same kinds of motivational and associative functions assigned to them in Hull's behavior theory

a negative tendency to discontinue reacting or a positive tendency to perform an incompatible act produces frustration. The elements at the left of the diagram indicate that both the initially dominant ongoing tendency and the incompatible competitive one are functions of their respective habit strengths (H_o and H_c) and of nonspecific drive (D). Drive and the habit strengths are in turn assumed to depend upon the antecedent manipulatable conditions of deprivation and noxious stimulation, and upon number of reinforcements, respectively. Likewise, the strength of the interfering inhibitory tendency is shown as varying with degree of response blocking or interference, with nonreinforcement, and with the amount of work involved in the execution of the responses. In this theory physical thwarting, prior to the development of learned tendencies to avoid the barrier, leads to a state of frustration because of the growth of inhibition which competes with the ongoing (thwarted) tendency. Thwarting characteristic of conflict situations is also assumed to produce frustration, since a competitive positive tendency can presumably be as effective as an inhibitory potential in negating an ongoing excitatory tendency.

The behavior-modifying consequences of frustration are shown at the right-hand side of Fig. 6:1. Frustration (F) is regarded as having two primary effects: (1) it results in an increment to general drive (ΔD), and (2) it provides distinctive internal stimuli (S_F). Within the theory, the increment to drive is assumed to have no new functions. It serves simply as another source of drive and thus combines multiplicatively with associative tendencies, whether learned or unlearned, to yield enhanced excitatory potentials. The frustration-generated stimuli, likewise, are assigned no special functions other than those commonly attributed to internal or external stimuli of any kind. Thus, as the diagram indicates, unlearned tendencies (Us) to react to the frustration stimuli may exist from birth, and/or new habit strengths can be built up to these internal stimuli by conditioning. The final elements of the diagram suggest that overt action will be a function of the relative strengths of the several excitatory tendencies aroused in the specific frustrating situation.

It should be clear from the preceding discussion that the Brown-Farber conception is neither purely motivational nor purely associative. It provides a place for both motivational increments and associative changes. In this respect it resembles other, more general, motivational theories of behavior.

Amsel's Frustration Theory. Much of this conception was presented originally by Amsel in 1951, but the most highly developed version appeared in 1958. For Amsel, the major source of frustration is nonreward in situations where the organism has learned to expect a reward. Thus, when a rat enters a goal box where it has been previously fed and finds no food in a customary location, the animal will be thwarted, and frustration will result. Frustration is described at one point as a "motivational condition," but it would appear from Amsel's development that frustration is essentially an *implicit reaction.*

In dealing with frustration as a behavior determinant, Amsel has stressed two major points that, while superficially somewhat different, are nonetheless related. First, the primary reaction of frustration resulting from nonreward is assumed to lead both to an increment in general drive and to frustration-specific internal cues. Moreover, if the enhanced drive persists for a period of time following frustration, whatever actions are elicited within that period should show augmentation, save when strongly competitive responses are evoked by frustration (or other) stimuli. As we shall note below, Amsel and his associates have devised a number of ingenious experiments, the results of which lend substantial support to this expectation.

The second major facet of Amsel's theory consists in the assumption that frustration, like other responses, can be conditioned, and that an organism may, therefore, after a series of nonrewarded trials, come to anticipate frustration. Seward (1951) has made a similar proposal, and Holder, Marx, Holder, and Collier (1957) have reported experimental evidence for the conditionability of frustration. The specific mechanism underlying this effect parallels Hull's r_g–s_g mechanism rather closely. On the first nonrewarded trial, the primary frustration reaction (F) is elicited in the goal box, and through the operation of classical conditioning it becomes associated with the stimulus complex present in the goal box. On subsequent trials, fractional components of the primary frustration reaction can be elicited in the alley (or elsewhere) by cues that are similar (stimulus generalization) to those that were present in the goal box. These anticipatory frustration reactions (r_f) are thus analogous to the anticipatory consummatory responses (r_gs) posited by Hull. Moreover, the r_fs, like the r_gs, are assumed to be accompanied by their own characteristic internal stimuli (s_fs).

Although Amsel does not deny that the arousal of the r_f–s_f sequence may lead to an increment in drive, as Hull and Spence have supposed to be true of the r_g–s_g sequence, the behavior-determining functions of the r_f–s_f mechanism are viewed primarily as the capacity of s_f to elicit specific inhibitory responses. For example, in dealing with behavior in partial reinforcement situations, Amsel assumes that frustration is inherently aversive and that tendencies to avoid a nonrewarding goal box can become associated with the frustration-response–produced stimuli (s_fs). On relatively early trials, therefore, performance tends to be poorer when the response is not rewarded on every occasion, because the s_f-elicited avoidance tendencies interfere with tendencies to approach. On later trials, however, since the animal usually does keep on running, the approach tendencies become more and more strongly attached to the frustration stimuli. When all reinforcement is omitted during extinction, partially reinforced animals perform more efficiently than continuously rewarded controls because the former subjects have associated the frustration stimuli with running, but the latter have not.

Incidentally, Amsel's assumption that frustration is both motivating and aversive is quite in accord with the views expressed here. Specifically, to assert that an animal tends to avoid a situation where frustration has been produced and drive has been increased is consistent with our third criterion for identifying motivational variables (Chapter 2). On this criterion a variable is identified as motivational if behavior antedating its introduction tends to be weakened or abandoned. It is not paradoxical, therefore, to say that an organism can learn to anticipate and to avoid frustration and yet exhibit response augmentation immediately following thwarting.

A detailed comparison of the Amsel and Brown-Farber theories would take us beyond the intended scope of this book, but it is interesting to observe that the appearance of anticipatory frustration can be explained by the latter theory without the added assumption that frustration is directly conditionable. On this view the introduction of nonrewarded trials after an animal has been repeatedly reinforced for approaching a goal would be expected to lead to the development of avoidance tendencies. Through the operation of stimulus generalization, these tendencies could be elicited, along with approach tendencies, in the alley leading to the goal box. Since frustration is assumed to arise from the competition between one excitatory tendency and another, it follows that frustration could thus be generated prior to reaching a goal. Apparent instances of conditioned frustration could in this way be explained in terms of conditioned and generalized response tendencies which produce frustration through their competitive interaction.

Evaluating the Motivational Effects of Thwarting

Should one proceed on the assumption that thwarting does, in fact, result in drive enhancement it becomes necessary to consider the practical question of how this phenomenon can be unambiguously demonstrated. In principle, of course, an experiment designed to reveal the presence of frustration-produced drive must be essentially the same as all other investigations purporting to show that variables are functioning motivationally. In terms of the position taken here, this means that frustration can be said to have led to an increment in drive when at least one of the basic criteria for the identification of a motivational variable has been met and when there is little reason to suppose that the observations are attributable solely to altered associative strengths.

Frustration Drive as a General Energizer. The large majority of experiments to be considered in the following pages have been designed on the assumption that intensified behavior should be exhibited at or near the time of thwarting. Implicitly, therefore, if not explicitly, most investigators have adopted a criterion for identifying frustration or frustration effects that is identical with our first criterion suggested in Chapter 2.

Prior to about 1950 the only evidence favoring the hypothesis of frustration-induced drive was casual and nonsystematic. Early workers in the field of learning frequently noted that when motivated subjects encountered obstructions in problem-solving and trial-and-error situations, highly energetic activity was the result. Thorndike (1898), for example, reported that cats in attempting to escape from the confinement of a problem box struggled with "extraordinary vigor." Likewise, Hamilton (1916), during his extensive comparative studies of reactions to insoluble problems, often observed that his subjects exhibited excited, emotional behavior. Moreover, an increase in response strength during the first few extinction trials has been reported for classically conditioned responses by Switzer, 1930, Hilgard and Marquis, 1935, and Hovland, 1936. Whether this phenomenon constitutes a legitimate instance of frustration drive is uncertain, although omitting the UCS may strengthen competitive inhibitory tendencies and thereby induce some measure of frustration.

Observations of increased response vigor following the thwarting of a well-learned response appear in increasing numbers during the third and fourth decades of the present century. For example, Skinner (1932) found the rat's rate of eating to be higher after a temporary period of enforced waiting than immediately prior to the beginning of the frustration period. Skinner used the term "emotional" in describing this effect, but he seems not to have considered the heightened rate to be a frustration-drive phenomenon. Miller and Stevenson (1936) and Finch (1942), whose studies we have already mentioned, reported a marked intensification of certain responses following nonreward in a situation where reward had formerly been consistently obtained. Others, such as Crespi (1944), had also observed intensified activity following both nonreward and a shift from large to small reward, and Brown and Gentry (1948) reported numerous instances in which periods of delay were preceded by heightened emotional behavior.

Perhaps the earliest experimental study directed specifically toward demonstrating the presence of frustration drive and toward the discovery of the variables on which it depends is that by Marzocco (1951). Basing his theorizing, in part, upon the suggestions of Brown and Farber (1951), Marzocco reasoned that the hypothetical state resulting from thwarting would function as an irrelevant drive to raise the organism's total effective drive level. Moreover, this heightened drive would be expected to increase the amplitude of any response evoked during thwarting, provided stimuli accompanying frustration did not lead to excessively strong competing responses. He also hypothesized that frustration would increase with degree of hunger and with amount of practice in making the frustrated response. And since the frustration state might be relatively transient, increasing the length of the interval between successive frustrated responses should weaken the effect of a previous frustration upon a subsequent reaction.

To test these predictions, Marzocco trained 81 rats in a modified Skinner box in which measures could be obtained of the force with which the rats depressed the bar. The general procedure involved a number of days devoted to habituation and taming followed by one day of training in bar-pressing and by a second day of testing for frustration-drive effects. On the frustration day, all animals were given three rewarded trials followed by a series of consistently nonrewarded (frustrating) trials. Three subjects were assigned at random to each of the cells of a $3 \times 3 \times 3$ factorial design. The variables of the design and their levels were: (1) hours without food at the time of frustration: 1, 16, and 22; (2) number of rewarded bar-pressing trials on the acquisition day: 8, 24, and 72; and (3) time (in seconds) between successive nonrewarded trials on the frustration day: 10, 20, and 40. Marzocco's measure of frustration-drive effects was a difference score obtained for each rat by subtracting the mean force it exerted on the bar during the first four trials of the frustration day from the mean force exerted on the next four. When the responses for all 81 rats were grouped together, the rise in force due to thwarting proved to be very striking and highly significant. Figure 6:2 shows this effect quite clearly. Here it will be seen that immediately following the fourth trial (the first nonrewarded one) the average force rises from 28 to 35.9 grams. Moreover, if 28 grams is taken as a reference level, it is apparent that in spite of continued nonreward the rats continued to press the lever with "supernormal" vigor until about the seventeenth trial.

When the data for the differently treated groups were analyzed, Marzocco found the frustration effect to be significantly related to

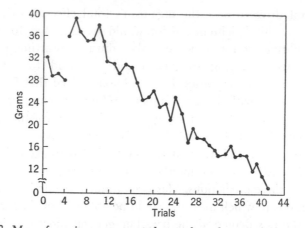

FIG. 6:2. Mean force in grams exerted on a lever by rats during a series of trials in which the first three trials were followed by food reward and the remainder were not. The marked increase in vigor of response after the first nonrewarded trial (trial 4) provides a clear example of the energizing effects of thwarting upon subsequent responses. (*From Marzocco, 1951.*)

hours of food deprivation at the time of frustration, with the frustration-produced increase in bar-pressing force rising with degree of hunger. He also found an increasing frustration effect as the intertrial interval was shortened, though the trend was not statistically significant. This relation had been predicted on the ground that the frustration generated on one nonrewarded trial should have a greater effect on the vigor of the following response when the interval between them was short. The frustration effect was also expected to increase directly with number of reinforced trials. Both the 24- and 72-reinforcement groups showed a greater increase in force than did the 8-reinforcement group, but the 72-trial group showed less of the effect than did the 24-trial animals.

Taken as a whole, Marzocco's study provides clear evidence for increased response vigor following thwarting. But his study does not prove that thwarting leads to an increment in drive. During their preexperimental history his animals could have learned in a variety of situations to exert more vigorous responses in order to circumvent barriers or to overcome resistance to the completion of a response. If so, and if the bar-pressing situation could be regarded as sufficiently similar to the situations in which such responses had been learned, the transfer of the learned reactions to the new situation could be explained. Alternatively, the animals might have learned during their bar-pressing acquisition trials that if no reward followed a weak response, a more vigorous press would successfully activate the food-release mechanism. Consequently, when no food appeared during extinction trials, its absence would provide cues tending to evoke more vigorous responses. If this were the correct interpretation, however, the experimental variable of number of reinforcements should have been more clearly related to the frustration effect. Finally, one might even look upon Marzocco's results as an instance of regression. His data show that the mean force exerted on the bar by a group of 27 rats during acquisition was 33.5 grams for the first 10 rewarded trials and 20.6 grams for the last 10 (of 72) trials. Thus the animals were apparently learning, during their bar-pressing trials, to exert less and less force on the bar. If pressing the bar vigorously is regarded as the "earlier habit" and weaker pressing as the "later habit," then the animals' frustration behavior might reasonably be described as "regression" to an earlier form of activity. These various interpretations of Marzocco's results reemphasize the point that experiments purporting to demonstrate the frustration-drive effect must be done with great care if the credibility of associative conceptions is to be minimized. That this is rather difficult to accomplish will become clearer as we examine additional studies of the frustration-drive phenomenon.

Amsel and Roussel's (1952) experiment constitutes an ingenious attempt to demonstrate the energizing effects of nonreward upon locomotor behavior in the rat. Initially, these investigators trained their rats to run down a short straight alley into a goal box for food and then out into a second connecting alley and to a second goal box for a second bit of food. Preliminary training consisted of 84 trials, on each of which the rats obtained food in both goal boxes. During an additional 36 trials, food was omitted from the first goal box on a randomly selected half of the runs. These 18 nonrewarded trials constituted the frustrating trials. The effects of thwarting were evaluated by measuring the rats' speed of running in the second section and comparing the values obtained on frustrating (nonrewarded) trials with those obtained on rewarded trials

On all trials food was present in the second goal box. The results of these manipulations upon the median running times of the 18 subjects in the second alley are summarized in Fig. 6:3. Here it will be seen that the rats' running time, when reward was provided in both goal boxes, had reached a stable level at the end of the 28 days (3 trials daily) of preliminary training. Shortly after the introduction of the frustration trials, however, running time on those trials dropped to a new level, which proved to be significantly lower than the level maintained on further reward trials. Amsel and Roussel concluded from these data that frustration due to non-reward in the first goal box produced an addition to the motivational complex, which resulted in the establishment of a new and higher maximum speed of running.

Taken at face value, this finding supports the frustration-drive hypothesis, but as Amsel and Roussel point out, other interpretations are possible. For example, they note that the difference in the performance of the animals on the rewarded and frustration

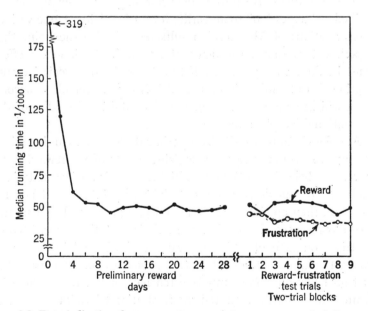

FIG. 6:3. Data indicating that rats tend to run faster on nonrewarded (frustrating) trials than on rewarded trials when the two kinds of trials are administered alternately following a long period of training during which every trial has been rewarded. (*Adapted from Amsel and Roussel, 1952.*)

test trials could mean either a depression of performance on rewarded trials or heightened performance on nonreward trials.
Speed of running during the preliminary reward days and on the
rewarded test trials might have been reduced because the animals
had eaten food in the first goal box just before entering the second alley. If this were correct, the frustration-drive hypothesis
would not be needed to explain faster running on nonrewarded
trials.

Amsel and Roussel suggest, however, that two factors support
the argument against this performance-depression hypothesis. First,
the omission of customary reward in the first goal box should have
altered the stimulus complex (taste of food in the mouth, for example) to which running had been conditioned, and this would
function to reduce running speed on nonrewarded trials. Second,
experimental evidence from other studies shows that a small
amount of prefeeding may increase the level of performance. Since
both of these factors would have an effect opposite to that described by the performance-depression explanation, Amsel and
Roussel do not consider that interpretation the only reasonable
one.

Support for the wisdom of their view has recently been obtained
by Wagner (1959). In a similar experiment, where the frustration-
drive effect was clearly demonstrated, he ran an additional control
group, whose members were detained for a few seconds in the first
goal box but were never fed therein. On the response-depression
hypothesis, these animals, whose hunger had not been reduced
just prior to running in the second alley, should have run faster
in that alley than rats that had been fed in the first goal box.
However, these control subjects of Wagner's ran at about the
same speed in the second alley as did the animals that consumed
a pellet in the first goal box.

Before turning to other types of studies purporting to demonstrate the frustration-drive effect, we should note that Amsel and
his associates (e.g., Roussel, 1952) have confirmed the main finding of the Amsel and Roussel study on a number of occasions.
Moreover, they have also shown (Amsel and Hancock, 1957) that
the frustration effect is more marked if the first alley is similar to
the first goal box than if it is different. This observation is consist-

ent with their assumption that frustration is a consequence of the thwarting of an expectancy (r_g-s_g) for a goal object. If the first alley is the same color as the first goal box it should elicit a stronger anticipation of food than if the two are different, and the frustration of the stronger expectancy should lead to a bigger increment in drive with a greater enhancement of running speed in the second alley.

Experimental attempts to demonstrate the presence of frustration-drive effects on human subjects, particularly children, have been reported quite frequently in recent times. It is impossible here to review each of these studies in detail, but those by Haner and Brown (1955) and by Holton (1956) serve as excellent representative examples.

One of the purposes of the Haner-Brown study was to try to extend and clarify the frustration-aggression hypothesis of Dollard, Doob, Miller, Mowrer, and Sears (1939). According to these latter writers, aggression is a function of, among other things, degree of *instigation to action*. But Haner and Brown regard instigation to action as being equivalent to Hull's excitatory potential, which includes both habit and drive, and hold that Dollard et al. fail, in their handling of this concept, to recognize the importance of the habit strength component. They make the prediction, therefore, that if behavior is frustrated near the goal, where habit strength is presumed to be stronger, the "amount of disturbance experienced" will be greater than if the sequence is interrupted at some point farther from the goal. Moreover, intensity of aggressive action should vary directly with "amount of disturbance experienced." In the terminology of this chapter, Haner and Brown are asserting that degree of frustration is directly related to habit strength at the time of thwarting and that the motivational increment is, in turn, a direct function of degree of frustration. This, it will be recalled, was essentially the position taken by Marzocco.

In attempting to test this assertion, Haner and Brown gave elementary school children a serial task in which they had to place 36 marbles, one at a time, into 36 holes in a board. They were told that four successful completions of the task would bring a prize but that the time allotted to each trial would be limited and variable. On certain trials the experimenter operated a mechanism which caused whatever marbles had been placed on the board to drop though the holes into a box below. On these frustration trials a buzzer would sound and the subjects had to depress a spring-loaded plunger to turn off the buzzer and initiate a new trial. Degree of frustration-induced drive was inferred from the amount of downward movement of the plunger. On various trials all subjects were frustrated at four points of proximity to the goal, that is, after 9, 18, 27, or 32 marbles had been placed in the holes on the board. The buzzer was also sounded after all 36 marbles had been used. But this, by definition, was not a frustration trial, since the goal (or a subgoal, at least) had been reached.

The results of the plunger-pushing measurements obtained by Haner and Brown are shown in Fig. 6:4. As this figure shows, when the point of frustration was moved closer and closer to the goal, as expressed by the number of marbles placed on the board, the mean amount of plunger depression increased progressively, reaching a peak at the 32-marble point, which was eight-ninths of the distance to the goal. But the displacement of the plunger dropped markedly when all 36 marbles had been placed and the goal had been reached. According to the authors, the increase in plunger force from the 9-marble point of interruption to the 32-marble point was highly significant statistically. Consequently, their hypothesis concerning the increase in motivational effects of frustration with increasing habit strength tended to be supported.

One of the noteworthy features of the Haner-Brown study is

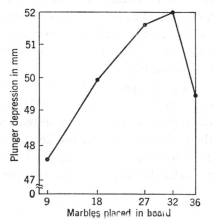

FIG. 6:4. Mean amplitude of plunger-depressing responses made by children following the induction of frustration at varying distances from a goal. Since the task was to place 36 marbles in holes in a board, the distance from the goal decreased with increasing numbers of marbles placed. (*Adapted from Haner and Brown,* 1955.)

that the response of plunger pressing, from which motivational effects were inferred, was clearly different from the thwarted instrumental response of marble placing. Because of this, an interpretation involving transfer of training rather than increased motivation does not seem highly plausible. On such a view, one would have to suppose that the children had learned in very similar situations that vigorous plunger-pressing responses or closely similar ones would enable them to circumvent or remove a thwarting agent more quickly than weak plunger presses. Some children, of course, might have had an opportunity to acquire such habits. But generally speaking, when an explanation rests upon the principles of stimulus generalization, regression, and the like, its plausibility is reduced if the indicator response differs from the thwarted instrumental response and if the indicator response is causally unrelated to the removal or circumvention of the barrier.

Holton (1956) has also obtained evidence favoring the hypothesis that frustration-drive effects become greater with increased nearness to a goal and with increasing numbers of reinforcements of the thwarted response. In the initial phase of her experiment, three groups of preschool children were taught to make a simple spatial discrimination. Two identical orange-colored stimulus patches were presented against a black background, and the child's task was to push against one of the patches. A correct response was followed by a marble reward, and a prize could be won by accumulating a stated number of marbles. Thwarting was induced by failure to reinforce the panel-pressing response with a marble. The apparatus was constructed so that accurate measurements could be made of the force with which each of the stimulus panels was pushed by the subjects during both rewarded and frustration trials.

Three groups of subjects were used by Holton. The members of one were permitted to make only 13 correct responses before being thwarted near the goal. A second group was also frustrated near the goal, but after making 26 correct responses. The third group was given 26 reinforced trials, but nonreward was introduced at a greater distance from the goal than in the case of the first two groups.

To evaluate the frustration-drive effects, Holton compared the mean force exerted on the four trials preceding nonreward with the mean force on the four trials following nonreward. The values obtained from these measurements for the three groups are plotted in Fig. 6:5.

As this figure shows, all three groups pushed harder on the stimulus panels on the first four nonrewarded trials than they did on the preceding rewarded trials. Actually, only one of the 45 subjects in the three groups failed to exhibit a higher mean score for the nonrewarded trials than for the rewarded ones. Thus the finding that nonreward leads to more vigorous responses receives further confirmation. Holton also found, as the figure indicates, that of the two groups blocked near the goal, the one given 26 reinforcements prior to blocking exhibited a significantly greater increase in response amplitude than the 13-trial group. In addition, the group blocked near the goal (26–N) showed a greater increase in force than the comparably trained group (26–F) that was blocked farther from the goal. This is consistent with the results

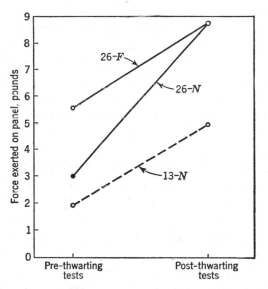

Fɪɢ. 6:5. Mean force exerted on response panels by children before and after thwarting. The curve marked 26–F denotes the responses of a group given 26 reinforcements and blocked far from the goal. The curves labeled 26–N and 13–N apply to groups blocked near the goal after 26 and 13 reinforcements, respectively. (*Adapted from Holton, 1956.*)

of the Haner-Brown experiment and with theoretical expectations.

Reduction in Frustration Drive as Reinforcement. The investigations reviewed in the preceding section all point to the conclusion that response enhancement at or near the time of thwarting fits the view of thwarting as a source of drive. It is also reasonable to suppose, if we bear in mind our second criterion for the identification of a motivational variable (Chapter 2), that a reduction in frustration drive should be reinforcing. Thus one would expect that the strength of a response would increase if that response were followed by a reduction in frustration.

As is sometimes the case with ideas such as this, the supporting evidence, though plentiful, is almost entirely anecdotal. In the typical trial-and-error situation, for instance, an organism tends to learn whatever response is successful in leading to the circumvention of the thwarting circumstances or to the correct solution of the problem. Such learning may be due, in part, to a reduction in frustration-produced drive following the performance of the correct reaction. But in these situations the problem-solving response nearly always leads to the receipt of food or to other reinforcers. This makes it difficult to decide whether the escape reaction is being reinforced by a reduction in frustration drive or by some quite different agent. There are instances, however, such as that reported by Guthrie and Horton (1946), in which animals learn to escape from a problem box by performing a specific act, yet do not consume the reward when they get out. In such cases the reinforcement may be provided by a decrease in frustration drive since hunger remains unaffected.

Negative Effects of Increases in Frustration Drive. Our third criterion for the identification of a motivational variable leads to the expectation that reactions followed by increased drive due to thwarting should tend to be weakened. As noted above, Amsel's supposition that frustration is an aversive condition is consistent with this view.

Probably the clearest evidence for the negative effects of thwarting upon prefrustration behavior is provided by an experiment of Holder, Marx, Holder, and Collier (1957). These investigators trained hungry rats to run down a 90-inch straight alley for food reward. During a series of 25 such training trials, administered one per day, the rats were detained for 1 second in a delay chamber at the middle of the runway. On subsequent test trials, one-third of the subjects continued to run under the same conditions as during training, another third were detained for 15 seconds in the delay box, and the remaining third were delayed for 45 seconds. Both running- and starting-time measures revealed that the increased delay led to better performance in the post-delay-box section of the alley—this supports the concept of frustration drive as an energizer—but to poorer performance in the pre-delay-box segment. Granting the plausibility of our third motivation-variable criterion, we may conclude that this latter effect, like the former, supports the assumption that thwarting serves as a source of drive. As Holder et al. point out, the reduction in response strength in the pre-delay segment can be explained, within Amsel's theory, as due to the growth of an anticipatory frustration reaction or, following Brown and Farber, as a consequence of the conditioning of avoidance responses to the noxious cues accompanying frustration. Further experimental evidence, indicating that delays lead to the weakening of pre-delay responses can be found in the studies of Cooper (1938), Gilhousen (1938), Brown and Gentry (1948), and Holder (1951).

Conflict as a Source of Drive. Throughout the foregoing pages we have proceeded on the assumption that frustrating conditions such as physical blocks, delays, and removal of rewards may all involve the development of tendencies that are antagonistic to the tendency being thwarted. And since the simultaneous arousal of competitive tendencies is also the definitive feature of conflict situations, no attempt has been made to distinguish between frustration and conflict. In so far as conflict and frustration cannot be differentiated, experiments purporting to have demonstrated that conflict leads to an increment in drive would necessarily be of the same general sort as those designed to detect frustration-generated drive. Studies by Hollenberg and Sperry (1951), and by Lowell (1952a), which rest on unpublished theoretical developments of J. W. M. Whiting, serve as examples of such research.

In concluding this chapter, we find it interesting to note that the conflict-drive hypothesis has been extended from individual behavior situations to social and cultural phenomena by Whiting and Child (1953). These authors tabulated the child-rearing practices of 75 primitive societies and then obtained ratings of "initial satisfaction" and "socialization anxiety." The term *initial satisfaction* refers to the positive (pleasant or rewarding) consequences of the socialization process at the individual level. *Socialization anxiety*, however, is the consequence of severity of discipline during child training and is approximately equivalent to an acquired-fear reaction. Ratings on each of these two variables were obtained for each culture in a number of different areas of parent-child interaction such as aggression, weaning, and toilet training. The ratings of initial satisfaction and socialization anxiety were then used by Whiting and Child to test a number of hypotheses about relations between child-rearing practices and various aspects of adult personality patterns.

The concept of conflict-produced drive is introduced in Whiting and Child's treatment of the origins of the fear of others. Here it is suggested that fears of human and animal spirits derive in considerable measure from anxieties about the expression of aggression. Individuals acquire anxieties concerning aggressive acts toward their parents during childhood as a result of the parents' punitive role in the socialization process. These fears of parents and near relatives, primarily, are assumed to generalize to other people and/or spirits (human or animal) to the degree that the generalized stimulus patterns resemble the persons originally responsible for frustration and punishment. From hypotheses such as these Whiting and Child predict, and confirm their prediction from child-rearing and other data, that members of primitive societies should exhibit a greater fear of human spirits than of animal spirits. Moreover, by the use of the conflict-drive hypothesis, they successfully predict that societies with high aggression anxiety will have more nearly equal tendencies to fear human and animal spirits than will societies with low aggression anxiety. The precise steps in this and in other deductions made by Whiting and Child are too detailed for presentation here; but it is significant that their conflict-drive concept leads to reasonably clear-cut, testable predictions, which apparently could not have been made without its use.

Summary

The problem of whether an increase in general drive is produced by frustrating or conflictful situations serves as the focal point for the discussions of this chapter. When recast into a form consistent with the conceptual framework of earlier chapters, this is the problem of whether a reference reaction, if it is elicited at about the time some other activity is thwarted, will be affected as though a motivational variable had been introduced. Throughout the chapter the terms thwarting and frustration are used, respectively, to designate the fact of response interference and the state or condition produced by interference.

A variety of methods may be employed to prevent the initiation, continuation, or completion of a response. In frustration experiments with animal subjects, physically restrictive devices are commonly used. These may take the form of solid barriers in a maze pathway, delay chambers, restraining harnesses, and locked food-dish covers. Thwarting may also be produced by removing some of the stimulus objects upon which the to-be-thwarted response depends or by introducing new stimuli to which incompatible reactions have been, or may become, conditioned. With human subjects, thwarting can be produced by verbal instructions to the effect that the subject has failed or has performed at an unsatisfactory level. In general, the ideal method for producing thwarting would seem to be one that interferes with a response or response chain while producing the least possible alteration of the normal, response-eliciting stimulus complex.

The introduction of experimental conditions believed to be thwarting is not alone sufficient to insure that the to-be-blocked response will indeed suffer interference. Typically, therefore, the success of a blocking operation is inferred from one or more overt behavioral changes. The observation that a subject repeatedly makes partial responses resembling his prethwarted reactions serves as one criterion for evaluating the success of thwarting operations. Abrupt response failure following the introduction of a frustrating condition and response resumption upon the removal of that condition may also indicate successful response blocking.

Motivational theorists, for the most part, are partial to the view that thwarting induces a state (sometimes a response) of frustration, which in turn raises the subject's level of drive. Nevertheless, interpretations containing no reference to drive as such may also provide satisfactory accounts of certain phenomena characteristic of thwarting. In general, such explanations of frustration-situation behavior rely on the view that thwarting must necessarily modify stimulus conditions and hence associative strengths. Increased vigor of responding, persistent trial-and-error behavior, and other activities typical of frustrating situations are thus seen as instances of transfer of training, stimulus generalization, and the learning of new responses to cues attending thwarting.

Writers favoring motivational views generally concur in assuming that frustration leads both to an increment in drive and to the production of frustration-specific stimuli. For some authors, however, frustration assumes the systematic status of a response. This leads to the conclusion that frustration can be conditioned and can therefore be elicited in complete or in fragmentary form by appropriate stimuli. The weakening of instrumental reactions antedating frustration is explained on this view as an instance of the occurrence of fractional anticipatory frustration reactions having inhibitory properties.

In the majority of experiments designed to reveal the motivating properties of frustration, an increase in the strength of an indicant response has been taken as the criterion of heightened drive. Thus, enhanced running speed following nonreward or delay, heightened vigor of lever pressing following extinction trials, and excited or exaggerated movements have all provided support for the frustration-drive conception. The weakening or abandonment of responses antedating an increase in drive is also a potentially useful criterion for the identification of motivational variables. Experimental data from studies in which delays are introduced in runways or mazes are coordinate with this criterion, since delay typically leads to poorer performance in pre-delay portions of a maze. Systematic data supporting the supposition that a reduction in frustration drive functions as reinforcement for the learning of new responses are conspicuously absent.

Thwarting may usually, if not always, give rise to the appearance of competitive reaction tendencies, and since conflict is commonly defined by reference to response competition, no attempt has been made here to differentiate between frustration and conflict. Some experimental findings suggest that situations labeled "conflictful," like those termed "frustrating," may generate increases in level of motivation.

CHAPTER 7

Motivational Variables and Human Performance

IN THE PRECEDING CHAPTERS the major portion of the experimental and illustrative material was drawn from investigations of animal behavior. This procedure can be justified on the ground that in large measure the problems and theoretical issues under examination arose from basic experiments with animal subjects and that these investigations have been more extensive and precise than studies of human motivation. Significant contributions have been made, of course, to our knowledge of motivation by research workers who have been concerned exclusively with human behavior. But human beings, probably because of the extensive role that language plays in their activities, present us with unique motivational problems requiring special consideration. This and the following chapter, therefore, are exclusively devoted to the analysis of these problems. Although a sharp distinction probably cannot be drawn between behavior that is perceptual and behavior that is not, material bearing on the relations of motivational variables to performance in perceptual tasks has been treated separately in Chapter 8.

In its organizational structure, this chapter parallels our earlier discussion of methods of defining drive. Thus, in Chapter 2, the assertion was made that drive can be independently defined by reference to antecedent conditions, to stimulus conditions, to organic states, or to subjects' responses in standardized test situations. Here, therefore, we shall consider some of the effects on human performance of drive-level variations believed to result from deprivation and from the administration of strong stimuli, as well as the effects of drive differences defined in terms of individual differences in test-situation behavior.

Deprivation-induced Motivation

Because of practical difficulties attending the induction of severe deprivation states in human subjects, research studies of the effects of such deprivations on performance are rare. Moreover, of relevant experiments, a majority have involved behavior that is typically termed "perceptual" and hence are discussed in the following chapter.

On purely theoretical grounds, whether of the motivational or associative variety, one would anticipate that specific behavioral changes would be exhibited when human subjects are deprived of food. For example, from the multiplicative-drive theory it would be predicted that food deprivation would lead to an increase in D and hence to an increase in the strengths of all excitatory tendencies. Performance level in a variety of situations should be improved by hunger, therefore, provided only that the tendencies to perform the correct responses are the dominant ones in the hierarchy of reactive tendencies. However, increased drive should lead to poorer performance whenever incorrect tendencies are stronger than correct ones. Coupled with the effects of increases in D are effects attributable to changes in internal stimuli (S_{MVS}), including self-administered verbal commands or instructions. With extended periods of deprivation, these cues may increase in intensity, numerosity, or persistence, and since specific correct or incorrect response tendencies may be associated with these stimuli, marked changes in the relative strengths of all reactive tendencies could accompany severe deprivation. As a consequence, definite predictions can be made only when knowledge of the comparative strengths of task-relevant and task-irrelevant tendencies is available. Behavior is jointly determined by external and internal stimuli, however, and hence the effects of deprivation should also depend, to a considerable degree, on the kinds of stimuli provided by the behavior-testing situation and on their relations to the subjects' learning history. Thus a stimulus such as a picture of spaghetti would presumably be more likely to elicit food-related responses from a hungry Italian child than from a child who has had fewer opportunities to associate such responses with both internal hunger stimuli and the visual cues of spaghetti.

The view that hunger should, as a consequence of intensified internal cues, lead to an increase in food-related verbal responses is supported in some degree by both anecdotal and experimental evidence. Historical reports of personal experiences during periods of famine or extended deprivation (Sorokin, 1942) indicate that at such times concern with food becomes a topic of overwhelming importance, toward which the individual's thoughts and activities are entirely and unceasingly directed. For the person who is starving food becomes the central focus of daydreams and conversations.

Of especial interest in this connection is a report by Brožek, Guetzkow, and Baldwin (1951) of a study of semistarvation conducted during the year 1944–1945. The subjects of this experiment, who were conscientious objectors, volunteered to undergo a period of greatly reduced food intake for a period of 24 weeks. Consistent with the reports of ill-fated expeditions by explorers and others, the 36 semistarved subjects gave clear evidence that much of their waking thoughts centered on food and on related matters such as cooking and agriculture. "They talked and read about food. Their attention was attracted by the scenes of food and eating in the movies. . . . Almost any discussion was likely to end by talking about food. Cook books, menus, even such dry information as reading bulletins on food production became fascinating subjects to men who, a few months earlier, gave little thought to the fine points of the culinary art or the intricacies of agricultural statistics" (p. 250). But these men, when examined by psychological instruments such as a free-association test, the

Rorschach test, and Rosenzweig's Picture Frustration Test, gave almost no indication of enhanced food-related responses. The only positive result was that they made significantly more uncommon (idiosyncratic) responses to the food words of the free-association test than did a group of nonhungry control subjects. The finding that a greater total number of responses was given to the Rorschach test after six months of starvation than during an initial control period is consistent with the idea that the drive due to hunger should enhance all responses. But similar increases were not found in the case of other measures, and it may be that this was simply a retest phenomenon, as Brožek et al. suggest.

Just why the psychological tests yielded negative results is unclear, but positive evidence for the effects of hunger on behavior might have been obtained had different tests been used. It is difficult, on intuitive grounds, to believe that either the Rorschach test or the Rosenzweig Picture Frustration Test provide stimuli capable of eliciting differential responses from hungry and nonhungry subjects. This is indicated by the fact that seven subjects never gave a food response to the Rorschach test, and only eight of the 100 stimulus words used in the free-association test were clearly related to food and eating. Perhaps, therefore, a closer relationship between the psychological-test data and other behavioral criteria would have been obtained had the tests contained a larger proportion of hunger-related stimulus items.

The investigation of Brožek et al. involved a more protracted and severe deprivation state than that of any other experimental study. Short-term deprivation effects, however, have been studied in a few instances. For example, Sanford (1936), in what may have been the first attempt to investigate the influence of hunger on imaginal processes, administered word-association and picture-interpretation tests to school children both before and after lunch. More than twice as many food-related responses were elicited by the prelunch tests as by the postlunch tests. In a subsequent study, using college students, Sanford (1937) found a progressively increasing tendency for food-relevant responses to occur on a battery of tests as deprivation was increased up to 24 hours.

In an experiment on food deprivation and imaginative processes, Atkinson and McClelland (1948) asked subjects who had been without food for 1, 4, and 16 hours to write short stories about pictures drawn principally from Murray's Thematic Apperception Test. The specific pictures were chosen to represent a variety of aspects of situations related to hunger, such as satiation, deprivation, food, and an eating place. The writers were asked to make their stories as imaginative and interesting as possible, and the results were scored by noting the percentage of writers whose stories exhibited certain characteristics. These characteristics or categories were, for example, story plots about food, statements about food deprivation, about activity instrumental to the securing of food, and about consummatory activity. Tabulations of responses in these categories revealed that as hunger increased, there was no over-all increase in the percentage of subjects who used food imagery or food themes (plots) in their stories. Moreover, there was a decided *decrease* in the number of references to the goal activity of eating as a function of deprivation time. Hunger was accompanied, however, by an increase in the percentage of stories in which *food-deprivation* plots and *deprivation-overcoming* instrumental activity appeared. The over-all findings were thus ambiguous, since the hypothesized relation between need and need-related imaginative responses was supported by the data from some scoring categories but not by the data from others.

The significance of the particular stimulus items used in tests designed to evaluate the effects of deprivation on performance is underscored by the results of the Postman-Crutchfield (1952) experiment. These investigators varied not only degree of hunger but also the probability that a stimulus would elicit a food response as well as the strength of the subject's set to make food responses. The stimuli were skeleton words, with blank spaces to be filled in by the subjects. Different types of lists having low, moderate, and high probabilities of eliciting food responses were used in conjunction with levels of hunger ranging from 0 to 6 hours. The degree of *selective set* to give food responses was varied by arranging the first few words of the lists so that 0, 1, 2, or 5 food responses would be elicited from different groups of subjects prior to their being presented with the principal items of the list.

Analyses of data from rather large numbers of subjects showed that when degree of food set and type of list (food-response probability) were held constant, no simple relation existed between intensity of need and frequency of need-related responses. Degree of set, however, as induced by increasing numbers of prelist food responses did lead to progressively more frequent food solutions to the skeleton words. The only way in which hunger affected performance was to produce slight changes in the relative effectiveness of the different levels of set. That is, for hungry subjects (4 to 6 hours of deprivation) the function relating degree of set to number of food responses was positively accelerated, whereas for nonhungry individuals (0 to 1 hour) the function was negatively accelerated. It was also found that the effect of set on frequency of word solutions was greater for skeleton items having a moderate probability of eliciting food words than for items with either a very low or a very high probability. Nonselective energizing effects of hunger could not, of course, be revealed by this experiment since every subject was required to complete the same total number of skeleton words.

Generally speaking, it is clear from the Postman-Crutchfield study that the selective effects of mild degrees of deprivation are slight and can be demonstrated only by carefully designed experiments in which a delicate balance is maintained among such variables as set and initial response probability. Quite certainly, if all skeleton words elicited food responses, or if none did, it would be impossible to demonstrate that variously deprived groups of subjects differ with respect to food-response output. The test items must be carefully chosen if group or individual differences are not to be obscured by either "ceiling" or "floor" effects. This is not, incidentally, a problem unique to the measurement of deprivation effects. It is characteristic of all measurement situations. It would be impossible, for example, to find out how well children solve arithmetic problems if the problems are either so easy that all children obtain scores of 100, or so difficult that none can be solved by any student.

In only one experiment, apparently, has the relation of hunger to eyelid conditioning been explored. Franks (1957) studied the acquisition and extinction of eyelid responses in nondeprived subjects and in subjects who had gone without food, water, and tobacco for approximately 22 hours. Since the two groups did not differ significantly in number of conditioned responses, the results failed to support the predictions of a multiplicative-drive theory. However, the procedures followed by Franks (massed acquisition trials, partial reinforcement, few reinforced trials) were rather unconventional, and the asymptotic conditioning levels for both groups were unusually low. A replication of this experiment under conditions more favorable to the development of conditioned responses is clearly indicated.

The possibility that hunger might selectively affect the retention of previously learned materials has been investigated by Williams (1950). In his studies hunger, which was introduced after original learning had been completed, had no effect upon the retention either of words that were directly related to the need or of neutral words that had been associated with need-related words.

By way of summary we are led to conclude that exceptionally little is known of the effects of deprivation on human performance in nonperceptual tasks. We do not know, for example, whether hunger tends to facilitate a broad diversity of responses, as a multiplicative-drive theory would predict, since most investigations have not been designed to reveal such effects. Nor can we assert with confidence that hunger always functions selectively. Moreover, experiments involving deprivation conditions other than hunger are practically nonexistent, and we possess neither reliable data on the learning of various tasks under different drive levels nor information on the effects of a reduction in a primary need following the performance of successful responses. The sum and substance of our current knowledge seems to be that under rather restricted conditions hunger sometimes exerts a mildly facilitative effect upon the tendency to give verbal responses related in one way or another to food and to the activities connected with its procurement and consumption. Under other experimental circumstances, however, no relation between hunger and performance has been observed.

Motivating Effects of Strong Stimuli

With human beings, as with other organisms, it has long been supposed that the intense stimulation provided by electric shocks, bright lights, loud noises, blasts of air, and internal tensions may function as a motivational variable.

Electric Shock. Probably because of the ease with which it can be administered, electric shock has been used with a wide variety of organisms and in almost every conceivable laboratory situation. In spite of its widespread use, however, standardized techniques are still not available for administering and measuring shock, and the results of different experiments, even when they purport to be investigating the same problem, are seldom in agreement.

Overt changes in behavior produced by electric shock are quite diverse, and depend not only on shock intensity but also upon its time of presentation with respect to a response or response sequence. Obviously shock can be administered consistently either before, during, or after a response has been elicited by other stimuli. Or it can be introduced at random intervals bearing no systematic temporal relation to any specific response. Let us consider these two modes of shock presentation in turn.

If one were to try to simulate, with electric shock, the motivating characteristics of hunger, it would probably be necessary to use a relatively mild continuous shock which would become progressively stronger over a period of hours. One might then study behavior in standardized situations with different initial and/or terminal levels of shock and with partial or complete shock reduction following the performance of specific responses. But since most human subjects object to such treatment, experimenters have typically used rather brief shocks, the interval between response and shock being held constant. On theoretical grounds we would anticipate that shock administered following a response would have a different effect on behavior than would shock presented while a response is in progress or prior to its appearance.

The consistent administration of shock following a particular response presents us with the typical paradigm of the punishment situation, and the observation that response strength is thereby weakened supports the belief that shock is functioning as a motivational variable, since one criterion (Chapter 2) for the identification of such variables is thereby met. The literature in this area is voluminous, but the experimental results are by no means uniform. Probably the most reasonable general conclusion one can draw from these studies is that behavior consistently preceding very strong shocks tends to be abandoned (cf. Postman, 1947), but there are numerous exceptions to this rule.

The weakening of a response as a consequence of subsequent punishment can be interpreted in several ways. For example, if shock regularly follows a response, the environmental cues eliciting that reaction, as well as internal response-produced cues, should acquire the capacity to evoke conditioned fear reactions (cf. Chapter 5). Initially, fear-produced increments in drive might augment the strength of the punished response, but subsequently, with extremely strong fear, competing responses might be aroused and their appearance in lieu of the punished response might be reinforced by a reduction in fear. Alternatively, postresponse shocks could elicit escape or withdrawal reactions that might be reinforced by shock cessation and might competitively interfere with the principal to-be-punished reaction. For instance, a subject may be shocked on the fingers each time he enters a blind alley in a finger maze. If the shock is terminated whenever he moves his hand away from the end of the alley, such escape movements may be reinforced; and since these newly acquired movements are oppositely directed to those involved in entering the blind, the latter may be overridden or weakened.

The administration of rather mild shocks after the occurrence of particular responses may serve simply to inform the subject as to the correctness or incorrectness of his reactions. Thus it has been shown, by Tolman, Hall, and Bretnall (1932), and by Muenzinger (1934), for example, that shocks following correct responses in a maze are sometimes as effective in producing learning as are shocks following errors. Shocks administered in this way may or may not have significant motivational effects, but they clearly qualify as associative variables since they provide specific knowledge of results. Weak shocks probably lead neither to escape reactions nor to increments in drive, and conditioned emotional reactions should seldom develop from their being paired with neutral cues.

The introduction of shock prior to the occurrence of a response might be expected to have motivational consequences if shock-induced emotionality or other processes persist until the response is evoked. Or if shock precedes a response by only a very brief interval, shock-elicited skeletal responses might perseverate for a time and interfere with the subsequently elicited criterion reaction. In this case, of course, the decline in response strength would qualify as an instance of competitive interaction among responses and hence as an example of an associative effect.

Precisely similar analyses would appear to be applicable to situations in which shock is administered coincidentally with an ongoing reaction. On a multiplicative-drive theory any shock should intensify whatever behavior is in progress and thereby fulfill the energizing criterion of motivational variables. But the more intense the shock, the higher the probability that it will elicit strenuous responses of vocalization or escape and thereby lead to a decline in the efficiency of overt performance. In every instance shock can apparently function both as a source of drive and as a specific stimulus capable of arousing a variety of defensive reactions. When behavior is facilitated by shock, the effect can be ascribed either to an increase in drive (motivational theory) or to the appearance of a facilitative response (associative theory). Likewise, performance degradation can be attributed to the appearance of shock-induced competing reactions, or to an initial superiority of task-irrelevant reaction tendencies in comparison with the correct ones.

If electric shocks are presented at random intervals they cannot provide reliable task-specific information to the subject nor is it likely that stable, stimulus-specific conditioned fear reactions will develop. Nonetheless, behavior might be affected either positively or negatively, since the subject's general drive level might be increased and/or competing responses might be evoked. Experimental evidence indicating that random shocks sometimes lead to improved performance has been reported by several investigators (e.g., Gilbert, 1936, 1937; Rosenbaum, 1953; Spence, Farber, and Taylor, 1954), but such shocks also have been found to disrupt the performance of some subjects (Deese, Lazarus, and Keenan, 1953). In so far as random shocks function facilitatively, support is provided for the multiplicative-drive view, since these shocks do not provide cues appropriate to the solution of a problem.

Unconditioned Stimuli as Sources of Drive. In the experiments we have just reviewed, the reference responses being studied were typically not elicited by shock. However, when shock is used as the UCS in human conditioning studies, it probably functions both as an elicitor of the to-be-conditioned reaction and as a source of drive. In a typical experiment (e.g., eyelid conditioning), if a response is to be counted as "conditioned," it must occur after the onset of the CS and, generally speaking, before the onset of the UCS. Consequently, on any one conditioning trial, the drive produced by the UCS cannot affect the latency, and perhaps not even the magnitude, of a foregoing, anticipatory CR. Both latency and amplitude could be affected, however, by residual drive from UCS presentations on earlier trials. Thus, as Spence (1958) has surmised, if one group of subjects is conditioned with a strong air puff and another with a weak air puff, the former should have a higher average drive level than the latter. Because of this the frequency of CRs should be directly related to the intensity of the puff, or more generally, to UCS intensity.

Available experimental data, though surprisingly sparse, support these expectations. In what may have been the first study of this kind, Passey (1948) reports that mean frequency of conditioned eyelid responses increases in an approximately linear manner as a function of the logarithm of air-puff intensity. Subsequently, Spence (1956, 1958) and his associates have repeatedly shown that conditioned eyelid responses are more frequent when strong rather than weak puffs are used. The dashed-line curve of Fig. 7:4, which appears in another context later on in this chapter, clearly shows this effect. In addition, acquisition curves obtained with different UCS intensities tend to diverge during the course of training. This finding is consistent with the assumption that the habit strengths for the groups under comparison are multiplied by different magnitudes of drive (D). Also relevant here is McAllister's (1953) study in which it was shown that the eyeblink response is extinguished far more rapidly when the UCS is omitted entirely, and hence drive level is lowered, than when the UCS continues to be presented, though separated from the CS by an interval too long to produce conditioning.

Unfortunately, no UCSs other than air puffs have apparently been systematically manipulated in classical conditioning experiments with human subjects. It remains to be seen, therefore, whether the consistent results obtained in the eyelid situation can be reproduced with other aversive stimuli and other responses.

It is also evident that other interpretations are possible beside that which attributes drive-arousing properties to the *UCS*. Variations in *UCS* level might affect performance not only by changing drive, but also by altering habit strength or by evoking different classes of unconditioned responses.

Noise. Industrial psychologists have long been concerned with the problem of how a worker's efficiency is affected by the loud noises that often accompany manufacturing processes. Experimental attempts to investigate this problem have not, however, pointed unambiguously to any one general conclusion. In some cases noise seems to have a facilitative, dynamogenic effect on performance, though marked increases in energy output and in fatigue are typical accompaniments of such effects. In other cases, especially where the noise, because of its intermittency or other special characteristics, appears to elicit competing reactions, performance declines. By and large, however, the most extensive studies of performance under noise, such as those of Stevens and his collaborators (1946), indicate that performance on a variety of psychomotor and intelligence tests is not significantly changed by prolonged exposure to noise. This may or may not mean that noise has no motivational effects. Quite possibly, noises of certain kinds may produce increments in drive strength, and yet, at the same time, elicit interfering responses. To date there are few experiments on performance under noise in which adequate numbers of subjects have been tested and in which irrelevant factors of suggestion and the like have been adequately controlled (cf. Chapanis, Garner, and Morgan, 1949). We must conclude, therefore, that while noise may function as a motivational variable, its effects are in marked degree a function of its specific characteristics, especially as these relate to the rhythm or other aspects of the task, to the operator's level of proficiency, and to numerous other variables.

Motivating Effects of Instructions

Verbal instructions, whether administered before, during, or after a bit of behavior has been exhibited, are stimuli, which, like electric shock and noise, may have motivational consequences. As we have already remarked in discussing acquired sources of drive, nonspecific "hurry-up" instructions seem to function motivationally to facilitate whatever behavior is taking place or is about to take place. Besides, individuals seem to learn to motivate their own activities by administering similar "try-hard" instructions to themselves. The laboratory psychologist is well aware that performance levels can be changed if subjects are told that the task is important (or unimportant), that the test is a measure of intelligence, that the results will affect their standing in class, or that they have failed or succeeded. As with all variables alleged to have motivational effects, however, instructions may modify performance either by virtue of their cue properties and the resulting changes in associative strengths or through a change in drive strength, or in both ways.

When verbal instructions contain specific cues appropriate to the responses being scored as correct, improvement in performance is expected and is seldom considered to be a motivational outcome. For example, if a subject were told which way to go at each choice point of a maze in order to stay on the true path, his improved performance in comparison with that of noninstructed subjects would not qualify as a motivational effect. But if he were simply told to do his best, and if this instruction were followed by superior performance, we would be more likely to conclude that a change in drive had been produced. Instructions to "do your best" provide no specific response-directing cues, and if improved performance follows it may be due to nonassociative processes. This is not to say, however, that a nonmotivational interpretation of such results could not be defended. One could always argue, for instance, that alleged motivation-inducing instructions augment performance not because they add an increment to drive, but because they arouse a whole family of learned facilitative responses such as sitting erect, concentrating on the task at hand, and suppressing inclinations to daydream.

Instructions to subjects to the effect that they have either failed or succeeded in the performance of an assigned task are commonly held to exert motivational influences on subsequent tasks. But here again, as Lazarus, Deese, and Osler (1952) and Farber (1955) have observed, it is desirable to distinguish between the purely motivational effects of such instructions and their associative (informative) consequences. For the most part, the kinds of instructions described by the terms *success* and *failure* tend to be unrelated to the particular responses involved in performing a just-completed task. They tend, that is, to be relatively general statements such as "You have done better (or worse) than most people do on this task." The nonspecific nature of such instructions minimizes, though it does not eliminate, the likelihood that subsequent behavior will be affected through associative channels. The most general finding of studies of instruction-induced failure seems to be that subsequent performance is impaired (cf. Farber, 1955), but this effect could be interpreted equally well by either a motivational or an associative theory. As Farber notes, ". . . the impairment of performance by failure does not necessarily demonstrate its associative effects, nor does the improvement of performance by failure demonstrate its drive effects. Just as the associative mechanism attending failure may either benefit or harm performance, so might an increase in drive, in and of itself, affect behavior either favorably or adversely, depending on the specific nature of the task and the experimental conditions involved" (p. 317).

Because of the conflicting nature of experiments designed to manipulate human motivational level by means of verbal instructions, and because none seems to have been designed so that the separate contributions of drive and associations can be evaluated, we have chosen not to review them in detail. Praise or reproof may lead either to better or poorer performance, depending upon the nature of the experimental conditions, which are as yet poorly understood, and upon the characteristic ways in which individual subjects react to those conditions, to the experimenter, and to his comments concerning the subject's performance. About all one can say with assurance is that associative factors probably play a dominant role when the instructions are related to the correctness or incorrectness of specific responses and that a concept of a nonspecific drive may be useful when success-failure statements are very general.

Response-defined Motivational Level

In the preceding sections of this chapter we have dealt briefly with some theoretical and experimental aspects of human motivational differences as defined by amount of deprivation and intensity of stimulation. The remainder of the chapter is devoted to studies in which degree of drive or motivation is defined, not by the manipulation of an external variable, but in terms of individual differences in responses to standardized tests. In the studies to be considered, motivation is said to differ among individuals who respond differently to the stimuli provided by projective or questionnaire tests.

As the reader may recall from Chapter 2, drive level can be operationally defined, independently of the behavior to be explained, by noting how different subjects react in a given situation. The finding of stable individual differences in reactivity permits us to rank-order our subjects with respect to test performance, and if we choose to define drive in terms of test scores, we can then rank-order our subjects with respect to drive. Drive differences thus defined may never, of course, turn out to be significantly related to performance in any other situation or to other theoretical concepts. If not, then other ways of defining drive may be tried and the most useful definition provisionally adopted.

Psychologists have sometimes claimed that the use of response-defined drive levels is to be avoided as not "truly experimental," since drive is not being manipulated directly. That this objection is unfounded can be made clear by the following example. Suppose we desire to vary the intensity of a stimulus light in our laboratory. We can achieve this variation either by adjusting the amount of electric current that is allowed to flow through the filament of a single lamp, or by selecting several different lamps from an available population of lamps. The first method parallels that in which drive is "manipulated" by, say, changing the strength of shock administered prior to a behavioral test. The second is like that in which individuals having specific degrees of the property in question, i.e., strength of drive, are chosen from a large population by means of a test. Since standardized instruments for measuring light intensity have been developed by the physicist, the readings of such instruments can be used to support the contention that selective and manipulative procedures can lead to the same outcome. In principle, the selective and manipulative methods of varying drive can also be equated, but until practical instruments for assessing drive strength have been developed and standardized, any assertion to the effect that a *particular* level of test-defined drive is identical with one produced experimentally must remain open to question.

Critics of the selective procedure have argued further that individuals who differ with respect to their responses on an alleged test of drive may also differ in a variety of other ways, thus confounding other variables with drive. The comment, though legitimate, is not a criticism uniquely relevant to the selective procedure. It applies with equal cogency to the manipulative methods as well. Thus when we try to change drive by experimentally altering deprivation time or by administering different strengths of shock, we may also be altering associative strengths, hormonal levels, and many other factors. Likewise, in manipulating the intensity of light from a single bulb, changes in the color of the light may be produced, just as bulb diameter may fluctuate when intensity is varied by the selection of particular lamps. However, if our standard light-measuring device is insensitive to color and to bulb diameter, then the presence of these confounding variables is of no consequence. And in the case of drive, if there is reason to believe that the behavior being studied is insensitive to the presence of known or suspected confounding variables, then changes in such ancillary factors, whether produced by manipulative or selective methods, can be ignored. In principle, therefore, there is as much justification for trying to vary drive by a process of selection as by seemingly more direct experimental manipulations. No one can predict, at present, which of the many varieties of each method will ultimately yield the most useful and significant estimate of drive, nor whether one of the methods will ultimately prove to be better than the other.

Motivation Defined by Imaginative Responses

One of the most extensive research programs directed toward evaluating human motivation by means of subjects' responses is that of McClelland and his principal associates, Atkinson, Clark, and Lowell (1953).

As we have already seen (Chapter 5), these authors use the word *motive* to designate learned, and only learned, anticipations (expectations) of rewards or punishments. An individual has a fear motive or an anxiety motive if, when exposed to cues that have previously been followed by punishment, he experiences an affective (emotional) arousal similar to, or representative of, the arousal produced by pain or punishment. An organism has a hunger motive when, as a consequence of repeated eating experiences, the internal cues accompanying deprivation or external cues (or both) arouse an affectively toned expectancy of the pleasurable consequences of eating. We have previously noted that these negative and positive motives are essentially identical, in their origins and affective aspects, with conditioned anticipatory fear reactions and anticipatory fractional goal responses, respectively. The achievement motive, which has been studied most extensively, is defined as a learned, affective anticipation of the pleasurable consequences of success in situations where the quality or efficiency of one's performance is to be evaluated. Overt behavior is assumed to be affected "motivationally," though in ways that are never clearly specified, by the arousal of one or more motives such as these.

Measuring Human Motive Strength. In attempting to develop an adequate definition of human motive strength, McClelland and his coworkers have concentrated their attention upon the content of imaginative responses given by subjects to a standardized test. Specifically, subjects are presented with a series of relatively uninformative pictures resembling those in the Thematic Apperception Test, and are asked to tell an imaginary story about each. The stories are then scored by counting, according to certain rules, the number of ideational items believed to be diagnostic of the presence of a specific motive. Individuals or groups can thus be rank-ordered with respect to the strength of a given motive as defined by the frequency of their motive-relevant reactions to the pictures. The performance of the same individuals under other conditions can then be studied to see whether it is meaningfully related to fantasy-defined motive strength.

This technique of defining individual differences in motive strength in terms of subjects' reactions to one situation (story telling) and of using such differences to explain performance variation in a second situation exemplifies the response-based method (Chapter 2) of independently defining drive. The procedure entails the working out of an R–R relation, and involves the assumption that the motive governs both imaginative reactions and test-situation performance.

In principle, any set of reactions to a standardized test can be used to define motive strength, but McClelland et al. regard the fantasy content of stories as uniquely suitable. Their preference for this method rests upon the traditional psychoanalytic view that unguarded free associations provide the richest material for studying human motives, upon their belief in the fruitfulness of the method, and upon the questionable assumption that fantasies are not affected by a subject's specific knowledge or factual information.

Experimentally Aroused Motive Strength. One of the first experiments in this area, one we have already briefly discussed, was performed by Atkinson and McClelland (1948). These investigators reasoned that if the content of imaginative thought reflects motive strength, changes in that content should follow from experimentally induced variations in the intensity of a motive. An adult human being who has been deprived of food should possess a hunger motive, and the presence and strength of this motive should be revealed through imaginative stories by an increase in the frequency of food- and/or eating-related items. As we have seen, Atkinson and McClelland's expectations were not borne out in the case of food-related responses, though increased hunger was accompanied by more frequent references to *food deprivation.* Nevertheless, this minimally satisfying relation was taken as confirming the hypothesis that with lengthened deprivation the hunger motive was aroused more vigorously by the combined action of deprivation and picture cues, and that the intensified motive enhanced the probability of occurrence of food-related imaginative responses.

By means of additional experiments McClelland and his collaborators have tried to show that conditions designed to induce the arousal of the motives of sex, fear, affiliation, and achievement also lead to corresponding increases in the motive-related content of imaginative stories. With the exception of Clark's (1952) experiment on the sex motive, stories produced under conditions regarded as motivating ". . . contained more imaginative responses dealing with thoughts, feelings, and actions related to the goal-directed sequence of the motive in question" (Atkinson, 1954, p. 66). For reasons not yet well understood, however, these results, obtained with male subjects, could not be replicated with women. When the same procedures were tried with female subjects, as many motive-related imaginative responses were obtained when the motives were supposedly aroused as in nonaroused control conditions.

With these experiments as a foundation, the conclusion was reached that the strength of almost any motive could be estimated from the frequency with which certain types of imagery appeared in subjects' stories about pictures. Thus if one person gives more food-related responses to pictures suggesting eating than does another, the inference is drawn that the former is hungrier, has a stronger motive to eat, than the latter. And the person whose imaginative stories contain frequent references to success and achievement is presumed to have a stronger motive to achieve than one whose imaginative output is less rich in words connoting goal attainment.

The Achievement Motive and Overt Behavior. Much of the research effort of the McClelland group has been directed toward determining the ways in which motives, especially the need for achievement, influence overt behavior other than that involved in the telling of imaginative stories. They have sought to determine whether groups of individuals defined as having strong need for achievement will perform more effectively on various tests or tasks than low-achievement groups.

That need for achievement apparently does not function as a nonspecific energizer after the manner of Hull's D is suggested by the data from several investigations. Thus Zatzkis (1949) failed to find a clear or significant relation between the mean number of words written in a class essay and the need-achievement scores of the student writers. Moreover, McClelland et al. (1953) reported that subjects with low need-achievement scores gave a greater mean number of responses to the 10 cards of the Rorschach test than did the high scorers, with moderate need-achievers giving more responses than either high or low. And finally, Atkinson (1950), in a study preparatory to one on the recall of completed and uncompleted tasks, found that with a limited number of tasks subjects who scored high on the need-achievement test never completed significantly more tasks than did subjects with low need-achievement scores. In fact, under instructions designed to be relaxing rather than motivating, the high need-achievers performed significantly fewer tasks than the low need-achievers.

Inasmuch as McClelland and his collaborators have never specified precisely what it is that a motive does when functioning as a motivator, considerable uncertainty remains as to how overt behavior should be affected by a motive such as the need for achievement. Generally speaking, however, these investigators appear to hold that increased motive strength should lead to faster performance and greater work output, or, under unspecified conditions, to more efficient performance.

Perhaps the best support for the expectation that high need-achievers should perform better than those with low scores is provided by Lowell's (1952b) experiment. His college student subjects were required to perform a simple arithmetic task for a period of ten minutes. Tabulations of the number of addition problems solved during each two-minute period showed that subjects high on the achievement scale performed more efficiently during each practice period than subjects who were low on the scale. These data, which are presented graphically in Fig. 7:1, are cited by Atkinson (1954) as the kind of relation that "has often been used

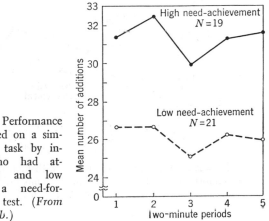

FIG. 7:1. Performance levels obtained on a simple addition task by individuals who had attained high and low scores on a need-for-achievement test. (*From Lowell, 1952b.*)

to illustrate the so-called 'energizing' function of motives" (p. 71).

Of special interest in connection with this experiment is the reported fact that the subjects of the two groups did not differ significantly in respect to their basic numerical skills as measured by the quantitative score on the ACE Psychological Examination. This would seem to imply that achievement motivation was functioning as a nonselective energizer to enhance performance, since it indicates that the basic skills (associative factors) of the two groups were equal. But from another point of view this is puzzling. On the basis of published statements concerning the nature of the achievement motive, one would expect the motive to be aroused during the taking of the ACE test to an even greater degree than during an experiment requiring the performance of simple additions. Consequently, it may be appropriate to ask why the high need-achievement group differed from the low group on the simple addition tests but not on the quantitative portion of the intelligence test. Performance on an intelligence test involves the efficient utilization of knowledge and conceptual skills as well as basic capacity, and highly motivated individuals should perhaps perform more efficiently on such tests.

In another part of Lowell's experiment, high and low need-achievers were required to reconstruct common words from scrambled arrangements of the letters. On this task, as Fig. 7:2 shows,

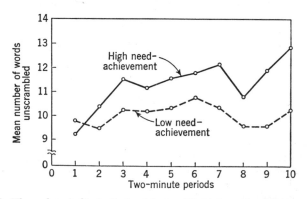

FIG. 7:2. These data indicate that subjects with high need-achievement scores tend to improve during the course of an anagrams task, whereas subjects with low scores do not. (*Adapted from Lowell, 1952b.*)

the two groups did not differ greatly at first, but the high need-achievement group showed a progressive increase in facility with practice while the other group did not. The difference between the over-all means for the two groups was not statistically significant, but the divergence of the two curves was said to be highly reliable. This finding has been interpreted (McClelland et al., 1953) to mean that where learning is possible, as in this scrambled-words task, subjects with strong achievement motivation learn as the task progresses, and the skills thus acquired are facilitated by the achievement motive. Moreover, the occurrence of learning is said to strengthen the view that need-achievement scores do indeed reflect level of motivation. The view is based on the supposition that the mere occurrence of learning constitutes a decisive criterion for evaluating the presence of a motive. Here the authors have failed to see that for most theorists learning provides an adequate criterion of motivation only when a *reduction* in motivation has clearly been involved.

Lowell's finding that the so-called highly motivated group performed more poorly than the low group during the first two minutes of the test is also rather puzzling. Assuming equal skills in unscrambling the mixed-up words, we should expect a more highly motivated group to do better initially than a poorly motivated one. The failure to find an initial difference is even more disturbing when we realize that relevant skills were probably not equal at the outset, since the group with high achievement scores was significantly superior to the low group on the linguistic score of the ACE test. The divergence of the curves probably can't be explained, however, in terms of differences in linguistic ability alone. When this "intelligence" factor was held constant by the technique of partial correlation, there was still a significant correlation ($r = .44$) between achievement motivation and output of scrambled words.

Additional evidence purporting to show that performance in certain situations is enhanced by high achievement motivation has been reported by McClelland and Liberman (1949). According to these investigators, subjects with high achievement motivation exhibit lower recognition thresholds for words denoting success than do subjects with low achievement motivation. This may or may not be a motivational phenomenon, however, since the two groups might not have been equally familiar with the critical stimulus words. Moreover, Veroff, Wilcox, and Atkinson (1953) showed that women with high achievement-motivation scores did better than those with low scores during the middle portion of an anagrams test when the general level of performance tended to lag. Hedlund (1953), however, was unable to replicate this finding. Evidently we cannot yet accept the conclusion that performance in a variety of situations is enhanced by high achievement motivation. Furthermore, as Atkinson (1954) has noted, a number of the supportive experiments involve behavioral measures concerning which the theoretical expectations are not especially clear.

How Motives Affect Behavior. In their early publications McClelland and his associates failed to indicate how motives, as defined by them, function as determinants of verbal fantasy responses or of responses in problem solving and other task situations. Atkinson (1954) has tried to fill this gap by relating the concept of motives to the expectancy theories of MacCorquodale and Meehl (1953) and of Tolman and Postman (1954). Considering first the question of how motives might affect imaginative responses to TAT-like pictures, it is clear that here Atkinson has adopted a straightforward associative view. Thus he maintains that while motives are being learned many additional reactive tendencies (response predispositions) are also becoming associated with the same cues. The internal stimuli of hunger, for example, tend to arouse not only the anticipation of food (the hunger motive) but also verbal and other responses that are related to eating, to a wide variety of different foods, and to the situations in which eating has frequently taken place. Consequently, when pictures containing food-related cues are presented to hungry subjects, the combination of internal and picture-provided cues tends to elicit food-related imaginative responses. In essence, the stronger the hunger motive, the stronger the learned predisposition to use words related to eating, and the greater the likelihood that such words will be evoked by the joint action of picture cues and the combination of hunger-produced and anticipation-of-food-produced cues. Similarly, a high achievement motive should be accompanied by strong predispositions to perform certain kinds of responses (including words), and in telling imaginative stories, therefore, subjects so motivated should be more likely to use words related to achievement. It is thus evident that a motive, defined as a learned, affective, anticipatory process does not function, with respect to fantasy responses, as a drivelike energizer, but only as a source of stimuli to which specific kinds of associations have been developed. Only the single principle of interactions among families of associative tendencies is involved in the theoretical explication of the alleged motivationlike effects of motives upon imaginative verbal responses.

In dealing with behavior in problem-solving and learning situations, Atkinson appeals to two different kinds of expectancies. One of these, the motive, is the affectively toned expectation of either good or bad things to come. The second kind of expectancy is described as cognitive or perceptual rather than affective. Such an expectancy is a consequence of the organism's repeated experiences with environmental objects and their interrelations. It is approximately equivalent to Tolman's (1948) notion of a "cognitive map" and to Hull's construct of habit strength. This cognitive expectancy, much like Hull's habit strength, is apparently incapable, when acting in isolation, of leading to overt behavior. A person may know that food can be obtained from a neighborhood store and precisely how to get there (cognitive expectancy), but he will not travel to the store to get food unless he has a desire to eat (motive-type expectancy). According to Atkinson, the final tendency to respond overtly depends jointly upon these two kinds of expectancies.

Atkinson's treatment still leaves us in doubt, however, as to the "motivating" role of the motive-type expectancy. In one of his diagrams the motive is shown as *multiplying* the environmentally cued performance expectancy, but in the accompanying text we are told only that "mutual facilitation" increases the strength of the disposition to respond. Apparently, the use of the multiplicative sign in this diagram was not intended to parallel Hull's use of the same symbol, since Atkinson holds that a motive facilitates only those instrumental reactive tendencies that have a terminal member, the goal concept, in common with the motive. This sort of selective enhancement is evidently more representative of an associative than of a motivational interpretation. On this view, if an animal is made hungry and is then placed into an alley where it has previously received only water when thirsty, the two expectancies would not have a common goal member. The environmental cues would arouse the expectation of obtaining water in the goal box, but the hunger motive would arouse the anticipation of eating food. Hence, this theory would seem to predict that the hungry animal's instrumental responses of running down the alley and especially his responses of drinking water would not be enhanced by the presence of the hunger motive. However, as we have seen in our review of Miller's (1948b) experiments (Chapter 3), hunger does seem to facilitate responses previously learned under thirst.

In summary, it appears that a motive, as defined by McClelland and his associates, always functions as a *selective* facilitator, capable of enhancing only restricted sets or classes of responses. In this respect a motive differs markedly from a motivational concept such as Hull's drive, which is assumed to multiply all learned and unlearned reactive tendencies. The two conceptions also differ, incidentally, in that Hull's theory predicts that increased drive will lead to poorer performance under certain conditions, whereas the motive theory always seems to predict enhanced performance. In addition, the mechanisms through which motives exert their selective effects either upon imaginative responses or upon behavior in learning and problem-solving situations seem to involve no principles other than those of conventional associative learning theory. This may be a virtue, but it has naturally led certain critics (e.g., Farber, 1954b) to wonder whether the term *motivational* is, strictly speaking, appropriate to either the theory or the research of McClelland and his coworkers.

Selective Response Facilitation. The view that a motive functions selectively to enhance motive-related responses presents an interesting problem for theoretical analysis. Let us suppose we were to perform an experiment like that of Atkinson and McClelland (1948), and that our subjects tended, as time of food deprivation increased, to give greater numbers of imaginative responses related to food and eating. If our pictures had been appropriately chosen, the cues they provided might have aroused learned associative tendencies to emit food responses which were equal in strength to the tendencies to give nonfood reactions. If hunger were functioning as a generalized drive (D), the excitatory tendencies to make both food-related and non-food-related responses should be strengthened equally as deprivation time increased. This would mean that although the *proportion* of food-related to non-food-related reactions would be the same for all our groups, the *total number of responses of each kind would increase with hunger.* Hence, if between-group comparisons were made on the basis of food-related words only, hunger would appear to have a selectively energizing effect, when in fact it had not. On the other hand, if our pictures elicited more food-relevant than non-food-relevant words, we should expect, from a multiplicative-drive theory, that the absolute difference between the number of food and nonfood responses would increase across groups with intensified hunger. In this case, increases both in the absolute number of food-related words and in their frequency compared with non-food-related words would be predicted as deprivation was lengthened. Apparently then, what seems to be a selective energizing effect can, in theory, be produced by an increase in generalized drive level. In one case this results from a comparison between groups when deprivation-relevant and deprivation-irrelevant response tendencies are equally strong, and in the other, from comparisons either between or within groups when deprivation-related tendencies are initially dominant.

Selective sensitization of food-related responses could also be produced, however, by the presence of specific associative tendencies established through prior learning to the cues accompanying hunger (cf. Brown, 1953a). Thus intensified hunger should lead to more food responses, provided food responses have been associated with the internal stimuli of deprivation. Were such a mechanism as this operating effectively, one would predict that the difference favoring food-related over non-food-related words would increase either within a single group or across groups as deprivation was extended. Moreover, the effect should be obtainable even when the external cues provided by test pictures tend to elicit initially as many food-related as non-food-related responses. Obviously this is an associative view, since selective sensitization is explained without invoking either a multiplicative drive or a motive.

One might maintain, of course, that increased deprivation leads, as in the above interpretation, to stronger internal cues and hence to stronger habits but that these habits are reflected in overt behavior via their effect upon other habits. Thus the tendencies to make food-related responses that are associated with deprivation stimuli might combine with the reactive tendencies incited by picture cues to increase relevant response frequency. This might be treated conceptually as a matter of stimulus summation or in terms of the facilitative effects of one habit set upon another. In either event, the interpretation, which closely parallels that proposed by Atkinson, would once again be associative rather than motivational.

Alternative Proposals for Measuring Achievement Motivation. According to McClelland (1956), he and his associates have investigated a variety of methods of measuring achievement motivation that do not involve imaginative stories. However, none of the substitute methods proved to be successful, the criterion of success being an appreciable correlation with achievement scores derived from the content analysis of fantasy. Among the methods tried were: (*a*) story alternatives to the pictures, presented in multiple-choice form; (*b*) word stems to be completed with achievement and nonachievement alternatives; and (*c*) agreement with achievement sentiments on a questionnaire. The only promising technique, one developed by Aronson (1956), is also a kind of projective or expressive test. This investigator finds that content analyses of spontaneous doodles yield consistent significant correlations with need-achievement scores over several samples of college students. It is McClelland's (1956) belief that this method is potentially valuable because it presumably can be used for children too young to tell stories, for civilizations without written records, for persons who are apparently too anxious about achievement to write of it fluently, and for groups who speak entirely different languages.

In spite of these failures to find other useful techniques for measuring the need for achievement, some progress has been reported by investigators outside of the McClelland group. Elizabeth French (1956), for example, reports some success in developing a measure of complex motives that does not involve the use of pictures. In her test, which is disguised as a test of insight, the subjects are presented with ten single-sentence descriptions of the behavior of hypothetical individuals. A sample sentence is "Ray works much harder than other people," and the subjects are asked to "explain" the behavior described therein. The rationale of the test is that subjects who have, say, high achievement motivation, will tend to project that motivation into their explanations of the hypothetical instances of behavior. Some of the test items were adapted from those used by Sheriffs (1948), and the method of scoring the subjects' answers was similar to that used by McClelland. By altering the nature of the scoring categories, estimates of either the achievement motive or the affiliation motive were said to be obtainable. It is too early to know how this type of test will compare with the more traditional method of measuring achievement motivation, but French has reported a significant correlation of .48 between performance on a digit-letter substitution test and test-defined achievement motivation under task-orienting instructional conditions.

After prolonged practice in the scoring of TAT stories following the procedure of McClelland and his associates, a satisfactory degree of interscorer agreement can apparently be obtained. Nevertheless, many workers have found that even after considerable training scoring reliabilities remain low. To circumvent this difficulty an objective form of the TAT called the Iowa Picture Interpretation Test (IPIT) was developed at the State University of Iowa. In this test, TAT pictures are presented singly, each one accompanied by a set of four verbal statements. Within each set of statements, one is designed to reflect achievement motivation and the other three to reflect insecurity, blandness, and hostility. The statements were selected as relevant to each of these four categories on the basis of judgments by clinical psychologists. The subjects' task is to look at each picture and indicate the degree to which the accompanying statements are appropriate to the picture by arranging them in rank order. Scores are computed by obtaining the sum of the ranks for each category.

Preliminary administrations of the test for standardization purposes revealed that the test-retest reliability of the achievement scores, though discouragingly low, was about the same as that of the standard story form of the TAT when scored by skilled raters. However, achievement imagery scores from the IPIT (Hurley, 1955) failed to correlate significantly ($r = .12$, $N = 45$) with scores obtained by means of McClelland's system of scoring. Nevertheless, Williams (1955) has reported that subjects with high achievement scores (IPIT-defined) worked significantly faster on a simple test of addition than subjects with low scores. This finding is similar to that reported by Lowell (1952b), using the McClelland method of scoring, and is supported further by Johnston's (1957) data showing that high achievement-imagery subjects of both sexes attempted significantly more simple addition problems over 10 two-minute trials than did subjects with low achievement ratings. In addition, Johnston (1955) found that high achievement subjects perform more efficiently on an electrical maze task, and Hurley (1957) reports a positive relation between IPIT achievement scores and the frequency of both correct and incorrect responses in a verbal learning task. It would seem, therefore, that IPIT achievement ratings may reflect, in part, individual differences in level of motivation. Nevertheless, considerable research remains to be done before it can be concluded that the IPIT is measuring a motivational variable rather than something else or that extensive similarities exist between whatever variable it does measure and other purported measures of achievement motivation. Encouraging evidence for the view that a good objective scoring method may eventually be developed has recently been presented by Johnston (1957), who showed that the test-retest reliability of the IPIT could be substantially improved by lengthening the test.

Finally, it is worth noting that Hedlund (1953) has made a serious effort to objectify the categories by which achievement scores are obtained from subjects who are exposed to achievement-type TAT pictures. He designed an objective multiple-choice test, called the Iowa Multiple-choice Achievement Imagery Test, which consisted of 70 three-foil items. One foil of the three was an achievement-related statement and the other two were unrelated. Ten such items were constructed for each of seven achievement-motive–arousing pictures. The result of parallel experimental administrations of both the objective test and of the standard story form was that the internal consistency of both tests over pictures was extremely low. That is, individual pictures did not tend in a consistent manner to yield comparable estimates of the relative need for achievement of different individuals. Moreover, neither Hedlund's objective test nor the standard story form was related in any clear-cut manner to several aspects of classroom perform-ance or to performance on an anagrams test. In this latter respect Hedlund's results failed to corroborate the relationship between achievement scores and anagrams performance previously reported by Clark and McClelland (1950). Hedlund concluded, therefore, that neither the objective form nor the story form of the need-achievement test had predictive utility for the specific performance criteria he chose to investigate.

Motivational Differences Defined in Terms of Scores on a Scale of Manifest Anxiety

In this section we shall consider theory and evidence relating to the view that individual differences in level of general drive can be usefully defined in terms of the responses of subjects to ques-tionnaire items purporting to reflect manifest anxiety. This con-ception, developed originally by Janet Taylor (1951), and by Spence and Taylor (1951), has led to an extensive amount of discussion and research, and only the barest outline of its many details and ramifications can be presented here.

Taylor's method of defining human drive level by means of an anxiety scale was grounded upon Hull's multiplicative-drive theory and upon the results of studies of the acquired drive of fear in animals (see Chapter 5). The extension of these principles and relations to human behavior suggests that those who differ in degree of fearfulness or anxiety should also differ correspondingly in general level of drive. And if drive strengths differ, then be-havior in diverse situations should be affected in a manner con-sistent with the assumption that drive (D) is a nonspecific factor affecting all reactive tendencies. Those who have studied the rela-tion between questionnaire-defined anxiety and performance have addressed themselves essentially to these problems.

Taylor's manifest anxiety scale (referred to hereafter simply as the MAS) was constructed in the form of a questionnaire-type personality inventory. Its component items, many of which were adapted from the Minnesota Multiphasic Personality Inventory, posed questions that clinical psychologists judged would elicit answers reflecting manifest emotionality or anxiety. Few if any of the individuals who have worked with the MAS, at least among those in the Iowa group, have ever been concerned with the problem of whether the test measures "true anxiety," whatever that may mean. Nevertheless, as Taylor (1956a) has shown, MAS scores correlate about as well with psychiatrists' judgments of manifest anxiety and with other criteria as do other tests purporting to measure anxiety. But these correlations are irrelevant to the central aim of most of the studies involving the MAS. The members of the Iowa group have simply assumed that it may be useful to *define* drive level (D) in terms of MAS scores. They have then proceeded to explore the utility of this definition by determining whether performance in a variety of situations is affected in ways that are consistent with the theoretical implications of this definition and of the system from which it springs.

Empirical Findings of MAS Studies. The first and still one of the most striking findings in the MAS literature is that reported in Taylor's original paper. She administered her test to members of an undergraduate class and on the basis of their answers picked out a high-drive (high anxiety) and a low-drive (low anxiety) group. The high-drive group consisted of those who fell in the upper 12 per cent of the distribution of MAS scores, and the low-drive group was made up of those in the lower 9 per cent. When both groups were run under identical conditions in an eyelid-conditioning situation, it was found that the high-drive subjects conditioned more rapidly than did the low-drive subjects. As the conditioning curves (Fig. 7:3) for these subjects show, the anxious subjects conditioned much more rapidly than did those in the nonanxious group. Presumably the habit strengths of the two groups were equal since both were given the same number of conditioning trials. The difference between the performance levels of the two groups is highly significant and is entirely consistent with the hypothesis that the groups differed in general drive strength.

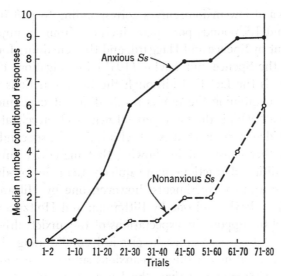

Fig. 7:3. Eyelid-conditioning curves for subjects with high (anxious) and low (nonanxious) scores on a questionnaire designed to measure degree of manifest anxiety. (*From Taylor, 1951.*)

Since the appearance of Taylor's paper, her principal finding that eyelid conditioning is better with high-anxious subjects has been confirmed in eight independent experiments (see Taylor, 1956a; Spence, 1956; Spence and Ross, 1957). In all but one of these studies the differences were statistically significant.

In a summary of experimental evidence bearing on the relation of anxiety to performance level in eyelid conditioning, Spence and Ross (1957) and Spence (1958) have pointed out that the agreement among studies from the Iowa laboratory has been suprisingly good. Not only has the anxiety-level variable yielded rather uniform results, but degree of conditioning has also been shown to vary with the strength of the UCS, a variable which, as we have noted above, is also presumed to affect drive level. Fig. 7:4, reproduced from Spence (1958), illustrates these rather remarkable interexperiment consistencies. The four points on the curve labeled "random subjects" are from four independent experiments in which randomly selected subjects were employed. As would be expected from the theory, these points define a curve falling between the curves for high and for low anxiety. The data-points on the high- and low-anxious curves corresponding to puff intensities of 0.25 and 1.5 pounds per square inch are from an unpublished experiment by Spence and Haggard, and the remaining four points are from the Spence and Taylor (1951) investigation. Especially impressive is the fact that although the three functions were obtained by combining the results of six different experiments, the functions all exhibit the same general negatively accelerated form.

The evidence from studies of classical defense conditioning, then, is rather consistent in showing that high-drive subjects acquire conditioned reactions more quickly than do low-drive subjects. At least two experiments, however, one by Hilgard, Jones, and Kaplan (1951) and one by Bitterman and Holtzman (1952) have failed to support the expectations of the anxiety-drive theory with respect to performance in classical conditioning situations. In the former, although the high-anxious subjects gave more conditioned eyelid responses than the low-anxious subjects, the difference was not statistically significant. And in the second study, in which the galvanic skin response rather than the eyelid re-

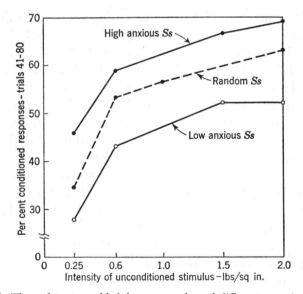

Fig. 7:4. These data, assembled from a number of different experiments, indicate primarily that the strength of conditioning increases with the intensity of the unconditioned stimulus. Also to be seen are unusually consistent differences attributable to level of manifest anxiety. (*From Spence, 1958.*)

sponse was being conditioned, college subjects in the upper 50 per cent of the distribution of MAS scores were slightly but not significantly superior with respect to conditionability. As Taylor (1956a) points out, however, the number of subjects in the first experiment was unusually small, and in the second moderately anxious subjects were included in both the high- and low-anxious groups by the procedure of selection.

Anxiety, Chronic or Acute? Concerning the general concept of anxiety and level of drive, it is of interest to note that two views of the process have been proposed by members of the Iowa group. Taylor, in her original article, suggested that subjects who scored high on her scale might be considered chronically anxious. If so, they would tend to behave as though they had a relatively high level of drive even in nonstressful situations. Alternatively, Rosenbaum (1953), and Spence, Farber, and Taylor (1954) have se riously entertained the possibility that persons who score high on the MAS are individuals who, though not especially anxious when performing simple, familiar tasks, become anxious or overreact emotionally when tested in unusual or threatening situations. On the first of these views, high anxiety is regarded as more or less chronically present in certain individuals; on the second, it is an acute emotional reaction or state aroused only in stressful kinds of situations.

The experimental evidence bearing upon these two views of the nature of anxiety is not yet sufficiently extensive to permit us to choose between them, though the weight of evidence seems to favor the acute theory. Rosenbaum, for example, in a study of stimulus generalization used either a buzzer, a weak shock, or a strong shock as a "punishing" stimulus for slow reactions. On the acute hypothesis, anxious subjects should differ from nonanxious subjects when a strong shock is used but not when a nonnoxious buzzer is used, provided the situation is, in other respects, devoid of threat. Rosenbaum found, in accord with this view, that the differences between high- and low-anxious subjects were not significant save under the strong-shock condition. Apparently the weak shock was so mild—it was described to the subjects as a "slight" skin stimulation—that it was no more stressful than the buzzer. Further support for the acute theory comes from a study of eyelid conditioning by Spence, Farber, and Taylor (1954). Anxious subjects, who were conditioned by these investigators under neutral conditions, showed only a slight (nonsignificant) superiority in response frequency when compared with nonanxious subjects. But when occasional shocks or threats of shocks were introduced between trials, the anxious individuals performed at a significantly higher level than those with low MAS scores. Finally, the experimental findings of Bindra, Paterson, and Strzelecki (1955) may also be interpreted as indirectly supporting the acute hypothesis. In their study, involving classical salivary conditioning, which is presumably nonstressful, the performance of the high- and low-anxious subjects did not differ. The chronic theory would predict, of course, that even in a nonemotional situation such as this, the high-anxious subjects should, because of their higher level of drive, perform more effectively, unless strong competing (task-irrelevant) responses are dominant.

Studies such as those of Wenar (1954) and of Spence and Farber (1953) can be interpreted as supporting either the acute or the chronic view. In the first of these investigations, which was concerned with the relation of anxiety to temporal generalization, the experimenter measured the reaction times of his subjects to a buzzer, a weak shock, and a strong shock. He failed to find, however, any increase in the difference between the mean reaction times of anxious and nonanxious subjects as a function of the intensity of the stimulus to which they were reacting. The finding that the groups differed even when reacting to the supposedly neutral buzzer fits the chronic theory, and if the buzzer and the two shocks are assumed to be equally stressful, the data could be made to conform to the acute theory. The findings of Spence and Farber (1953) compare with those of Wenar and require somewhat similar interpretations. These experimenters did not find the difference between the conditioning scores of anxious and nonanxious subjects to be a function of an increase in the intensity of airpuff used as the unconditioned stimulus. Again, one might try to support the acute theory by declaring that all puffs were equally noxious, though this seems unlikely. But the fact that even with the weakest puff the high-anxious subjects conditioned more readily than those with low MAS scores is coordinate with the chronic-anxiety theory.

Anxiety and Complex Learning Situations. Nearly all of the MAS experiments we have discussed can be regarded as ones in which few competitive tendencies to make task-irrelevant responses were present. In the eyelid-conditioning situation there is doubtless some tendency for a subject to inhibit his blinking reactions to the CS, and some writers (Hilgard and Marquis, 1940) have maintained that conditioned responses always develop in the face of an inhibitory set. Nevertheless, through the use of appropriate instructions and by having the subject make a voluntary blink to a ready signal, the typical tendency to hold the eye open can be largely eliminated. When this has been done, it seems reasonable to regard the situation as one in which the indicator response is essentially the dominant member of the hierarchy. In these cases, the theoretical expectation is that high-anxious subjects should perform better than low-anxious subjects. But when the task is such as to permit or support the appearance of strong interfering responses, the theory becomes more complex and the predictions change. It is to a consideration of these situations and the theory appropriate to them that we now turn. Our treatment of these matters rests in considerable degree upon that presented by Spence (1956) in his Silliman lectures.

In a stimulus-response theory of the Hull-Spence variety, overt performance on any task is a consequence of complex interactions and competitions among task-relevant (correct) and task-irrelevant (incorrect) response tendencies. Other factors equal, the stronger the drive, the stronger all excitatory tendencies become, but also, as a result of the multiplicative assumption, the greater the disparities among the absolute strengths of all members of the hierarchy. If tendencies dominant under low drive are relevant to successful performance of the assigned task, an increase in drive should lead to improved performance. But when the dominant tendencies are those regarded as incorrect by the experimenter, an increase in drive will lead to the relative strengthening of these incorrect tendencies, and performance should become worse. This theory, as we have seen, enables one to maintain that drive always functions as an energizer, while providing an adequate explanation for the observation that high drive, on occasion, leads to poorer rather than to better overt performance.

In the earliest experiments designed to study the relation of anxiety level to performance in complex situations, both verbal (serial learning) and motor tasks (finger maze) were used. From analyses of these tasks, it was predicted that high-drive (anxious) subjects should perform more poorly than low-drive subjects. This expectation was based on the known fact that, because of the serial nature of these tasks, rather strong perseverative and antici-patory tendencies are often present. Such tendencies—an intrusion error in serial verbal learning is a good example—are, by definition, task-irrelevant, and their presence should always tend to degrade performance. Furthermore, the disruptive effect of these conflicting tendencies should be greater for the high-drive than for the low-drive subjects.

Within limits, these predictions have been borne out. Thus, Taylor and Spence (1952), using a special type of serial-verbal maze, and Farber and Spence (1953) with a finger maze, have found that low-drive subjects tend to be the better performers. In the second of these studies, however, it was noted that some of the choice points elicited very few errors, and it seems reasonable, therefore, to regard them as choices where the correct tendency was dominant. At such points the high-anxious subjects should have performed better than low-anxious ones, but they did not. Nega-tive results have also been reported by Hughes, Sprague, and Ben-dig (1954), who failed to obtain significant differences between the performance levels of extreme MAS groups who were tested with several serial-verbal mazes.

At this point appears the perennial problem of whether the obtained effects of anxiety differences could be due in part to factors other than differences in drive. Obviously they could, and those who have worked with the MAS have been quite aware that individuals lying at the extremes of the scale may differ not only with respect to drive intensity but also with respect to a variety of other traits or characteristics. One of the several pos-sibilities that has been pointed out (Spence, 1956) is that people who score at the high end of the MAS may be those who would also rank high on a scale of "degree of susceptibility to distraction." Should this be the case, then anxious subjects may do more poorly on serial learning tasks because they are paying attention to stimuli that are irrelevant to successful task performance and not because their drive level is high. This is clearly an associative interpretation of performance differences, since it appeals to stable individual differences in habits of "distractibility." Child and Waterhouse (1953) have similarly sought to explain certain instances of so-called motivated behavior by reference simply to number and strength of task-interfering tendencies.

In order to be able to control and to manipulate the relative associative strengths of task-relevant and task-irrelevant tendencies, Spence, in his more recent studies (1956), has turned to the paired-associates method of verbal learning. This task requires the subject to form associations between the component members of each of several pairs of words. Upon seeing the first member of each pair, the subject must speak the second word (usually within about two seconds) before it is presented. On successive runs through the list of paired words, the order of the pairs is changed to minimize the likelihood that associations from one pair to another will be formed within the list. Of special importance is the fact that rather wide variations in the strengths of the correct and incorrect tendencies can be experimentally produced. For instance, the strength of the association between the stimulus and response elements of each pair can be increased by picking out response words having a high probability of being given as associations to the stimulus words. Presumably, the stronger the tendency for the stimulus item to call out its particular response word prior to training in the laboratory, the less the likelihood that incorrect responses will be dominant. Competitive responses can also be minimized by making certain that the stimulus members of the different pairs are neither synonymous nor formally similar.

Spence (1956) has performed a number of experiments designed to explore the consequences of varying the strength of competitive tendencies in a paired-associates task. Figure 7:5 shows the results of one of these investigations in which competition between pairs of words was minimized while the strength of the tendency for each stimulus word to elicit its paired response word was maxi-

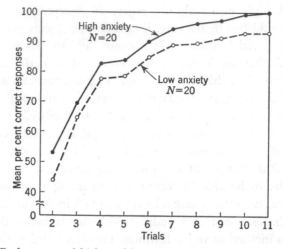

FIG. 7:5. Performance of high- and low-anxious subjects on a verbal learning task. The paired-associate items being learned were selected to minimize competition between separate pairs of words and to maximize the tendency for each stimulus word to elicit its paired response word. (*From Spence, 1956.*)

mized. As predicted from the theory, the high-anxious subjects learned to perform this task significantly better than did low-anxious subjects. Presumably this is because the lists were successfully structured to minimize the appearance of incorrect competing reactions, even though the task, taken as a whole, was relatively complex.

Several additional studies have been reported by Spence, in which increases in the strength of interfering tendencies were deliberately produced by using response words that were unlikely to be elicited by their paired stimulus words and by using stimulus words that were synonyms for one another. With this type of paired-associates list, the low-anxious subjects tended to perform better on the strong-interference pairs than did the highly anxious subjects. In this respect the results of three different experiments were consistent, but in none was the effect statistically significant.

In concluding this section, we find it interesting to note that Castaneda, McCandless, and Palermo (1956) have developed a modified form of the MAS for use with fourth-, fifth-, and sixth-grade children. Moreover, these investigators have shown that the performance of anxious children on difficult tasks is significantly worse than that of nonanxious children (Palermo, Castaneda, and McCandless, 1956), that anxiety level is negatively correlated with intelligence test scores, at least for girls (McCandless and Castaneda, 1956), and that when task difficulty is varied there is a significant interaction between anxiety and task difficulty, anxious subjects doing relatively superior work on easy items and inferior work on difficult ones (Castaneda, Palermo, and McCandless, 1956). Thus, the empirical relationships found for anxious and nonanxious adults tend to be confirmed with children.

Summary

The present chapter deals with theoretical and experimental aspects of the problem of how motivational variables affect the performance of human subjects in a variety of situations. The effects on performance of drive, defined in terms of severity of deprivation, in terms of exteroceptive stimulation and verbal instructions, and in terms of responses to standardized tests, are considered in turn. To reduce the enormous literature in this area to more manageable proportions, experiments dealing with the effects of motivational variables upon perceptual behavior have been treated separately in the following chapter.

Investigations in which attempts have been made to vary human motivation by manipulating severity of food deprivation are relatively scarce, and the results are far from consistent. According to generalized drive theory, hunger should enhance all reactive tendencies, thereby leading to better performance when correct habits are strongest and to poorer performance when incorrect tendencies are dominant. Experiments designed to evaluate these expectations have seldom been conducted, however, and most investigators have proceeded on the assumption that hunger or other needs should augment only those responses that are related to the need. When subjects are maintained on a semistarvation schedule for prolonged periods it is found that much of their waking time is indeed devoted to thoughts and daydreams about food and eating. But efforts to obtain more objective evidence for this phenomenon through the administration of standardized psychological tests have generally been unsuccessful. Similarly, attempts to show that relatively short periods of complete deprivation will enhance the frequency of food-related responses to TAT-like pictures, to word-completion test items, and to free-association stimulus words have failed to provide consistent or conclusive support for the hypotheses under investigation.

The administration of electric shock to human subjects either before, during, or after the elicitation of certain responses produces significant effects, which, in certain instances, are like those to be expected of motivational variables. Specifically, reactions that are consistently followed by shock reduction tend to be learned, and those followed by shock induction tend to be abandoned. Moreover, randomly administered shocks sometimes appear to produce an enhanced emotional or motivational level that is generally facilitative of performance. Under a variety of conditions, however, these generalizations do not hold. Not only does shock tend to elicit responses that interfere with the successful performance of some tasks, but it may also serve, particularly with human subjects, as a source of specific knowledge concerning the correctness or incorrectness of various responses. Although the motivational consequences of other strong stimuli have not been extensively studied with human subjects, we may note that the intense noises associated with industrial or military operations do not, for the most part, appear to function as motivational variables.

Attempts to manipulate human motivation by the use of "ego-involving" or "success" and "failure" instructions have produced diverse results. Where these instructions are relatively nonspecific and are accompanied by improved performance, the arousal of a general drive may be indicated. In other instances, however, instructions seem to function associatively, either because they contain problem-solving hints or because they have a capacity to evoke facilitating habits or attitudes. But few studies of this type have been designed so that a choice might be made between motivational and associative interpretations.

The procedure of defining degree of motivation in terms of responses to standardized tests has been widely used with human subjects, although the method has been criticized on the ground that it is not truly experimental and that it is especially likely to involve the confounding effects of other variables. Upon careful analysis, however, these objections appear to be unsupportable. In principle, adequately rigorous operational definitions of drive can be based upon either manipulative or selective methods.

The assumption that human motive strength can be usefully defined by analyzing the content of subjects' imaginative stories underlies the extensive work of McClelland and his associates. For the members of this group all motives are learned, and all are affectively toned expectations of the coming of pleasant or unpleasant consequences. As determinants of behavior, motives apparently always function as facilitators, although the effect is limited to responses that are in some way relevant to the motive. Moreover, the mechanisms involved in the facilitative action of motives are simply those of associative learning theory, and no explicit appeal is made to a concept of drive or motivation as such. The theory is thus seen to be associative rather than motivational, though the intricacies of the associative interactions have not been presented in detail.

Another large group of investigations, in which drive level has been defined by test-situation behavior, consists of the work of Taylor and Spence and their collaborators. These investigators have proceeded on the assumption that subjects with different drive strengths can be selected on the basis of their responses to a scale of manifest anxiety, and that the behavior of such subjects in diverse test situations should be deducible from the basic relations of Hull's multiplicative-drive theory. Although failures to confirm these expectations have been noted, the theory is well supported by a substantial body of positive experimental findings. Generally speaking, both adults and children who are defined as having high drive perform more efficiently than do low-drive subjects on tasks involving few competing responses. But where strong interfering tendencies are present low-drive subjects tend to be superior, precisely as predicted. The underlying theory may be characterized as primarily motivational, since appeal is made to a concept of nonspecific drive, but associative principles also play an important supplementary role.

CHAPTER 8

Motivational Variables and Perception

IT HAS LONG BEEN KNOWN that sensory and perceptual experiences are largely determined by the properties of the stimulus energies impinging upon sensory receptors. And every student of psychology has some acquaintance with the specific stimulus-response relations or psychophysical laws that have been painstakingly determined by psychologists and physiologists. Less firmly established, however, and of more recent vintage, is the view that the reactions of subjects in perceptual experiments depend not only upon stimulus variables but also upon the personality, attitudes, associative predispositions, and level of motivation of each and every subject. In this chapter our attention is focused upon the last of these relations, that between motivational variables and behavior in situations described as perceptual.

The Problem of Perception in the Study of Behavior

When pressed for an exact account of the nature of perception, psychologists rather generally tend to favor either of two somewhat disparate views. The first of these views is that perception can be construed most adequately as the private experience of the perceiver. To understand what perception is like, it is only necessary that one engage in perceiving for himself. Perception, according to this phenomenological position, thus turns out to be whatever the individual perceiver perceives perception to be. Those who favor this interpretation appear to be enchanted by the wonders of perception and regard the solution of its mysteries as the key to the understanding of all psychological problems. On this view, all the phenomena of learning, motivation, personality, adjustment, and social behavior can be reduced to, or best understood as, examples of the operation of perception.

The second, less sanguine view of perception begins by rejecting the notion that perception can ever make scientific sense so long as its essential nature lies hidden within the private experiential world of the perceiver. Perceiving *in someone else* is not an activity that is visible to the naked eye of the scientist. If one is to use the word "perceiving" at all, therefore, with reference to organisms other than one's self, the term must be introduced by means of a formal definition, the elements of which are ultimately reducible to directly indicatable things. One can observe the behavior but not the experiences of one's subjects; hence any assertion about the perceptions of these subjects must be based ultimately upon how they behave. According to this second point of view, perception must have the status of a scientific inference or construct, and like so many other constructs (e.g., motivation, habit strength, and cognition), perception is real only to the degree that its presence as a component of our explanatory accounts of behavior serves to enrich our understanding of that behavior. Moreover, if perception is to function as an element in a systematic account of behavior it must be defined independently of the behavior it is presumed to be affecting, and it must have behavior-determining properties, or relations to antecedents and other constructs, that are different from those ascribed to other postulated entities or processes. If not, then perception, which is inherently no less expendable than any other scientific term, need not be invoked as a component of any behavior system.

Is a Concept of Perception Ever Needed? Those who hold to

the second of the above views tend also toward the opinion that many, if not all, of the investigations commonly described as perceptual can be carried to successful completion without appealing to a concept of perception. This is especially true, it would seem, of studies in which subjects respond *immediately* and *overtly* to the presentation of stimulus objects of one kind or another. Suppose, for instance, that subjects are asked to identify simple geometrical forms. If certain responses are elicited by particular forms in a regular manner, then empirical relations can be established between physically definable stimulus objects, on the one hand, and frequencies and/or kinds of responses, on the other. Subsequently, almost unlimited experimentation can be conducted to determine the conditions under which these relations do or do not hold. One can vary the size, color, shape, intensity, texture, and distance of the figures, or note whether the responses are affected by training, by the use of inverting lenses, by the level of dark adaptation, and so on. The goal of such research is to determine the range of conditions across which the stimulus-response function remains invariant; or, alternatively, to outline the boundary conditions that must be fulfilled if the stimulus-response law is to hold true. This can be done quite successfully without, at any time, referring to or invoking a concept of perception. Innumerable studies could be cited to support the contention that a construct of perception is not essential either to the formulation of many stimulus-response laws or to the determination of the interactive effects upon them of motivational, associative, and other variables. Moreover, highly detailed and satisfactory physiological interpretations of the manifold organic events intervening between stimulus and response can be developed without including perception as a link in the explanatory chain.

The preceding arguments suggest that the concept of perception may be superfluous in many situations, but the possibility remains that the concept might play a useful explanatory role in *some* situations. One such situation is that in which a stimulus is presented but no overt response appears until some time after the stimulus has been removed. In attempting to interpret this behavior one might assume that during the initial stimulus-exposure period, a covert perceptual response or process was aroused. And this internal, perseverating sequel to stimulation might then be treated as the immediately effective determinant of the subsequently evoked overt response. This view has the virtue of permitting us to incorporate into an objective theory of behavior any instance in which a subject says that he perceived something (in the past) even though at the time the stimulus was presented he made no overt reaction whatever.

Defining Perception. If perception is to serve as a conceptual bridge in such delayed-response experiments and in others, it must be operationally defined, the definition being structured so as to contain no reference to the particular behavior that is alleged to be determined by perception. In defining intervening variables such as drive, one can formulate acceptably independent definitions in several ways, and the same variety of definition is apparently acceptable for the concept of perception. To take a single example, a subject might be defined as "perceiving" in one situation on the basis of his behavior under other conditions. To make this clear, let us suppose that we have determined for a given subject an empirical relation between the verbal response "triangle" and a physical stimulus having a triangular form. If this subject is now presented with a triangle, but for one reason or another makes no overt verbal response, we can still assert that he perceived the triangle, *by definition.* These relations are shown in schematic form in Fig. 8:1. The S_T ------ R_V linkage at the top of this diagram is the empirical law relating the triangular stimulus (S_T) to the overt verbal response (R_V). This law is then used as the basis for the assertion that a covert perceptual response (r_p) is evoked in the stimulus-presentation situation where no overt reaction occurs. If, as is shown in the bottom line of the diagram, the verbal response is evoked subsequently when the subject is instructed to recall, even though S_T is not present, then this response may be attributed to the perceptual reaction. The occurrence of R_V is in no way essential to the structure of the definition of r_p, however, and it can be asserted, therefore, that the subject has perceived, irrespective of whether R_V, some other response, or even no response at all is elicited during the recall phase. Thus this definition of r_p is seen to be, as it must be, entirely independent of whatever behavior one might choose to attribute to r_p.

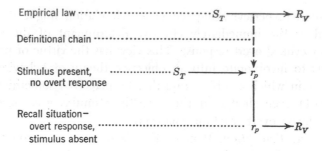

Fɪɢ. 8:1. This diagram summarizes the several steps and relations that would be involved in one kind of definition of perception. First of all, an empirical law relating the presentation of the triangle (S_T) to the occurrence of an overt, identifying verbal response (R_V) must have been firmly established. This law then provides the grounds for the statement that the perceptual response (r_p) has been evoked, *by definition*, when the triangle is presented but the overt response is absent. Finally, it may prove useful to invoke r_p in interpreting instances in which R_V appears in the absence of the triangle.

Inasmuch as perception can be defined in a variety of different ways, the results obtained with one definition may differ substantially from those obtained with another. For instance, if a child is presented with a number of circles and is told to draw what he sees, he may draw a number of ovals. If these responses are then used to define the child's perceptions, it is necessary to conclude that circles are perceived as ovals. And this conclusion must stand until some other definition of the child's ability to perceive can be formulated, which can be shown to have more scientific utility and significance than the first. For example, if the child shows under other conditions that he is capable of sorting circles into one pile and ovals into another, we may find it profitable to redefine his perceptions accordingly. By one of these criteria the subject perceives circles as ovals, but by the other he does not. When two definitions of perception fail to coincide in this manner, however, neither is "right" and the other "wrong." A correctly formulated definition is "wrong" only in the sense that in the interpretation of a broad range of behavior it may be less useful than some other definition. The well-known psychophysical methods, with their emphasis on the precise control and measurement of stimuli, on repeated observations, and on the use of statistically grounded inferences, provide us with our most trustworthy methods of deciding what is perceived and when.

Motivational Variables and Perception. Any experiment in which subjects are asked to identify, detect, or compare physically present stimuli would qualify, according to many writers, as being concerned in some way with perception. Inasmuch as the subjects in such experiments are responding overtly, it seems reasonable to expect that the introduction of motivational variables might produce changes in the frequency, latency, and/or correctness of the subjects' responses. The responses involved are the customary ones of labeling, naming, and discriminating, by saying "same," "different," "larger than," and the like. Consequently, if one chooses to define perception in terms of these responses, one must conclude that perception has been modified by a motivational variable whenever that variable is accompanied by changes in such responses.

Although experiments such as the above are often labeled "perceptual," they possess no unique attributes or characteristics by means of which they can be unambiguously distinguished from the so-called "discrimination" or "choice" experiments. Moreover, if perception is regarded as a covert response or process (e.g., r_p in Fig. 8:1) intervening between the external stimulus (S) and an overt response (R), and if *a motivational variable is operating throughout the entire S - - - - R sequence,* then any effect of that variable upon R may be attributable either to a change in the relation of S to r_p, or to a modification of the relation of r_p to R. Apparently, most studies of the effects of motivation on perception have been designed so that *the motivational variable is present both while the stimuli are being presented and while the response is being evoked.* None of these studies can be said, therefore, to have answered the question of whether perception, as well as overt behavior, can be modified by motivation.

In principle, however, an experiment designed to provide this information appears to be feasible. For example, one might present identical, impoverished stimuli to two groups of subjects, one operating under high drive, the other under low. Overt responses would be prevented by instructions during this initial stimulus-presentation phase. Then at a later time the drive level of both groups would be equated, and they would be given some kind of recall or recognition test. If drive affects perception, the performance of the two groups should differ during the second test phase, and such performance differences could not be ascribed to the effects of drive upon the relation of r_p to R. Effects of this latter variety could be detected, however, by equating drive during the stimulus-exposure phase and varying it during recall.

From these considerations the conclusion is reached that irrespective of how the motivation-perception problem is formulated, perception cannot be said to have been affected by motivation unless behavior is affected. *To study the role of motivational variables in perception is to study the changes wrought by these variables in the frequencies or kinds of responses exhibited by subjects in so-called perceptual experiments.* Whether these changes in response are to be ascribed to modified perceptions or to changes in response systems other than perception hinges on the design and interpretation of one's experiments.

Multiplicative-drive Theory and Perceptual Behavior. Hull, in theorizing about behavior in classical and instrumental conditioning situations, did not include the construct of perception in his group of intervening variables. But the responses evoked in perceptual experiments are clearly items of behavior, and it is appropriate, therefore, to inquire as to how such responses might be affected by changes in Hull's drive (D).

Let us consider, by way of example, a psychophysical (perceptual) experiment in which a subject's absolute threshold for visual stimuli is determined by the method of constant stimuli. With this method, a number of discrete stimuli, whose intensities range above and below threshold, are presented singly to a subject. Usually he is instructed to say "yes" if he sees the stimulus and "no" if he does not. The experimenter tabulates the frequencies of "yes" and "no" responses corresponding to each of the stimuli and after converting these frequencies into percentages plots them against the stimulus values to obtain the usual psychophysical function. The solid-line curve of Fig. 8:2 is a fictitious example of such a function. As this curve shows, the hypothetical subjects seldom perceive (say "yes" to) the faintest stimulus and almost always say "yes" when the brightest stimulus is presented. By convention, the absolute threshold is defined as the value of stimulus intensity that elicits "yes" responses 50 per cent of the time. In this graph, the threshold lies at stimulus 4 since the solid curve

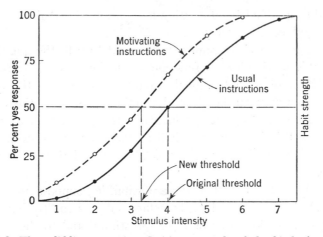

FIG. 8:2. The solid-line curve is a fictitious example of the kind of psychophysical function commonly obtained when the method of constant stimuli is used to determine an absolute threshold. The dashed-line curve, with its corresponding threshold, is the predicted outcome of the assumption that instructions alleged to be motivating actually serve to affect the associative strengths of the "yes" response to all stimulus intensities while leaving drive level unaltered.

intersects the horizontal 50 per cent response line directly above 4. Responses of saying "no" are not plotted in the figure, but these would decrease from a maximum at the left to a minimum at the right and would form a mirror image of the "yes"-response curve.

To apply Hull's multiplicative-drive theory to observations such as these we must first obtain some estimate of the relative habit strengths of the responses being recorded. On the simplifying assumption that drive does not vary with stimulus intensity, it follows that the habit strength of the "yes" response must vary directly with the frequency with which that response appears. The habit strength to say "yes" must be greatest, therefore, for stimulus 7 and weakest for stimulus 1. This fundamental assumption of a direct relation between empirical response percentages and habit strength is indicated by the "habit-strength" legend on the right-hand ordinate. It is not necessary, for purposes of this analysis, to specify the mechanisms by which these habits have been developed. It must be presumed, however, that these associative tendencies have been acquired prior to the experiment and are transferred to specific laboratory stimuli by means of verbal instructions to the subjects.

Having made this assumption, we next turn to the question of how this psychophysical function would be affected by the manipulation of a motivational variable. Within the theory two distinct answers can be given, depending on whether the variable leads primarily to a change in habit strength or to a change in drive. In this discussion we shall not consider instances in which motivational variables might affect both associative strength and drive.

To illustrate the first of these possibilities, suppose an attempt is made to raise drive level by telling subjects to "try hard" and to "pay very close attention" to the stimuli and to the assigned task. Instead of affecting drive, such instructions may function simply to elicit specific receptor-adjustive acts (cf. Spence, 1951a; Wycoff, 1952) such as blinking less often, moving the head less, and fixating the center of the exposure field more consistently. Or they may evoke tendencies to repress thoughts of impending social activities, classroom examinations, and so forth. If such responses are elicited by the alleged motivating instructions, the subjects should indeed show improved performance in detecting faint stimuli. In this instance better performance would be indicated by an increase in the frequency of "yes" responses and a corresponding decrease in "no" reactions. And since, by assumption, response frequency reflects habit strength, it must be concluded that the instruction-induced adjustive acts have led to an effective increase in the habit strength of the "yes" response for all stimuli save those of maximum initial strength. The observable result of such an over-all increase in habit strength would be a leftward shift of the psychophysical function and a corresponding drop in the threshold. This is shown in Fig. 8:2 by means of the dashed-line curve.

Several studies designed to test these expectations have been conducted in the psychological laboratories of the State University of Iowa. The results of two of these are shown in Fig. 8:3. The data plotted in the upper panel were obtained by Bechtoldt and McDonough (1958) in a situation in which the subjects were asked to report whether a faint gray spot could be seen when

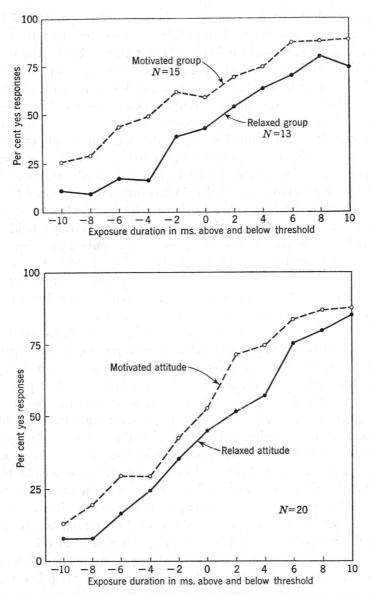

Fig. 8:3. The data plotted in the upper panel were obtained by Bechtoldt and McDonough (1958) and those in the lower panel by Ludvigson (1958). In both instances, attempts to increase the subjects' level of motivation by verbal instructions shifted the psychophysical functions toward the left and lowered the absolute thresholds. These empirical curves may be compared with the theoretically predicted results shown in Fig 8·7

presented at very brief exposures in a tachistoscope. The right-hand curve was obtained from subjects who were told to relax and take it easy, and the left-hand curve from subjects who were told to do their very best. Comparable results from an investigation by Ludvigson (1958) are shown in the lower panel. In his experiment a single group of subjects performed a tachistoscopic identification task under instructions designed to be motivating at one time and nonmotivating at another. The results of both of these studies are consistent with the hypothesis that "pay-attention" instructions can alter behavior in a perceptual experiment by affecting associative tendencies. When instructions produce these effects they should not, in all strictness, be described as "motivating," and interpretations of their influence on behavior should be carefully identified as associative, since they contain no reference to a motivational concept. Incidentally, there is little reason to suppose that instructions to try harder will always lead to better performance. Such instructions might actually arouse interfering tendencies and thereby produce a decrease in efficiency.

The second answer to the question of how an alleged motivational variable might affect behavior in a psychophysical experiment involves the assumption that the variable produces a change in drive strength alone. Referring to the hypothetical data plotted as the solid line in Fig. 8:4, it is apparent that the empirical frequencies of "yes" and of "no" responses are exactly equal for the threshold stimulus, and that therefore the associative strengths must also be equal at that point. Under these conditions an increase in drive should not produce any change in the relative frequencies of the "yes" and "no" responses, since the corresponding excitatory potentials will remain equal. Consequently, the threshold in a psychophysical experiment of this kind should not be affected if the motivational variable leads only to a change in drive.

When the "yes" and "no" habit strengths are not equal, however, an increase in drive, on the multiplicative assumption, will magnify the absolute difference between the two excitatory tendencies and thereby increase the frequency with which the dominant reaction is evoked. This condition of habit-strength inequality is met for all stimuli save 4. At stimuli 5, 6, and 7 the "yes-response" habit is stronger than the "no-response" habit, and an

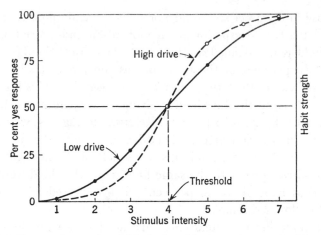

FIG. 8:4. If a motivational variable leads solely to an increase in drive, without affecting associative strengths, then the accompanying theoretical analysis suggests that the psychophysical function relating percentage of "yes" responses to stimulus intensity should become steeper. This is indicated here by the dashed-line curve. The absolute threshold, however, should not be affected by changes in drive alone.

increase in drive should enhance the frequency of "yes" responses at those points. By the same reasoning, intensified drive should reduce the frequency of "yes" responses to stimuli 1, 2, and 3, since the dominant tendency at these points is to say "no." These predicted effects, which are shown in Fig. 8:4 by means of the dashed-line curve labeled "high drive," should be negligible, of course, at stimuli 1 and 7 because of "floor" and "ceiling" effects, respectively. On the multiplicative-drive theory then, *intensified drive should increase the steepness of the slope of the psychophysical function throughout the middle portions of the stimulus range, but the absolute threshold, if defined in the conventional manner, should not change.* Since an increase in slope means a decrease in response variability, this indicates, in one sense, an increase in "perceptual sensitivity." This prediction may be less intuitively reasonable than our first, and the writer knows of no experimental data that clearly support it, but it does fit with the commonly held view that lackadaisical (unmotivated?) subjects yield flatter psychophysical functions than those who attend strictly to business.

Under the conditions specified in the foregoing example, an

increase in drive per se should not reduce the absolute threshold. But in the typical experiment on motivation and perception, the threshold is not defined as the point where the stimulus is perceived 50 per cent of the time, but as the point at which it is perceived two or three times correctly in succession. This is equivalent to defining the threshold as lying somewhere above the 50 per cent level, e.g., at 75 per cent. Referring to Fig. 8:4, we can see that the intersection of the high-drive curve with the horizontal line at the 75 per cent level falls to the left of the intersection of the low-drive curve with the same line. If the threshold were thus defined as lying above 50 per cent, then increased drive should lead to a lower threshold.

The foregoing interpretations have dealt only with the effects of motivational variables upon *absolute thresholds*, but similar principles can be applied to experiments in which the method of constant stimuli is used to determine *difference limens*. In such experiments, each of several comparison stimuli is repeatedly paired with a standard, the subject being asked to judge whether the comparison stimuli are "greater" or "less" than the standard with respect to some property such as loudness, length, brightness, or weight. The introduction of a motivational variable into an experiment of this kind would be expected to produce an over-all displacement of the psychophysical function, provided the variable leads to a general change in the strength of the associative tendency to say "larger than" (or "smaller than"). The practical outcome of such a displacement would be a shift in the point of subjective equality and the appearance of a constant error. (In a subsequent section of this chapter it is noted that the "value" of a stimulus object might affect a psychophysical function in this manner.) The *slope* of the function should not be altered, however, by habit-strength modifications alone, save in the unlikely event that associative tendencies corresponding to stimuli that are greater and less than the standard are affected in opposite directions.

If the motivational variable enhances drive, leaving associative strengths unchanged, then an increase in slope is the only predicted outcome. Initially, associative tendencies to say "greater than" should be stronger than tendencies to say "less than" for stimuli greater than the standard, and the reverse should be true for stimuli less than the standard. An increase in drive should function, therefore, on the multiplicative assumption, to increase the excitatory potentials of correct responses relative to incorrect ones, thereby reducing the size of the difference limens and improving accuracy of discrimination. Conversely, decreased drive should result in less accurate discriminations. However, the point of subjective equality, where "greater than" and "less than" responses are equally frequent and their associative strengths are presumably equal, should not be affected by modifications in drive strength.

The results of several studies conducted at the State University of Iowa are consistent in showing that the psychophysical function tends to become steeper under high drive when the method of constant stimuli is used to determine difference limens. The data from two of these experiments, by Clark (1958) and by Tandler (1958), are shown in Fig. 8:5. The same task, that of judging whether each of a number of comparison circles was larger or smaller than a standard, was used in both studies. And in both experiments drive level was supposedly lowered by pretending that the subjects' responses were not being recorded on certain trials and that these trials served only as rest-period activity. It is clear from these experiments that under the alleged high-drive condition the frequency of larger-than responses for stimuli larger than the standard was increased and the frequency of larger-than responses for stimuli smaller than the standard was diminished. However, the issue of whether the observed effects are due to changes in drive per se or to modified habit strengths is not settled by these results.

Throughout the foregoing theoretical development, it was assumed that the stimuli were relatively simple events such as faint lights or tones. In most experiments relating perception to motivation, however, words, nonsense syllables, or complex forms are used instead of lights or tones, and the subjects are required to name or identify the stimuli. When such stimuli are presented clearly and for relatively long periods of time, the correct responses, with rare exceptions, are evoked 100 per cent of the time. Hence if one is to study the effects of motivational or other variables on perception, the stimuli must be presented unclearly or in some

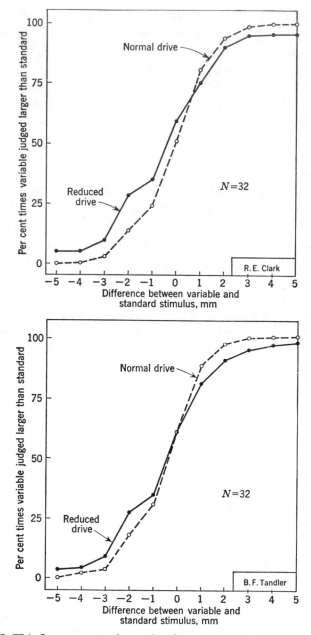

Fig. 8:5. This figure presents the results of two independent but identical experiments (Clark, 1958; Tandler, 1958) on the role of motivation in visual judgments of area. The method of constant stimuli was employed to determine difference limens, some observations being made under "normal" conditions and others (reduced drive) when the subjects were led to believe that their responses were not being recorded.

impoverished form so that identification is not always perfect. Impoverishment can be effected by blurring the outlines of visual forms, by shortening exposure times, by reducing stimulus intensity, or by various combinations of these methods.

To extend the multiplicative-drive theory to responses elicited by such impoverished stimuli, it is necessary first to consider the effect of impoverishment upon the habit strength of the identifying response. One possible assumption is that impoverishment produces no change other than a decline in habit strength. If so, then increased drive should magnify the values of the excitatory potentials for all impoverished forms of the stimulus, and performance in identifying the stimulus should improve. Moreover, this conclusion should hold for any stimulus to which a naming response has been strongly associated, irrespective of whether the stimulus is or is not related to the drive-producing conditions.

Alternatively, impoverishment might lead not only to a decline in the strength of the habit for the correct response, but also to a rise in the strength of other competitive habits. For instance, if the printed word *house* were made fainter and fainter, the middle letter might disappear sooner than the rest. Hence, for the impoverished stimulus, the strength of the habit to say "hose" might become stronger than that to say "house." Should impoverishment have this effect, accuracy of identification should decline under high drive, since the associative tendencies to utter the wrong words would be stronger than those to speak the correct words. The effect of drive upon the absolute threshold for simple physical stimuli (see Fig. 8:4) may also be regarded as an instance of habit-strength reversal of this kind, the habit strength for a response of "no" being presumed to exceed the "yes" response habit for all subthreshold stimulus values.

These expectations from the multiplicative-drive theory may or may not prove accurate when subjected to experimental test. For our present purposes, however, this is of minor importance. Of more significance is the fact that these limited predictions illustrate the application of a motivational theory to behavior which, if one chooses, may be described as "perceptual." While these guesses have been made without reference to a concept of perception, it is entirely possible that performance in psychophysical tasks will ultimately demand such reference.

Facilitative effects of motivational variables upon identifying responses to impoverished stimuli can be interpreted associatively as well as motivationally (cf. Brown, 1953a). Through past learning, need-related responses are more likely than others to have become associated with stimulus aggregates composed of both internal and external cues. When the strong supportive function of unambiguous external stimuli is weakened through impoverishment, the *relative* importance of internal cues will be enhanced, and if the motivational variable alters these internal stimuli, selective facilitative effects may be observed. In every instance, therefore, where motivational variables appear to have modified the responses that define perception, it is imperative to inquire whether the effect was indeed motivational or whether it could have been due to existing differences among, or changes in, the relative strengths of associative tendencies.

Primary Sources of Drive and Perception

The studies evaluated in this section are necessarily limited to those involving hunger and thirst as primary sources of drive for the reason that almost no other primary sources of motivation have been manipulated in studies of perception. Electric shock, which also seems to qualify as a primary source of drive, has often been used in perceptual experiments but in a manner that makes the treatment of such studies more appropriate to a later section on perception and secondary sources of motivation. Specifically, electric shocks have nearly always been paired with visual stimuli during preperception phases of experiments, and have usually not been administered while perceptual proficiency is being measured.

The Effects of Deprivation upon Perceptual Responses. An experiment by McClelland and Atkinson (1948) provides us with an example of investigations of the effects of food deprivation upon behavior in a perceptual situation. In this study subjects who had gone without eating for periods of from 1 to 2, 4 to 5, and 16 to 18 hours were asked to report what they saw at various times on a dimly illuminated screen. On most occasions no pictures of any kind were projected on the screen, but the subjects were made to believe that extremely faint pictures were indeed being shown. This belief was strengthened by the initial showing of a recognizable object and by occasional hints from the experimenter as to the nature of the "objects" being shown. Under these conditions, subjects who had been without food for 16 to 18 hours gave significantly more food-related responses than did those with 1 to 2 hours of deprivation, the number of responses made by the 4 to 5-hour group falling in between. The results were not entirely consistent, however, since in some cases, in answer to questions posed by the experimenter, increasingly hungry subjects gave more frequent responses related to instrumental acts of securing food, but did not give more frequent responses dealing with food items as such. Moreover, as the experimenter's hints contained increasingly direct references to food, the number of food responses increased, but not *differentially* as a function of hunger. And when vaguely defined blots were projected on the screen instead of blank slides, the frequency of food-related responses diminished.

According to some critics, the McClelland-Atkinson investigation is not "perceptual," since when blank slides were projected on the screen there was "nothing there" save a dim "blob" of light for the subjects to perceive. Nevertheless, the subjects were told that very faint pictures would be projected and that guesses might often have to be made as to the nature of the pictures. Under these conditions the subjects did report seeing things, and, with the exceptions noted above, the more severe their hunger the more numerous their food-related responses. Thus an empirical relationship was obtained between a motivational variable and responses by which perception could be defined. The question of whether it would be scientifically useful to define perception in terms of responses occurring in the absence of structured external stimuli can be answered only by a careful evaluation of the relative merits of this and of alternative definitions.

Lazarus, Yousem, and Arenberg (1953) have reported that the recognition of tachistoscopically presented pictures of food objects improves with hunger. This conclusion was based on data obtained from four groups of subjects whose tachistoscopic recognition thresholds for both food and nonfood objects were tested under 0 to 1, 2, 3 to 4, and 5 to 6 hours of food deprivation, respectively. The trend of the data for the first three groups was clearly in a direction to support the authors' conclusions, but a decline in performance was observed in the case of the hungriest group. Because of this reversal, conclusions from this study as to the sensitizing effect of hunger on perception must be limited to short periods of deprivation. Nevertheless, the tendency for recognition accuracy to improve with mild degrees of hunger was observed in two independently conducted experiments, and somewhat similar findings have been reported by Levine, Chein, and Murphy (1942). According to Lazarus et al. the drop in perceptual efficiency at the longer deprivation intervals may be a consequence of a conditioned hunger cycle, a possibility previously suggested by Sanford (1937).

That the facilitative effect of hunger on perception is relatively ephemeral is suggested by the results of a further study by Lazarus et al. This investigation was identical with the first, save that fewer subjects were run in each group and all observers were required, after each stimulus presentation, to select a response from a list containing the names of the 10 pictures plus six additional items. When freedom of choice was restricted in this way, recognition of food objects became increasingly worse, though not significantly so, as the period of deprivation was lengthened. No evidence was found in either study to indicate that hungry subjects make more food-related, prerecognition responses or give more food associations to the stimulus words of a free-association test than non-hungry subjects. Thus the findings of these several studies, though suggestive of a relation between hunger and tachistoscopic recognition thresholds, are not, because of reversals of direction and interexperiment inconsistencies, entirely convincing.

Two additional experiments, by Wispé and Drambarean and by Taylor have yielded contradictory results. Wispé and Drambarean (1953) asked subjects who had been without food and water for 0, 10, and 24 hours to identify tachistoscopically presented words. Both common and uncommon words, some related and some unrelated to food and water deprivation, were used. Analyses of recognition thresholds revealed that degree of "commonness" was the most important factor determining word recognition. Among both the common and uncommon words, however, significant interactions were obtained between severity of deprivation and need relatedness of the stimulus words. That is, recognition times for neutral words were unaffected by deprivation, whereas times for need-related words dropped markedly from the 0-hour to the 10-hour condition, thereafter remaining at about the same level for the 24-hour group. The authors conclude from these data that need-related words are recognized more easily as deprivation increases. Although the subjects' previous experience with words would account for their ability to recognize common words more readily than uncommon ones, the apparently positive effects of deprivation could scarcely be ascribed to the factor of familiarity since the differently deprived groups were presented with the same words.

Taylor (1956b), however, in an experiment similar to that of Wispé and Drambarean failed to confirm their findings. In her study the subjects' set to expect the presentation of food words was manipulated in addition to their degree of physiological need. In two replications of the experiment, with different orders of stimulus presentation, Taylor observed that the recognition thresholds of deprived subjects for need-related words did not differ significantly from those of satiated subjects. Subjects who had been set to expect need-related words, however, did have lower thresholds than control subjects.

A series of experiments by Gilchrist and Nesberg (1952) provides some final examples of studies relating need to perception. These investigators attempted to avoid certain of the methodological deficiencies of previous experiments by studying the short-term perceptual recall of both need-related and neutral objects. Specifically, their subjects were shown colored slides of food objects (or neutral objects), the intensity of the projector lamp being set at a standard level. Subsequent to the projection of each slide, the lamp voltage was either raised or lowered and subjects were asked to readjust the voltage until the projected image looked the same as when first presented. A stable result from an integrated series of four experiments was that all subjects tended to make positive time errors. That is, they tended to make the projected image brighter than the standard level. The positive time errors for satiated subjects remained constant, whereas those for deprived subjects increased progressively with hours of food deprivation up to a limit of 20 hours. In effect, therefore, performance became progressively worse as a function of increasing hunger. In one experiment involving pictures of fluids, increasingly severe thirst (for subjects who were also hungry) was accompanied by higher and higher voltage settings, whereas for satiated subjects no such progressive increase in positive time error appeared. Figure 8:6 shows the lamp-voltage settings made by thirsty and satiated subjects as a function of time since the start of the experiment.

Of special interest here is the dashed-line portion of the curve for the thirsty subjects. As the label indicates, the final point on the curve was obtained after the thirsty subjects had been permitted to drink as much ice water, orange juice, and/or milk as they wished. This strikingly precipitous drop was highly significant and was replicated in two further experiments. In these, Gilchrist and Nesberg showed that the increasingly positive time error associated with increased need was not due merely to the visually patterned nature of the food pictures but was dependent specifically on their need-related characteristics. From these studies the authors concluded that as need increased, positive time errors in the illuminance matches of objects relevant to that need tended to increase.

Since Gilchrist and Nesberg offer no theoretical interpretations of their rather dramatic findings, it is of interest to see whether

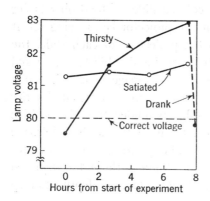

FIG. 8:6. Average lamp-voltage settings made by thirsty and satiated subjects in adjusting the brightness of a projected image of thirst-related objects to subjective equality with a previously seen image. True physical equality would have been obtained if the voltages had been set at 80. The drop at the right-hand side for the thirsty group coincided with their having drunk fluids ad libitum. (*From Gilchrist and Nesberg, 1952.*)

the type of explanation proposed earlier in this chapter can be expanded to encompass their results. We note first of all that even satiated subjects consistently made positive constant errors in their illuminance matches. This means that if two equally bright stimulus objects are presented, one after the other, the second is judged dimmer than the first. Or it means that if a subject is allowed to adjust the brightness of a second object to subjective equality with a first, he tends to set the second brightness level higher than that of the first. Thus a positive time error implies that the tendency to make adjustive response settings above the "true" value is stronger than the tendency to make adjustive reactions below the "true" value. Hence the two corresponding habit strengths must be unequal. But, as we have repeatedly noted, when habit strengths are unequal, increasing drive produces an increasing disparity between the corresponding excitatory tendencies and thereby an increase in the predominance of one overt response over another. Thus the finding that positive errors increase in magnitude with hunger but not under satiation follows as a logical consequence of the multiplicative-drive hypothesis. On this view, drive variations should have no effect when constant errors are absent. This theory does not, of course, encompass the data at the 0-hour point in Fig. 8:6. However, the surprisingly low voltage settings made at that point by the subjects who were later to become thirsty may well have been due to sampling fluctuations. At the start of the experiment both groups were equal with respect to level of deprivation, and hence their lamp-voltage settings should have been approximately identical.

This interpretation, though applicable to the difference between deprived and satiated subjects, must be modified to fit the data obtained by Gilchrist and Nesberg when the illuminance levels of need-related and non-need-related pictures were matched by the same subjects. These findings, shown in Fig. 8:7, would probably call for the introduction of an *incentive motivation factor*. Thus, as deprivation becomes more severe, the need-related items may elicit anticipatory responses of enhanced vigor, and greater and greater increments might be added to drive. This should lead, as indicated above, to an increase in the relative strength of the dominant response and hence to progressively larger constant

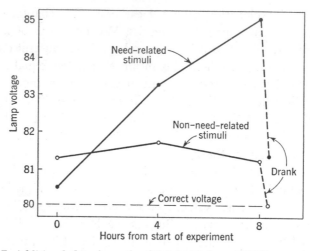

Fig. 8:7. Additional data from the Gilchrist-Nesberg (1952) experiment. In this phase a single group of subjects was tested with both need-related and non-need-related stimulus objects. Quite clearly, the magnitude of the positive error increases for need-related items but not for neutral items as a function of hours of water (and food) deprivation. The effect seems to disappear immediately, however, when the subjects are permitted to drink.

errors. By contrast, non-need-related items should not produce incentive-generated motivational increments. At this point, however, the theory seems to fall short; for although increasing thirst should have progressively magnified the constant errors even for non-need-related items, it did not do so (see Fig. 8:7, lower curve). Nevertheless, the terminal drop of the curve for non-need-related pictures, like that for need-related stimuli, is consistent with theoretical expectations.

We conclude this section with the following summarizing comments. Research purporting to have shown a relationship between intensity of physiological need and responses in perceptual situations has yielded suggestive and stimulating, though controversial and inconsistent, results. In some instances, deprivation seems to facilitate the identification of need-related pictures or words presented at near-threshold levels. Rather often, however, inconsistent or negative results have followed from the use of similar methods. Indeed, in experiments such as those of Gilchrist and Nesberg, increased deprivation has been shown to lead to poorer rather than better "perceptual" performance. All in all, therefore, experimental findings in this area, as well as theories as to their nature and relationships to other varieties of motivated behavior, must be viewed with reservations.

Secondary Sources of Drive and Perception

Up to this point, we have dealt only with experiments in which deprivation has served as the principal motivational variable, and in which motivational properties of the to-be-perceived stimuli, if any, have tended to play a secondary role. By far the largest group of experiments, however, consists of those in which the stimuli serve both as to-be-perceived cues and as the principal determinants of level of motivation. In nearly all of these cases the presumed capacity of the cues to function as motivational variables can reasonably be attributed to processes of learning. Such studies can legitimately be treated, therefore, as instances of the influence of secondary or learned sources of drive on perceptual behavior.

Motivation and Judgments of Magnitude. Most investigators whose studies fall in this category have been concerned with the problem of whether visual estimates of size are significantly affected by the value of the objects being judged. Usually, the stimulus objects have been coins, subjects being asked to equate coin size to that of a neutral disk, whose diameter can be varied. Unfortunately, many of the early experiments were characterized by methodological, experimental, and statistical inelegancies, and little confidence can be placed in the results. For example, in some studies an illuminated patch of light served as the variable stimulus, the diameter of which was adjusted by the subject to equal that of a relatively dark coin seen against a light background. This deviation from conventional psychophysical practice was sometimes further magnified by permitting subjects to hold the coins in their hands, tactual cues thereby being added to one stimulus complex but not to the other. Moreover, adequate controls were seldom included for the effects of the inscriptions on the coins or for differences among them in color, thickness, and weight. In spite of these defects, or perhaps because of them, the results of early studies (e.g., Bruner and Goodman, 1947) were so strik ing that, if they did nothing else, they aroused widespread interest and stimulated others to perform parallel experiments. In subsequent investigations the introduction of methodological refinements has, in some instances, reduced or obliterated the supposed enhancing effect of value on size. But positive results have also been obtained under more carefully controlled conditions and the phenomenon may well be genuine.

Although the majority of experiments have been directed toward determining the effects of value on estimates of size, it has also been reported that judgments of weight, numerosity, and brightness are altered by so-called motivational factors. The motivational state is most commonly assumed to be aroused by the specific stimuli being judged, though it has sometimes been varied by the selection of subjects whose socioeconomic needs are presumed to differ.

Value as a Source of Drive. One of the major conceptual problems attending studies of the perception of valued objects is that of specifying the mechanism by which variations in value might produce changes in drive. Inquiries as to the nature of value raise many complex questions that have intrigued and baffled economists and philosophers for generations. For the student of behavior, however, it seems apparent that value cannot meaningfully be treated as a property of physical objects as such, and that the most useful definition would be structured in terms of an object's power to elicit preferential approach and seizing responses from organisms. This would imply, incidentally, that value is always relative. A lump of sugar has more positive value to a rat than a block of wood if and only if the rat approaches and seizes the sugar instead of the wood. A 50-cent coin is more valuable than a dime only to the degree that individuals prefer the former to the latter. If the individuals are infants rather than adults, or if they have not been raised in our culture, or if the test is conducted during a period of severe inflation, neither coin may have more value than the other, and neither coin may have more value than a blank disk of paper or metal. To say, then, that a coin or any other object has value is to assert that it elicits responses of certain kinds, at certain times, and from certain individuals, and in addition, that these responses are different from those elicited by other coins or other objects. *A physical object is valuable only to the extent that organisms approach and choose it in preference to other objects.*

Defining value in terms of behavior helps to clarify the problem of how a valuable stimulus object might produce an increase in drive. The behavior of approaching and seizing objects such as coins, jewelry, new cars, and the like, which is characteristic of adults in our culture, is evidently learned as a consequence of the rewards provided by society. When a subject in an experiment on judgment of size is presented with both a coin and a neutral disk, the coin must, if it is to be defined as having positive value, elicit stronger tendencies of approaching and choosing than does the neutral disk. And since the coin has become a positive goal object, the sight of it may well elicit learned tendencies to make anticipatory goal reactions $(r_g s)$, which in turn may contribute increments to the subject's general level of drive (D). When the problem is structured in this manner, value becomes covariant with strength of incentive motivation, a topic discussed in detail in Chapter 5.

In brief, when the value of a stimulus object is manipulated, simultaneous (and correlated) changes are presumed to be induced in the strengths of learned tendencies to approach and possess the object. And in so far as anticipatory goal reactions occur, their vigor, and hence the drive increments they provide, should also increase with the value of the goal object.

A parallel interpretation can be made of studies in which motivational or affective levels have been manipulated by the selection of groups alleged to differ in personality or in social position. Thus, if judgments of coin size are made by poor and rich children, it might be argued that *the groups differ with respect to the strengths of their habits to seek and secure coins, and perhaps also, therefore, in the intensities of their anticipatory (drive-contributing) responses.* However, variations in drive strength alone should not affect judgments of coin size if the associative tendency to say "larger than" is equal in strength to the tendency to say "smaller than" when a coin is compared to a neutral disk of identical size. Presumably, therefore, differences in the strengths of linguistic habits must be invoked as an adjunct to the preceding interpretation. This matter will be treated in more detail after the consideration of additional illustrative investigations.

Experimental Studies of the Judged Size of Coins. If the value of an object determines its apparent size to any degree, the effect must be revealed through changes in the nature of subjects' responses concerning the size of that object. Phrased in this way, the problem seems relatively straightforward, but the design of an experiment adequate to provide unequivocal results is far from simple. It would not do, for example, to present a coin to a subject and ask him simply to estimate its size in inches or millimeters. Even if the mean of his judgments differed significantly from true physical size, one would have no way of knowing whether the discrepancy was due to value, to the presence of a picture on the coin, to the subject's lack of practice in making such estimates, or to any of a number of other factors. In principle, there is only one way in which the effects of value on judged size can be unambiguously assessed: *judgments must be made of the relative size of a valued object when it is compared with less valued objects having essentially identical physical properties.* By this criterion, an ideal experiment on size as a function of monetary value, would be one in which subjects are required to say whether genuine coins (or bills) looked larger or smaller than counterfeit moneys. Were an experiment done in this way, all sources of variability save value would be properly controlled. Conclusions based on the use of control objects whose physical properties or backgrounds deviate substantially from those of the valued objects cannot be regarded as definitive. Moreover, for complete confirmation of the value-size hypothesis, increases in value would have to be accompanied by progressively greater distortions of apparent size, at least over a certain range of sizes. The greater an object's value, the greater should be the distortion of its apparent size when compared with suitable control objects. Unfortunately, nearly all existing studies have failed, in one respect or another, to meet these ideal conditions, and we must content ourselves with suggestive rather than conclusive findings.

Confining our attention for the moment to studies of common coins, we find scant evidence that when they are physically present their size is enhanced. In their initial investigation Bruner and

Goodman (1947) reported astonishingly large overestimations of coin sizes when compared with judgments of cardboard disks. But findings of subsequent studies in which the controlling base line has been more appropriately provided by metal disks have, in the main, been negative.

Carter and Schooler (1949), seeking to check the Bruner-Goodman results, asked children to adjust the size of a circular patch of light to correspond to the sizes of various coins, metal disks, and cardboard disks. Their results, for coins and aluminum disks only, are presented in Fig. 8:8. The cardboard-disk data have been omitted on the ground that cardboard disks are less suitable as control objects than aluminum disks. As these curves reveal, the sizes of the penny, dime, and nickel were all *underestimated*, though not significantly, both with reference to true size and to aluminum disks. Both the 25- and 50-cent pieces were overestimated, the latter significantly so. Subsequently, Bruner and Rodrigues (1953) also found the penny and nickel to be judged smaller than worthless metal counterparts, only the quarter being estimated as larger (nonsignificantly) than its corresponding metal disk. Both coins and metal disks, however, were judged as larger

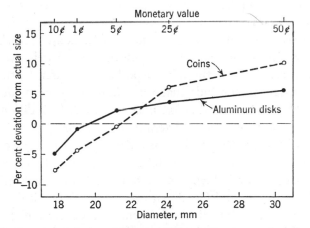

Fɪɢ. 8:8. Experimental data indicating that small coins tend to be judged smaller and large coins larger than aluminum disks equal in size to the various coins. These results were derived from tests in which physically present coins and disks were matched to a circular patch of light, whose diameter could be controlled by the subjects. (*Adapted from Carter and Schooler, 1949.*)

than paper disks. The rather commonly held view that coins, when *physically present*, tend to be judged larger than metal disks of comparable size is thus apparently supported by the data for only one coin (50-cent piece) from a single experiment (Carter-Schooler). And even this effect may be due less to value per se than to other factors such as the design on the coin.

Whether available data support the notion that degree of over-estimation of size increases with value is also questionable. In the Carter-Schooler study, the effect was indeed greater for the more valuable of the two coins that were overestimated. But in the Bruner-Rodriguez study, since only the quarter was overestimated (the 50-cent piece was not used) relative degree of *overestimation* cannot be determined. These latter authors, finding little evidence for absolute overestimation, suggest that when the members of a stimulus series are valuable, the *differential* enhancement between the terminal members of that series will be greater than between corresponding members of a neutral series. But their data, cited to support this contention, do not show differential *enhancement*, if this is taken literally to mean that all coins are enhanced in some degree, higher valued ones being enhanced more. Rather, their findings, like those of Carter and Schooler, are that negative enhancement (underestimation) occurs for small coins and positive enhancement for larger ones. To explain this by the value hypothesis one would have to contend that coins of little value have even less value than metal disks; but such a twist would impose a severe strain on the value hypothesis. Apparently, therefore, it is necessary to conclude that *when judgments are made of the size of physically present coins, under controlled conditions, their value is an as-yet-unproved determinant of their apparent size.*

Before leaving this problem of judged size of coins, we should note that the socioeconomic status of the subject, his age, and other factors may influence his estimates. Children described as "poor" by Bruner and Goodman overestimated physically present coins more than did "rich" children. But Carter and Schooler, who used larger groups, obtained no significant differences between the judgments of rich and of poor children under coins-present conditions. To confound the issue further, Rosenthal (1951) reports the size estimations of rich ten-year-olds to be greater than those of poor subjects for every coin, but the reverse to hold for six-year-olds. In many studies, judgments have also been made of the remembered sizes of coins by both rich and poor subjects. These memory judgments have not been treated here since they fall outside the conventionally defined area of perception, but it appears likely that value has a more marked effect upon judgments of remembered size than upon the apparent size of physically present objects (e.g., Carter and Schooler, 1949).

Other Studies of Apparent Magnitude and Value. We turn now to other studies, in which, for the most part, coins were not used as stimulus objects or in which unusual techniques were adopted. In this latter respect the investigation of Ashley, Harper, and Runyon (1951) is of special interest. Seeking to control attitudes towards money, these investigators told hypnotized subjects to forget their previous life histories. On some occasions the subjects were told they really had lived very poverty-stricken lives, and at other times that they had been reared in extremely well-to-do homes. All subjects were also tested in the normal waking state. When the "poor" state was induced, subjects tended slightly to overestimate the sizes of all coins, relative to true size, and when the subjects were "rich," they tended to underestimate all sizes.

The results of this experiment, for responses made with coins present, are shown in Fig. 8:9. The differences between the subjects' responses when "poor" and when "rich" were statistically significant, but the differences between "poor" and "normal,"

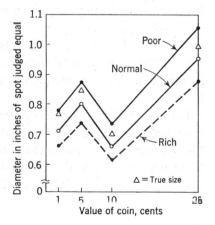

Fig. 8:9. Judgments of the size of physically present coins made by subjects under normal conditions and under hypnotically induced "rich" and "poor" attitudes. (*Adapted from Ashley, Harper, and Runyon, 1951.*)

"poor" and "true" size, "rich" and "normal," and "rich" and "true" size were not evaluated by Ashley et al. and were presumably not significant. Indeed, for three of the coins, the subjects, when "poor," came closer to the true sizes than when "normal," and the size exaggerations produced by the "poor" instructions, though they occurred for every coin, were of doubtful significance. Moreover, the tendency of the subjects (adults) when in the "rich" state to underestimate all sizes is consistent with neither Rosenthal's data from ten-year-old subjects nor with the results provided by Bruner and Goodman's rich subjects. Very possibly, as Ashley et al. have noted, their findings may be due in part to the fact that their subjects when "poor" were very attentive and hence more accurate, whereas the same subjects when in the "rich" state were relatively careless, responded quickly, and only "condescendingly cooperated."

A final phase of the Ashley, Harper, and Runyon study marks the use of a new and ingenious procedure. In this phase the hypnotized subjects, under both "rich" and "poor" instructions, were required to match the diameters of a variable circle of light and a metal slug. At diverse times the slug was described to the subjects as either lead, silver, white gold, or platinum. The results of this test, reproduced in Fig. 8:10, show that estimated size tended to increase with the declared value of the metal and that "poor" judgments inclined more toward overestimation than "rich" ones. Because the same slug was used under all conditions, one cannot appeal to uncontrolled external stimulus factors to explain the results. Unfortunately, since we have so little knowledge of what takes place during hypnosis, these findings cannot readily be generalized to "normal" subjects. Nevertheless, tests conducted under hypnosis may reveal the operation of processes whose effects in waking subjects are usually obscured by sets, attitudes, and the like.

Experimental results entirely negative with respect to the size-value hypothesis have been reported by Lysak and Gilchrist (1955). Using paper currency rather than coins, they required adult subjects to match the bills against control rectangles bearing designs of varying complexity. Estimates of size were found to be unaffected

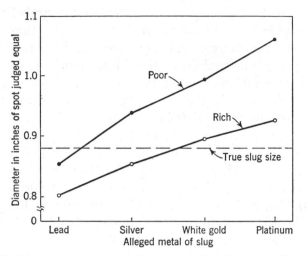

F<small>IG</small>. 8:10. Subjects under hypnotically induced "rich" and "poor" attitudinal states made judgments of the size of a gray iron slug. The effects upon their judgments of being told that the slug was made of lead, silver, white gold, or platinum are shown in the figure. (*Adapted from Ashley, Harper, and Runyon, 1951.*)

by the monetary value of the bills, though apparent size increased with increasing complexity of patterns on the control rectangles.

In some experiments essentially valueless objects have been artificially endowed with symbolic "value" by inscribing them with marks such as the dollar sign. This procedure was followed by Solley and Lee (1955). In their study white cardboard disks bearing the dollar sign were found to be significantly overestimated even though the nonmonetary symbols used on control disks had been judged to have the same degree of "perceptual closure" as the dollar sign. These data were interpreted to mean that symbolic value affects perceived size, but the brevity of the original report, which describes only one other symbol (swastika), makes critical appraisal difficult. The disks were equated for degree of closure, but this may not have eliminated the kinds of stimulus variables which, in perceptual illusions, lead to nonveridical report.

The hypothesis that symbolic value affects apparent size is supported to some degree, however, by a study of Dukes and Bevan (1952). Their subjects participated in a "gambling" game involving cards of identical size but of different symbolic value, as indicated by printed numbers ranging from − 300 through 0 to + 300. These cards were randomly chosen, and the subject won or lost amounts determined by the printed numbers. After each such trial, the subjects selected, from a graduated series of blank control cards, one which they judged equal in size to the value card. As the monetary value printed on the test card increased from 0 to + 300 the subjects tended to select larger reference cards. That is, the estimates of size were smallest for test cards of 0 (printed) value and increased in a negatively accelerated manner as symbolic value was heightened. However, the subjects also tended to select larger and larger blank reference cards as the value of the printed cards changed from 0 to − 300. If one regards this as decreasing positive value, as seems reasonable, then the results for the negative cards fail to conform to the value-size hypothesis. These results might be due in part to the fact that the physical length of the numbers stamped on the cards increased with both positive and negative value. Consequently, the tendency to overestimate the size of the cards at the extremes of the scale, whether positive or negative, may have been dependent on the size of the printed numbers rather than on "subjective value." No nonvalued control cards were used to evaluate the significance of this factor.

Additional positive results have been reported by Beams (1954), who observed that children with strong food preferences tended to make significantly more frequent larger-than judgments of their favored foods. Mausner and Siegel (1950), however, using stamps of similar size and shape, but of alleged values ranging from 5 cents to $12, found no evidence for the alteration of recognition thresholds by value.

Similar studies, in which factors other than value have been manipulated, have produced both positive and negative results. Thus Bruner and Postman's (1948) subjects judged tokens inscribed with positive symbols as larger than tokens bearing negative or unpleasant inscriptions. Klein, Schlesinger, and Meister (1951), however, in a comparable study were unable to demonstrate that the apparent size of neutral objects was changed by affective symbols. Young children may be more susceptible to these effects, since Lambert, Solomon, and Watson (1949) report enhanced estimates of the size of neutral disks that have been associated with rewards, and diminutions of size when rewards are withdrawn.

Though lack of space does not permit a full report of other studies relevant to the problem of size as a function of value, it seems fair to conclude that, *at best, the effect is relatively slight especially when the valued objects are physically present.* Value seems to exert its greatest effects upon the judgments of children and hypnotized adults, and individual differences in the need for money influence judged size, provided that estimates are made from memory.

An Interpretation of Size-Value Relations. The data we have reviewed on the size-value hypothesis, though leaving many questions unanswered, are sufficiently suggestive to warrant further research as well as the development of theories as to how value might affect apparent size. In this latter area little has been done, and Jenkin (1957), in his comprehensive review, lists only two such attempts. One of these is a single sentence by Bruner and Rodrigues suggesting that the effect may be due somehow to the frequent pairing in the environment of size and value. The other, a proposal of Dukes and Bevan, is that value, like certain parameters of electronic circuits, functions to "tune" the organism to respond selectively and with "amplification" to valued objects. In an earlier section of this chapter it was suggested that valued objects might function after the manner of incentives to arouse anticipatory drive-producing reactions. However, the details of the process through which value might affect size-estimating behavior were not presented, and it is to this task that we now turn.

In a psychophysical study employing the method of constant stimuli, accentuated size would be revealed as a displacement of the function toward the region of the stimulus dimension composed of large comparison objects. Such a shift has been diagramed in Fig. 8:11, the assumption being that the solid-line curve was obtained when a metal disk the size of a 50-cent piece was compared, as the standard stimulus, with other metal disks. The dashed-line curve is assumed to have resulted from the use of a real half dollar as the standard stimulus. In this imaginary experiment, the point of subjective equality (PSE) falls at stimulus 4

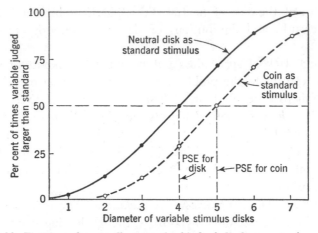

FIG. 8:11. Fictitious data to illustrate the kind of displacement of a psychophysical function that should be obtained with the method of constant stimuli if a coin tends to be judged larger than a neutral disk of equal diameter. It is assumed here that the point of subjective equality (PSE) shifts from variable stimulus 4 to stimulus 5 when the coin is used as the standard stimulus.

with a metal-disk standard stimulus and at stimulus 5 with the coin as a standard. For simplicity, no change in slope is assumed to have accompanied the rightward displacement of the curve. In interpreting the dashed-line curve we must remember that the decreased percentages of "larger than" judgments for all the comparison metal-disk stimuli mean a general increase in the tendency to judge the valued coin as "larger."

As a result of our previous analyses the conclusion was reached that an increase in drive alone should increase the steepness of a psychophysical function, but should not displace the entire function in the manner shown in Fig. 8:11. Altered habit strengths, however, could have this effect. The necessary steps in developing this argument are as follows:

First, we reiterate the view that an object such as a coin has positive value only because individuals approach and select it in preference to other objects. Consequently, objects can only be rank-ordered with respect to value when we know the rank orders of their capacities to elicit choosing and seizing responses. Secondly, in a great many instances, objective size tends to vary directly with value, especially when similar types of objects are grouped together. Houses, cars, diamonds, ranches, TV sets, candy bars, and bundles of money are, for the most part, more valuable when large than when small. Consequently, it seems reasonable to expect that tendencies to make *verbal responses* such as "large," "impressive," "bigger," "heavier," "broader," and "higher," should become strongly associated through learning with those objects toward which strong habits of approach are being established. Hence it follows that any object of demonstrable value must be one tending strongly to evoke instrumental choice reactions and, in addition, verbal responses of the general class "large." Finally, a shift of the point of subjective equality must occur if a valued object elicits more "larger-than" responses than a neutral object of equal size. To find such a shift is to obtain empirical evidence that "value leads to a perceptual accentuation of size."

It will be seen that this interpretation of the effects of value upon judgments of size is purely associative, since it contains no reference to a specific motivational entity. Moreover, this view is similar in some respects to the Bruner-Rodrigues conception, mentioned earlier, and to suggestions presented by Lambert, Solomon, and Watson (1949). Our interpretation is also consistent with the findings of experiments such as that of Proshansky and Murphy (1942), in which perceptual judgments were altered by rewards and punishments.

The Perception of Stimuli Associated with Noxious Events. As we have seen, it may be possible, by manipulating the value of a stimulus object, to vary habit strengths and/or incentive motivation and hence to change the nature of the responses defining perceived magnitude. If a subject is repeatedly punished rather than rewarded for responding to certain stimuli, one would expect that avoidance behavior and emotionality would become strongly associated with such stimuli and that changes in drive and habits resulting from such learning might also affect perceptual behavior.

Existing experiments in which anxiety-arousing stimuli have been used as the to-be-perceived cues may be divided into two broad classes. In one the perceptual identification of initially neutral cues is tested following a training period in which noxious stimuli —usually electric shocks—have been paired with the neutral cues

—usually words. Studies constituting the second group are distinguished by the use of stimuli such as vulgar words, which, as a consequence of socialization training, have supposedly acquired tendencies to evoke emotional reactions of disgust, apprehension, or anxiety. (The present section deals with only the first group, the second being covered subsequently.) Though superficially different, both groups of experiments pose the *question of whether a conditioned stimulus for an emotional response can be more (or less) readily identified than an equally familiar neutral stimulus.* Or, when account is also taken of typical experimental procedures, the question becomes that of whether responses of identifying and naming impoverished forms of a given stimulus will be altered when that stimulus also elicits an emotional response.

Conceptualizing the problem in this manner permits us to relate this kind of perceptual research to other traditionally nonperceptual problems. For one thing, it becomes clear that in this area the student of perception and the student of conditioned fear or anxiety are dealing with much the same phenomena, though the former individual is less interested in the strength of the emotional response than in its effects on identifying reactions. The student of perception asks whether a learned emotional tendency functions as a motivational variable in modifying the effective strength of a nonemotional associative tendency (the identifying response) when both tendencies are attached to the same stimulus. But this, as has been noted in Chapter 5, is very similar to the *acquired-drive problem.* It is this relation that has led us to treat these perceptual tasks as activities involving secondary sources of drive.

Studies of the perception of threatening stimulus objects are also similar to experiments on *stimulus generalization,* save that in the former studies the stimulus in its clearly identifiable form elicits both a learned identifying response and an emotional reaction that may function motivationally. In presenting generalized (impoverished) versions of that stimulus, therefore, one seeks to determine whether the generalized identifying response will be modified in motivational ways by the simultaneously elicited generalized emotional response. A so-called neutral control stimulus is presumably one whose impoverished versions elicit a generalized identifying response but little or no emotion.

The problems that arise in studying the identification of inimical cues are also related to those that attend research on *stimulus distinctiveness*. The central problem in the latter investigations is whether the identifiability of a stimulus, as estimated from the ease with which new responses can be attached to it, can be enhanced by associating other distinctive (often nonverbal) responses with that cue. Here, however, in contrast to the so-called perceptual experiments, the added associative connections are typically neutral emotionally.

In the light of the preceding analysis, and assuming that emotional arousal often has motivational-variable-like effects, we must go on to specify the mechanism or mechanisms underlying emotionally altered perceptions.

Mechanisms of Emotionally Modified Perceptual Behavior. It is an unfortunate fact that in the studies under consideration one finds few specific statements or hypotheses as to how emotionality may affect perception. Although it is usually assumed that emotionality is motivating, almost nothing is said about either the nature of motivation or its relation to perception. In general terms, motivation is alleged to function either to prevent the individual from seeing the stimulus clearly—this is termed *perceptual defense* —or to help him to see the stimulus more clearly—this is *perceptual vigilance* or *sensitization*. As numerous writers have noted, however, specific hypotheses as to which of the two effects will occur under a given set of conditions are singularly rare.

On the assumption that a perceptual situation involves the sequence of the stimulus (S), a covert perceptual response (r_p), and an overt (usually verbal) identifying response (R_V), there appear to be two possible ways in which R_V can be affected by stimulus-evoked emotionality. First, if the emotional response (r_e) occurs either before, or concomitantly with, r_p, then the development of r_p, and ultimately of R_V, could either be hindered or facilitated by r_e, depending upon the properties assigned to r_e. Second, if r_e has a longer latency than r_p, as would certainly be the case if the occurrence of r_e were contingent upon r_p, then any effects of r_e upon overt behavior would have to be due to modifications of the functional linkage between r_p and R_V or to direct effects upon R_V. According to some authors, it is only when behavior is affected in the first of these ways that one can properly speak of "pure" perceptual defense or vigilance. For such writers alterations in behavior attributable to the second of the above mechanisms should be regarded as instances of response suppression or augmentation, since the alleged perceptual response (r_p) is not directly affected by r_e.

To clarify the implications of this interpretation, let us suppose that a single taboo word is presented *just once* at near threshold level to each of a group of subjects. If this word is identified less often than an equally familiar neutral word (presented in the same way to other subjects), either the hypothesis of "pure" perceptual defense or the hypothesis of response suppression could account for the results. But if each subject is presented with only one word on a single occasion, the emotionality produced by that word can only affect r_p, and thereby produce "pure" perceptual defense or vigilance, if r_e occurs as soon as or before r_p. Unfortunately, little can be said about the *relative* latencies of emotional and perceptual responses. But from what is known concerning the latencies of peripheral autonomic reactions (cf. Solomon and Wynne, 1954) it would appear that emotional responses *may* develop too slowly to affect perception itself in a single-trial situation such as this.

Stimulus- induced emotionality may not, therefore, affect perception in this kind of single-trial experiment, but the procedures followed in actual experiments are such that even if r_e does have a long latency, it nevertheless can affect perception. Thus it is customary in studies of perceptual defense to present each word a number of times, exposure durations being increased progressively, as in the ascending order of the method of limits, until recognition occurs. Obviously even a long-latency r_e, provided it persists for several seconds, can, under these conditions, antedate and thereby modify perceptual responses elicited by subsequent presentations of the same or different words. Moreover, the emotionality generated by additional taboo words in a list could serve either to heighten the average emotional level or to prevent its decline. Conventional experimental procedures, therefore, insure that r_p can be affected by emotionality, though they do not insure that the influence of r_e will be confined to r_p alone, since a persisting r_e could also affect the relation of r_p to R_V.

Evidence to support this hypothesis of persisting emotionality is provided by the McGinnies and Sherman (1952) study, in which recognition thresholds for neutral words were found to be elevated by the prior presentation of taboo words. They used the term "generalization" for this effect, but it seems more appropriate to describe it as persisting or residual emotionality. Incidentally, the hypothesis of persisting emotionality leads to the methodological recommendation that neutral words should not be interspersed among nonneutral words in the same list if one wishes to maximize differences in the thresholds for the two kinds of words.

Turning now to the specific roles that might be played by r_e, it is clear that both its possible contribution to general drive and its associative effects merit consideration. On the assumption that drive varies directly with the strength of r_e, the problem is reduced to the more general one that we have already discussed of word-identification thresholds as a function of drive intensity. Thus if the associative strengths of the neutral and taboo words in a single list are simply weakened by impoverishment rather than supplanted by other (incorrect) associative tendencies, then all thresholds should be lowered by heightened drive. Or if taboo words alone are presented to one group of subjects and neutral words to another group (familiarity equated) then only the taboo-word thresholds should be lowered, provided additional qualifying assumptions such as the above are also met.

Any associative interpretations that one might formulate of the effects of r_e upon word-identification thresholds would probably follow the general lines of reasoning presented in Chapter 4 and in earlier portions of this chapter. For example, it might be postulated that r_e leads to, or produces, distinctive internal stimuli (s_e) and that either facilitative or competitive reaction tendencies have been, or can become, attached to s_e through learning. From these assumptions, defenselike or vigilancelike effects, that are either selective or nonselective with respect to taboo and neutral words, could be satisfactorily explained. It should be noted, however, that the concept of emotionality is not crucial to associative interpretations such as these, and in a later section of this chapter it will be shown that some of the findings of perceptual experiments can be deduced from nonemotional assumptions resembling those of modern conflict theory.

The Perception of Stimuli That Have Been Paired with Shock. We turn now to specific laboratory studies in which recognition thresholds have been determined for stimuli with which electric shocks have been associated. Investigations of the *recall* of shocked words or syllables are omitted on the ground that they are related only indirectly to perceptual behavior.

In an experiment whose major purpose was not the investigation of perceptual accuracy as a function of conditioned emotionality, Lazarus and McCleary (1951) nevertheless obtained some relevant evidence. In the standardization phase of their experiment, 10 five-letter nonsense syllables were presented tachistoscopically at near threshold levels. On the basis of the subjects' responses, two groups of five syllables each were equated with respect to the number of times they were correctly recognized and also with respect to the frequency of their use by the subjects. Thus possible differences in familiarity between the two sets of syllables were minimized. Then, with the syllables clearly exposed for one-second periods, galvanic skin responses (GSRs) were conditioned to five of the syllables by the use of electric shock. Finally, all syllables were again presented in a tachistoscope at short exposure times, GSRs were recorded, and five seconds after each exposure the subjects made verbal reports of what they had seen.

The results obtained from tabulations of verbal reports are of immediate relevance here. These data, when corrected for response preference, *failed to indicate significant differences in the recognition of shock and nonshock syllables.* However, when no correction for response frequency was made, seven of nine subjects identified the shock syllables more accurately than the nonshock syllables, though again the differences were not significant. These data are consistent with the view that success in perceptual identification depends, in part, upon response frequency, but they yield no support for the supposition that the addition of an emotional tendency to a stimulus (by conditioning) modifies the accuracy of identifying responses.

From analyses of their GSR data, Lazarus and McCleary concluded further that even when subjects are unable to make correct verbal identifying responses, autonomic discrimination may be possible. This judgment was based on the fact that all nine of their subjects gave larger GSRs to shock than to nonshock syllables even when the syllables were incorrectly reported verbally. This effect was termed *subception* to indicate that "perceptual" discrimination, defined by autonomic activity, apparently takes place, even when "perceptual" discrimination, defined by verbal report, does not.

The subception effect and comparable effects reported by McGinnies (1949) and others have generated considerable argument and counterargument. The findings place some theorists in the difficult position of having to hold that a shock syllable is in a sense "perceived" as a shock syllable (and hence the subject reacts to it emotionally), and yet that it is not "perceived" since the subject cannot identify it correctly. Thus subjects are both discriminating and not discriminating.

This seeming paradox disappears if we reject the notion that all behavior, including autonomic activity, is a reflection of perception and that the "real" nature of perception can be appraised only through phenomenological statements concerning conscious awareness. In perception, as in all other subject-matter areas of psychology, there is no one "true" measure, and inferences based on any particular measure need not, and often do not, correlate perfectly with inferences grounded in a second measure. A subject in a verbal learning experiment, for example, may appear to have learned nothing if we estimate his learning by means of the *method of recall*. But with the *savings* method, we may be able to show quite clearly that practice has led to considerable learning. Similarly, a rat in a *T* maze may choose one side as often as the other, and from this we would conclude that no differential response tendency has been established. Measurements of running time, however, may indicate significantly longer times on one side than on the other, and quite different conclusions may be indicated. By analogy, the subjects of the Lazarus-McCleary experiment were not "discriminating" when verbal reports were taken as the criteria of differential response, but when reference was made to the average amplitudes of their autonomic reactions, they were "discriminating." The fact that the two measures yield different results should cause little surprise in the light of our experience in other research areas. Bewilderment ensues only when we speak in non-operational terms of "awareness." Unless we are to abandon the principle of scientific determinism we must maintain, as Bricker and Chapanis (1953) have insisted, that when responses to shock syllables are genuinely greater than those to nonshock syllables, and if other factors are equal, then the stimuli provided by the two kinds of syllables must be unequal. The fact that verbal-identifying responses to shock and nonshock syllables do not differ is indeed interesting, but it is paradoxical only when we champion the view that such responses constitute the only "true" mirror of perception as it "really" is.

Returning now to additional experiments involving electric shock, we find several of interest. Murphy (1953), for example, obtained evidence that shock may facilitate the perceptual identification of nonsense syllables. However, the tachistoscopic thresholds for shock syllables were not significantly lower than those for nonshock syllables, save when a normal scale-value transformation was made of the original data. Thus the degree of generality of his results may be somewhat limited. Lysak (1954) has also reported that previously shocked nonsense syllables are more readily seen than neutral syllables if punishment is not administered in the recognition situation. When shocks are given both during training and recognition phases, however, significantly higher thresholds are obtained for shock syllables than for nonshock syllables.

Reece (1954) has described an investigation purporting to demonstrate a relation between the reinforcement occasioned by shock reduction following the pronunciation of a nonsense syllable and the visual recognition threshold for that syllable. He used a paired-associates verbal learning task in which electric shocks were administered on half of the pairs of syllables. For one group of subjects shock was terminated (shock-escape condition) as soon as the response syllable was pronounced. But for a second group the shock was kept on (nonescape condition) for the entire duration of syllable presentation. On the tachistoscopic tests the shock-escape group exhibited generally lower thresholds than the group for whom shock escape was not possible. The thresholds for the shock-escape group, however, did not differ from those of a nonshocked control group. Apparently the thresholds of the shock-escape group were not lowered by reinforcement, but rather the thresholds of the nonescapable-shock group were raised. During the course of the paired-associates learning task, shock escape produced significantly better learning than did the inescapable shock condition, but not better than the nonshock condition. Thus the obtained differences in thresholds appeared to be due, not to improvement resulting from shock escape, but to interference generated by inescapable shock. Poorer performance during learning would indicate weaker associative strengths, and hence the recognition scores for the nonescapable-shock group should be lower. (This would qualify, evidently, as an associative, not a motivational, interpretation.) Finally, Reece found *no significant differences between the recognition thresholds for shocked and neutral syllables* within each group, regardless of whether the syllables were the "stimulus" or the "response" members of the pair. This is consistent with the negative findings of the Lazarus-McCleary study described above, and with the theoretical analysis in the preceding section.

In a more recent study of shock and perception, Pustell (1957) employed geometrical figures (diamond, circle, square, triangle) rather than taboo words or nonsense syllables. In a pretest phase, a tachistoscope was used to present cards, on each of which were mounted three grey forms and one black form. The subjects' task was to identify the spatial position of the darker figure on each card. Then in a training phase various subgroups of subjects were shocked while looking at each of the different black figures. Tests for the effects of shock were conducted by presenting cards on which all four figures were black, the requirement now being to point out the section of the card "which stood out" most. Because of the brief stimulus exposures, the subjects never realized that the all-black sets of forms were different from the original training sets having only one black figure. Significant changes in perceptual thresholds were obtained with male but not female subjects. As the result of shock, the males became more "vigilant," the particular form previously associated with shock being more often denoted as "standing out" than nonshock forms. Women, however, were affected in the opposite direction, tending to become "defensive." For them the shock figures were less likely (not significantly) to be seen as "outstanding." Pustell, in attempting to account for these findings, has postulated that perhaps anxiety provides a facilitative *cue* for men which helps them to identify the shock figure, whereas anxiety (in a way that is not explained) provides *drive* for women and thus leads them to be defensive.

The Perception of Socially Taboo Stimuli. Current interest in the problem of the perception of socially taboo words stems largely from an investigation by Bruner and Postman (1947), in which elevated thresholds for taboo as compared with neutral words were ascribed to perceptual defense. Although the literature on perceptual defense is very extensive, explicit definitions of the term are rare, a fact which may account, in part, for the frequent debates the field has witnessed in recent years. From implicit statements, however, it is evident, as we have already indicated, that perceptual defense means quite different things to different writers. For some the term is appropriate only to those incidents in which the preperception is both unconscious and specific to the preperceived stimulus, and in which the defensive reaction affects perception itself. For other workers perceptual defense seems to denote simply the empirical finding of higher recognition thresholds for inimical than for neutral stimuli. And in other instances the term is used to refer to a more or less conscious avoidance, of the sort made by individuals when they catch a fleeting glimpse of a gruesome or revolting scene. Closing the eyes, looking askance, or thinking of other things are, in this special sense, instances of perceptual defense. The term *perceptual vigilance* has also been variously and vaguely used, though it has received less attention than the concept of defense, perhaps because vigilance is less dramatically related to psychoanalytic theory.

During the years since defense and vigilance first came into psychological prominence, two major trends have developed in research and interpretation. The first is characterized by investigations and explanations designed to prove that the phenomena of both defense and vigilance can be adequately explained by appeal to conventional principles of associative learning. The aim of these studies has been to show that differences in the learning history of subjects prior to their entering the laboratory can account for what may appear to be laboratory-induced changes in perceptual processes. In essence, this is simply an associative view of the mechanisms mediating either raised or lowered identification thresholds.

The second stream of research arises from the premise that defensiveness and vigilance are not adjustive reactions of the population at large but attributes of individual personalities. On this view some subjects will be defensive, some vigilant, and others may be both, depending on the nature of the stimulus material and the circumstances under which it is presented. Our treatment of research in this area will involve the consideration of these two major trends.

Perception of Taboo Materials as an Associative Phenomenon. The first and most devastating blows against the view that defense is an unconscious, motivationally determined effect on perception per se were struck by Howes and Solomon (1950) and by Solomon and Howes (1951). These authors approached the problem from a strictly operational point of view, much as we have approached it in earlier sections of this chapter. This led them to the conclusion that perception is not studied directly, but is inferred from, or defined by, characteristics of the subject's responses and of the stimuli presented to him. In the majority of experiments on human perception, moreover, the subject's responses are verbal or linguistic, and hence it is only when linguistic responses change that one can properly speak of changes in perception. Thus, to study perception in these situations is to investigate the manifold variables of which linguistic behavior is a function. As Solomon and Howes (1951) have phrased it, ". . . *any variable that is a general property of linguistic responses must also be a property of any perceptual concept that is based upon those responses*" (p. 257).

The principal conception to which this line of attack leads is that the perception of printed words must depend, in considerable degree, upon the frequency with which the individual has seen, pronounced, and used those words in the past. That is, the stronger the learned associative tendency to give a linguistic response to a certain cue, the more readily will impoverished forms of that cue elicit the correct response, provided impoverishment does not itself alter relative associative strengths. In the typical perceptual experiment, this means that recognition thresholds should decrease as familiarity increases. In the terminology of this book, Howes and Solomon were simply asserting that the thresholds for linguistic identifying responses are inversely related to the habit strengths of those responses.

In criticizing previous studies in which perceptual defense was alleged to have been operating, Solomon and Howes noted that the taboo words might have been in many cases less familiar to college subjects than were the neutral control words. Where this was true, higher thresholds for taboo words could easily be explained without invoking the notion of defense. And by a similar line of reasoning one could also account for instances of perceptual vigilance, provided only that cogent evidence for the greater familiarity of the stimuli could be adduced.

This criticism of the concept of perceptual defense has undoubtedly had a widespread salutary effect upon research in this area. Almost without exception, some attempt is made in current investigations of the phenomenon to equate taboo and neutral words for familiarity and/or frequency of usage prior to determining their relative recognition thresholds. Familiarity values are most commonly allotted to stimulus words on the basis of their frequency of occurrence in written English, as determined by Thorndike and Lorge (1944). However, there is some question whether the Thorndike-Lorge counts are representative of word frequencies in today's written English. The word "Kotex," for example, which is sometimes used as a taboo word, does not appear in these counts. Moreover, it is doubtful whether any index of frequency based on written English is entirely adequate as an estimate of word familiarity in the population at large and especially among college students. As a consequence, those who defend the concept of perceptual defense (e.g., McGinnies, 1950) can assert with some confidence that the words whore, bitch, and belly are far more familiar, at least in spoken English, than the words beatific, elegies, and vignettes, even though the Thorndike-Lorge semantic counts show them all to be equally frequent. If the thresholds for taboo words such as these are elevated, the champion of defense may declare that this is in spite of their relatively high familiarity as estimated, perhaps, from frequency of usage in bull sessions and bars. And the opponent of defense, relying upon a different criterion of familiarity, may reason that the elevated thresholds are due simply to weaker associative strengths. Opinions differ, therefore, with respect to the appropriateness of various methods of defining familiarity. But it is generally conceded that any alleged instance of perceptual defense is suspect in the absence of evidence that the associative strengths of critical and neutral words have been equated.

Perhaps the best control of the frequency variable has been achieved in studies where the same words have been used under conditions designed to make them either threatening or neutral. McGinnies and Sherman (1952), as we have pointed out, found that neutral words, when preceded by taboo words, exhibited higher thresholds than when the neutral words were preceded by other neutral words. An interpretation in terms of differential familiarity cannot reasonably be applied to this experiment though residual emotionality might account for the findings. Wienar (1955) endowed words with either threatening or nonthreatening characteristics by imbedding them in different contexts for different groups. His subjects exhibited sensitization, however, rather than defense, a threat group requiring fewer recognition trials than a nonthreat group. This finding is consistent with the supposition that threat leads to an increment in drive, which in turn magnifies tendencies to make appropriate linguistic responses in the recognition situation.

A survey of experiments in which adequate controls for familiarity were lacking indicates that, with unselected populations, both higher and lower thresholds are reported for taboo words, the first result being more frequent than the second. The preponderance of defensive indications is not great, however, and even if the familiarity variable were not involved in important degree, processes other than defense may have been operating. One plausible explanation, also proposed by Howes and Solomon, is that subjects may resist saying a taboo word in the presence of an experimenter even for several trials after the word has been covertly identified. Thus, for example, a subject might well hesitate to say the word *penis* aloud even though reasonably certain that this specific word had been presented. Since the tendency to inhibit the overt enunciation of taboo words in certain kinds of social situations is unquestionably learned, it is not unreasonable to regard this "defensive mechanism" as fundamentally associative.

That response suppression of this kind may often function to produce "apparent perceptual defense" is indicated by a variety of studies. Chief among these is the investigation of Whittaker, Gilchrist, and Fischer (1952), in which it was found that Negro subjects deliberately refrained from making verbal identifications of words derogatory to their race until the stimuli became unambiguously clear. This conclusion was based on verbal statements of the subjects and on the fact that the effect was observed when the experimenter was white but not when he was a Negro. Evidence for comparable effects comes from other studies in which subjects have reported withholding responses or where significant subject-experimenter interactions have been observed. The act of refraining from overt enunciation because of felt or imagined social threats is itself quite obviously a kind of defense against anticipated embarrassment. It does not qualify as perceptual defense, however, if by this term one means the selective filtering of incoming inimical stimulus patterns.

In trying to keep subjects from withholding overt verbal responses, experimenters have devised a number of different procedures. For example, subjects may be instructed to respond in writing rather than orally; they may be told ahead of time that vulgar words are to be presented and that they should not be concerned over speaking them; or they may be given facilitative sets through instructions which allege that hesitation in uttering the critical words is a sign of maladjustment and neuroticism. The results obtained with procedures such as these favor the conclusion that as the tendency to withhold overt responses diminishes, differences between recognition thresholds for taboo and neutral words tend to disappear. Postman, Bronson, and Gropper (1953), for example, whose subjects responded in writing, actually found taboo words to have lower thresholds than neutral words, a difference which they attributed to an initial underestimation of the relative familiarity of the inimical words. Moreover, Freeman (1954) reported that when subjects were set to look for taboo words, recognition thresholds were no different than for neutral words. It also seems likely that taboo-word thresholds tend to be higher than neutral-word thresholds at the start of an experimental session, the difference disappearing progressively as the subjects come to expect and get set to report the taboo items (Bitterman and Kniffen, 1953; Lacy, Lewinger, and Adamson, 1953).

The fact that subjects who are told to expect socially unaccept able words tend not to exhibit perceptual defense does not, however, constitute a crucial argument against perceptual defense. When subjects are so instructed, they are thereby predisposed toward the making of one or more of a relatively limited number of responses. This set to respond, which seems to qualify as an associative process, might facilitate the identification of critical words. But if the taboo and neutral thresholds do not differ significantly under conditions such as these, the advocate for defense could certainly argue that if the "bad" words had not been selectively favored their thresholds might well have been higher.

In summary, it can be stated with reasonable confidence that in many instances where an unconscious mechanism of perceptual defense is alleged to have been involved, the results can be explained more simply and more parsimoniously by appeal to well-known principles of associative learning. Among these principles are those of frequency of exposure to a stimulus, frequency of previous elicitation of the response, learned tendencies to withhold socially inappropriate responses, and selective sets which predispose subjects either to look for or not to look for taboo words. There are few experiments, indeed, in which none of these associative interpretations has proved reasonable and in which perceptual defense stands out as the most acceptable hypothesis.

Competing Response Theory of Perceptual Defense. We shall conclude this chapter shortly with a brief look at studies purporting to show that perceptual defense and/or vigilance are characteristic modes of adjustment of individual personalities. First, however, let us see whether some of the findings of the experiments we have just considered can be interpreted in somewhat different associative terms than those proposed by Solomon and Howes.

Initially, let us assume that printed vulgar words arouse tendencies both to speak and not to speak. Vulgar words (or shocked words) are thus the counterparts of ambivalent stimuli in a conflict situation (cf., e.g., Miller, 1944; Brown, 1957). They tend, as a result of socially administered reinforcements and punishments, to elicit incompatible positive and negative responses. Moreover, since severity of punishment for saying a vulgar word probably varies directly with its degree of vulgarity, it is further hypothesized that the tendency for such words to elicit avoidance or nonspeaking responses also varies directly with vulgarity.

These postulated relationships are shown graphically in Fig. 8:12. Here the base line denotes degree of vulgarity, and the ordinate shows the strength of the positive and negative tendencies corresponding to each word. To simplify matters, all words are regarded as being equally familiar and hence as possessing identical, strong, positive tendencies. The inhibitory tendency is indicated as weaker than the positive for each word, whether vulgar or not, since in actual experiments nearly all subjects do speak such words when they are clearly presented. These assumptions permit one to deduce, among other things, that overt responses to "dirty" words should have a longer latency than responses to neutral words, even when all are presented clearly. To deduce the phenomenon

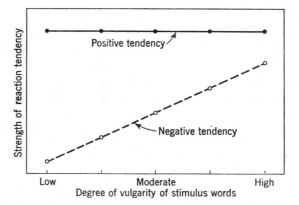

Fig. 8:12. Relative strengths (assumed) of positive tendencies to speak and negative tendencies not to speak when stimulus words of varying degrees of vulgarity are clearly presented (i.e., long exposure times are used). The curves are constructed on the premise that all of the words are equally familiar (flat positive-tendency curve), but differ in the degree to which they elicit tendencies to inhibit overt expression.

of higher tachistoscopic recognition thresholds for taboo words, however, we need additional concepts.

One principle that seems to hold considerable promise here is that of *stimulus generalization*. To apply this principle, let us suppose that the tendency to speak a written word is maximal when tachistoscopic exposure time is long, but that as the stimulus becomes impoverished with reduced exposures, the strength of the tendency decreases. In short, *the function relating exposure time to strength of reaction tendency is assumed to be similar to a gradient of stimulus generalization.* This supposition is portrayed graphically in Fig. 8:13, where the upper curve is the strength of the tendency to speak a moderately vulgar word for each of a number of different exposure times. (The highest point on this curve has been set to equal the height of the horizontal positive-tendency curve in Fig. 8:12.) This figure illustrates the further hypothesis that the tendency not to speak the off-color word also generalizes along the dimension of exposure time. (The maximum strength of the weak negative tendency equals that for a moderately vulgar word in Fig. 8:12.) Were we to combine this generalization figure with the previous one, these gradients would extend out toward the viewer at a right angle from the surface of

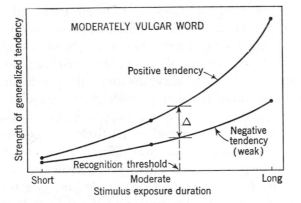

FIG. 8:13. Hypothetical generalized tendencies to pronounce and to refrain from pronouncing a moderately vulgar word. Both tendencies are assumed to become weaker as the stimulus is impoverished by reducing exposure duration. The distance (Δ) between the points of the double-headed arrow denotes the assumed amount by which the positive tendency must exceed the negative for the response to become overt.

Fig. 8:12. Similar pairs of generalization curves could obviously be constructed for each of the words of Fig. 8:12.

Assume now that the positive and negative tendencies summate algebraically and that the positive must exceed the negative by a certain fixed amount for the response to become overt. As has been noted, in determining thresholds with a tachistoscope, a word is usually presented for increasingly long exposures until the subject correctly identifies the word on two or three occasions. In terms of Fig. 8:13, this means that over successive trials there will be a progressive increase in the difference between the positive and negative tendencies. This increase is clearly consistent with the fact that correct recognition responses become more probable with increased exposure duration. It has been assumed that the identifying response will not be elicited until the positive tendency exceeds the negative by a certain definite amount, which is indicated in Fig. 8:13 by the double-headed arrow identified by a delta (Δ). For this off-color word, therefore, the recognition threshold should lie at an exposure duration just slightly greater than one of moderate length.

Suppose, however, that an unusually vulgar word is substituted for the off-color one. For such a very vulgar word, assuming equal familiarity, we should expect the positive tendency to be the same as before but the negative tendency to be greater for all exposure times. This is schematized in Fig. 8:14, where the negative tendency at maximum is about equal to that for the most vulgar word in Fig. 8:12. Since the generalized inhibitory tendency is stronger, as is shown here, for all exposure durations, the positive and negative curves lie closer together throughout the range of the exposure-duration dimension than was the case for the off-color word. With the very dirty word, therefore, relatively long exposure durations must be reached before the difference (Δ) between the positive and negative tendencies becomes sufficient to permit the verbal (recognition) response to occur. As this diagram shows, the double-headed arrow lies farther to the right than it did in the previous figure, and since this corresponds to increased exposure durations, a higher threshold for a very dirty than for an off-color or neutral word can thus be deduced. Of especial significance, here, is the fact that neither emotion, nor drive, nor

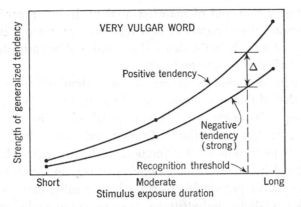

FIG. 8:14. Hypothetical gradients in the strength of generalized positive and negative linguistic tendencies for a very vulgar word. Here the difference between positive and inhibitory tendencies (Δ) that is arbitrarily assumed to be required for the evocation of an overt reaction falls at a longer exposure duration than in the case of a less vulgar word (cf. Fig. 8:13). A higher recognition threshold for very vulgar than for equally familiar neutral or moderately vulgar words can thus be deduced.

perceptual defense, nor differential familiarity has been invoked as a necessary adjunct to the deduction.

Personality Characteristics and the Perception of Taboo Materials. Those who currently favor the concept of perceptual defense emphasize the notion that defense is an individual mode of adjustment to threat. If their idea is tenable, then an unselected population of subjects would not be expected to exhibit perceptual defense. Rather, since some individuals react in a defensive manner and others in a sensitized manner, randomly chosen subjects should show neither defense nor vigilance, their distinct modes of reacting being concealed by the process of averaging.

This view, that reactions to threatening stimuli differ considerably from individual to individual and from situation to situation, leads to research procedures which differ from those we have previously discussed. The principal change is that subpopulations of subjects are chosen initially from larger groups by means of tests purporting to reveal characteristic personality differences. Perceptual tests are then carried out to determine whether the personality attributes correlate with degree of defensiveness or vigilance. In principle this method is like that used in studies of need achievement and of manifest anxiety. It is a procedure directed toward the discovery of R-R relationships, since it is hoped that responses made to the items of one test will be correlated with responses elicited by a second test.

This general approach appears to have stemmed from studies such as that of Postman, Bruner, and McGinnies (1948), in which an attempt was made to relate perceptual selectivity to a factor described as "personal values." By personal values these authors apparently mean individual differences in the degree to which one is interested in, or places high value upon certain things or ideas. Thus a scientist presumably places a higher value upon scientific principles, relations, and attitudes, than on comparable aspects of other areas such as religion, economics, or politics. Similarly, the artist, the politician, and the businessman each has his own characteristic value or interest patterns. And even individuals who cannot be identified in terms of professional affiliation presumably have higher values for some areas than for others, and these high- and low-value areas should be detectable by means of suitable tests.

In the Postman, Bruner, and McGinnies experiment, college subjects were tested by means of the Allport-Vernon Study of Values, a test designed to yield value ratings in areas described as economic, theoretical, religious, social, esthetic, and political. Each subject was also given the perceptual task of identifying words in each of the six value areas. The results of the perceptual test indicated that there was some tendency for the subjects to see words in their own high-value categories more readily than those in their low-value groups. Thus an individual with a high religious-value score was described as having been sensitized to religious words. Conversely, for such a person, scientific or theoretical words might be threatening, and if so, he should exhibit perceptual defense for such words.

Although some of the statistical and graphic procedures of this study can be seriously questioned, similar results have been reported by Haigh and Fiske (1952), Solomon and Howes (1951), and others. It is of interest, therefore, to consider some of the factors that might produce a positive correlation between test-defined value orientation and perceptual identifying responses.

For most writers "value orientation" refers to a kind of inner personalistic factor capable of organizing both the perceptions and the overt actions of the individual. Thus, for example, Brown and Adams (1954) assert that a value area is a "central, cognitive, affective construct." As such, it is given the properties of determining both selective responses made to value-test items and selective perceptions of value-related stimulus words. Postman, Bruner, and McGinnies say little concerning the nature of value orientation per se, save that it results from a long process of socialization and functions to modify perception by means of selective, accentuative, and fixative mechanisms.

The results of studies relating perception to value orientation can probably be explained, however, without appealing to value as such. Thus it might be supposed that a high aesthetic (or other) value orientation, as defined by scores on the Allport-Vernon test, means simply that one is interested in, and devotes considerable attention to aesthetic matters. But a strong interest in aesthetic and artistic subjects would lead one to read articles and books on such topics to the relative exclusion of other works. Consequently the person with a high aesthetic-value score should become more familiar with the particular words used in writings on aesthetics than with words in, for example, the areas of science and politics. If he had such familiarity, then he would more readily identify aesthetic words when they were presented tachistoscopically than words of other value areas. And this should hold true even though the aesthetic and nonaesthetic words occurred with equal frequency in printed English and hence would be defined as "equally familiar" in terms of a criterion such as the Thorndike-Lorge word count.

This interpretation, it may be seen, is essentially the associative, nonmotivational one proposed by Solomon and Howes (1951) and reiterated by Postman (1953a), and by Farber (1955). It is the view that recognition thresholds are determined by familiarity, that unequal familiarity with words of different value groupings depends upon one's interests or preferences, and that interests or preferences might be detected by responses to the items of the Allport-Vernon scale.

Whether value as a special-purpose cognitive construct need

be evoked in connection with such an interpretation remains a matter of individual preference. One could argue, in the interest of parsimony, that the concept of value is quite superfluous since its alleged functions as a determinant of behavior can be explained by assuming that individuals have learned through socially administered rewards and punishments to be interested in different kinds of things. Or it might be argued that value orientation is somehow an antecedent to, and a determinant of, one's differential interests, and that these in turn determine familiarity and hence differential recognition thresholds.

Eriksen (1954) has been an active exponent of the view that defense and vigilance are idiosyncratic rather than universal modes of response to threat. He has criticized the conventional procedures in which "dirty" words are presented to randomly selected subjects on the ground that such words are probably not anxiety arousing for all or even most typical college subjects. Moreover, he maintains that an adequate test of the perceptual defense hypothesis necessarily demands some evaluation of the ways in which individual subjects handle or react to anxiety. On this view one must demonstrate that individuals differ in degree of defensiveness to anxiety-arousing stimuli presented in nonperceptual situations. Subjects cannot be said to be perceptual defenders unless some independent support is thus provided for the assumption that they are *generally* defensive.

The adoption of this theoretical position generally leads to distinctive kinds of research. For example, Lazarus, Eriksen, and Fonda (1951) used, with neurotic subjects, a sentence-completion test in which some of the sentences could easily be filled out with sexual or aggressive solutions. Subjects who, on the basis of this test, could be defined as "expressive" with respect to sex were able to perceive auditorily presented sexual sentences as well as neutral sentences. But subjects who tended to block or give distorted endings to the sexual sentences could not hear the sexual sentences as well as they could hear the neutral ones. In another study, Eriksen (1951) has reported that some subjects show signs of blocking or emotional upset to TAT pictures which usually elicit aggressive reactions, whereas other subjects express aggression quite freely in their stories. When tested on a perceptual recognition test, the former subjects had higher thresholds for aggressive than for neutral pictures, whereas the latter subjects had relatively low thresholds for the aggressive scenes.

Research studies designed along similar lines have been carried out by Stein (1953), Chodorkoff (1956), and Neel (1954), all of whom have found defensiveness or vigilance, as revealed by perceptual thresholds, to be correlated with the results of other tests purporting to identify personality characteristics of individual subjects.

By way of conclusion it may be noted that although the study of perceptual defense and/or vigilance as an individual-difference phenomenon seems like an attempt to prove the reality of perceptual defense in the face of such criticisms as those of Solomon and Howes, it is nevertheless a perfectly acceptable way of proceeding. The fact that randomly chosen subjects may not exhibit defense, particularly when frequency of prior experience with the stimuli has been properly controlled, does not mean that *some* individuals might not exhibit the effect. Clearly, one can *define* defensiveness in terms of responses to a sentence-completion test or to a test of some other kind, and then proceed to study the relation of defensiveness thus defined to reactions evoked in other test situations. The individual-difference method does not, however, preclude the possibility that the reactions to all tests are due to differential experiences with the materials of the tests rather than to perceptual defense. When individuals who are "expressive" with respect to sexual matters are selected out of a group, we may simply be selecting those who, in addition to being expressive, or perhaps because of their expressiveness, have had more extensive experience with sexual words, symbols, and ideas. On the other hand, the test-defined "sexual inhibitor" might well have had fewer exposures to, and experiences with, materials of a sexual nature. If such groups differ in their ability to identify sexual words, it might be more sensible to explain these results by referring to individual differences in associative strengths rather than to traits of defensiveness or to value systems with vague motivational overtones.

Summary

Of central importance to the discussions in this chapter is the general problem of the effects of motivational variables upon perception. However, the perceptions of subjects whose behavior is being studied by the psychologist cannot be observed directly by him, and perception must therefore enter into theories of behavior in the role of a scientific construct. Like other constructs, e.g., motivation and associative strength, perception must be explicitly defined within scientific language, and it must prove its significance through its capacity to enhance our understanding of behavior. That a construct of perception may not be needed in behavior theory is suggested by the fact that many so-called perceptual experiments, in which subjects are required to identify or compare physically present stimulus objects, can be successfully conducted and useful stimulus-response laws determined without any reference to perception. Nevertheless, perception may serve a useful explanatory purpose in some situations, especially those in which overt identifying responses do not occur until some time after a stimulus has been withdrawn. Inasmuch as perception is often defined in terms of subjects' linguistic responses, a motivational variable may be said to have affected perception when its introduction leads to changes in the kinds or frequencies of linguistic responses exhibited by subjects in so-called perceptual experiments.

In an effort to relate the motivation-perception problem to material contained in earlier chapters, an attempt is made to apply the multiplicative-drive hypothesis to behavior in psychophysical test situations. From the assumption that empirically determined response frequencies provide evidence of relative habit strengths the conclusion is reached that absolute thresholds may either be elevated or depressed if a motivational variable leads solely to the arousal of competitive or facilitative habits. But if the variable affects drive alone, the slope of the psychophysical function should become steeper, the threshold, as conventionally defined, remaining unaffected. Similar lines of reasoning are applied to the interpretation of data obtained from studies of differential sensitivity and of recognition thresholds for meaningful stimuli.

Studies of the effects of primary sources of drive upon behavior in perceptual situations have yielded suggestive but inconsistent results. Some observations suggest that food and/or water deprivation enhances the frequency with which need-related words are given as responses to unstructured stimuli and to near-threshold presentations of need-related words or pictures. Deprivation operations have also produced contradictory results, both within and between experiments, and in some cases deprivation leads to poorer performance even with need-related stimulus items.

A large majority of studies relating motivational variables to perception consist of those in which the to-be-perceived stimuli themselves are thought to function as motivational variables. Thus words that have been associated with positive rewards, with electric shock in the laboratory, or with social punishments have been used as to-be-identified stimuli on the assumption that the perception of such words will be modified by their acquired motivational properties. Analyzed in this way, the problem may be described as that of the influence of secondary sources of drive upon perceptual behavior.

A review of representative investigations purporting to show that the judged size of objects is affected by their value leads to the conclusion that the effect at best is slight, especially when the valued objects are physically present. The judgments of children and of hypnotized adults appear to be most readily affected by the variable of object value, and individual differences in the need for money affect judgments of remembered coin size. It is suggested, by way of interpretation, that because of socialization processes, objects of value tend to evoke both stronger instrumental preference responses and more frequent verbal responses of the general class "large" than do comparable nonvalued objects. The elicitation of more frequent "larger-than" responses by valued objects in a psychophysical investigation is the basic datum indicating that value leads to an accentuation of judged size.

Interpretations of differences in the recognition thresholds for emotion-arousing and for neutral words have commonly involved appeal to mechanisms of perceptual defense or perceptual sensitization (vigilance). Defense is usually described as an unconscious process akin to repression that functions to protect one from perceiving things that are distasteful or anxiety-arousing. Early studies purporting to have demonstrated this phenomenon have been criticized for failing to equate the familiarity of taboo and neutral stimuli. Later investigations, in which different criteria of familiarity have been employed, have yielded inconsistent results, defense being reported in some cases and vigilance in others. In most instances interpretive mechanisms other than defense or vigilance, such as response suppression, familiarity, and predisposing sets, appear to provide more parsimonious interpretations of lowered or raised recognition thresholds. Higher recognition thresholds for taboo words might also be explained on the grounds that tendencies both to speak and not to speak such words have been established through learning and that these tendencies generalize along the dimension of exposure duration. Assuming that an identifying response will not become overt until the tendency to speak exceeds the tendency not to speak by a given fixed amount, it is concluded that recognition thresholds would fall at longer exposure durations for taboo than for neutral words.

The final section of this chapter contains a brief review of investigations designed to show that perceptual defense and vigilance are idiosyncratic phenomena. Underlying these studies is the view that an individual is defensive only with respect to certain kinds of taboo items and that perceptual defense cannot be demonstrated, therefore, unless the subjects' defensive areas have been appropriately identified. Experimental findings have supported this contention, since defensiveness (or vigilance), as defined by selection procedures of a nonperceptual nature, has been found to correlate with perceptual thresholds. Even in these instances, however, alternative interpretations couched in terms of individual differences in familiarity with certain classes of stimuli merit careful appraisal.

‖‖

CHAPTER 9

Miscellaneous
Motivational Problems

THIS FINAL CHAPTER deals with a variety of problems, which, though only tenuously related to one another, are all of considerable interest to the student of motivation. Each of these topics might have been woven into the fabric of the preceding chapters, but only, it was felt, with some loss of continuity and over-all unity. As we shall see, the bearing of the questions considered here upon previously discussed problems, though somewhat tangential, is nevertheless significant.

Approach-eliciting Stimuli as Motivational Variables

At several places in the foregoing pages (especially in Chapters 3 and 7) it has been noted that motivational properties are commonly attributed to such external stimuli as intense electric shocks, bright lights, blasts of air, loud noises, and acrid odors. Presumably these stimuli are regarded as motivators because, as experimental variables, they satisfy one or more criteria (cf. Chapter 2) for the identification of motivational variables. In addition, these stimuli tend to evoke responses of escape or withdrawal, a characteristic that results in their being described as noxious or aversive.

There are many other external stimuli, however, that tend to evoke approach rather than escape reactions. These "benign" stimuli are often described as lures or incentives, suggesting that they, like their more intense noxious counterparts, may also function as motivational variables. Since we have not yet considered this problem in detail, we turn now to the question of whether and under what conditions approach-eliciting stimulus objects do indeed serve as motivational variables in addition to fulfilling their obvious role as behavior directors.

The large majority of instances in which appeals have been made to the drive-arousing functions of approach-evoking cues are to be found in studies of so-called exploratory, manipulatory, and curiosity behavior. Investigators responsible for such studies have typically postulated the existence of special-purpose drives that are named in terms of the observed behavior. Thus, exploratory, manipulatory, and curiosity drives have been proposed as explanatory concepts. And in most instances the impression is conveyed that the external, mild, stimulus objects "pull" the organism toward them, exemplifying a motivating property that is "attractive" rather than "repellent." Though the theoretical implications and formal details of this view have not been as carefully elaborated as might be desired, the general conception has proved appealing to those who insist that behavior is motivated as much by "positive" goals as it is by internal disquietudes.

Existing studies in which concepts of exteroceptively aroused drives have been invoked may be roughly divided into two groups. First, there are those in which the behavior-directing goal object has, in the past, either functioned repeatedly as a reward or has been closely associated with reward. In these studies, whatever drive-arousing properties the lure may possess are typically attributed to learning. In the second group of experiments, the remote stimulus object is either completely or relatively novel to the subject; in fact, its capacity to arouse drive is said to be contingent upon its novelty. When such an object is first seen by the organism, a drive of "curiosity" or "exploration" is allegedly aroused. This new drive is said to impel the individual to move toward, and to touch, smell, manipulate, or inspect the object. In the one case, therefore, drive increments are aroused by highly familiar objects that have often served as, or have been associated with, empirically reinforcing conditions; and in the other, entirely unfamiliar sources of stimulation generate special-purpose drives to explore and/or to manipulate. We consider each of these possibilities in turn.

Incentive-aroused Drive. The general idea that an event such as the sight of familiar food may heighten one's motivational level is by no means recent, but relatively precise, systematic formulations of this idea appear to have been first presented by Spence (1951*a*) and by Hull (1951). As we have already observed (e.g., in Chapter 5), these theorists contend that appetitive responses composing the final consummatory chain become classically conditioned to the stimuli provided by food and its environs. Through stimulus generalization, primarily, certain fractional components of the consummatory response sequence will be elicited even when the animal is yet some distance from the goal. These reactions (r_gs) are thought to produce a drive increment (K) which combines additively with D and which, like D, multiplies all associative tendencies. The anticipatory goal reaction (r_g) is also said to produce characteristic interoceptive stimuli (s_gs) to which a variety of responses (either learned or unlearned) may be associated. The expectation of food is thus seen as a learned tendency to make anticipatory, partial responses of the kind involved in eating. These responses can affect other behavior either motivationally or associatively or in both ways.

Inasmuch as we have already remarked upon the relation of the r_g–s_g mechanism to the general problem of acquired sources of drive and to such conceptions as McClelland's affective arousal, only a few additional comments need be made here. First, proponents of the view that motivation stems from external sources as well as from bodily disequilibria have largely ignored the possibility that the r_g–$s_g \rightarrow K$ mechanism might fulfill some of their needs. Harlow (1953), for example, in a paper that heartily endorses the importance of external cues as sources of drive makes no reference to this mechanism. This omission may be due to his desire to stress the instinctive aspects of the process as well as to a conviction that the so-called secondary sources of drive are of little theoretical significance. Second, an important implication of the r_g–s_g conception is that it provides a means whereby the organism's level of motivation can be enhanced while the goal is being approached, even though the lure itself remains hidden until the final moment of goal attainment. One who holds that external stimuli are drive arousing only while they are actually impinging upon the subject's distance receptors could scarcely maintain that invisible lures are motivating. Third, since K, the D-like factor, is the result of conditioning, its magnitude can be relatively independent of the intensity of the conditioned stimulus. The motivational increment is triggered, as it were, by external stimuli, but its magnitude is primarily a function of the intensity of the learned internal reactions (r_gs) rather than of the intensity of the external stimulus. To the extent that this may be true, these instances of externally aroused drive reduce in the final analysis to internal disquietudes that may be similar to those attending hunger, thirst, and emotionality.

Novel Stimuli as Sources of Drive. The view that *unfamiliar* stimulus objects are approached, explored, and manipulated rests upon a variety of well-authenticated observations. Specifically, it has been noted that rats and a number of other organisms, including man, will move toward some, though by no means all, strange or novel objects. Upon arrival the organism may touch, push, pull, sniff at, manipulate, mouth, bite, or lick the previously remote object. Thus, exploratory, manipulatory, and curiosity behavior consists of two phases: an initial phase of orienting toward and approaching a given region or object, and a secondary phase composed of a variety of nonlocomotor reactions that appear after the novel object has been reached. The reaction patterns of the second phase are typically described as "manipulatory," especially when exhibited by monkeys or men who are capable of complicated manual acts. To the degree that exploration-eliciting objects are indeed novel, interpretations based on learned, object-specific, anticipatory responses (e.g., r_gs) are patently inappropriate. In fact, as familiarity with the novel object increases, exploration declines. Recourse is sometimes had, therefore, to the special-purpose concepts of curiosity or exploratory drives.

Experimental Studies of Exploratory and Manipulatory Behavior. The rather extensive literature descriptive of experiments on exploration and manipulation has been summarized by Glanzer (1958), Butler (1958), Berlyne (1958), and Dember and Fowler (1958). Further detailed review of these studies cannot be undertaken here, but a knowledge of some of their principal findings is essential to a further discussion of theoretical issues.

Perhaps the most general statement one can make about these experiments is that *in a wide variety of situations animals often behave so as to reduce contacts with familiar stimuli or locales and to increase contacts with novel objects or regions.* As an example, when rats are permitted to run freely through a simple T or Y maze, they tend, on any given trial, to enter a different arm from that chosen on the preceding trial. As a result, alternation of sides is often exhibited on successive trials. Apparently this is not a result of fatigue or inhibition specific to a particular response, since the same reaction, e.g., right turning, will be repeated if the stimuli are changed from trial to trial (Montgomery, 1952). The rat seems to get tired of looking at the same environment, not tired of making the same response. The fact that percentage alternation increases when rats are detained in the goal box of the chosen T maze arm (Glanzer, 1953), supports this "stimulus satiation" hypothesis, especially since increases in intertrial intervals produced by detention outside the maze typically reduce alternation. Moreover, response alternation is observed whether food is provided for either choice, or for neither. Also related to the alternation phenomenon is the finding that rats are more likely to enter and explore a compartment if it contains a variety of objects such as wooden blocks than if it contains few or none (Berlyne, 1955).

Not only do animals exhibit preferences for new as opposed to old environments and sources of stimulation, but the opportunity to explore new situations appears to have rewarding value for the learning of instrumental responses. Thus Montgomery (1954) reports that rats will learn to choose the arm of a Y maze leading to a large open box containing numerous rectangular blocks (the Dashiell maze) or, for the same reward, will learn a black-white discrimination (Montgomery and Segall, 1955). Myers and

Miller (1954), moreover, found that rats would learn to touch a door in order to open it to get to the other side of a two-compartment box. And Kish (1955), among others, has shown that rats will learn to press a lever if the act is followed by an increase in illumination.

One of the most reliable findings of experiments on exploration is that with repeated exposures novel objects rather quickly lose their power to elicit approach and exploration. When periods of rest are introduced following the "extinction" of exploration, a kind of "spontaneous recovery" takes place, though recovery is seldom complete. Moreover, the decrement in exploration resulting from frequent presentations of one set of objects or situations generalizes to other similar objects (Montgomery, 1953).

The most dramatic experiments on the rewarding properties of visually presented stimuli are probably those of Butler (1953) and of Butler and Harlow (1954). In these investigations, monkeys were placed one at a time in a dimly lighted, opaque-walled box. Two small doors were situated on one wall of the box, and if either of these was unlatched, the monkey could push it open and look out into the surrounding monkey-laboratory world. When the doors were painted yellow and blue, and the blue door was always unlocked, the monkeys learned to open the blue door and ignore the other, the only apparent reward for this response being the opportunity to look through the door for about 30 seconds. This door-pushing behavior was remarkably persistent, most monkeys showing a willingness to perform the response for many hours without flagging (Butler and Harlow, 1954). Harlow (1953) has suggested that this exemplifies the operation of a "drive to explore the visual world outside the box" and that the opportunity to do so is reinforcing. He has also stated that this is an instance of the arousal of a drive by an external stimulus. In other experiments Butler (1957) has shown that the frequency of door-pushing responses increases with hours of deprivation of visual experience, and that auditory stimuli may also serve as incentives and/or rewards.

Manipulatory activity is similar, in certain respects, to the kinds of exploratory behavior we have just been considering. If sticks, mechanical puzzles, or other manipulatable objects are presented to a monkey, it will sooner or later approach and handle them. If the object consists of several separable components, the monkey will eventually disassemble it and in this way "solve" the problem. Moreover, as with visual exploratory actions, these disassembling reactions can be elicited over and over again (Harlow, 1953). Typically, none of the conventional appetitive or social rewards is administered following a successful puzzle-disassembling response, and yet proficiency in this activity may increase significantly over trials. The persistence of the behavior and its improvement with practice are considered to support the contentions that the animal has a manipulatory drive and is rewarded by performing manipulations. The greater perseveration of manipulatory activities in monkeys, as compared with exploratory behavior in rats, may be ascribed to species differences or perhaps to the greater reinforcing power of manual manipulation as compared with mere visual inspection.

That the research findings are not always as consistent as the foregoing experiments might suggest is indicated by reports of occasional failures to obtain approach and exploration with respect to strange objects. Young chimpanzees, for instance, do not look at novel objects and do not approach and explore them until they have been exposed to such objects for prolonged periods (Welker, 1956). Rats also resist leaving the home cage in order to explore an elevated runway (Montgomery, 1955), and monkeys will not learn to open a door to look out at a large dog or to hear recorded vocalizations of a monkey colony whose members are being molested (Butler, 1958). Some stimuli, therefore, even though unfamiliar, do not elicit exploratory behavior or function as reinforcers for the acquisition of new responses. In some experiments repeated presentations of such avoidance-eliciting objects are accompanied by an initial, progressive increase in exploration, followed by a terminal decline. This has been interpreted to mean that exploration increases as fear is extinguished, with exploration then declining in the usual manner as stimulus novelty wears off.

Though advocates of the concepts of exploratory and curiosity drives have pressed their views with vigor and enthusiasm, numerous problems remain to be solved before their interpretations can be said to carry complete conviction. For one thing, the conditions under which these alleged special drives are aroused have not been carefully specified. As a consequence, one cannot be certain which bits of behavior require the postulation of these special-purpose drives and which do not. The topographical properties of the so-called exploratory behaviors and of other, nonexploratory activities are in many respects identical. For example, if a rat moves from one end of a box to the other, one has no way of knowing, from the behavior alone, whether the rat is motivated by the sight of the other end of the box, by dissatisfaction with the end where he is, or simply by a tendency to become active. Moreover, as Berlyne (1958) has pointed out, a specific behavior pattern may be scored as exploratory if it is exhibited in one part of the test apparatus but not if it appears in another. If a rat runs down an alley and sniffs at an object at the end, he is usually said to be exploring, but if he stays in the starting compartment and sniffs at the walls, he is not exploring (by the usual criteria) since he hasn't gone anywhere.

Most frequently the label "exploratory" is applied when an animal does something in a situation where he receives no obvious reward for his performance. But the presence or absence of an exploratory drive is not announced until after the behavior has been observed to occur. If a strange object is approached, curiosity drive is invoked; but if the same object is not approached, the existence of a fear drive is asserted. Thus the presence of a drive to explore is sometimes inferred from, and at the same time used to explain, behavior of moving from one place to another, especially if there is no other apparent reason for the movement. The postulation of an exploratory drive in this way is quite circular, and therefore of questionable worth as a scientific explanation. Not all assertions concerning the presence of exploratory or curiosity drives are as clearly circular as this, but the problem has not been squarely faced nor adequately solved.

Another difficulty arises when one attempts to define stimulus novelty. Is a block of wood a novel object for the rat? If so, how novel? Probably if a rat has been raised in the usual way in the laboratory, it has seen other objects resembling, to a greater or less degree, a block of wood. Pellets of laboratory chow are often fashioned in rectangular form, and their color is similar to that of natural wood. So when a rat approaches and sniffs at a small block of wood in a maze, how can we be certain that this is not an instance of transfer of training, mediated by stimulus similarity? If so, need we worry either about stimulus novelty or about the curiosity drive that novelty is alleged to arouse? As with exploratory drive, the specification of stimulus novelty rests, to an unsatisfactory degree, upon the observation that the expected behavior has indeed occurred. Novel objects are supposed to arouse a drive to explore such objects, but degree of novelty is typically not evaluated independently of exploration.

Of extant theories of exploratory and curiosity behavior, Berlyne's (1955) is probably the most carefully and precisely structured. According to this theory, which in its formal properties resembles the Hull-Spence r_g–s_g formulation, when novel stimuli fall upon an organism's receptors, a drive-stimulus-producing response labeled "curiosity" will be evoked. The "drive-to-explore" or the drive of "perceptual curiosity" acts, apparently, to facilitate behavior of exploring the objects that generate the response-produced drive. Exploratory activities reduce the drive to explore, and when this occurs following a response, that response will tend to be learned. In addition to functioning as a reinforcing agent, exposures to novel stimuli through exploratory activities, bring about a weakening of the curiosity drive. According to Berlyne, the process of curiosity diminution can be described by Hull's model for the extinction of conditioned responses, a model in which permanent decrements are explained by the concept of conditioned inhibition and temporary diminutions by reactive inhibition.

Because of the similarity of this conception to the r_g–s_g expectancy mechanism, it is of interest to compare the two in more detail. First, whereas the r_g–s_g configuration clearly refers to a learned reaction, the drive-producing curiosity response must be instinctive, since only *novel* stimuli can arouse curiosity, and only objects that the organism has never seen are really novel. Second, although expectancy-produced drive becomes stronger as a function of the number of encounters with a rewarding object, curiosity drive is weakened by the same variable. Repeated experiences with food that is assumed to be drive reducing strengthen the expectancy mechanism; but repeated exposures to a novel stimulus, which in a comparable manner reduces the curiosity drive, weaken the power of the stimulus to arouse the drive. Conversely, anticipatory goal responses are extinguished when the rewarding object is omitted, while curiosity is extinguished when the rewarding object is kept in the situation.

Although Berlyne has tried to cast his views into a form consistent with Hullian theory and to extend it into the general area of perception, his usage of the term *drive* is not coordinate with Hull's. Berlyne's curiosity drive is apparently a drive to perform a specific act or a specific group of acts. Conceived in this manner, it is a special-purpose drive incorporating directive properties, and is therefore not the same as Hull's general D. Perhaps Berlyne adopted this position because one cannot explain why a subject approaches a novel object instead of doing something else, if one assumes that the sight of the object leads only to heightened D. An increase in D does not activate or multiply approach tendencies alone, and reactions of exploring and manipulating would not be facilitated by intensified D unless these responses were, for other reasons, the dominant members of the response hierarchy. Nevertheless, in the typical exploratory situation, approaching may often be the dominant response. An animal, when placed into a maze at the starting point, obviously cannot back up. If he moves at all it must be *away* from his initial position and therefore toward the remotely located, to-be-explored objects.

Another account of exploratory behavior requiring analysis is that proposed by Butler and Harlow in conjunction with their experiments on the "visual-exploration drive." According to these writers, visual exploratory responses are members of a broad family of curiosity or exploratory drives (including manipulatory drives) that are elicited by external stimuli. This interpretation has been suggested as an explanation of the behavior of the monkeys who learned new discriminatory reactions for visual rewards.

That this view leads to difficulties should be clear from the following: If the act of looking out of the window at the outside (laboratory) world is the specific event that arouses the visual-exploration drive, then the monkeys do not have this drive until they have succeeded in opening the correct window. The drive aroused by the final act of visual exploration cannot, therefore, provide the impetus for the response of window opening. External stimuli, when seen, may indeed incite a drive to explore with the eyes, but it is illogical to say that those stimuli, *while they are invisible to the monkey*, actively function to arouse the drive to work in order to see.

But the panel-pushing and latch-manipulating activities of Butler's monkeys were presumably motivated in some way, and the *motivating agency must have been functioning prior to the time the monkeys obtained their visual rewards*. Several possibilities suggest themselves. For one, being unable to see may be the crucial variable. This possibility is supported by Butler's study (1957), in which visual exploratory responses were found to increase in frequency as a function of the amount of visual deprivation. Or since, in the typical experimental setup, auditory stimuli are not excluded, and the confined monkey can hear the sounds produced by other members of the colony and by numerous people in the laboratory, these noises could serve as drive-producing incentive stimuli. Still another view is that confinement in an opaque box is a mild anxiety-inducing variable for the monkey (Brown, 1953b). When coupled with the auditory cues, this might be sufficiently motivating to explain the observed behavior. And finally, it might even be supposed that if seeing is rewarding, for whatever reasons, then eye movements and other components of the sequence of looking responses could become conditioned to environmental stimuli in much the same way as consummatory responses. Were this the case, then generalized, fractional, anticipatory seeing responses (r_s–s_s) might be elicited in visually restrictive environments and, like the analogous r_g–s_g mechanism, might add an increment to drive. Perhaps in this way one could speak more precisely of the motivating properties of the "expectation of seeing."

Harlow (1953) has maintained that exploratory and manipulatory activities weigh strongly against a drive-reduction theory of reinforcement, since these actions do not produce immediate diminutions in any of the primary physiological needs. There is no existing experiment, however, in which the possibility that some kind of drive reduction has occurred has been completely ruled out. Thus if a monkey becomes anxious when confined in a dimly lighted box, a reinforcing reduction in anxiety may occur when it gets a chance to see other monkeys and/or the familiar laboratory environment. Supporting this view are the previously cited observations that monkeys will not learn responses that are followed by such stimuli as the sight of a large dog or the sounds of other monkeys being molested (Butler, 1958). It is also apparent, in this connection, that if a confined monkey has a drive to see, as Harlow asserts, then the act of seeing must reduce this drive. One might thus be led, oddly enough, to a drive-reduction theory, albeit not a need-reduction theory, of the reinforcing effects of visual exploration. On these grounds the external stimulus becomes a drive-to-see reducer, not a drive-to-see arouser. Incidentally, Berlyne holds that external cues play both of these roles, arousing a drive when first seen and reducing that drive with further seeing.

It seems justifiable to conclude from this analysis that while animals do indeed engage in activities of approaching and exploring biologically neutral objects, it is far from certain that a special-purpose exploratory drive need be invoked to explain such activities. Moreover, though monkeys and other animals do learn new responses for rewards of visual stimulation, the nature of the motivation underlying the evocation of these responses remains unclear. Before the visually rewarding events are seen, motivational processes other than those aroused by to-be-seen stimuli must be in operation. Apprehension due to isolation and confinement, anticipation of seeing, or auditory stimuli may serve in this role as motivators. Lastly, although there are many reports of instances in which animals will learn to solve a T maze or a discrimination problem for an exploratory reward, alternative explanations have seldom been carefully ruled out. Thus the presentation of novel, reinforcing stimuli has typically been confounded with an increase in space (cf. Montgomery, 1954), and hence the reinforcement may have been provided by escape from confinement or by the opportunity to run, which is known to be reinforcing (Kagan and Berkun, 1954), rather than by the sight of unfamiliar objects. Experimenters such as Chapman and Levy (1957) have considered this problem and have concluded that novelty may be reinforcing even when increased space is controlled, although the effect disappears when the animals are made hungry. Considerable research remains to be done, therefore, before we can be entirely certain that novel stimuli per se are reinforcing and that no negative factors such as confinement, anxiety, or stimulus deprivation are also involved. Nearly all currently available studies can be interpreted as supporting either the hypothesis that the animals are tired of looking at one portion of their world (stimulus satiation) and hence are relieved to get out, or that they are excited and pleased (curiosity drive) to see something new.

On the Conditioning of Emotional Responses

As we have noted, principally in Chapter 5, there is reason to suppose that fears and other emotional reactions can become associated, through learning, with biologically neutral stimuli and may thereby come to serve as acquired sources of drive. But the problem of how such emotional responses are learned has been postponed to the present chapter. Since most of the written material on this topic deals with the learning of fear, we shall restrict our discussion to this emotion, omitting the problem of whether positive affective responses are acquired by processes other than those involved in fear conditioning.

Theories of Fear Conditioning. Theorists who have concerned themselves with the question of how emotional reactions are learned may be divided into two broad groups on the basis of the answers they have suggested. One group consists of those who hold that the acquisition of conditioned emotional responses is governed by the *same* processes that control the learning of nonemotional responses. The members of the second group maintain that *different* processes control the learning of the two kinds of reactions. The members of both groups, however, disagree among themselves as to which mechanisms should be assigned positions of central importance.

Probably the best-known members of the first group are Guthrie (1935) and Hull (1943, 1951, 1952). According to Guthrie, an association is formed between a stimulus and a response, whether the response is a skeletal movement or an internal emotional activity, whenever the response occurs in the presence of the stimulus.

The mere contiguity, or the occurrence together in time, of stimulus and response is sufficient to produce the associative bonding that is the essence of learning. For Hull also, stimuli and responses must be contiguous if stimuli are to acquire tendencies to elicit reactions. But in addition to contiguity, a reduction in drive following the elicitation of the response is regarded by Hull as an essential condition for the formation of associations. During the conditioning of fear, the noxious *UCS* is assumed to serve as a primary source of drive, and its termination, therefore, constitutes a reduction in drive. Both Hull and Guthrie thus agree that contiguity is a necessary condition for the growth of associations. They disagree in that Hull considers drive reduction to be an additional necessary condition, whereas Guthrie does not. As members of the "same-processes" group, these theorists believe that the learning both of emotional and nonemotional responses can be explained in terms of one set of principles.

Notable members of the second, or "different-processes," group are Schlosberg (1937), Skinner (1938), and Mowrer (1947). For Mowrer, whose views we have chosen to examine in detail, S-R contiguity is both the necessary and the sufficient condition for the learning of emotional responses. Instrumental reactions involving skeletal muscles are not learned, however, unless a reduction in drive follows such acts. The fear-conditioning aspect of Mowrer's interpretation, which in general closely resembles the views of Schlosberg and Skinner, is thus seen to be essentially Guthrian, whereas Mowrer's position with respect to instrumental learning is identical with Hull's. Although Spence (1956) has not seriously concerned himself with this problem, he has tentatively proposed a different-process theory that is the exact opposite of Mowrer's. According to Spence, instrumental actions are perhaps learned through the operation of contiguity alone, whereas the acquisition of autonomically controlled reactions may rest upon the occurrence of drive reduction in addition to contiguity.

Apparently, then, learning theorists, at least those who regard learning as involving associations between responses and stimuli, concur in the belief that contiguity is an indispensable condition for the acquisition of emotional reactions. They do not agree, however, as to whether additional variables, particularly those upon which the immediacy or completeness of drive reduction might depend, are also necessary. Thus the issue is reduced to this basic question: What empirical variables determine the conditioning of emotional responses?

Those who, like Mowrer, hold to a strict contiguity view of emotional conditioning would probably maintain that the following experimental variables are of primary importance for the growth of emotional associative strengths: (1) the interval between the onset of the CS and the onset of the UCS (degree of contiguity); (2) the intensities of the CS and the UCS; and (3) the frequency and recency of S-R pairings. Presumably, any variable that might affect the time of occurence, or the abruptness or the completeness of the drive-reduction process would be rejected as of no significance for emotional conditioning. One such variable is UCS duration. If drive reduction occurs when the UCS is terminated and if drive reduction is reinforcing, then the more protracted the UCS the greater the delay of reinforcement. From the viewpoint of a contiguity theorist, however, varying the interval between the emotional response and a reduction in the drive, other things constant, should have no effect upon the strength of the conditioned emotional associative tendency.

Theorists who do not hold that mere contiguity is a sufficient condition for the formation of emotional associations would nevertheless grant the importance of the above variables of contiguity, stimulus intensity, frequency, and recency. But in addition they would maintain that variables such as UCS duration, which might affect the drive-reduction process, should not be dismissed until careful experiments have shown them to be irrelevant or insignificant.

If isolating significant variables lies at the heart of the problem of emotional conditioning, then it would appear that definitive answers could be obtained from straightforward experimental investigations. But such inquiries could provide us with a complete list of relevant variables without resolving the issue. Those concerned with this problem might agree on a group of variables and yet disagree as to the nature of the mechanisms activated by those variables. For example, the time at which an electric shock is terminated might be shown to affect emotional conditioning, but the question could still be raised as to whether drive reduction does or does not accompany shock termination. Perhaps for the masochist, shock cessation is drive arousing rather than drive reducing. Similarly, an increase in the duration of an electric shock may result in augmented pain, or, if adaptation occurs, in diminished pain. And the variable of degree of S-R contiguity may affect learning through any one of a variety of mechanisms of which we know nothing as yet.

Mowrer, for example, made no distinction between empirical variables and the hypothetical mechanisms underlying those variables. Consequently, in rejecting the assumption that the *mechanism* of drive reduction was necessary for emotional conditioning, he also rejected all of the *empirical variables* on which drive reduction might depend. This he need not have done. Like Guthrie, he could have maintained that certain of the "law-of-effect" or drive-reduction variables influence the strength of an emotional response by protecting associations from unlearning rather than by strengthening them in the first place. By this stratagem Mowrer could have retained any of the empirical drive-reduction variables while rejecting the drive-reduction mechanism.

Illustrative Investigations. Concerning experimental attempts to determine whether contiguity alone is sufficient for the learning of fear reactions, none has thus far yielded unambiguous results. This is a difficult field, however, in which to design crucial experiments, since none of the alternative hypotheses has been stated with sufficient precision to make exact tests possible.

To illustrate the vexing nature of the problem, let us examine the procedures used in studies purporting to bear on the issue. One of the experimental designs often used to evaluate the relative merits of the contiguity-alone versus the contiguity-plus-drive-reduction conceptions is shown in Fig. 9:1. Here it will be seen that the classical aversive conditioning procedures used with the two groups are identical in all respects save that the duration of the UCS is longer in the case of group II than in the case of group I. That is to say, the CSs are identical, and the contiguity variable is also presumably identical, since, with the CS-UCS intervals equal, the time between the CS and the unconditioned response must also be the same for the two groups.

Now on a drive-reduction hypothesis it might be predicted that the members of group I would show more fear conditioning than the members of group II because the drive-reducing event (shock cessation) occurs more immediately in group I than in group II. The assumption that associative strength varies inversely with delay of reinforcement is, of course, also involved in this prediction. Thus, if it can be shown that a short-shock group is no more fearful than a long-shock group, this evidence would weigh against Hull's delay-of-reinforcement hypothesis and against the drive-reduction view. But this conclusion would be justified only if one could be sure that the delay-of-reinforcement variable had not been overridden by other factors. One such factor is shock intensity. Thus, if shock duration is permitted to vary while delay-of-reinforcement is being manipulated, this variation may lead to changes in effective shock strength. As common sense would seem to suggest, a CS that signals the coming of a long shock might well arouse *more* fear than one that is premonitory of brief shock (cf. Miller and Dollard, 1941, p. 58). Perhaps the unconditioned pain is more intense with long shock, even with physical intensity held constant, or the drive reduction occasioned by the cessation of a longer shock may be greater than that following the offset of brief shock. If a short-shock group shows more conditioned fear than a long-shock group, the drive-reduction theorist may feel encouraged. But his theory is not refuted even if a significant difference in the reverse direction is obtained. If long

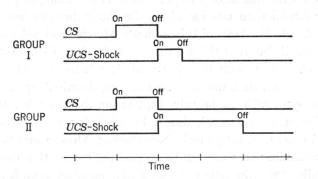

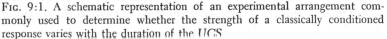

FIG. 9:1. A schematic representation of an experimental arrangement commonly used to determine whether the strength of a classically conditioned response varies with the duration of the UCS

shock leads to more fear than short shock, this effect may mean that *events associated with the termination of shock are affecting the process of emotional conditioning.* And if they are, then fear conditioning may be a function of other variables than the mere contiguity of the CS and the unconditioned response.

Experimental studies employing designs much like that in Fig. 9:1 have been reported by Sullivan (1950), Bitterman, Reed, and Krauskopf (1952), Mowrer and Solomon (1954), and Zeaman and Wegner (1954). Sullivan's experiment, involving the conditioning of the GSR in human subjects, with short and long intense auditory stimuli as UCSs, provided suggestive but not conclusive evidence that the short-duration stimulus was more effective in producing conditioned GSRs. Bitterman et al. attempted to condition GSRs by means of short and long shocks. While the long-shock procedure tended to yield responses of larger amplitude than the short shock, the differences fell far short of statistical significance. Unfortunately, the subjects in this study served as their own controls, the short shock being paired with the lighting of one 15-watt lamp on one half of the 16 trials and the long shock being paired with the lighting of an identical lamp on the other half of the trials. Hence, the failure to obtain differences in either direction, in spite of the fact that all subjects whose records were used said they knew one light was followed by long and the other by short shock, is not surprising. In the Mowrer-Solomon experiment, rats given fear-conditioning training with 10-second shock showed some indication (10 per cent level of confidence) of being more fearful than rats for whom the shock duration was only 3 seconds. On the basis of this evidence Mowrer and Solomon suggest that if the short shock had been as brief as 0.5 second, ". . . it is virtually certain that it would be reliably less effective in producing fear than would a shock of long duration" (p. 21). This is consistent with the intuitive expectation that cues denoting the coming of a short shock should be less fear arousing than cues that forewarn of long shock. Nevertheless, Mowrer and Solomon still maintain that these results support their views that the events attending the termination of a UCS have no effect upon fear learning. This conclusion is puzzling, since if one group does exhibit more fear than the other, with S-R contiguity equated, then, contrary to Mowrer's interpretation, contiguity is not the whole story. If genuine differences in fear can be produced by the use of long and short shocks, then the variable of *UCS* duration, involving as it does the time at which the noxious stimulus goes off, may indeed have something to do with fear learning.

Zeaman and Wegner, in a study of conditioned cardiac responses, have found that a relatively short shock of 2 seconds duration leads to conditioned acceleration during the *CS-UCS* interval. With a 6-second shock, however, the conditioned response is a deceleration in heart rate. This difference in the form of the conditioned responses is ascribed to the fact that the heart is accelerating at the time of shock reduction in the short-shock condition, but is decelerating at the time the long shock terminates. The authors interpret their results as supporting the view that drive reduction is the mechanism of conditioning in the case of this autonomically mediated response.

In connection with designs of the type illustrated in Fig. 9:1, it should be noted that, with the exception of Sullivan's experiment, apparently none of the investigations has been conducted with an optimal *CS-UCS* interval. The work of White and Schlosberg (1952) and of Moeller (1954) indicates that a *CS-UCS* interval of about 0.5 second yields optimal GSR conditioning. In the study of Bitterman et al., this interval was set at 5 seconds. According to White and Schlosberg, this should yield no conditioning at all, and some question can be raised whether in fact Bitterman et al. did indeed obtain conditioned responses, since their design included no controls for pseudoconditioning. It may also be observed, as Miller (1951) has pointed out, that it is not always certain, when shock duration is being varied in animal experiments, that drive reduction occurs only at the instant when the experimenter terminates the shock. If an animal is free to move about on an electrified grid, the shock may actually be intermittent, for the rat can momentarily escape shock by leaping and running. This could mean that a long shock, in effect, is a series of short shocks involving multiple drive reductions and reinforcements. In rat experiments some control over this factor has been provided by the use of shock compartments with low ceilings, but so long as the animals are free to move and the shock electrodes are not fixed to the animal, the control may be less than perfect. In any event, very carefully designed and well-controlled experiments will be needed before we can be sure that long shocks do not produce a degree of fear different from that produced by short shocks, and that delay of reinforcement is not a significant factor.

An investigation by Mowrer and Aiken (1954) provides an additional example of problems attending the design of crucial experiments on the contiguity-alone versus the contiguity-plus-drive-reduction views. Figure 9:2 shows the various fear-conditioning procedures used by Mowrer and Aiken. As this figure indicates, UCS duration was the same for all groups, but the position of the CS with respect to the UCS was varied progressively from group I through group IV. In a fifth group, not shown in the figure, the CS was withheld until two minutes after the UCS terminated.

In explaining this experimental design, Mowrer and Aiken state that according to Hull, the nearer the CS is in time to the termination of the UCS, the greater should be the capacity of the CS to

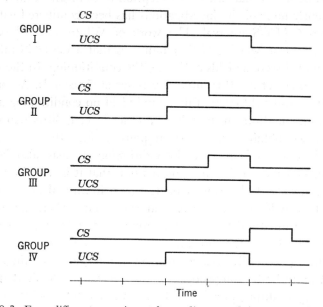

Fig. 9:2. Four different experimental paradigms used in an experiment designed to evaluate the relative merits of the contiguity-alone versus the contiguity-plus-drive-reduction views of emotional conditioning. (*Adapted from Mowrer and Aiken, 1954.*)

evoke fear. The alleged expectation from Hull's views, therefore, is that fear should be conditioned more strongly in group III, say, than in group I. Unfortunately, this is a misinterpretation of Hull's position, since for him the interval of importance for fear conditioning is not the time between the CS and the offset of the UCS. Rather, Hull holds that the significant intervals are (1) that between the CS and the *response*, and (2) that between the *response* and the *reinforcing state of affairs*. In the Mowrer-Aiken design, if it is assumed that the response is always aroused shortly after the onset of the UCS, then, since the UCS duration is held constant, the interval between response and reinforcement is also constant. However, as the position of the CS relative to the UCS is progressively shifted from that used with group I to that used with groups IV and V, there is clearly a change in the temporal separation of CS and response. But on Hull's views, this change in the position of the CS would be expected to lead to poorer and poorer conditioning, since *it involves a change from a forward conditioning procedure to an extreme degree of backward conditioning*. It is not surprising, therefore, that Mowrer and Aiken found group I to be the most fearful, with fear becoming progressively less in the groups for whom the procedure became more and more "backward." It is well known to students of conditioning that backward conditioning arrangements yield little if any stable conditioned responses. Davitz (1955), using stimulus presentation orders like those of Mowrer and Aiken's groups I and III, also reports that more fear is conditioned when the CS precedes the onset of the UCS than when it coincides with UCS termination. However, Davitz also fails to note that the manipulation of the position of the CS relative to the UCS involves a shift from forward to backward conditioning. Strouthes and Hamilton (1959) have also employed experimental procedures like those used with groups I and II of the Mowrer-Aiken study. Their animals, however, showed enhanced bar pressing during the presentation of the fear-arousing CS rather than inhibition, as in the Mowrer-Aiken investigation. But Strouthes and Hamilton's group-II animals were more fearful than their group-I subjects, as estimated by degree of bar-pressing facilitation. Arguing from the position that delay of reinforcement is shorter for group II than for group I, and from the further assumption that the best index of the delay interval is provided by the time from CS onset to UCS termination, Strouthes and Hamilton conclude that their results tend to support the drive-reduction position. Finally, Gerall, Sampson, and Boslov (1957) have clearly shown that a known reinforcer (electric shock) affects the conditioning of pupillary dilation, which is a response controlled by the autonomic nervous system. Light offset was found to be an adequate UCS for the evocation of the pupillary response, but no conditioning occurred when the CS was paired with light offset alone. However, when the UCS consisted of shock paired with light offset, or shock alone, conditioning of pupillary dilation was readily obtained.

Physiological Studies Related to the Concept of General Drive

When Hull (1943) outlined his concept of a nonspecific drive (D), his speculations rested entirely upon observations of gross, molar behavior. At that time there were scant grounds for supposing that a general-purpose motivating function of this sort could be meaningfully ascribed to the activities of any particular neural system or group of systems. In recent years, however, this picture has been altered as a result of the discovery of new facts concerning the physiological and neurological mechanisms of motivation. Of special relevance for the hypothesis of nonspecific drive are data that have been interpreted to mean that the brain-stem reticular system has widespread motivational functions. Additional findings, particularly those from studies of intracranial electrical stimulation, have shed new light on such matters as the drive-reduction theory of reinforcement and the tendencies of organisms to avoid some stimuli and approach others. We shall discuss these several matters in the sections to follow.

Drivelike Functions of Reticular System Activity. A detailed elaboration of the anatomical minutiae of the reticular formation is clearly beyond the scope of this book, and for such information the reader must consult other sources (e.g., Rossi and Zanchetti, 1957, and Jasper, 1958). In broad outline, however, the brain-stem reticular formation consists, according to Lindsley (1957),

". . . of a rather dense network of neurons which forms a kind of central core extending from the medulla of the lower brain stem to the thalamus in the diencephalon. It extends through the regions of the pons and the midbrain tegmentum upward through the caudal portions of the hypothalamus and subthalamus" (p. 57). Activity in the brain-stem reticular system can affect the function of structures lying both below and above. In particular, fibers passing downward from the reticular formation into the spinal cord carry impulses that assist in the regulation (either by inhibition or facilitation) of complex postural and phasic muscular reactions Additionally, and perhaps more importantly for our purposes, other fiber systems composing the so-called ascending reticular activating system pass upward to basal ganglia, thalamus, hypothalamus, hyppocampus, and cortex.

As a consequence, apparently, of the anatomical diffusion of these ascending reticular system fibers, impulses from lower segments of the reticular formation can bring about widespread changes in cortical activity. This "activation effect," as it has been called, which was first reported by Moruzzi and Magoun (1949), is a modification of the waveform pattern of the electrical potentials recorded from the brain. When a subject is asleep, the form of these electrical impulses differs markedly from that characteristic of waking or excited states. Electrical stimulation in the region of the reticular system was found by Moruzzi and Magoun to change the cortical brain wave from the "sleep" pattern to the "waking" or "excited" form. Of possible significance, for theories of motivation, is the fact that this "electrocortical activation" is widespread, being observed at numerous points on the cortical surface. Moreover, as Lindsley, Bowden, and Magoun (1949) have shown, a progressive decline in amount of "electrocortical activation" is associated with increasingly widespread destruction of the reticular system. At the very least, then, the nonspecific activating effects of ascending reticular system activity appear to be consistent with the construct of a general-purpose drive.

That the arousal functions of the ascending reticular formation are analogous to, if not completely commensurate with, the notion of a nonspecific drive was apparently first noted by Hebb (1955), though Lindsley (1951) had seen the broad implications of reticular system activity for problems of emotion and motivation. According to Hebb, activation produced by the diffuse bombardment of the cortex by the arousal system is ". . . synonymous with a general drive state, and the conception of drive therefore assumes anatomical and physiological identity" (p. 249). Schlosberg (1954) has also stressed the emotional and motivational aspects of arousal activity, but he has not written expressly of its possible relations to Hull's general-purpose drive. These writers, and others (e.g., Malmo, 1958), have also observed that performance decrements characteristic of "overly motivated" subjects might reasonably be attributed to excessive bombardment of the cortex by the ascending reticular activating system. On this view, performance is related to motivation (activation) level by an inverted U-shaped function, performance being optimally efficient when amount of activation is neither too weak (the subject is drowsy or relaxed) nor too strong (the subject is angry, fearful, or enraged).

Support for the view that impulses in the ascending reticular system function in a relatively nonspecific fashion is provided primarily by observed changes in electrocortical potentials. But scattered data of a more molar nature are also consistent with this view. For example, it has long been known that responses of flight, rage, and generally heightened "emotionality" can be produced by intracranial stimulation; and it is responses of this sort that have often been seen as reflecting heightened drive. Moreover, according to Ingram, Knott, and Chiles (1953) and Lindsley (1957), electrical stimulation of the brain-stem reticular system has alerting or arousing effects upon overt behavior as well as upon the pattern of the electroencephalogram. Perhaps the most interesting data of this kind are those reported by Fuster (1958). According to this investigator, stimulation of the reticular formation of monkeys (at the mesencephalic level) while they are engaged in the performance of visual discrimination tasks increases their speed of reacting, improves their discriminatory accuracy, and lowers their tachistoscopic recognition thresholds. Precisely what the mechanism of this effect may be is not clear, but it seems to be congruent with the idea of a nonspecific drive. In several studies, however (e.g., Chiles, 1954; and Knott, Ingram, and Correll, 1960), lever pressing in cats tends to be arrested rather than augmented by electrical stimulation in the region of the hypothalamus.

Several investigators (Delgado, Roberts, and Miller, 1954; Cohen, Brown, and Brown, 1957; Roberts, 1958; Bursten and Delgado, 1958) have shown that intracranial stimulation may function in much the same way as peripheral shock. To take a single example, Delgado and his associates have noted that electrical stimulation of certain thalamic, mesencephalic, and rhinencephalic structures elicits fearlike responses in cats. The resultant emotionality can be conditioned to external stimuli; it can function to motivate the learning of instrumental acts; and it can serve as punishment in training hungry cats to avoid food. Although part of this effect may have been due to cerebral pain, similar results were not obtained from the stimulation of sensorimotor areas. Apparently, therefore, centrally introduced stimuli, when applied to certain structures and under certain learning conditions, play a role in the determination of behavior comparable to that of peripheral shocks or other drive-arousing unconditioned stimuli.

The above discussion has stressed the nonspecific consequences of central stimulation, but quite specific responses are also frequently evoked. According to Samuels (1959), relatively specific effects of central stimulation are more probably reflections of activity in the thalamic reticular system than of action in the brain-stem reticular system. As an example of such effects, Miller (1958) reports the elicitation of well-integrated eating and drinking responses in satiated rats as the result of central (hypothalamic) stimulation. This specificity of action is not of primary concern here, but it may constitute the physiological basis for such behavior-directing effects as are commonly ascribed to drive-variable stimuli (S_Ds).

Considered as a receiving station for incoming impulses, the reticular system is thought to be affected primarily by signals diverted via collaterals from the primary sensory pathways and, in addition, by impulses descending from the cortex. This means, as Lindsley (1957), Samuels (1959), and others have indicated, that the activity level of the multineuronal, multisynaptic reticular formation can be modified by both exteroceptive and interoceptive stimuli and even by "ideational" impulses presumed to originate in the higher cortical centers. From this the conclusion may be drawn that, in so far as the alerting and arousing effects of reticular system discharges can be equated to nonspecific drive, then level of drive is *under the control of external and/or internal stimuli.* The implications of this suggestion are widespread and of considerable importance, since, if this is indeed the case, plausible mechanisms are provided for (1) increasing drive by presenting the *CS* for an aversive response or by presenting an incentive object, (2) reducing drive by presenting a secondarily reinforcing stimulus, or (3) changing drive in almost any manner by verbal instructions or self-induced ideations. As we have previously observed in our discussion of the concepts of drive and need (Chapter 3), the possibility that drive strength can be changed by exteroceptive or proprioceptive stimuli may clarify some of the problems posed by the view that drive reduction is essential for learning.

It also seems probable that activity in the reticular system can control the sensitivity of peripheral receptors and, at a more central level, can integrate and coordinate receptor-generated information. The verification of these functions by further research may provide us with mechanisms by which drive can affect sensation, perception, memory, and a variety of other processes.

Reinforcing Properties of Intracerebral Stimuli. Although the behavioral effects of electrical stimulation of the brain have been studied in both acute and chronic preparations for many years, Olds and Milner (1954) were apparently the first to show that such stimuli can function as reinforcers for instrumental acts. This finding has provided the impetus both for considerable further research and for theoretical reappraisals of the mechanisms of reinforcement.

In the Olds-Milner demonstrations, electrodes were permanently implanted in the brains of rats in such a manner as not to interfere with normal daily activities. A pair of thin, flexible wires could be attached, as desired, to the electrodes where they emerged from the skull. These wires were suspended from above and hence did little to hamper the rat's movements in a Skinner box or through simple mazes. This arrangement made it possible for the experimenters to administer intracerebral electric stimuli of any strength or duration, at any moment, and in any relation to the overt actions of the rat.

The most interesting finding reported by Olds and Milner was that after appropriate conditions of pretraining, some subjects, particularly those having electrode tips in the limbic system, would press a Skinner-box lever repeatedly and for long periods of time, even though each lever-pressing response was accompanied by an intracranial shock. In some cases the shocks lasted until the lever was released, but usually their duration was fixed at 0.5 or 1.0 second. Under these conditions, with no rewards other than electrical stimuli being provided, rats would continue to press the lever for periods of several hours and at rates as high as approximately 30 responses per minute. Unquestionably, "masochistic" behavior of this kind is puzzling, since electric shock has been so widely used as an aversive or punishing stimulus. Nevertheless, the phenomenon is now well authenticated, having been repeatedly demonstrated in rats (Olds, 1956a, 1956b; Reynolds, 1958; Bower and Miller, 1958), in cats (Sidman, Brady, Boren, Conrad, and Schulman, 1955; Roberts, 1958), and in monkeys (Bursten and Delgado, 1958). There is also fairly general agreement that stimulation of the limbic system, and especially in the ventral region of the anterior hypothalamus, is more likely to yield positive reinforcement effects than the stimulation of other regions. The effect is not confined, however, to a single sharply circumscribed area, and since rather high intensities of shock are often used, structures other than those adjacent to the electrode tips may be involved.

When consideration is given to the question of why these subcortical stimuli function as reinforcers, no entirely convincing answers are forthcoming. One suggestion is that pleasurable sensations or experiences are aroused when known reinforcing areas are excited. On this view, certain portions of the brain are seen as "pleasure centers," since organisms do perform responses accompanied by the stimulation of these regions. Other areas, the stimulation of which seems to evoke avoidance and withdrawal rather than approach, would qualify as "pain centers." This conception is attractive to advocates of hedonistic theories of reinforcement and is supported by introspective reports of "pleasurable" sensations by human subjects who, while conscious, have been stimulated in or near the septal region (Heath, 1954). The view is also consistent with the notion that some of the reinforcing areas of the brain may exert a quieting or inhibiting effect on behavior. Thus Brady and Nauta (1953) have shown that extirpation of the septal area leads to an increase in activity, and that perhaps, therefore, the normal function of that area is generally inhibitory. As Olds (1955) remarks, ongoing activity usually stops abruptly when the septal region is stimulated electrically.

Weighing against this pleasure-center view are the findings of Roberts (1958), Bower and Miller (1958), and Brown and Cohen (1959). All these investigators have shown that stimulation of a given region, even with intensity held constant, may be either reinforcing or inhibiting depending upon the training procedures used and upon such factors as stimulation duration and the testing environment. Roberts, for instance, reports that cats in a Y maze will learn to enter one arm of the maze where shock to the posterior hypothalamus is turned on but will also learn to enter a second arm to turn off the shock. Apparently the onset of excitation is reinforcing, since the animals repeatedly enter the maze arm where shock is turned on; but continuation of the stimulus seemingly becomes aversive, because the cats also learn to enter the only arm of the maze where the shock is always terminated. Of special interest is Roberts's finding that increases in stimulus intensity affect the approach and escape responses differentially. With relatively weak shocks the response leading to shock onset is readily learned, whereas the turning-off response is not. But with high-voltage stimulation marked improvement is shown in the learning of the turning-off response while the turning-on reaction is performed more slowly and with clear indications of conflict.

Qualitative reports of the behavior of animals stimulated in reinforcing areas also weigh against any simple pleasure-center interpretation. Thus Olds (1955) observes that, following prolonged periods of reinforcing self-stimulation in the septal area, rats become vicious and are dangerous to handle. This seems to contradict the notion that septal stimulation has pleasurable or soothing consequences. Moreover, the typical behavior pattern exhibited by both rats and cats during periods of intermittent self-stimulation is often described as "agitated searching" or even as "flight," which scarcely suggests relaxation and contentment. If the self-stimulation of the sort investigated in these studies is pleasurable, it is the frenetic, compulsive pleasure of the masochist or the neurotic. Apparently neither rats nor cats, when stimulus duration is made to coincide with bar-depression time, hold the bar down for protracted periods so that the self-stimulation can be prolonged. Were this the case, *rate* of lever pressing should be extremely low, since the subject should have little tendency to release the lever and thereby terminate the "pleasant" experience. High rates of lever pressing are usually obtained with high voltages, indicating that the subjects, though they repeatedly approach and depress the lever, must be *releasing* it quickly and thus terminating the shock. Why should the lever be released if this act eliminates a genuinely pleasurable stimulus? The answer to this question is no clearer than that to the question of why the rat depresses the lever in the first place. In any event, although rats certainly develop a strong tendency to approach and press the lever, they also learn to release it after experiencing a relatively brief shock.

It is also quite probable that the success of self-stimulation demonstrations depends in considerable degree upon the voltage levels used during early training trials, upon the rapidity with which the voltage is increased over trials, and upon other aspects of the training and testing procedures. Olds (1955), for instance, reports that his rats were manually placed upon the bar to receive their first shock, that they were replaced thereon whenever they were not responding regularly, and that the progressive upward shifting of voltages had to be carefully executed in order to achieve maximum response rates. As yet no one seems to have set the shock at a high level initially and then left the animals alone to see whether they would then learn to press the lever to stimulate themselves. Judging from Roberts's results, if strong shock were used from the outset, it would probably not be reinforcing, though the same intensity of stimulation, if arrived at through a series of carefully graded steps, might so function. Such an experiment has apparently not even been done with mild shock, and, to the writer's knowledge, no learning curves have been published in which data from every shock trial (including the first) have been presented.

The importance of training and testing procedures is further high-lighted by the work of Bursten and Delgado (1958), who failed in a preliminary attempt to teach monkeys to press a lever for intracranial shock reward but succeeded in demonstrating the reinforcing effects of shock by the use of a shuttle box.

There is also merit in an interpretation proposed by Cohen, Brown, and Brown (1957). These investigators have observed that stimulation of intracranial structures such as the hypothalamus, though it may produce motivational increments, does not immediately and consistently evoke *directed* escape responses. The fearlike or ragelike emotionality cannot be referred by the animal to any specific objects or regions in his environment. Central shock is thus unlike grid shock, since the latter, because of the direction-giving peripheral pain cues, regularly elicits movements of leaping, hopping, or running that are directed away from the source of irritation. On this view, when animals are reinforced with central stimuli, as in the Olds-Milner study, they do not avoid the lever, because the central shock provides the animal with no information to indicate that the lever or any other particular feature of the testing environment is the source of the stimulus. Or to phrase it differently, mild central shock does not elicit lever-escape responses, and until these are evoked and are reinforced, the animals have no reason to refrain from approaching the lever. The fact that animals *learn* to press the lever is not, of course, explained by this interpretation. It is conceivable that factors such as those operating in studies of experimental masochism (see below) may be of significance in connection with this problem.

In the early flush of enthusiasm generated by studies of intracranial reinforcing stimuli, the fact that quite similar effects have been reported for externally administered shock and other strong stimuli seems to have escaped notice. Masserman (1946), for instance, in his studies of "experimental masochism," trained cats to obtain food by operating a lever. Blasts of air of gradually increasing intensity were then administered each time the lever was depressed. At the end of training, the cats were not only not disturbed by airblasts intense enough to evoke violent avoidance in nontrained animals, but they even operated the switch lever in the absence of food reward, the airblast having apparently acquired the properties of a substitute reward. Likewise, Farber (1948) and Miller and Davis (1943) have demonstrated that after rats have been trained to run down an alley for food, mild electric grid shock can be introduced in the middle of the alley without disrupting the approach behavior. The latter investigators also report that if shock strength is then increased gradually over trials, it can eventually reach a very high level without causing the animals to cease running, and that, in fact, their speed of running is increased. But if the voltage is raised precipitously, abrupt cessation of running is the result. A comparable phenomenon, observed a number of years ago by the writer, has been described as the "vicious-circle" phenomenon by Mowrer (1950). Rats were trained initially to run down a short straight alley to escape shock by reaching a nonelectrified section at the end. After this behavior was firmly established, the electrical connections to the first three feet of the grid were removed to make it "safe," while the last three feet were left electrified. Some rats, when placed into the safe section at the start, continued to run from the no-shock starting section and across the shock section to the safe goal region. With some animals this behavior persisted for literally hundreds of trials without the slightest sign of abatement. Mowrer has suggested that conditioned fear provides the motivation for running out of the safe starting section, that strength of fear is maintained by the shock encountered on the way to the safe goal, and that fear reduction, operating through the law of effect, continues to reinforce running. If to this is added the consideration that shock reduction also provides a powerful and continuing reinforcement for running, the plausibility of the theory is enhanced. Be that as it may, when rats exhibit this "vicious-circle" behavior they are responding quite like the animals in the intracranial self-stimulation experiments. It is even possible that an interpretation such as Mowrer's, which seems to provide a satisfactory explanation for one of these phenomena, can be extended to encompass the other.

We have already noted in discussing the so-called manipulatory and exploratory drives that rats will learn to press a lever when each press is followed by the onset of a light (Kish, 1955). This phenomenon, sometimes described by the phrase "sensory-change reinforcement," has been amply confirmed by Marx, Henderson, and Roberts (1955), by Kling, Horowitz, and Delhagen (1956), and by Barnes and Kish (1957). It is of interest here because of the ways in which it parallels the phenomena of reinforcement by central stimulation. For one thing, if the light is made too bright, its onset ceases to be reinforcing and becomes aversive (Marx et al.). Clearly, this is similar to Roberts's (1958) observation that when a central stimulus is intense, "turning-off" responses are easily learned but "turning-on" responses are not. Moreover, lever pressing both for central stimulation (Brady, Boren, Conrad, and Sidman, 1957; Olds, 1958) and for light onset (Forgays and Levin, 1959) is increased by food deprivation. And both types of stimulation, if administered under the proper conditions, can apparently reinforce more complicated responses than lever pressing, for example, maze behavior (Olds, 1955) and discrimination learning (Forgays and Levin, 1959). In the light of these similarities, it is conceivable that both types of experiments involve the operation of basically similar mechanisms of reinforcement.

The implications of findings like these for the drive-reduction hypothesis of reinforcement have been pointed out elsewhere (Brown, 1955). The fact that organisms will perform responses leading to, or accompanied by, increased intensity of stimulation is not especially damaging to this hypothesis. In the first place, there are many instances in which enhanced physical stimulation need not, and probably should not, be described as leading to or generating increments in magnitude of drive. In each particular case one must consider not only the amount of physical change but also the adaptation level of the subject's sense organs, the nature of his ongoing responses, his homeostatic balances, and his previous experiences with the stimulus. If, when evaluated in terms of these and other factors, a stimulus does not qualify as a source of drive, then the continued appearance of responses that are followed by that stimulus is not conclusive evidence against the drive-reduction position. In the second place, we must insist once more that the concepts of drive and need are not identical or at least do not have to be identical. A bodily need may function as a source of drive, but the class of drive-reducing operations contains more members than the class of need-reducing conditions. The body's need for water can be eliminated only by water or by fluids containing water, but the drive arising from that need can perhaps be partially reduced, at least temporarily, by such activities as turning one's attention to other matters, by chewing a stick of gum, by swallowing repeatedly, and so on. Inasmuch as all these activities involve an increase in stimulation, it again becomes apparent that drive level can probably be modified by either external or internal stimuli. It would be premature, therefore, to insist that drive is not reduced in self-stimulation demonstrations simply because no biological need is apparently satisfied. But it would be equally unwise to hold stubbornly to a drive-reduction view until one can point with some assurance to the source of the drive that is being reduced by self-stimulation and to the mechanisms by which this reduction might be achieved.

As a third and final point, one must bear in mind that neither self-administered intracranial stimuli nor exteroceptive stimuli can serve to motivate the behavior of approaching and pressing a bar, if, as is usually the case, they are not turned on until after the to-be-learned response has been initiated. In this respect, the self-stimulation studies are like the Butler-Harlow experiments on visual rewards with monkeys. The motivation underlying prestimulation behavior may be a kind of conditioned anxiety, or a positive expectancy (r_g-s_g) of anticipated pleasure, or perhaps simply the animal's normally present general drive. The first of these possibilities is consistent with Mowrer's interpretation of the "vicious-circle" phenomenon, and the second with the view that the onset of some stimuli may be "pleasurable" and that classically conditioned fractional responses anticipatory of such pleasure might serve as sources of drive. As to the third possibility, little need be said save that normal, healthy, awake organisms may always be operating under moderate drive even when no extreme biological imbalances exist. Taken in conjunction with the manifold stimuli provided by the usual environment, this persisting drive may suffice to activate a wide variety of behaviors, whose probabilities of appearance are subsequently modified by reinforcements of one sort or another.

Summary

It has been our purpose in this final chapter to expand our treatment of motivation by considering several topics that could not conveniently have been included in earlier chapters.

One of these topics involves the problem of whether nonnoxious stimuli that evoke responses of approaching, exploring, and manipulating also tend to function as motivational variables. Spence and Hull hold that such stimuli may indeed generate increments to drive, provided they have been closely associated in the past with reinforcing events. Thus responses composing appetitive consummatory sequences are thought to become conditioned to any stimuli present when those responses occur, and fractional components of the sequences can also be evoked by similar stimuli even prior to the time the goal is reached. These fractional anticipatory goal reactions (r_gs) are said to affect behavior both associatively, because of the characteristic stimuli (s_gs) they are assumed to provide, and motivationally, by adding an increment to drive.

Since organisms may approach, inspect, and manipulate unfamiliar as well as familiar objects, the possibility must be entertained that *novel* stimuli also function motivationally. With unfamiliar stimuli, however, interpretations involving acquired, anticipatory responses are clearly inappropriate. As a result, various writers (Montgomery, Harlow, Berlyne, and others) have urged that the postulation of special-purpose exploratory, curiosity, or manipulatory drives is desirable. These drives, however, are drives to perform only those specific kinds of acts that are evoked by the presentation of novel stimulus objects. Thus they involve both behavior-directing and motivating functions; and in the role of systematic concepts, these behavior-specific drives suffer from the fact that they are seldom defined in terms of observable events other than the particular actions they are alleged to produce.

Representative experiments dealing with exploratory, investigative, and manipulatory behavior indicate that rats, as well as higher organisms, do approach and investigate some, though by no means all, strange or novel objects. However, when such behavior is not evoked, or when actual withdrawal occurs, a fear drive is invoked in lieu of an exploratory drive. Nevertheless, numerous investigations can be cited which support the conclusion that organisms often behave so as to increase their contacts with unfamiliar stimuli or locales and to reduce their contacts with familiar objects or regions. And although exploratory and investigative behavior weakens rather quickly as novelty diminishes, manipulatory behavior in monkeys is remarkably persistent. In addition, some students of behavior have concluded that an opportunity to investigate a strange environment serves as a reinforcing agent for the learning of new responses.

Our analyses of these experiments and their interpretations indicate that in most instances it is difficult to reject the hypothesis that motivational factors of an aversive nature have been present in addition to, or instead of, the alleged investigative or manipulatory drives. Continued contact with, or confinement in, one segment of a maze may be an aversive condition that is alleviated by movement to other segments. It is also uncertain, in the case of experiments in which monkeys are reinforced by the act of looking out of an opaque-walled box, whether appeal must be made to the drive-arousing attributes of the external cues. At the very least, the drive underlying the performance of responses occurring prior to seeing cannot be ascribed to the effects of stimuli encountered only after seeing is permitted. However, mild anxiety due to isolation and confinement, or auditory stimuli, might function in such situations as motivators of preseeing behavior. It remains to be demonstrated, therefore, that special-purpose drives must be invoked to explain the variety of actions usually described as exploratory and/or manipulatory.

Learned emotional reactions are said by many to have significant motivational properties. The question of how such responses are learned, therefore, merits consideration in any theory of motivation. Some theorists (e.g., Guthrie and Hull) find no reasons for supposing that the learning of autonomically governed reactions is due to factors or processes different from those involved in the learning of skeletal (instrumental) responses. Others, however, maintain that different principles apply to the learning of the two classes of reactions. For example, Mowrer regards stimulus-response contiguity as both the necessary and the sufficient condition for the learning of fears, but drive reduction is seen as a further necessary condition for the acquisition of instrumental acts. This view contrasts with Hull's supposition that both drive reduction and S-R contiguity are necessary for the learning of all reactions.

Our analysis of these views and of experiments designed to support them reveals that a lack of precision in the structure of all extant theories makes crucial tests difficult. Experiments that have been reported appear to be unusually susceptible to interpretations other than those presented by the investigators and are marred by misconstructions of opposing theories and by the confounding effects of uncontrolled variables.

In the third major section of the chapter, evidence from physiological studies of central nervous system activity is reviewed with respect to its implications for a concept of general drive. Here the most significant finding appears to be that stimulation in the region of the brain-stem reticular formation can change electrical potentials at many parts of the cortex from a pattern characteristic of sleep to one associated with alert wakefulness. The motivational implications of this widespread bombardment of the cortex by the ascending reticular activating system have been widely noted, and Hebb has specifically identified this activity with a general-drive state. Apparently, these alerting functions can be modified by a wide variety of influences, including internal and external stimuli, and even the so-called ideational and attitudinal factors presumably mediated largely by cortical processes. It thus appears that drive level, to the extent that it may be identified with arousal activity of the ascending reticular system, can either be raised or lowered by a multiplicity of events. The potential significance of this possibility for such problems as those of secondary reinforcement, perceptual defense or vigilance, and the drive-reduction theory of reinforcement remains to be explored.

The final section of the chapter deals with studies of the reinforcing and inhibiting effects of centrally administered brain stimuli. The fact that animals can learn to perform acts such as lever pressing when the only consequence of the act is a subcortical electric shock is the empirical phenomenon of central interest. The basic finding has been repeatedly confirmed in rats and cats and, with some success, in monkeys. Some investigators have been led to the conclusion that reinforcing regions of the brain might be construed as "pleasure centers," whereas other areas, the stimulation of which leads to inhibition of activity, might be termed "pain centers." Support for this view has been provided by introspective reports from human subjects who have been stimulated while undergoing brain surgery under local anesthesia. In a variety of studies, however, it has been found that an animal can be taught either to perform an act to turn the brain stimulus on, or to perform a different act to turn it off. Since in these demonstrations the electrode placement and shock intensity is the same, any simple concept of pleasure or pain centers becomes relatively untenable. Apparently brain stimuli can have either rewarding or punishing effects, depending upon the kinds of behavior that are elicited by the test situation and upon temporal and other relations between the stimuli and the behavior.

REFERENCES

Adolph, E. F. (1941): The internal environment and behavior: III. Water content. *Amer. J. Psychiat.*, 97, 1365–1373.

Adolph, E. F. (1943): *Physiological regulations.* New York: The Ronald Press Company.

Amsel, A. (1950*a*): The combination of a primary appetitional need with primary and secondary emotionally derived needs. *J. exp. Psychol.*, 40, 1–14.

Amsel, A. (1950*b*): The effect upon level of consummatory response of the addition of anxiety to a motivational complex. *J. exp. Psychol.*, 40, 709–715.

Amsel, A. (1951): A three-factor theory of inhibition: an addition to Hull's two-factor theory. *Amer. Psychologist*, 6, 487. (Abstract.)

Amsel, A. (1958): The role of frustrative nonreward in noncontinuous reward situations. *Psychol. Bull.*, 55, 102–119.

Amsel, A., and W. Hancock (1957): Motivational properties of frustration: III. Relation of frustration effect to antedating goal factors. *J. exp. Psychol.*, 53, 126–131.

Amsel, A., and I. Maltzman (1950): The effect upon generalized drive strength of emotionality as inferred from the level of consummatory response. *J. exp. Psychol.*, 40, 563–569.

Amsel, A., and J. Roussel (1952): Motivational properties of frustration: I. Effect on a running response of the addition of frustration to the motivational complex. *J. exp. Psychol.*, 43, 363–368.

Anand, B. K., and J. R. Brobeck (1951): Hypothalamic control of food intake in rats and cats. *Yale J. Biol. and Med.*, 24, 123–140.

Anderson, E. E. (1941): The externalization of drive: III. Maze learning by non-rewarded and by satiated rats. *J. genet. Psychol.*, 59, 397–426.

Armus, H. L. (1954): *The effect of percentage of reinforcement and distribution of trials on resistance to extinction of a conditioned fear response.* Unpublished doctoral dissertation, State University of Iowa.

Aronson, E. (1956): *The need for achievement as measured by graphic expression.* Unpublished master's thesis, Wesleyan University. Cited in McClelland, 1956.

Ashley, W. R., R. S. Harper, and D. L. Runyon (1951): The perceived size of coins in normal and hypnotically induced economic states. *Amer. J. Psychol., 64,* 564–572.

Atkinson, J. W. (1950): Studies in projective measurement of achievement motivation. University of Michigan. Abstract in *University Microfilms,* Vol. X, N. 4; Publication No. 1945. Cited in McClelland, Atkinson, Clark, and Lowell, 1953.

Atkinson, J. W. (1954): Explorations using imaginative thought to assess the strength of human motives. In M. R. Jones (ed.), *Nebraska symposium on motivation.* Lincoln, Nebr.: University of Nebraska Press.

Atkinson, J. W., and D. C. McClelland (1948): The projective expression of needs. II. The effect of different intensities of the hunger drive on thematic apperception. *J. exp. Psychol., 38,* 643–658.

Bahrick, H. P. (1953): Sensory preconditioning under two degrees of deprivation. *J. comp. physiol. Psychol., 46,* 39–42.

Bakan, D. (1953): Learning and the scientific enterprise. *Psychol. Rev., 60,* 45–49.

Baker, R. A. (1955): The effects of repeated deprivation experience on feeding behavior. *J. comp. physiol. Psychol., 48,* 37–42.

Barnes, G. W., and G. B. Kish (1957): Reinforcing properties of the termination of intense auditory stimulation. *J. comp. physiol. Psychol., 50,* 40–43.

Barry, H., III (1958): Effects of strength of drive on learning and extinction. *J. exp. Psychol., 55,* 473–481.

Bass, Bettina (1958): *The effect of drive variation within and between subjects on conditioning performance.* Unpublished doctoral dissertation, State University of Iowa.

Beams, H. L. (1954): Affectivity as a factor in the apparent size of pictured food objects. *J. exp. Psychol., 47,* 197–200.

Bechtoldt, H. P., and J. S. McDonough (1958): *The effects of motivating instructions upon visual identification thresholds.* (Unpublished. Personal communication.)

Bergmann, G. (1944): An empiricist's system of the sciences. *Sci. Monthly, 59,* 140–148.

Berkun, M. M., M. L. Kessen, and N. E. Miller, (1952): Hunger-reducing effects of food by stomach fistula versus food by mouth measured by a consummatory response. *J. comp. physiol. Psychol., 45,* 550–554.

Berlyne, D. E. (1955): The arousal and satiation of perceptual curiosity in the rat. *J. comp. physiol. Psychol., 48,* 238–246.

Berlyne, D. E. (1958): The present status of research on exploratory and related behavior. *J. indiv. Psychol.*, 14, 121–126.

Bills, A. G. (1927): The influence of muscular tension on the efficiency of mental work. *Amer. J. Psychol.*, 38, 227–251.

Bindra, D. (1959): Stimulus change, reactions to novelty, and response decrement. *Psychol. Rev.*, 66, 96–103.

Bindra, D., A. L. Paterson, and J. Strzelecki (1955): On the relation between anxiety and conditioning. *Canad. J. Psychol.*, 9, 1–6.

Birch, D., E. Burnstein, and R. A. Clark (1958): Response strength as a function of food deprivation under a controlled maintenance schedule. *J. comp. physiol. Psychol.*, 51, 350–354.

Bitterman, M. E., and W. H. Holtzman (1952): Conditioning and extinction of the galvanic skin response as a function of anxiety. *J. abnorm. soc. Psychol.*, 47, 615–623.

Bitterman, M. E., and C. W. Kniffin (1953): Manifest anxiety and "perceptual defense." *J. abnorm. soc. Psychol.*, 48, 248–252.

Bitterman, M. E., P. Reed, and J. Krauskopf (1952): The effect of the duration of the unconditioned stimulus upon conditioning and extinction. *Amer. J. Psychol.*, 65, 256–262.

Bolles, R. C. (1958): Comments on Professor Estes' paper. In M. R. Jones (ed.), *Nebraska symposium on motivation.* Lincoln, Nebr.: University of Nebraska Press.

Bower, G. H., and N. E. Miller (1958): Rewarding and punishing effects from stimulating the same place in the rat's brain. *J. comp. physiol. Psychol.*, 51, 669–674.

Brady, J. V., J. J. Boren, D. Conrad, and M. Sidman (1957): The effect of food and water deprivation upon intracranial self-stimulation. *J. comp. physiol. Psychol.*, 50, 134–137.

Brady, J. V., and W. J. H. Nauta (1953): Subcortical mechanisms in emotional behavior: affective changes following septal forebrain lesions in the albino rat. *J. comp. physiol. Psychol.*, 46, 339–346.

Brady, J. V., W. C. Stebbins, and R. Galambos (1953): The effect of audiogenic convulsions on a conditioned emotional response. *J. comp. physiol. Psychol.*, 46, 363–367.

Brandauer, C. M. (1953): A confirmation of Webb's data concerning the action of irrelevant drives. *J. exp. Psychol.*, 45, 150–152.

Braunstein, E. P. (1923): Zur Lehre von den kurzdauernden Lichtreizen der Netzhaut. *Zsch. f. Sinnesphysiol.*, 55, 185–229. Cited by S. Hecht (1934): The nature of the photoreceptor process. In C. Murchison (ed.), *Handbook of general experimental psychology.* Worcester, Mass.: Clark University Press, 1934.

Bricker, P. D., and A. Chapanis (1953): Do incorrectly perceived tachistoscopic stimuli convey some information? *Psychol. Rev.*, 60, 181–188.

Broadhurst, P. L. (1957): Emotionality and the Yerkes-Dodson law. *J. exp. Psychol.*, 54, 345–352.

Brobeck, J. R. (1955): Neural regulation of food intake. In R. W. Miner (ed.), *The regulation of hunger and appetite*. Ann. N. Y. Acad. Sci., 63, Art. 1, New York: N.Y. Acad. Sci.

Brown, D. R., and J. Adams (1954): Word frequency and the measurement of value areas. *J. abnorm. soc. Psychol.*, 49, 427–430.

Brown, G. W., and B. D. Cohen (1959): Avoidance and approach learning motivated by stimulation of identical hypothalamic nuclei. *Amer. J. Physiol.*, 197, 153–157.

Brown, J. S. (1948): Gradients of approach and avoidance responses and their relation to level of motivation. *J. comp. physiol. Psychol.*, 41, 450–465.

Brown, J. S. (1953a): Problems presented by the concept of acquired drives. In *Current theory and research in motivation: a symposium*. Lincoln, Nebr.: University of Nebraska Press.

Brown, J. S. (1953b): Comments on Professor Harlow's paper. In *Current theory and research in motivation: a symposium*. Lincoln, Nebr.: University of Nebraska Press.

Brown, J. S. (1955): Pleasure-seeking behavior and the drive-reduction hypothesis. *Psychol. Rev.*, 62, 169–179.

Brown, J. S. (1957): Principles of intrapersonal conflict. *Conflict Resolution*, 1, 135–154.

Brown, J. S., and I. E. Farber (1951): Emotions conceptualized as intervening variables—with suggestions toward a theory of frustration. *Psychol. Bull.*, 48, 465–495.

Brown, J. S., and A. Jacobs (1949): The role of fear in the motivation and acquisition of responses. *J. exp. Psychol.*, 39, 747–759.

Brown, J. S., H. I. Kalish, and I. E. Farber (1951): Conditioned fear as revealed by magnitude of startle response to an auditory stimulus. *J. exp. Psychol.*, 41, 317–328.

Brown, J. S., J. W. Meryman, and F. N. Marzocco (1956): Sound-induced startle response as a function of time since shock. *J. comp. physiol. Psychol.*, 49, 190–194.

Brown, W. L., and G. Gentry (1948): The effects of intra-maze delay. II. Various intervals of delay. *J. comp. physiol. Psychol.*, 41, 403–407.

Brožek, J., H. Guetzkow, and M. V. Baldwin (1951): A quantitative study of perception and association in experimental semistarvation. *J. Pers.*, 19, 245–264.

Bruner, J. S., and C. C. Goodman (1947): Value and need as organizing factors in perception. *J. abnorm. soc. Psychol.*, 42, 33–44.

Bruner, J. S., and L. Postman (1947): Emotional selectivity in perception and reaction. *J. Pers.*, 16, 69–77.

Bruner, J. S., and L. Postman (1948): Symbolic value as an organizing factor in perception. *J. soc. Psychol.*, 27, 203–208.

Bruner, J. S., and J. S. Rodrigues (1953): Some determinants of apparent size. *J. abnorm. soc. Psychol.*, 48, 17–24.

Bugelski, R., and N. E. Miller (1938): A spatial gradient in the strength of avoidance responses. *J. exp. Psychol.*, 23, 494–505.

Burros, R. H. (1949): *Quantitative studies in secondary drive.* Unpublished doctoral dissertation, Yale University.

Bursten, B., and J. M. R. Delgado (1958): Positive reinforcement induced by intracerebral stimulation in the monkey. *J. comp. physiol. Psychol.*, 51, 6–10.

Butler, R. A. (1953): Discrimination learning by rhesus monkeys to visual-exploration motivation. *J. comp. physiol. Psychol.*, 46, 95–98.

Butler, R. A. (1957): The effect of deprivation of visual incentives on visual exploration motivation in monkeys. *J. comp. physiol. Psychol.*, 50, 177–179.

Butler, R. A. (1958): Exploratory and related behavior: a new trend in animal research. *J. indiv. Psychol.*, 14, 111–120.

Butler, R. A., and H. F. Harlow (1954): Persistence of visual exploration in monkeys. *J. comp. physiol. Psychol.*, 47, 258–263.

Calvin, J. S., E. A. Bicknell, and D. S. Sperling (1953): Establishment of a conditioned drive based on the hunger drive. *J. comp. physiol. Psychol.*, 46, 173–175.

Campbell, B. A., and D. Kraeling (1953): Response strength as a function of drive level and amount of drive reduction. *J. exp. Psychol.*, 45, 97–101.

Campbell, B. A., and D. Kraeling (1954): Response strength as a function of drive level during training and extinction. *J. comp. physiol. Psychol.*, 47, 101–103.

Campbell, N. R. (1921): *What is science?* London: Methuen & Co., Ltd.

Cannon, W. B. (1929): *Bodily changes in pain, hunger, fear, and rage*, 2d ed. New York: Appleton-Century-Crofts, Inc.

Carlton, P. L. (1955): *The effect of time of food deprivation on selective learning.* Unpublished doctoral dissertation, State University of Iowa.

Carter, L. F., and K. Schooler (1949): Value, need, and other factors in perception. *Psychol. Rev.*, 56, 200–207.

Castaneda, A., B. R. McCandless, and D. S. Palermo (1956): The children's form of the manifest anxiety scale. *Child Develpm.*, 27, 317–326.

Castaneda, A., D. S. Palermo, and B. R. McCandless (1956): Complex learning and performance as a function of anxiety in children and task difficulty. *Child Develpm.*, 27, 327–332.

Champion, R. A. (1954): *Drive-strength and competing response tendencies.* Unpublished master's thesis, State University of Iowa.

Chapanis, A., W. R. Garner, and C. T. Morgan (1949): *Applied experimental psychology.* New York: John Wiley & Sons, Inc.

Chapman, R. M., and N. Levy (1957): Hunger drive and reinforcing effect of novel stimuli. *J. comp. physiol. Psychol.*, 50, 233–238.

Child, I. L., and I. K. Waterhouse (1953): Frustration and the quality of performance: II. A theoretical statement. *Psychol. Rev.*, 60, 127–139.

Chiles, W. D. (1954): Performance during stimulation of the diencephalic activating system. *J. comp. physiol. Psychol.*, 47, 412–415.

Chodorkoff, B. (1956): Anxiety, threat, and defensive reactions. *J. gen. Psychol.*, 54, 191–196.

Clark, R. A. (1952): The projective measurement of experimentally induced levels of sexual motivation. *J. exp. Psychol.*, 44, 391–399.

Clark, R. A., and D. C. McClelland (1950): A factor analytic integration of imaginative, performance, and case study measures of the need for achievement. Unpublished paper, cited in McClelland, Atkinson, Clark, and Lowell, 1953.

Clark, R. E. (1958): Size estimation limens as a function of level of motivation. (Unpublished. Personal communication.)

Cohen, B. D., G. W. Brown, and M. L. Brown (1957): Avoidance learning motivated by hypothalamic stimulation. *J. exp. Psychol.*, 53, 228–233.

Cohen, M. R., and E. Nagel (1934): *An introduction to logic and scientific method.* New York: Harcourt, Brace and Company, Inc.

Conger, J. J. (1951): The effects of alcohol on conflict behavior in the albino rat. *Quart. J. Stud. Alcohol*, 12, 1–29.

Cooper, J. B. (1938): The effect upon performance of introduction and removal of a delay within the maze. *J. comp. Psychol.*, 25, 457–462.

Cotton, J. W. (1953): Running time as a function of amount of food deprivation. *J. exp. Psychol.*, 46, 188–198.

Courts, F. A. (1942): Relations between muscular tension and performance. *Psychol. Bull.*, 39, 347–367.

Cowles, J. T. (1937): Food-tokens as incentives for learning by chimpanzees. *Comp. Psychol. Monogr.* 14, No. 5 (Whole No. 71).

Crespi, L. P. (1944): Amount of reinforcement and level of performance. *Psychol. Rev.*, 51, 341–357.

Davenport, J. W. (1956): *Choice behavior as a function of drive strength and rate of learning.* Unpublished doctoral dissertation, State University of Iowa.

Davis, J. D. (1958): The reinforcing effect of weak-light onset as a function of amount of food deprivation. *J. comp. physiol. Psychol.*, 51, 496–498.

Davis, R. C. (1953): Physical psychology. *Psychol. Rev.*, 60, 7–14.

Davis, R. H. (1957): The effect of drive reversal on latency, amplitude, and activity level. *J. exp. Psychol.*, 53, 310–315.

Davitz, J. R. (1955): Reinforcement of fear at the beginning and at the end of shock. *J. comp. physiol. Psychol.*, 48, 152–155.

Deese, J., and J. A. Carpenter (1951): Drive level and reinforcement. *J. exp. Psychol.*, 42, 236–238.

Deese, J., R. S. Lazarus, and J. Keenan (1953): Anxiety, anxiety reduction, and stress in learning. *J. exp. Psychol.*, 46, 55–60.

Delgado, J. M. R., W. W. Roberts, and N. E. Miller (1954): Learning motivated by electrical stimulation of the brain. *Amer. J. Physiol.*, 179, 587–593.

Dember, W. N., and H. Fowler (1958): Spontaneous alteration behavior. *Psychol. Bull.*, 55, 412–428.

Dinsmoor, J. A. (1952): The effect of hunger on discriminated responding. *J. abnorm. soc. Psychol.*, 47, 67–72.

Dodson, J. D. (1917): Relative values of reward and punishment in habit formation. *Psychobiology*, 1, 231–276.

Dollard, J., and N. E. Miller (1950): *Personality and psychotherapy.* New York: McGraw-Hill Book Company, Inc.

Dollard, J., L. W. Doob, N. E. Miller, O. H. Mowrer, and R. R. Sears (1939): *Frustration and aggression.* New Haven, Conn.: Yale University Press.

Duffy, E. (1934): Emotion: an example of the need for reorientation in psychology. *Psychol. Rev.*, 41, 184–198.

Duffy, E. (1951): The concept of energy mobilization. *Psychol. Rev.*, 58, 30–40.

Duffy, E. (1957): The psychological significance of "arousal" or "activation." *Psychol. Rev.*, 64, 265–275.

Dukes, W. F., and W. Bevan, Jr. (1952): Size estimation and monetary value: a correlation. *J. Psychol.*, 34, 43–53.

Eisman, E. (1956): An investigation of the parameters defining drive (D). *J. exp. Psychol.*, 52, 85–89.

Eisman, E., A. Asimow, and I. Maltzman (1956): Habit strength as a function of drive in a brightness discrimination problem. *J. exp. Psychol.*, 52, 58–64.

Eriksen, C. W. (1951): Some implications for TAT interpretation arising from need and perception experiments. *J. Pers.*, 19, 282–288.

Eriksen, C. W. (1954): The case for perceptual defense. *Psychol. Rev.*, 61, 175–182.

Estes, W. K. (1950): Toward a statistical theory of learning. *Psychol. Rev.*, 57, 94–107.

Estes, W. K. (1958): Stimulus-response theory of drive. In M. R. Jones (ed.), *Nebraska symposium on motivation.* Lincoln, Nebr.: University of Nebraska Press.

Estes, W. K., and B. F. Skinner (1941): Some quantitative properties of anxiety. *J. exp. Psychol.*, 29, 390–400.

Farber, I. E. (1948): Response fixation under anxiety and non-anxiety conditions. *J. exp. Psychol.*, 38, 111–131.

Farber, I. E. (1954a): Anxiety as a drive state. In M. R. Jones (ed.), *Nebraska symposium on motivation*. Lincoln, Nebr.: University of Nebraska Press.

Farber, I. E. (1945b): Comments on Professor Atkinson's paper. In M. R. Jones (ed.), *Nebraska symposium on motivation*. Lincoln, Nebr.: University of Nebraska Press.

Farber, I. E. (1955): The role of motivation in verbal learning and performance. *Psychol. Bull.*, 52, 311–327.

Farber, I. E., and K. W. Spence (1953): Complex learning and conditioning as a function of anxiety. *J. exp. Psychol.*, 45, 120–125.

Finch, G. (1942): Chimpanzee frustration responses. *Psychosom. Med.*, 4, 233–251.

Forgays, D. G., and H. Levin (1959): Discrimination and reversal learning as a function of change of sensory stimulation. *J. comp. physiol. Psychol.*, 52, 191–194.

Franks, C. M. (1957): Effect of food, drink, and tobacco deprivation on the conditioning of the eyeblink response. *J. exp. Psychol.*, 53, 117–120.

Fredenburg, N. C. (1956): *Response strength as a function of alley length and time of deprivation*. Unpublished master's thesis, State University of Iowa.

Freeman, J. T. (1954): Set or perceptual defense? *J. exp. Psychol.*, 48, 283–288.

French, E. G. (1956): Development of a measure of complex motivation. Research Report TN-56-48, AF Personnel and Training Research Center, Lackland AF base, Texas.

French, J. R. P., Jr. (1944): Organized and unorganized groups under fear and frustration. In R. R. Sears (ed.), *Authority and frustration: Studies in topological and vector psychology. III. University Iowa Stud. Child Welfare*, 20, 231–308.

Freud, S. (1905, First German ed.): *Three essays on sexuality*. In Standard Edition. Vol. VII. London: Hogarth Press, Ltd., 1953.

Freud, S. (1936): *The problem of anxiety*. New York: W. W. Norton & Company, Inc.

Fuster, J. M. (1958): Effects of stimulation of brain stem on tachistoscopic perception. *Science*, 127, 150.

Gardiner, H. M., R. C. Metcalf, and J. G. Beebe-Center (1937): *Feeling and emotion*. New York: American Book Company.

Gerall, A. A., P. B. Sampson, and G. L Boslov (1957): Classical conditioning of human pupillary dilation. *J. exp. Psychol.*, 54, 467–474.

Ghent, L. (1957): Some effects of deprivation on eating and drinking behavior. *J. comp. physiol. Psychol.*, 50, 172–176.

Gilbert, R. W. (1936): The effect of noninformative shock upon maze learning and retention with human subjects. *J. exp. Psychol.*, 19, 456–466.

Gilbert, R. W. (1937): A further study of the effect of noninformative shock upon learning. *J. exp. Psychol.*, 20, 396–407.

Gilchrist, J. C., and L. S. Nesberg (1952): Need and perceptual change in need-related objects. *J. exp. Psychol.*, 44, 369–376.

Gilhousen, H. C. (1938): Temporal relations in anticipatory reactions of the white rat in a maze. *J. comp. Psychol.*, 26, 163–175.

Glanzer, M. (1953): The role of stimulus satiation in spontaneous alternation. *J. exp. Psychol.*, 45, 387–393.

Glanzer, M. (1958): Curiosity, exploratory drive, and stimulus satiation. *Psychol. Bull.*, 55, 302–315.

Grice, G. R., and J. D. Davis (1957): Effect of irrelevant thirst motivation on a response learned with food reward. *J. exp. Psychol.*, 53, 347–352.

Grice, G. R., and E. Saltz (1950): The generalization of an instrumental response to stimuli varying in the size dimension. *J. exp. Psychol.*, 40, 702–708.

Grossman, M. I. (1955): Integration of current views on the regulation of hunger and appetite. In R. W. Miner (ed.), *The regulation of hunger and appetite. Ann. N. Y. Acad. Sci.*, 63, Art. 1, New York: N. Y. Acad. Sci.

Guthrie, E. R. (1935): *The psychology of learning*. New York: Harper & Brothers.

Guthrie, E. R., and G. P. Horton (1946): *Cats in a puzzle box*. New York: Holt, Rinehart and Winston, Inc.

Gwinn, G. T. (1951): Resistance to extinction of learned fear-drives. *J. exp. Psychol.*, 42, 6–12.

Haigh, G. V., and D. W. Fiske (1952): Corroboration of personal values as selective factors in perception. *J. abnorm. soc. Psychol.*, 47, 394–398.

Hall, C. S., and G. Lindzey (1957): *Theories of personality*. New York: John Wiley & Sons, Inc.

Hall, J. F., and P. V. Hanford (1954): Activity as a function of a restricted feeding schedule. *J. comp. physiol. Psychol.*, 47, 362–363.

Hamilton, G. V. (1916): A study of perseverance reactions in primates and rodents. *Behav. Monogr.*, 3, No. 2 (Whole No. 13).

Haner, C. F., and P. A. Brown (1955): Clarification of the instigation to action concept in the frustration-aggression hypothesis. *J. abnorm. soc. Psychol.*, 51, 204–206.

Harlow, H. F. (1953): Motivation as a factor in the acquisition of new responses. In *Current theory and research in motivation: a symposium*. Lincoln, Nebr.: University of Nebraska Press.

Heath, R. G. (1954): Behavioral changes following destructive lesions in the subcortical structures of the forebrain in cats. In R. G.

Heath (ed.), *Studies in schizophrenia; a multidisciplinary approach to mid-brain relationships.* Cambridge, Mass.: Harvard University Press.

Heathers, G. L., and P. Arakelian (1941): The relation between strength of drive and rate of extinction of a bar-pressing reaction in the rat. *J. gen. Psychol.,* 24, 243–258.

Hebb, D. O. (1949): *The organization of behavior.* New York: John Wiley & Sons, Inc.

Hebb, D. O. (1955): Drives and the c.n.s. (conceptual nervous system). *Psychol. Rev.,* 62, 243–254.

Hedlund, J. L. (1953): *Construction and evaluation of an objective test of achievement imagery.* Unpublished doctoral dissertation, State University of Iowa.

Hilden, A. H. (1937): An action current study of the conditioned hand withdrawal. In L. E. Travis (ed.), *Studies in Clinical Psychology. Psychol. Monogr.,* 49, No. 1 (Whole No. 217).

Hilgard, E. R., and D. G. Marquis (1935): Acquisition, extinction, and retention of conditioned lid responses to light in dogs. *J. comp. Psychol.,* 19, 29–58.

Hilgard, E. R., and D. G. Marquis (1940): *Conditioning and learning.* New York: Appleton-Century-Crofts, Inc.

Hilgard, E. R., L. V. Jones, and S. J. Kaplan (1951): Conditioned discrimination as related to anxiety. *J. exp. Psychol.,* 42, 94–99.

Hillman, B., W. S. Hunter, and G. A. Kimble (1953): The effect of drive level on the maze performance of the white rat. *J. comp. physiol. Psychol.,* 46, 87–89.

Holder, E. (1951): *Response strength as a function of changes in the length of the delay interval.* Unpublished master's thesis, New Mexico State College. Cited in Holder, Marx, Holder and Collier, 1957.

Holder, W. B., M. H. Marx, E. E. Holder, and G. Collier (1957): Response strength as a function of delay of reward in a runway. *J. exp. Psychol.,* 53, 316–323.

Hollenberg, E., and M. Sperry (1951): Some antecedents of aggression and effects of frustration in doll play. *Personality: topical symposia,* 1, 32–43.

Holton, R. B. (1956): *Variables affecting the change in instrumental response magnitude after reward cessation.* Unpublished doctoral dissertation, State University of Iowa.

Horenstein, B. R. (1951): Performance of conditioned responses as a function of strength of hunger drive. *J. comp. physiol. Psychol.,* 44, 210–224.

Hovland, C. I. (1936): "Inhibition of reinforcement" and phenomena of experimental extinction. *Proc. Nat. Acad. Sci.,* Washington, 22, 430–433.

Hovland, C. I., and A. H. Riesen (1940): Magnitude of galvanic and vasomotor response as a function of stimulus intensity. *J. gen. Psychol.*, 23, 103–121.

Howes, D. H., and R. L. Solomon (1950): A note on McGinnies' "Emotionality and perceptual defense." *Psychol. Rev.*, 57, 229–234.

Hughes, J. B., II, J. L. Sprague, and A. W. Bendig (1954): Anxiety level, response alternation, and performance in serial learning. *J. Psychol.*, 38, 421–426.

Hull, C. L. (1931): Goal attraction and directing ideas conceived as habit phenomena. *Psychol. Rev.*, 38, 487–506.

Hull, C. L. (1937): Mind, mechanism, and adaptive behavior. *Psychol. Rev.*, 44, 1–32.

Hull, C. L. (1943): *Principles of behavior.* New York: Appleton-Century-Crofts, Inc.

Hull, C. L. (1951): *Essentials of behavior.* New Haven, Conn.: Yale University Press.

Hull, C. L. (1952): *A behavior system.* New Haven, Conn.: Yale University Press.

Hunt, H. F., and J. V. Brady (1951): Some effects of electroconvulsive shock on a conditioned emotional response ("anxiety"). *J. comp. physiol. Psychol.*, 44, 88–98.

Hunt, H. F., and L. S. Otis (1953): Conditioned and unconditioned emotional defecation in the rat. *J. comp. physiol. Psychol.*, 46, 378–382.

Hurley, J. R. (1955): The Iowa picture interpretation test: a multiple-choice variation of the TAT. *J. consult. Psychol.*, 19, 372–376.

Hurley, J. R. (1957): Achievement imagery and motivational instructions as determinants of verbal learning. *J. Pers.*, 25, 274–282.

Ingram, W. R., J. R. Knott, and W. D. Chiles (1953): Behavioral and electrocortical effects of diencephalic stimulation in unanesthetized, unrestrained cats. *XIX Internat. Physiol. Congr.*, 487–488.

Janowitz, H. D., and M. I. Grossman (1949): Some factors affecting the food intake of normal dogs and dogs with esophagostomy and gastric fistula. *Amer. J. Physiol.*, 159, 143–148.

Jasper, H. H., (ed.) (1958): *Reticular formation of the brain.* Boston: Little, Brown & Company.

Jenkin, N. (1957): Affective processes in perception. *Psychol. Bull.*, 54, 100–127.

Jerome, E. A., J. A. Moody, T. J. Connor, and M. B. Fernandez (1957): Learning in a multiple-door situation under various drive states. *J. comp. physiol. Psychol.*, 50, 588–591.

Johanson, A. M. (1922): The influence of incentive and punishment upon reaction time. *Arch. Psychol.*, 8, No. 54.

Johnston, R. A. (1955): The effects of achievement imagery on maze-learning performance. *J. Pers.*, 24, 145–152.

Johnston, R. A. (1957): A methodological analysis of several revised forms of the Iowa Picture Interpretation Test. *J. Pers.*, 25, 283–293.

Jones, M. C. (1924): The elimination of children's fears. *J. exp. Psychol.*, 7, 382–390.

Kabrick, R. P., and I. E. Farber (1952): Effect of electric shock on speed of reaction. *Amer. Psychologist*, 7, 586. (Abstract.)

Kagan, J., and M. Berkun (1954): The reward value of running activity. *J. comp. physiol. Psychol.*, 47, 108.

Kalish, H. I. (1954): Strength of fear as a function of the number of acquisition and extinction trials. *J. exp. Psychol.*, 47, 1–9.

Kaplan, M. (1952): The effects of noxious stimulus intensity and duration during intermittent reinforcement of escape behavior. *J. comp. physiol. Psychol.*, 45, 538–549.

Kendler, H. H. (1945): Drive interaction: I. Learning as a function of the simultaneous presence of the hunger and thirst drives. *J. exp. Psychol.*, 35, 96–109.

Ketchel, R. G. (1955): *Performance in instrumental learning as a function of shock intensity.* Unpublished master's thesis, State University of Iowa.

Kimble, G. A. (1951): Behavior strength as a function of the intensity of the hunger drive. *J. exp. Psychol.*, 41, 341–348.

Kish, G. B. (1955): Learning when the onset of illumination is used as reinforcing stimulus. *J. comp. physiol. Psychol.*, 48, 261–264.

Klein, G. S., H. J. Schlesinger, and D. E. Meister (1951): The effect of personal values on perception: an experimental critique. *Psychol. Rev.*, 58, 96–112.

Kling, J. W., L. Horowitz, and J. E. Delhagen (1956): Light as a positive reinforcer for rat responding. *Psychol. Rep.*, 2, 337–340.

Knott, J. R., W. R. Ingram, and R. E. Correll (1960): Some effects of subcortical stimulation on the bar press response. *A. M. A. Arch. Neurol.*, 2, 476–484.

Koch, S., and W. J. Daniel (1945): The effect of satiation on the behavior mediated by a habit of maximum strength. *J. exp. Psychol.*, 35, 167–187.

Lacy, O. W., N. Lewinger, and J. F. Adamson (1953): Foreknowledge as a factor affecting perceptual defense and alertness. *J. exp. Psychol.*, 45, 169–174.

Lambert, W. W., R. L. Solomon, and P. D. Watson (1949): Reinforcement and extinction as factors in size estimation. *J. exp. Psychol.*, 39, 637–641.

Lawrence, D. H., and W. A. Mason (1955): Intake and weight

adjustments in rats to changes in feeding schedule. *J. comp. physiol. Psychol.*, *48*, 43–46.

Lawson, R., and M. H. Marx (1958): Frustration: theory and experiment. *Genet. Psychol. Monogr.*, *57*, 393–464.

Lazarus, R. S., J. Deese, and S. F. Osler (1952): The effects of psychological stress upon performance. *Psychol. Bull.*, *49*, 293–317.

Lazarus, R. S., C. W. Eriksen, and C. P. Fonda (1951): Personality dynamics and auditory perceptual recognition. *J. Pers.*, *19*, 471–482.

Lazarus, R. S., and R. A. McCleary (1951): Autonomic discrimination without awareness: a study of subception. *Psychol. Rev.*, *58*, 113–122.

Lazarus, R. S., H. Yousem, and D. Arenberg (1953): Hunger and perception. *J. Pers.*, *21*, 312–328.

Levine, R., I. Chein, and G. Murphy (1942): The relation of the intensity of a need to the amount of perceptual distortion: a preliminary report. *J. Psychol.*, *13*, 283–293.

Lewin, K. (1931): Environmental forces in child behavior and development. In C. Murchison (ed.), *A handbook of child psychology*. Worcester, Mass.: Clark University Press.

Lewin, K. (1938): The conceptual representation and the measurement of psychological forces. *Contr. Psychol. Theor.*, I, No. 4.

Libby, A. (1951): Two variables in the acquisition of depressant properties by a stimulus. *J. exp. Psychol.*, *42*, 100–107.

Lindsley, D. B. (1951): Emotion. In S. S. Stevens (ed.), *Handbook of experimental psychology*. New York: John Wiley & Sons, Inc.

Lindsley, D. B. (1957): Psychophysiology and motivation. In M. R. Jones (ed.), *Nebraska symposium on motivation*. Lincoln, Nebr.: University of Nebraska Press.

Lindsley, D. B., J. Bowden, and H. W. Magoun (1949): Effect upon EEG of acute injury to the brain stem activating system. *EEG clin. Neurophysiol.*, *1*, 475–486.

Lindzey, G. (ed.) (1959): *Assessment of human motives*. New York: Holt, Rinehart and Winston.

Loess, H. B. (1952): *The effect of variation of motivational level and changes in motivational level on performance in learning*. Unpublished doctoral dissertation, State University of Iowa.

Logan, F. A. (1952): The role of delay of reinforcement in determining reaction potential. *J. exp. Psychol.*, *43*, 393–399.

Logan, F. A., D. L. Olmstead, B. S. Rosner, R. D. Schwartz, and C. M. Stevens (1955): *Behavior theory and social science*. New Haven, Conn.: Yale University Press.

Lowell, E. L. (1952a): *The effect of conflict on motivation*. Unpublished doctoral dissertation, Harvard University. Cited in Whiting and Child, 1953.

Lowell, E. L. (1952b): The effect of need for achievement on learning and speed of performance. *J. Psychol.*, *33*, 31–40.

Ludvigson, W. H. (1958): *Visual identification thresholds as a function of attitude.* (Unpublished. Personal communication.)

Lysak, W. (1954): The effects of punishment upon syllable recognition thresholds. *J. exp. Psychol.*, *47*, 343–350.

Lysak, W., and J. C. Gilchrist (1955): Value, equivocality, and goal availability as determinants of size judgments. *J. Pers.*, *23*, 500–501.

McAllister, W. R. (1953): The effect on eyelid conditioning of shifting the CS-US interval. *J. exp. Psychol.*, *45*, 423–428.

McCandless, B. R., and A. Castaneda (1956): Anxiety in children, school achievement, and intelligence. *Child Develpm.*, *27*, 379–382.

McClelland, D. C. (1951): *Personality*. New York: William Sloane Associates.

McClelland, D. C. (1956): *The measurement of human needs*. Final Report, Contract N7 onr 463, NR 171–363, Office of Naval Research, Aug. 31, 1956.

McClelland, D. C., and J. W. Atkinson (1948): The projective expression of needs: I. The effects of different intensities of the hunger drive on perception. *J. Psychol.*, *25*, 205–222.

McClelland, D. C., J. W. Atkinson, R. A. Clark, and E. L. Lowell (1953): *The achievement motive*. New York: Appleton-Century-Crofts, Inc.

McClelland, D. C., and A. M. Liberman (1949): The effect of need for achievement on recognition of need-related words. *J. Pers.*, *18*, 236–251.

MacCorquodale, K., and P. E. Meehl (1953): Preliminary suggestions as to a formalization of expectancy theory. *Psychol. Rev.*, *60*, 55–63.

McDougall, W. (1917): *An introduction to social psychology*, 12th ed. Boston: Luce.

McGinnies, E. (1949): Emotionality and perceptual defense. *Psychol. Rev.*, *56*, 244–251.

McGinnies, E. (1950): Discussion of Howes' and Solomon's note on "Emotionality and perceptual defense." *Psychol. Rev.*, *57*, 235–240.

McGinnies, E., and H. Sherman (1952): Generalization of perceptual defense. *J. abnorm. soc. Psychol.*, *47*, 81–85.

Madsen, K. B. (1959): *Theories of motivation*. Copenhagen: Munksgaard.

Malmo, R. B. (1957): Anxiety and behavioral arousal. *Psychol. Rev.*, *64*, 276–287.

Malmo, R. B. (1958): Measurement of drive: an unsolved problem in psychology. In M. R. Jones (ed.), *Nebraska symposium on motivation*. Lincoln, Nebr.: University of Nebraska Press.

Marx, M. H. (1956): Some relations between frustration and drive. In M. R. Jones (ed.), *Nebraska symposium on motivation*. Lincoln, Nebr.: University of Nebraska Press.

Marx, M. H., R. L. Henderson, and C. L. Roberts (1955): Positive reinforcement of the bar-pressing response by a light stimulus following dark operant pretests with no aftereffect. *J. comp. physiol. Psychol.*, 48, 73–76.

Marzocco, F. N. (1951): *Frustration effect as a function of drive level, habit strength, and distribution of trials during extinction*. Unpublished doctoral dissertation, State University of Iowa.

Masserman, J. H. (1946): *Principles of dynamic psychiatry*. Philadelphia: W. B. Saunders Company.

Mausner, B., and A. Siegel (1950): The effect of variation in "value" on perceptual thresholds. *J. abnorm. soc. Psychol.*, 45, 760–763.

Melton, A. W. (1941): Learning. In W. S. Monroe (ed.), *Encyclopedia of educational research*. New York: The Macmillan Company.

Meryman, J. J. (1952): *Magnitude of startle response as a function of hunger and fear*. Unpublished master's thesis, State University of Iowa.

Meryman, J. J. (1953): *The magnitude of an unconditioned GSR as a function of fear conditioned at a long CS-UCS interval*. Unpublished doctoral dissertation, State University of Iowa.

Meyer, D. R. (1951): Food deprivation and discrimination reversal learning by monkeys. *J. exp. Psychol.*, 41, 10–16.

Meyer, D. R. (1953): On the interaction of simultaneous responses. *Psychol. Bull.*, 50, 204–220.

Meyer, D. R., and M. E. Noble (1958): Summation of manifest anxiety and muscular tension, *J. exp. Psychol.*, 55, 599–602.

Miller, N. E. (1944): Experimental studies of conflict. In J. McV. Hunt (ed.), *Personality and the behavior disorders*. Vol. I. New York: The Ronald Press Company.

Miller, N. E. (1948a): Studies of fear as an acquirable drive: I. Fear as motivation and fear-reduction as reinforcement in the learning of new responses. *J. exp. Psychol.*, 38, 89–101.

Miller, N. E. (1948b): Theory and experiment relating psychoanalytic displacement to stimulus-response generalization. *J. abnorm. soc. Psychol.*, 43, 155–178.

Miller, N. E. (1951): Learnable drives and rewards. In S. S. Stevens (ed.), *Handbook of experimental psychology*. New York: John Wiley & Sons, Inc.

Miller, N. E. (1958): Central stimulation and other new approaches to motivation and reward. *Amer. Psychologist, 13*, 100–108.

Miller, N. E. (1959): Liberalization of basic S-R concepts: Extensions to conflict behavior, motivation, and social learning. In S. Koch (ed.), *Psychology: a study of a science*. Vol. 2. *General systematic formulations, learning, and special processes*. New York: McGraw-Hill Book Company, Inc.

Miller, N. E., and M. Davis (1943): A theoretical and experimental analysis of conflict behavior: IV. The influence of the positions of reward and punishment in the response sequence. (Unpublished paper. Cited in Miller, 1944.)

Miller, N. E., and J. Dollard (1941): *Social learning and imitation*. New Haven, Conn.: Yale University Press.

Miller, N. E., and D. H. Lawrence (1950): Studies of fear as an acquirable drive: III. Effect of strength of electric shock as a primary drive and of number of trials with the primary drive on the strength of fear. (Unpublished paper. Cited in Miller, 1951.)

Miller, N. E., R. I. Sampliner, and P. Woodrow (1957): Thirst-reducing effects of water by stomach fistula vs. water by mouth measured by both a consummatory and an instrumental response. *J. comp. physiol. Psychol.*, 50, 1–5.

Miller, N. E., and S. S. Stevenson. (1936): Agitated behavior of rats during experimental extinction and a curve of spontaneous recovery. *J. comp. Psychol.*, 21, 205–231.

Miller, W. C., and J. E. Greene (1954): Generalization of an avoidance response to varying intensities of sound. *J. comp. physiol. Psychol.*, 47, 136–139.

Miner, R. W. (ed.) (1955): The regulation of hunger and appetite. *Ann. N.Y. Acad. Sci.*, 63, Art. 1., New York: N.Y. Acad. Sci.

Moeller, G. (1954): The CS-UCS interval in GSR conditioning. *J. exp. Psychol.*, 48, 162–166.

Montgomery, K. C. (1952): A test of two explanations of spontaneous alternation. *J. comp. physiol. Psychol.*, 45, 287–293.

Montgomery, K. C. (1953): Exploratory behavior as a function of "similarity" of stimulus situations. *J. comp. physiol. Psychol.*, 46, 129–133.

Montgomery, K. C. (1954): The role of the exploratory drive in learning. *J. comp. physiol. Psychol.*, 47, 60–64.

Montgomery, K. C. (1955): The relation between fear induced by novel stimulation and exploratory behavior. *J. comp. physiol. Psychol.*, 48, 254–260.

Montgomery, K. C., and M. Segall (1955): Discrimination learning based upon the exploratory drive. *J. comp. physiol. Psychol.*, 48, 225–228.

Morgan, C. T. (1943): *Physiological psychology*. New York: McGraw-Hill Book Company, Inc.

Morgan, C. T. (1957): Physiological mechanisms of motivation. In M. R. Jones (ed.), *Nebraska symposium on motivation*. Lincoln, Nebr.: University of Nebraska Press.

Morgan, C. T., and E. Stellar (1950): *Physiological psychology*, 2d ed. New York: McGraw-Hill Book Company, Inc.

Moruzzi, G., and H. W. Magoun (1949): Brain stem reticular formation and activation of the EEG. *EEG clin. Neurophysiol.*, *1*, 455–473.

Mowrer, O. H. (1939): A stimulus-response analysis of anxiety and its role as a reinforcing agent. *Psychol. Rev.*, *46*, 553–565.

Mowrer, O. H. (1947): On the dual nature of learning—a re-interpretation of "conditioning" and "problem-solving." *Harvard Educ. Rev.*, *17*, 102–148.

Mowrer, O. H. (1950): *Learning theory and personality dynamics*. New York: The Ronald Press Company.

Mowrer, O. H. (1951): Two-factor learning theory: summary and comment. *Psychol. Rev.*, *58*, 350–354.

Mowrer, O. H., and E. G. Aiken (1954): Contiguity vs. drive-reduction in conditioned fear: temporal variations in conditioned and unconditioned stimulus. *Amer. J. Psychol.*, *67*, 26–38.

Mowrer, O. H., and R. R. Lamoreaux (1942): Avoidance conditioning and signal duration—a study of secondary motivation and reward. *Psychol. Monogr.*, *54*, No. 5 (Whole No. 247).

Mowrer, O. H., and L. N. Solomon (1954): Contiguity vs. drive-reduction in conditioned fear: the proximity and abruptness of drive-reduction. *Amer. J. Psychol.*, *67*, 15–25.

Muenzinger, K. F. (1934): Motivation in learning. II. The function of electric shock for right and wrong responses in human subjects. *J. exp. Psychol.*, *17*, 439–448.

Murfin, F. L. (1954): *The relationship of fear to the CS-UCS interval in acquisition and the CS-duration in extinction*. Unpublished doctoral dissertation, State University of Iowa.

Murphy, D. B. (1953): Recognition and recall as a function of frequency, shock, and individual differences variables. Unpublished doctoral dissertation, State University of Iowa.

Murray, H. A. (1938): *Explorations in personality*. New York: Oxford University Press.

Myers, A. K., and N. E. Miller (1954): Failure to find a learned drive based on hunger; evidence for learning motivated by "exploration." *J. comp. physiol. Psychol.*, *47*, 428–436.

Myers, T. I. (1952): *An experimental investigation of the effect of hunger drive upon the brightness discrimination learning of the rat*. Unpublished doctoral dissertation, State University of Iowa.

Nagaty, M. O. (1951): The effect of reinforcement on closely follow-ing S-R connections: I. The effect of a backward conditioning procedure on the extinction of conditioned avoidance. *J. exp. Psychol.*, 42, 239–246.

Neel, A. F. (1954): Conflict, recognition time and defensive behavior. *Amer. Psychologist*, 9, 437–438. (Abstract.)

Nissen, H. W. (1954): The nature of the drive as innate determinant of behavioral organization. In M. R. Jones (ed.), *Nebraska symposium on motivation*. Lincoln, Nebr.: University of Nebraska Press.

Olds, J. (1955): Physiological mechanisms of reward. In M. R. Jones (ed.), *Nebraska symposium on motivation*. Lincoln, Nebr.: University of Nebraska Press.

Olds, J. (1956a): A preliminary mapping of electrical reinforcing ef-fects in the rat brain. *J. comp. physiol. Psychol.*, 49, 281–285.

Olds, J. (1956b): Runway and maze behavior controlled by basomedial forebrain stimulation in the rat. *J. comp. physiol. Psychol.*, 49, 507–512.

Olds, J. (1958): Effects of hunger and male sex hormone on self-stimulation of the brain. *J. comp. physiol. Psychol.*, 51, 320–324.

Olds, J., and P. Milner (1954): Positive reinforcement produced by electrical stimulation of septal area and other regions of rat brain. *J. comp. physiol. Psychol.*, 47, 419–427.

Osgood, C. E. (1953): *Method and theory in experimental psychology*. New York: Oxford University Press.

Palermo, D. S., A. Castaneda, and B. R. McCandless (1956): The relationship of anxiety in children to performance in a complex learning task. *Child Develpm.*, 27, 333–337.

Passey, G. E. (1948): The influence of intensity of unconditioned stimulus upon acquisition of a conditioned response. *J. exp. Psychol.*, 38, 420–428.

Pavlov, I. P. (1927): *Conditioned reflexes*. London: Oxford University Press.

Perin, C. T. (1942): Behavior potentially as a joint function of the amount of training and the degree of hunger at the time of ex-tinction. *J. exp. Psychol.*, 30, 93–113.

Postman, L. (1947): The history and present status of the law of effect. *Psychol. Bull.*, 44, 489–563.

Postman, L. (1953a): The experimental analysis of motivational fac-tors in perception. In *Current theory and research in motivation: a symposium*. Lincoln, Nebr.: University of Nebraska Press.

Postman, L. (1953b): Comments on papers by Professors Brown and Harlow. In *Current theory and research in motivation: a sym-posium*. Lincoln, Nebr.: University of Nebraska Press.

Postman, L., W. C. Bronson, and G. L. Gropper (1953): Is there a mechanism of perceptual defense? *J. abnorm. soc. Psychol.*, 48, 215–224.

Postman, L., J. S. Bruner, and E. McGinnies (1948): Personal values as selective factors in perception. *J. abnorm. soc. Psychol.*, 43, 142–154.

Postman, L., and R. S. Crutchfield (1952): The interaction of need, set and stimulus-structure in a cognitive task. *Amer. J. Psychol.*, 65, 196–217.

Powloski, R. F. (1953): The effects of combining hunger and thirst motives in a discrimination habit. *J. comp. physiol. Psychol.*, 46, 434–437.

Proshansky, H., and G. Murphy (1942): The effects of reward and punishment on perception. *J. Psychol.*, 13, 293–305.

Pustell, T. E. (1957): The experimental induction of perceptual vigilance and defense. *J. Pers.*, 25, 425–438.

Ramond, C. K. (1954): Performance in selective learning as a function of hunger. *J. exp. Psychol.*, 48, 265–270.

Reece, M. M. (1954): The effect of shock on recognition thresholds. *J. abnorm. soc. Psychol.*, 49, 165–172.

Reese, T. W. (1943): The application of the theory of physical measurement to the measurement of psychological magnitudes, with three experimental examples. *Psychol. Monogr.*, 55, No. 3 (Whole No. 251).

Reynolds, R. W. (1958): The relationship between stimulation voltage and rate of hypothalamic self-stimulation in the rat. *J. comp. physiol. Psychol.*, 51, 193–198.

Richter, C. P. (1933): The effect of early gonadectomy on the gross bodily activity of rats. *Endocrinology*, 17, 115–450.

Roberts, W. W. (1958): Both rewarding and punishing effects from stimulation of posterior hypothalamus of cat with same electrode at same intensity. *J. comp. physiol. Psychol.*, 51, 400–407.

Rohrer, J. H. (1949): A motivational state resulting from non-reward. *J. comp. physiol. Psychol.*, 42, 476–485.

Rosenbaum, G. (1953): Stimulus generalization as a function of level of experimentally induced anxiety. *J. exp. Psychol.*, 45, 35–43.

Rosenthal, B. G. (1951): Attitude towards money, need, and methods of presentation as determinants of perception of coins from six to ten years of age. *Amer. Psychologist*, 6, 317. (Abstract.)

Rossi, G. F., and A. Zanchetti (1957): The brain stem reticular formation: anatomy and physiology. *Arch. ital. Biol.*, 95, 199–435.

Roussel, J. (1952): Frustration effect as a function of repeated non-reinforcements and as a function of the consistency of reinforcement prior to the introduction of nonreinforcement. Unpublished master's thesis, Tulane University. Cited in Amsel, 1958.

Saltzman, I., and S. Koch (1948). The effect of low intensities of hunger on the behavior mediated by a habit of maximum strength. *J. exp. Psychol.*, *38*, 347–370.

Samuels, I. (1959): Reticular mechanisms and behavior. *Psychol. Bull.*, *56*, 1–25.

Sanford, R. N. (1936): The effects of abstinence from food upon imaginal processes: a preliminary experiment. *J. Psychol.*, *2*, 129–136.

Sanford, R. N. (1937): The effects of abstinence from food upon imaginal processes: a further experiment. *J. Psychol.*, *3*, 145–159.

Schlosberg, H. (1937): The relationship between success and the laws of conditioning. *Psychol. Rev.*, *44*, 379–394.

Schlosberg, H. (1954): Three dimensions of emotion. *Psychol. Rev.*, *61*, 81–88.

Seward, J. P. (1951): Experimental evidence for the motivating function of reward. *Psychol. Bull.*, *48*, 130–149.

Seward, J. P. (1956): A neurological approach to motivation. In M. R. Jones (ed.), *Nebraska symposium on motivation.* Lincoln, Nebr.: University of Nebraska Press.

Sheffield, V. F. (1950): Resistance to extinction as a function of the distribution of extinction trials. *J. exp. Psychol.*, *40*, 305–313.

Sheriffs, A. C. (1948): The "intuition questionnaire": a new projective test. *J. abnorm. soc. Psychol.*, *43*, 326–337.

Shirley, M. (1928): Studies in activity. II. Activity rhythms; age and activity; activity after rest. *J. comp. Psychol.*, *8*, 159–186.

Sidman, M., J. V. Brady, J. J. Boren, D. G. Conrad, and A. Schulman (1955): Reward schedules and behavior maintained by intracranial self-stimulation. *Science*, *122*, 830–831.

Siegel, P. S. (1943): Drive shift, a conceptual and experimental analysis. *J. comp. Psychol.*, *35*, 139–148.

Siegel, P. S. (1947): The relationship between voluntary water intake, body weight loss, and number of hours of water privation in the rat. *J. comp. physiol. Psychol.*, *40*, 231–238.

Siegel, P. S., and J. J. Brantley (1951): The relationship of emotionality to the consummatory response of eating. *J. exp. Psychol.*, *42*, 304–306.

Siegel, P. S., and M. F. MacDonnell (1954): A repetition of the Calvin-Bicknell-Sperling study of conditioned drive. *J. comp. physiol. Psychol.*, *47*, 250–252.

Siegel, P. S., and M. Steinberg (1949): Activity level as a function of hunger. *J. comp. physiol. Psychol.*, *42*, 413–416.

Skinner, B. F. (1932): Drive and reflex strength. *J. gen. Psychol.*, *6*, 22–37.

Skinner, B. F. (1933): The measurement of spontaneous activity. *J. gen. Psychol.*, *9*, 3–24.

Skinner, B. F. (1938): *The behavior of organisms*. New York: Appleton-Century-Crofts, Inc.

Slonaker, J. R. (1912): The normal activity of the albino rat from birth to natural death, its rate of growth and the duration of life. *J. anim. Behav.*, 2, 20–42.

Smith, M., R. Pool, and H. Weinberg (1959): The effect of peripherally induced shifts in water balance on eating. *J. comp. physiol. Psychol.*, 52, 289–293.

Smith, M. P., and P. J. Capretta (1956): Effects of drive level and experience on the reward value of saccharine solutions. *J. comp. physiol. Psychol.*, 49, 553–557.

Solley, C. M., and R. Lee (1955): Perceived size: closure versus symbolic value. *Amer. J. Psychol.*, 68, 142–144.

Solomon, R. L., and D. H. Howes (1951): Word frequency, personal values, and visual duration thresholds. *Psychol. Rev.*, 58, 256–270.

Solomon, R. L., L. J. Kamin, and L. C. Wynne (1953): Traumatic avoidance learning: the outcomes of several extinction procedures with dogs. *J. abnorm. soc. Psychol.*, 48, 291–302.

Solomon, R. L., and L. C. Wynne (1953): Traumatic avoidance learning: acquisition in normal dogs. *Psychol. Monogr.*, 67, No. 4 (Whole No. 354).

Solomon, R. L., and L. C. Wynne (1954): Traumatic avoidance learning: the principles of anxiety conservation and partial irreversibility. *Psychol. Rev.*, 61, 353–385.

Sorokin, P. A. (1942): *Men and society in calamity*. New York: E. P. Dutton & Co., Inc.

Spence, K. W. (1944): The nature of theory construction in contemporary psychology. *Psychol. Rev.*, 51, 47–68.

Spence, K. W. (1948): The postulates and methods of 'behaviorism.' *Psychol. Rev.*, 55, 67–78.

Spence, K. W. (1951a): Theoretical interpretations of learning. In C. P. Stone (ed.), *Comparative psychology*. Englewood Cliffs, N.J.: Prentice-Hall, Inc.

Spence, K. W. (1951b): Theoretical interpretations of learning. In S. S. Stevens (ed.), *Handbook of experimental psychology*. New York: John Wiley & Sons, Inc.

Spence, K. W. (1956): *Behavior theory and conditioning*. New Haven, Conn.: Yale University Press.

Spence, K. W. (1958): A theory of emotionally based drive (D) and its relation to performance in simple learning situations. *Amer. Psychologist*, 13, 131–141.

Spence, K. W., and I. E. Farber (1953): Conditioning and extinction as a function of anxiety. *J. exp. Psychol.*, 45, 116–119.

Spence, K. W., I. E. Farber, and E. Taylor (1954): The relation of electric shock and anxiety to level of performance in eyelid conditioning. *J. exp. Psychol.*, *48*, 404–408.

Spence, K. W., and L. E. Ross (1957): Experimental evidence on the relation between performance level in eyelid conditioning and anxiety (drive) level. Technical Report 5, Studies of influence of motivation on performance in learning, Contract N9 onr 93802, Project NR 154–107, Office of Naval Research.

Spence, K. W., and J. A. Taylor (1951): Anxiety and strength of the UCS as determiners of the amount of eyelid conditioning. *J. exp. Psychol.*, *42*, 183–188.

Stein, K. B. (1953): Perceptual defense and perceptual sensitization under neutral and involved conditions. *J. Pers.*, *21*, 467–478.

Stellar, E. (1954): The physiology of motivation. *Psychol. Rev.*, *61*, 5–22.

Stevens, S. S. (1946): The science of noise. *Atlantic Monthly*, *178*, 96–102, July, 1946.

Stevens, S. S. (1951): Mathematics, measurement, and psychophysics. In S. S. Stevens (ed.), *Handbook of experimental psychology*, New York: John Wiley & Sons., Inc.

Strouthes, A., and H. C. Hamilton (1959): Fear conditioning as a function of the number and timing of reinforcements. *J. Psychol.*, *48*, 131–139.

Sullivan, J. J. (1950): *Some factors affecting the conditioning of the galvanic skin response.* Unpublished doctoral dissertation, State University of Iowa.

Switzer, S. A. (1930): Backward conditioning of the lid reflex. *J. exp. Psychol.*, *13*, 76–97.

Tandler, B. F. (1958): *Judgments of circular area and of line length under high and low levels of motivation.* (Unpublished. Personal communication.)

Taylor, J. A. (1951): The relationship of anxiety to the conditioned eyelid response. *J. exp. Psychol.*, *41*, 81–92.

Taylor, J. A. (1956a): Drive theory and manifest anxiety. *Psychol. Bull.*, *53*, 303–320.

Taylor, J. A. (1956b): Physiological need, set, and visual duration threshold. *J. abnorm. soc. Psychol.*, *52*, 96–99.

Taylor, J. A., and K. W. Spence (1952): The relationship of anxiety level to performance in serial learning. *J. exp. Psychol.*, *44*, 61–64.

Teel, K. S. (1952): Habit strength as a function of motivation during learning. *J. comp. physiol. Psychol.*, *45*, 188–191.

Teel, K. S., and W. B. Webb (1951): Response evocation on satiated trials in the T-maze. *J. exp. Psychol.*, *41*, 148–152.

Thorndike, E. L. (1898): Animal intelligence; an experimental study of the associative processes in animals. *Psychol. Rev. Monogr. Suppl.*, *2*, No. 4 (Whole No. 8).

Thorndike, E. L., and I. Lorge (1944): *The teacher's word book of 30,000 words*. New York: Teachers College, Columbia University.

Tolman, E. C. (1932): *Purposive behavior in animals and men*. New York: Appleton-Century-Crofts, Inc.

Tolman, E. C. (1942): *Drives toward war*. New York: Appleton-Century-Crofts, Inc.

Tolman, E. C. (1948): Cognitive maps in rats and men. *Psychol. Rev.*, 55, 189–208.

Tolman, E. C. (1949): There is more than one kind of learning. *Psychol. Rev.*, 56, 144–155.

Tolman, E. C. (1951): A psychological model. In T. Parsons and E. A. Shils (eds.), *Toward a general theory of action*. Cambridge, Mass.: Harvard University Press.

Tolman, E. C. (1952): A cognition motivation model. *Psychol. Rev.*, 59, 389–400.

Tolman, E. C., and H. Gleitman (1949): Studies in spatial learning: VII. Place and response learning under different degrees of motivation. *J. exp. Psychol.*, 39, 653–659.

Tolman, E. C., C. S. Hall, and E. P. Bretnall (1932): A disproof of the law of effect and a substitution of the laws of emphasis, motivation, and disruption. *J. exp. Psychol.*, 15, 601–614.

Tolman, E. C., and L. Postman (1954): Learning. In C. P. Stone (ed.), *Annual review of psychology*. Palo Alto, Calif.: Annual Reviews, Inc.

Troland, L. T. (1928): *The fundamentals of human motivation*. Princeton, N.J.: D. Van Nostrand Company, Inc.

Veroff, J., S. Wilcox, and J. W. Atkinson (1953): The achievement motive in high school and college age women. *J. abnorm. soc. Psychol.*, 48, 108–119.

Verplanck, W. S., and J. R. Hayes (1953): Eating and drinking as a function of maintenance schedule. *J. comp. physiol. Psychol.*, 46, 327–333.

Wagner, A. R. (1959): The role of reinforcement and nonreinforcement in an "apparent frustration effect." *J. exp. Psychol.*, 57, 130–136.

Warden, C. J. (1931): *Animal motivation. Experimental studies on the albino rat*. New York: Columbia University Press.

Warner, L. H. (1927): A study of sex behavior in the white rat by means of the obstruction method. *Comp. Psychol. Monogr.*, 4, No. 5 (Whole No. 22).

Webb, W. B. (1949): The motivational aspect of an irrelevant drive in the behavior of the white rat. *J. exp. Psychol.*, 39, 1–14.

Welker, W. I. (1956): Effects of age and experience on play and exploration of young chimpanzees. *J. comp. physiol. Psychol.*, 49, 223–226.

Wenar, C. (1954): Reaction time as a function of manifest anxiety and stimulus intensity. *J. abnorm. soc. Psychol.*, *49*, 335–340.

White, C. T., and H. Schlosberg (1952): Degree of conditioning of the GSR as a function of the period of delay. *J. exp. Psychol.*, *43*, 357–362.

Whiting, J. W. M., and I. L. Child (1953): *Child training and personality: a cross-cultural study*. New Haven, Conn.: Yale University Press.

Whittaker, E. M., J. C. Gilchrist, and J. W. Fischer (1952): Perceptual defense or response suppression. *J. abnorm. soc. Psychol.*, *47*, 732–733.

Wiener, M. (1955): Word frequency or motivation in perceptual defense. *J. abnorm. soc. Psychol.*, *51*, 214–218.

Williams, J. E. (1955): Mode of failure, interference tendencies and achievement imagery. *J. abnorm. soc. Psychol.*, *51*, 573–580.

Williams, M. (1950): The effects of experimentally induced needs upon retention, *J. exp. Psychol.*, *40*, 139–151.

Wispé, L. G., and N. C. Drambarean (1953): Physiological need, word frequency, and visual duration thresholds. *J. exp. Psychol.*, *46*, 25–31.

Wolfe, J. B. (1936): Effectiveness of token-rewards for chimpanzees. *Comp. Psychol. Monogr.*, *12*, No. 5 (Whole No. 60).

Woodworth, R. S. (1918): *Dynamic psychology*. New York: Columbia University Press.

Wycoff, L. B., Jr. (1952): The role of observing responses in discrimination learning. Part I. *Psychol. Rev.*, *59*, 431–442.

Yamaguchi, H. G. (1951): Drive (D) as a function of hours of hunger (h). *J. exp. Psychol.*, *42*, 108–117.

Yamaguchi, H. G. (1952): Gradients of drive stimulus (S_D) intensity generalization. *J. exp. Psychol.*, *43*, 298–304.

Yerkes, R. M., and J. D. Dodson (1908): The relation of strength of stimulus to rapidity of habit formation. *J. comp. Neurol.*, *18*, 459–482.

Young, P. T. (1936): *Motivation of behavior*. New York: John Wiley & Sons, Inc.

Young, P. T. (1949): Food-seeking drive, affective process, and learning. *Psychol. Rev.*, *56*, 98–121.

Young, P. T. (1955): The role of hedonic processes in motivation. In M. R. Jones (ed.), *Nebraska symposium on motivation*. Lincoln, Nebr.: University of Nebraska Press.

Zatskis, J. (1949): *The effect of the need for achievement on linguistic behavior*. Unpublished master's thesis. Wesleyan University. Cited in McClelland, Atkinson, Clark, and Lowell, 1953.

Zeaman, D., and N. Wegner (1954): The role of drive reduction in the classical conditioning of an autonomically mediated response. *J. exp. Psychol.*, *48*, 349–354.

NAME INDEX

Adams, J., 321
Adamson, J. F., 315
Adolph, E. F., 68, 72
Aiken, E. G., 346
Amsel, A., 83, 84, 108, 132, 133, 155, 156, 163, 195, 205, 211–213
Anand, B. K., 66
Anderson, E. E., 187
Arakelian, P., 80
Arenberg, D., 283
Armus, H. L., 167
Aronson, E., 250
Ashley, W. R., 295, 297
Asimow, A., 91
Atkinson, J. W., 131, 180, 184, 227, 239, 241–244, 246, 248, 282

Bahrick, H. P., 132
Bakan, D., 3
Baker, R. A., 76
Baldwin, M. V., 226
Barnes, G. W., 358
Barry, H., III, 120
Bass, B., 78, 120
Beams, H. L., 298
Bechtoldt, H. P., 274, 275
Beebe-Center, J. G., 24
Bendig, A. W., 260
Bergmann, G., 46
Berkun, M. M., 65, 338
Berlyne, D. E., 331, 334, 335
Bevan, W., Jr., 297
Bicknell, E. A., 189

Bills, A. G., 185
Bindra, D., 131, 258
Birch, D., 178, 179, 187
Bitterman, M. E., 256, 315, 344
Bolles, R. C., 131
Boren, J. J., 132, 353, 358
Boslov, G. L., 348
Bowden, J., 349
Bower, G. H., 86, 353, 354
Brady, J. V., 132, 163, 168, 353, 354, 358
Brandauer, C. M., 122
Brantley, J. J., 132, 156
Braunstein, E. P., 19
Bretnall, E. P., 232
Bricker, P. D., 308
Broadhurst, P. L., 85
Brobeck, J. R., 66, 69
Bronson, W. C., 314
Brown, D. R., 321
Brown, G. W., 86, 351, 354, 356
Brown, J. S., 70, 108, 148, 150, 151, 156, 157, 166, 172, 182, 195, 201, 203, 208, 249, 282, 316, 337, 357
Brown, M. L., 86, 351, 356
Brown, P. A., 214
Brown, W. L., 208, 219
Brozek, J., 226
Bruner, J. S., 289, 293, 298, 310, 320
Bugelski, R., 148
Burnstein, E., 178, 187
Burros, R. H., 168
Bursten, B., 351, 353, 356
Butler, R. A., 331–333, 337, 338

389

SUBJECT INDEX